MILITARY LAW

MILITARY LAW

A HANDBOOK
FOR THE NAVY
AND MARINE CORPS

LCDR Edward M. Byrne, JAGC, USN

UNITED STATES NAVAL INSTITUTE

Annapolis, Maryland

COPYRIGHT © 1970
by the UNITED STATES NAVAL INSTITUTE
Annapolis, Maryland
Library of Congress Catalogue Card 75–104005
ISBN 0–87021–377–6

Printed in the United States of America

Designed by HARVEY SATENSTEIN

Edited by LOUISE GERRETSON

*Composed in ten point Linotype Baskerville leaded two points
by Monotype Composition Company, Inc., Baltimore,
Maryland*

*Printed by offset on sixty pound Finch Tradebook Offset
and bound in G.S.B. Navy
by The Maple Press Company, York, Pennsylvania*

to Dorothy, Kathy, and Eddie

Foreword

This reference book is being published at the close of perhaps the most significant decade in the development of criminal law. The brisk pace of change has affected all stages of the criminal process, from the behavior of the policeman on the street to the technical rules of courtroom procedure. It has also sparked intensive public debate which has challenged traditional assumptions as well as every innovation. The ferment of this period has been unprecedented, and it has preoccupied—and occasionally agonized—those persons involved in the criminal process.

In this time of change the military has been centrally involved. Through decisions of the U.S. Supreme Court, decisions of the U.S. Court of Military Appeals, legislative amendments to the Uniform Code of Military Justice, two new Manuals for Courts-Martial and a host of regulatory modifications, military justice has paralleled, and in many instances anticipated, new developments in the criminal law.

At such a time, this book on military law will prove a useful tool for line officers. Even more than civilian citizens, military officers need to be familiar with the criminal process, for during their careers they may be called upon to participate in it at various stages. Whereas a civilian may be called upon to perform jury duty or to testify as a witness, a military officer has other responsibilities. During the course of his military career he may serve as a pretrial investigating officer, accuser, convening authority, or supervisory authority. As convening authority, he must determine whether to refer a case to trial and what type of court-martial, if any, would be appropriate. As a reviewing authority, he must examine a case for legal accuracy, sufficiency of the evidence, and appropriateness of the sentence. A comprehensive understanding of military justice is essential for the judicious performance of these responsibilities. It is equally necessary for an appreciation of the interaction of command discipline and military justice.

This instructive text will serve well to familiarize its readers with these concepts. It is thorough, readable, and up to date. Navy and Marine Corps officers who become conversant with its content will be better prepared to further the objectives of both the Naval Service and its system of criminal law. Consequently, this book is a welcome and valuable addition to the literature on military justice.

JOSEPH B. McDEVITT
Rear Admiral, JAGC, U.S. Navy
Judge Advocate General
of the Navy

Preface

This book is intended to serve the needs of Navy and Marine Corps officers who are not military lawyers. Its purpose is to serve both as a textbook and a professional handbook in military law.

It is specific in those areas where an officer's knowledge must be specific: for example, the preliminary inquiry officer must know how to take a statement from an accused and to conduct a legal search. It is general in those areas where an officer need only have a general knowledge of the subject matter.

Discussion cases are included to enable the student of military law to visualize the application of military law and the philosophy of those who have a role in interpreting and formulating it. Self-quizzes at the end of each chapter are designed to illustrate further application of the law and point up the magnitude and complexity of our present military justice system.

To accomplish its purpose, the book covers specifically the "nuts and bolts" of the duties of the preliminary inquiry officer, court member, president of a court-martial, convening authority, summary court officer, legal officer, line of duty/misconduct investigation officer, and the trial and defense counsel. The 22 appendices include samples of the forms and reports needed by an officer when fulfilling his various duties relating to military justice. Unauthorized absence and larceny are discussed in detail to permit an understanding of these common offenses and to assist in understanding how to plead and research other offenses.

Therefore, although this is a book for nonlawyers, this is not an easy book. It is doubtful if an "easy" book can be written on such a complex subject without its being technically inaccurate and totally valueless as a working tool.

In the future, the effectiveness of the military justice system will be directly proportionate to the interest and knowledge of the naval officer. If his interest wanes, so will his involvement in the judicial process and the responsiveness of the system to the military's special needs for good order and discipline. Consequently, basic understanding of military law is essential to the future of the naval service.

EDWARD M. BYRNE
Lieutenant Commander
JAGC, U.S. Navy

7 January 1970
Annapolis, Maryland

Acknowledgments

An acknowledgment is made to those persons whose generosity facilitated and expedited the creation of this book.

Commander Thomas J. Johnson, U.S. Navy, Course Coordinator of the Leadership and Military Law course at the U.S. Naval Academy, Annapolis, Maryland, thoroughly reviewed the manuscript and provided numerous constructive suggestions.

Lieutenant Homer E. Moyer, JAGC, U.S. Navy, attached to the Military Justice Division of the Office of the Judge Advocate General of the Navy, and a Navy member of the Ad Hoc Committee which compiled the *Manual for Courts-Martial, United States, 1969* (Revised), served as a technical editor.

Commander Robinson Lappin, JAGC, U.S. Naval Reserve, Academic Director of the United States Naval Justice School in Newport, Rhode Island, and Lieutenant Craig V. Dana, JAGC, U.S. Naval Reserve, Command Judge Advocate, U.S. Naval Station, Annapolis, Maryland, reviewed the manuscript. Captain Homer A. Walkup, JAGC, U.S. Naval Reserve, Deputy Assistant Judge Advocate General (Investigations) reviewed Chapters XIV and XV. Colonel Richard C. Boys, U.S. Air Force (Retired), Assistant Professor, U.S. Naval Academy, and Captain Christian L. Harkness, U.S. Marine Corps, reviewed the first several chapters of the original manuscript. I am also indebted to Captain Paul C. Boyd, U.S. Navy; Lieutenant Colonel Don D. Beal, U.S. Marine Corps; Commander Eugene J. Christensen, U.S. Navy; and Lieutenant Colonel George J. Ertlmeier, U.S. Marine Corps; Commander S. P. Halle, U.S. Navy; and Senior Professor Gregory J. Mann, U.S. Naval Academy, for their leadership and encouragement.

Most of all, I appreciate the help and encouragement of my wife Dorothy, who initially reviewed the manuscript, typed and retyped it, assisted with the index, and finally, read proof.

Extensive assistance and enthusiastic support have been received from the Military Justice and Investigations Divisions of the Office of the Judge Advocate General of the Navy and from the Judge Advocate General's School, U.S. Army, Charlottesville, Virginia. I have drawn deeply upon the excellent printed notes and some of the appendices utilized by the United States Naval Justice School.

E. M. B.

Contents

FOREWORD vii

PREFACE ix

ACKNOWLEDGMENTS xi

CHAPTER I   THE HISTORY AND BACKGROUND OF MILITARY LAW   3
101   Early Military Law   3
102   The English   4
103   Early Origins of American Naval Law   5
104   The Uniform Code of Military Justice   7
105   The Military Justice Act of 1968   8
106   The Officer and the Code   8
107   Authoritative Structure and Basic Sources of
      Military Law   9
108   Publications Relating to Military Law   11
109   The Present Military Justice System   12
110   Summary   14
DISCUSSION CASE: The Spencer Case   14
DISCUSSION AND SELF-QUIZ   18

CHAPTER II   APPREHENSION AND RESTRAINT   20
201   Apprehension   20
202   Custody   21
203   Probable Cause for Pretrial Restraint   21
204   Who May Restrain   22
205   Types of Pretrial Restraint   22
206   Release from Restraint   23
207   Offenses Connected with Apprehension and Restraint   24
208   Speedy Trial   24
209   Summary   25

Discussion Case: *United States* v. *Ellsey*   26
Discussion and Self-Quiz   28

CHAPTER III   The Preliminary Inquiry, Statements, and
                Search and Seizure 30
301   Initiation of Charges   30
302   Duty to Initiate Charges   31
303   Action Upon Receipt of Charges   31
304   Investigation   32
305   Preliminary Inquiry   32
306   Obtaining a Statement from the Accused   33
307   The Voluntary Statement   33
308   Search and Seizure   35
309   Legal Objects of a Search   35
310   The Search Authorized by a Commanding Officer   36
311   "Shakedowns" and the Area Search   38
312   Other Lawful Searches   39
313   "Fruit of the Poison Tree" Doctrine   40
314   Completion of the Preliminary Inquiry   41
315   Final Pre-mast Screening   42
316   Commanding Officer's Action   42
317   Summary   43
Discussion Case: *United States* v. *Tempia*   44
Discussion and Self-Quiz   51

CHAPTER IV   A Study of Offenses and Drafting
                Specifications: Unauthorized Absence 54
401   Article 86   54
402   Elements of Unauthorized Absence   55
403   Duration of the Absence   56
404   Defenses   57
405   The Defense of Impossibility   58
406   The Defenses of Mistake and Ignorance of Fact   59
407   Some Rules of Thumb   59
408   Defenses Barring Trial   60
409   Drafting Charges and Specifications   62
410   Proving the Unauthorized Absence   65
411   Summary   65
Discussion Case: *United States* v. *Holder*   66
Discussion and Self-Quiz   69

CHAPTER V   A Study of Offenses and Drafting
                Specifications: Larceny 72
501   The Nature of Larceny   72

502   Types of Larceny   72
503   The Elements of Larceny   73
504   Wrongful Appropriation   76
505   Defenses to Larceny and Wrongful Appropriation   76
506   Drafting the Larceny and Wrongful Appropriation
      Specifications   78
507   Summary   79
DISCUSSION CASE: *United States* v. *O'Hara*   80
DISCUSSION AND SELF-QUIZ   83

CHAPTER VI   NONJUDICIAL PUNISHMENT AND NONPUNITIVE
                MEASURES   85
601   A Discussion of Nonpunitive Measures   85
602   The Nature of Nonjudicial Punishment   86
603   Who May Impose Nonjudicial Punishment   87
604   Persons Upon Whom Nonjudicial Punishment May Be
      Imposed   87
605   Right to Demand Trial   87
606   The Hearing   88
607   Mast Alternatives   89
608   The Nature of Mast Punishments   89
609   Amount, Combination, and Apportionment   92
610   Post Mast Procedures and Appeal   94
611   Service Record Entries   95
612   The Unit Punishment Book   95
613   Suspension, Mitigation, Remission, and Setting Aside   96
614   Other Types of Mast   97
615   Summary   98
DISCUSSION CASE: *United States* v. *Fretwell*   100
DISCUSSION AND SELF-QUIZ   104

CHAPTER VII   THE SUMMARY COURT-MARTIAL 105
701   The Nature of a Summary Court-Martial   105
702   Responsibility of a Summary Court   106
703   Convening a Summary Court-Martial   106
704   Examination of the Case File   107
705   The Pretrial Conference   108
706   The Trial   109
707   The Sentence   111
708   The Court-Martial Record   112
709   Review of Summary Courts-Martial   112
710   Summary   114
DISCUSSION AND SELF-QUIZ   114

CHAPTER VIII   THE CONVENING AUTHORITY 116
    801   The Authority to Convene   116
    802   Jurisdiction   117
    803   The Detailing of Members   119
    804   Defense Counsel and Military Judge Requirements
          For a BCD Special Court-Martial   120
    805   Defense Counsel Requirements for a Non-BCD
          Special Court-Martial   122
    806   Physical Conditions or Military Exigencies   123
    807   Command Influence   124
    808   The Legal Officer   126
    809   Summary   127
    DISCUSSION CASE: *United States* v. *Cole*   128
    DISCUSSION AND SELF-QUIZ   130

CHAPTER IX   THE TRIAL AND DEFENSE COUNSEL 133
    901   Trial Counsel's Ethics and Conduct   133
    902   Defense Counsel's Ethics and Conduct   134
    903   Trial Counsel's Preparation   137
    904   Defense Counsel's Preparation   145
    905   Counsel's Relationship with the Judge, Members, and
          Opposing Counsel   152
    906   Arguments of Counsel   153
    907   Summary   154
    DISCUSSION CASES: *United States* v. *Lewis*   154
                      United States v. *Gardner*   158
    DISCUSSION AND SELF-QUIZ   161

CHAPTER X   MEMBERS, PRESIDENT, AND MILITARY JUDGE 162
    1001   Who May Serve as Members   162
    1002   Absence of Members   163
    1003   Responsibilities Prior to Assembly   164
    1004   Duties After Assembly   165
    1005   Determining Guilt or Innocence   168
    1006   Voting on Findings   170
    1007   Determining the Sentence   172
    1008   Duties of the Non-presiding President   173
    1009   Duties of the Presiding President   174
    1010   Duties of the Military Judge   175
    1011   Summary   176
    DISCUSSION CASE: *United States* v. *Lynch*   177
    DISCUSSION AND SELF-QUIZ   180

CHAPTER XI   BASIC RULES OF EVIDENCE 181
1101   Direct and Circumstantial Evidence   182
1102   The Purposes of the Rules of Evidence   182
1103   An Orderly Presentation   183
1104   Ensuring Reliability of Evidence—Authenticity 186
1105   Wasting Time and Confusing the Issues—Relevancy 190
1106   The Exclusionary Rules of Evidence—Competency 191
1107   Summary   199
DISCUSSION CASE: *United States* v. *Gerlach*   200
DISCUSSION AND SELF-QUIZ   203

CHAPTER XII   TRIAL PROCEDURE 206
1201   The General Court-Martial   206
1202   Setting the Trial Date   207
1203   The Article 39(a) Session   207
1204   Trial Before a Military Judge Alone   208
1205   Initial Informal Inquiry   208
1206   Calling the Court to Order   208
1207   Announcing the Personnel of the Court   209
1208   The Qualifications of Counsel   209
1209   Oaths of the Military Judge, Counsel, and Members   210
1210   Challenges   211
1211   Withdrawal of Charges and Specifications   212
1212   The Arraignment   212
1213   Motions   213
1214   The Plea   214
1215   The Guilty Plea   215
1216   The Not Guilty Plea   216
1217   Opening Statements   217
1218   Summary   217
DISCUSSION CASE: *United States* v. *Chancelor*   218
DISCUSSION AND SELF-QUIZ   223

CHAPTER XIII   TRIAL PROCEDURE AND REVIEW 224
1301   Proposed Instructions   224
1302   Arguments   225
1303   Instructions   225
1304   Findings   227
1305   Pre-sentencing Procedure   230
1306   Instructions on Sentence   231
1307   Punishments   232
1308   Recommendation for Clemency   235
1309   The Record of Trial   235

1310   Initial Review   236
1311   Subsequent Review   239
1312   Deferment of Confinement   240
1313   Article 69 Relief and New Trial Petitions   240
1314   Court-Martial Orders   241
1315   Summary   241
DISCUSSION CASE: *United States* v. *Wheeler*   243
DISCUSSION AND SELF-QUIZ   248

CHAPTER XIV   ADMINISTRATIVE FACT-FINDING BODIES 250
1401   Necessity of Administrative Fact-Finding Bodies   250
1402   Types of Administrative Fact-Finding Bodies   251
1403   Selection of Type of Fact-Finding Body   252
1404   Parties   252
1405   Courts of Inquiry   254
1406   Formal Investigations   255
1407   Informal Investigations   256
1408   Investigative Report   257
1409   Summary   258
DISCUSSION AND SELF-QUIZ   259

CHAPTER XV   LINE OF DUTY AND MISCONDUCT
               DETERMINATIONS 260
1501   Misconduct/Line of Duty   261
1502   The 24-Hour Rule   263
1503   Investigation Requirement   263
1504   Responsibilities When Investigation Is Not Required   264
1505   Diseases   264
1506   Convening Authority's Action   265
1507   Summary   265
DISCUSSION AND SELF-QUIZ   266

APPENDICES
 1. Locally Prepared Report Form   271
 2. Report and Disposition of Offenses—NAVPERS 2696   272
 3. Suspect's Rights Acknowledgment/Statement   274
 4. Record of Authorization for Search   275
 5. Consent to Search   278
 6. Completed Charge Sheet (DD Form 458)   279
 7. Directions for Completing Charge Sheet and Sample Summary
    Court-Martial Record   282
 8. Administrative Remarks (Page 13)   286
 9. NJP Punishments   287
10. Limits of Punishments under Article 15   288

11. Table for Combining Restraint 289
12. Table for Combining Punishments 290
13. Court Memorandum (Page 6) for CO's NJP 291
14. Summary Court-Martial Convening Order 292
15. Trial Guide for Summary Court-Martial 293
16. Court Memorandum (Page 6) for Summary Court-Martial 322
17. Special Court-Martial Convening Order 323
18. Modification to Convening Order of Special Court-Martial 324
19. Checklist for Trial Counsel 325
20. Checklist for Defense Counsel 333
21. Informal One Officer Investigation Appointing Order 340
22. Informal Investigative Report 341

ANSWERS TO SELF-QUIZZES 343

GLOSSARY 363

BIBLIOGRAPHY 376

INDEX 378

MILITARY LAW

CHAPTER I

The History
and Background
of Military Law

Military law may be defined as the *law regulating the military establishment.* Included within this rather broad definition is the military justice system. It is designed to preserve good order and discipline within the military service in much the same manner as state and federal laws are designed to preserve law and order in the civilian community. Military law, like civilian law, requires that the rights of the individual be protected and seeks to assure every serviceman equal justice under the law.

Military authority may at times be exercised in the event the United States occupies the territory of another (military government); or governs our civilian forces in dire emergency (martial law); or takes action against nationals of another country who violate the laws of war, but these matters will not be discussed in this publication.

101 Early Military Law

Military law had its origins in ancient history. There were two distinct bodies of military law: that of the sea and that of land armies. The law of the sea developed from the necessity of protecting ships and their cargoes in international commerce. The law of land armies was based upon theories of vengeance and prevention. However, military law had one ultimate purpose throughout history insofar as it applied to warships and land armies: it had to maintain a high level of discipline both in war and peace. In order to achieve that goal, it had to be able to function under adverse conditions when ships were at war at sea and when vast armies were locked in combat on land.

To achieve this ultimate purpose the military law of the sea and that of the land took different paths, reflecting the nature of their circumstances. Land armies were greatly affected by the rise and fall of governments, while the law of the sea, because of distance alone, developed in its own manner. Brigadier General James Snedeker, U.S. Marine Corps (Ret.), in his book, *A Brief History of Courts-Martial,* describes it thus:

> A body of sea-law began to take shape under the Phoenicians. It was a unique system, independent and unchallenged, because its jurisdiction was in a region owned by no king or local chieftain. The mariners who lived aboard the galleys shared a common life and experience. Their dangers, trials, and tribulations were similar, regardless of their origin, race, or creed. Although the empires ashore rose and fell, one after another, the growing body of sea-law continued to mature, independent of dynastic changes.

The sea law was incorporated into codes issued by successive maritime powers, such as Rhodes, Amalfi, Barcelona, and the Island of Oléron. These codes combined the case law of the local maritime courts, local regulations, treatises and compilations by authors. In essence, they incorporated the customary law of the sea. (Custom may be defined as that usage which by common consent and long-established practice becomes law.)

The codes of the law of the sea changed with the rise and fall of great maritime nations, but the continuity of each successive code remained, as each relied on the other for its background and authority. The continuity of the law of the sea was essential, as maritime nations did not retain standing navies during peacetime, but disbanded them until a war situation arose.

Out of the sea law developed a branch peculiarly related to the military, which we shall term "naval law."

102   The English

It was inevitable, that as England began to become the mistress of the high seas, her naval laws and customs would influence those of other nations.

The English derived their customary sea law from the established codes of Oléron and the sea law of Wisby. At first, the maritime courts of the English seacoast towns, each with their own variation of law, determined the law that was to be followed on board the ships which they furnished to the king for his use in wartime. Eventually, the uncertainty and lack of uniformity created by such a situation encouraged the English Navy to take jurisdiction when a vessel was at sea.

As a result, a publication entitled the *Black Book of the Admiralty* was compiled during the first half of the fourteenth century. It stated that the administration of justice "according to the law and ancient customs of the sea" was among an admiral's duties. Eventually, the admirals began to issue regulations upon assuming command of a fleet, and although they did cover some offenses, "the laws and customs of the sea" were still applicable to most situations.

In describing punishments during this period, General Snedeker states the following:

> Punishments of this period were, however, barbarous. A thief was tied up to the capstan, and every man in the ship gave him five lashes on his bared back with a three-thonged whip. The habitual thief, after flogging, was dragged ashore astern of a boat, and there ignominiously dismissed. For sleeping on watch the offender had three buckets of water poured over his head and into his sleeves; but for a fourth such offense he was placed in a basket hung from the bowsprit, with a can of beer, a loaf of bread, and a knife, and left to starve or drown at his own election.

Another common punishment was keelhauling, which was the process of drawing a man by rope under the ship from one side of the ship to the other.

In 1649, the British Parliament adopted rules for the governing of a fleet which were subsequently revised and made applicable to all British naval forces three years later. These articles, promulgated during the Cromwell era, constituted the first British naval code enacted by its national legislative body. The code had universal and continuous authority over the Royal Navy. As such, it was the ancestor of all British and American naval law. The articles were modified many times prior to the American Revolution.

103 Early Origins of American Naval Law

Early in the fall of 1775, the Continental Congress began to pay serious attention to naval affairs and, after weeks of debate, it determined that if a successful war of independence was to be waged against England, an armed navy was an absolute necessity. On 13 October 1775, a Naval Committee was authorized to arm two merchant vessels—our first navy. Subsequently, the Naval Committee was authorized to arm two more merchant vessels. John Adams was one of the members of the committee. On 10 November 1775, the Continental Congress authorized the raising of two battalions of Marines—the birth of the Marine Corps.

Shortly thereafter, in December of 1775, the "Rules for the Regulation of the Navy of the United Colonies" was distributed following enactment by the Continental Congress. They were largely the work of John Adams and were based almost entirely on British law. Those regulations that were changed were done so to the extent that American political philosophy demanded. There were only 44 articles, many of which were unrelated to military law. Except for enumerating the punishments for such offenses as mutiny, murder, drunkeness, swearing, striking or quarrelling with an officer, and retreating in the face of the enemy, this first legislation provided that the "laws and customs of the sea were to predominate." The only procedure for courts-martial prescribed in these regulations was a statement as to how many officers constituted a court-martial and a recitation for the oath of members and witnesses. Therefore, the fledgling United States Navy followed the customary law of the Royal Navy.

The Articles of Confederation, adopted in 1781, provided that Congress shall have the power to make "rules for the government and regulation of the land and naval forces." The ships of the Navy had begun to fade away with the end of the Revolutionary War. Consequently, when the Constitution of the United States was established in June 1788, the Navy had no ships. Section 8 of Article I of the Constitution provides that "Congress shall have power . . . to make rules for the government and regulation of the land and naval forces."

It is very significant to the course of the development of naval law that the representatives of the people (Congress) were to determine the naval service's rules and regulations. One reason for this decision was perhaps the fact that the British Parliament was now enacting the rules and regulations for the Royal Navy. A more basic reason was the reluctance to place the military under the *complete* power of the executive branch and a desire that the military forever be subordinate to the will of the people (the President of the United States, under Article II of the Constitution, is commander in chief of the armed forces). This decision, as we shall see, eventually led to the virtual extinction of naval law as a separate body of law.

Once Congress had begun to enact legislation in the area of naval law, it began to evolve into a system of statutory law versus custom. Through this method, the new judicial and moral procedures relating to the rights of the accused and those rights afforded an individual under common law began to be reflected in naval law. As custom became more and more uncertain, the demand grew for more and more statutory regulation.

Between 1775 and 1862, at least six changes were made to naval law, continually adding to its scope and content. Flogging was abolished by Congress in 1850. In 1862, the pressures of the Civil War and the problems of administering law which was partially statutory and partially custom encouraged Congress to pass the "Articles for the Government of the Navy." These articles were traditionally called the "Rocks and Shoals." In the same enactment, Congress abolished the traditional spirit ration and, to compensate the sailor, increased his pay by five cents per day.

The Articles for the Government of the Navy, although revised several times, remained in effect until 1951. By that time the 25 articles passed in 1862 had been expanded to 70 articles.

104 The Uniform Code of Military Justice

World War II subjected the Rocks and Shoals to its most severe test and public opinion found it wanting. By 1951, naval law with its customs and traditions had been largely superseded by enactments of Congress. The net result was patchwork legislation that was inconsistent and difficult to administer. General Snedeker describes the situation in the following manner:

> The Articles for the Government of the Navy had suffered even more interpretation than amendment. Adaptation of ancient language to a modern navy was taken care of administratively, often through strained interpretation. In an air age, the articles nowhere mentioned aircraft, and the language of sailing-ship days was stretched to cover the realities of the present. The stretch had reached its elastic limit when the Navy, after reviewing the reports and recommendations of various boards, drafted a bill to amend every article in the Articles for the Government of the Navy save one.

Many of the Navy's proposed changes were enacted. However, this did not stem the tide of public opinion. There were many complaints from veterans about military law in all three services, and Congress was responsive. Congress had been contemplating further unification of the services, and it appeared that the application of the same basic law to all three services was a satisfactory step in that direction. In April of 1950, Congress passed the Uniform Code of Military Justice (hereinafter called the Code) and it became law on 5 May 1950. It was in full force and effect on 31 May 1951. The Code primarily was based upon the Army's "Articles of War" which had been amended and had served as a test of many new concepts. Consequently, "naval law," in effect, died, and in its place the Uniform Code of Military Justice, applicable to all three services, was born.

The Code was indeed a change. For example, it provided for a highest court called the United States Court of Military Appeals, which was composed of three civilian judges. It was, in effect, the supreme court of the military. Command influence was specifically condemned and sanctions imposed for its exercise. A law officer was appointed for general courts-martial who had authority similar to that of a civilian judge.

105 The Military Justice Act of 1968

From 1951 to 1968, Congress enacted only relatively minor changes to the Code. However, in 1968 Congress again made significant changes in the Uniform Code of Military Justice. The changes again reflected the application of civilian concepts of jurisprudence to the military. With these changes, it appeared that military law itself was losing more of its identity as a separate body of law.

For example, the *law officer* is now a *military judge*. An accused, in any special court-martial must be offered the services of a lawyer qualified in the sense of Article 27(b) of the Code (hereinafter called a certified military lawyer). A military judge must now be detailed to every special court-martial in which an accused can be awarded a bad conduct discharge, unless physical conditions or military exigencies prevent such detailing.

Indeed, the distinctions between a United States federal court and a special or general court-martial have been greatly lessened. Now, offenses, procedure, and evidence are based upon federal law, and the "laws and customs of the sea" discussed in the "Rules for the Regulation of the Navy of the United Colonies" are a dim memory.

106 The Officer and The Code

Today all the armed forces have the same basic statute known as the Code, and the same basic Manual for Courts-Martial implementing this Code. (There are some minor variations in each service which will be discussed later.)

Unlike his civilian counterpart, the average officer is continually called upon to perform his part in the administration of military justice. For example, Navy Regulations require him to enforce the law, to report violations of the law, and to apprehend violators of the law.

An officer may be required to serve in a police function as a shore patrol or security officer. He may become legal officer, responsible for a myriad of details involving military law that occur each day and for advising the commanding officer as to the law. Certainly at some time in his career he will be expected to conduct a preliminary inquiry into the facts of an offense and to write up a report of those facts on a NAVPERS 2696 (Report and Disposition of Offenses form). He probably will be called upon to sit as a member of a court-martial. Although the possibility is not as great under the new Code, he may have to act as the trial or defense counsel in a special court-martial.

As he becomes more senior, the officer will be expected to conduct summary courts-martial, to act as president of courts-martial, and eventually to act as the convening authority and to perform his judicial and command responsibilities in a manner that will promote discipline and high morale in his command.

107 Authoritative Structure and Basic Sources of Military Law

Military law comes from many sources. However, there is a certain precedence in these sources which must be delineated; otherwise, in the event of conflict, there is no way to determine which source prevails.

1. *The Constitution.* The Constitution of the United States is the *supreme* law of the land. From the Constitution the President, Congress, and the Supreme Court of the United States derive their authority. As previously mentioned, Article I, Section 8 of the Constitution grants Congress the authority to make rules for the regulation of the land and naval forces. The U.S. Constitution is contained in Appendix 1 of the MCM.

2. *The Uniform Code of Military Justice.* Congress, pursuant to this authority, eventually enacted the Uniform Code of Military Justice, the "Code." It is contained, with its amendments incorporated therein, in Appendix 2 of the MCM of 1969.

3. *The Manual for Courts-Martial, United States, 1969 (Revised Edition).* Congress in writing the code did not write a book for the military; it only passed 140 articles. It delegated to the President of the United States the following authority:

> Article 36. President May Prescribe Rules. (a) The *procedure* including modes of proof, in cases before courts-martial, courts of inquiry, military commissions, and other military tribunals may be prescribed by the President by regulations which shall, so far as he considers practicable, *apply the principles of law and the rules of evidence generally recognized in the trial of criminal cases in the United States district courts,* but which may not be contrary to or inconsistent with this chapter. (Emphasis added.)

Consequently, Congress has delegated authority to the executive branch of the government to establish the rules of evidence and the procedures before courts-martial, with the requirement that they should follow the *federal* rules of evidence and procedure *except* where they may be inconsistent with the Code.

The President responded to this authority vested in him by Congress by prescribing the Manual for Courts-Martial (MCM). The MCM is the basic directive implementing the Code. It is available on all ships and stations in the naval service. Every Navy and Marine Corps officer has a responsibility to have at least a working knowledge of the MCM.

4. *The Manual of the Judge Advocate General.* In drafting the Code and MCM it was recognized that there were certain matters that were peculiar to the individual services that the MCM could not adequately prescribe. Consequently, the Code and the MCM permit the "Secretary concerned" to prescribe regulations in certain areas. For example, the Secretary of the Navy, under Article 23 of the Code, has the authority to designate other commanding officers or officers in charge who may convene a special court-martial, in addition to those discussed in Article 23 of the Code. The Manual of the Judge Advocate General (the JAG Manual) contains most of these designations and other minor variations in the manner of administering justice which are peculiar to the Navy and Marine Corps. This JAG Manual is, therefore, a direct source of military law as it is a directive of the Secretary of the Navy.

5. *The U.S. Court of Military Appeals (COMA).* Next to Congress, the most predominate factor in military law is the U.S. Court of Military Appeals. The court, established by Congress, is a United States court and not an administrative agency. Unlike other United States courts, which derive their authority from Article III of the Constitution, its authority is derived from Article I of the U.S. Constitution under the authority of Congress to make rules for the regulation of the land and naval forces.

It is the highest appeals court in the military judicial system. It consists of three civilian judges who are appointed by the President of the United States with the advice and consent of Congress. They are appointed for a term of fifteen years. Article 67 of the Code discusses the court.

The U.S. Court of Military Appeals basically determines questions of law. In determining what the law is, the court interprets and, if necessary, modifies the Code, the MCM, the JAG Manual and other regulatory publications. It applies Supreme Court decisions of constitutional import to the military judicial system unless they are excluded directly or by necessary implication by the provisions of the Constitution itself.

In *United States* v. *Tempia* (a Discussion Case at the end of the third chapter) the Court of Military Appeals applied a Supreme Court decision *(Miranda* v. *Arizona)* to the military. Briefly, it required that an accused be advised of his right to a lawyer free of charge before he makes any statement. This decision necessitated the revision of the MCM. The Court has consistently reviewed the provisions of the Code and MCM to determine their constitutionality.

6. *The Courts of Military Review.* These courts are lower courts one level below the U.S. Court of Military Appeals. They are established within the office of each Judge Advocate General. They review questions of both law and fact. Sentences, as approved, that extend to dishonorable

or bad conduct discharge; dismissal of an officer, cadet, or midshipman; confinement for one year or more; or which affect a general or flag officer, must be reviewed by a Court of Military Review.

7. *United States Navy Regulations 1948.* These regulations are applicable to all personnel within the Department of the Navy (which includes the Navy and Marine Corps). They are issued by the Secretary of the Navy. They are a direct source of military law in those matters in which the Code or the MCM permit the Secretary of the Navy to prescribe the law.

For example, paragraph 20 of the MCM provides that a man under arrest "is subject to the restrictions incident to arrest prescribed in regulations of the Secretary concerned." Article 1405 of Navy Regulations does provide guidelines, that have the force of law, relating to the limits for an arrest of an officer.

Navy Regulations also prescribe the rights, duties, and responsibilities of members of the naval service (the Navy and Marine Corps). For example, the possession of alcoholic liquors for beverage purposes on board a ship or aircraft (with certain exceptions) is prohibited by Article 1269 of Navy Regulations. If a person violates this article, he is charged with a violation of an article of the Code (Article 92). This article provides for the failure to obey a lawful order or regulation.

As a practical matter, Navy Regulations and other instructions and notices of local commands are a very important source of law. Of course, they must be lawful to be enforceable.

108 Publications Relating to Military Law

All decisions of the Court of Military Appeals (except for the most recent) may be found in two basic authoritative publications: the *United States Court of Military Appeals* and *Court-Martial Reports.* The *Court-Martial Reports* (CMR's) also contain selected cases decided by the Courts of Military Review and are most commonly used in those naval service libraries fortunate enough to possess them.

Throughout the book the reader will note that cases are described as follows: *United States v. Parish,* 17 USCMA 411, 38 CMR 209 (1968). This means that the case of United States versus Parish may be found on page 411 of Volume 17 of the book, the *United States Court of Military Appeals.* It may also be found on page 209 of Volume 38 of the *Court-Martial Reports.*

The *JAG Journal,* published periodically by the Office of the Judge Advocate General of the Navy, contains authoritative discussions of specific problems in military law. It is available throughout the naval service and is highly informative.

The Digest of Opinions, which contained digests of selected opinions of the three JAGS, the Treasury Department, the CMR's and other governmental departments and agencies, discontinued publication in 1968.

Other regulatory publications, such as the BUPERS Manual, Marine Corps Personnel Manual, and instructions and directives from higher authority, should always be consulted when they may be relevant to a particular issue. For example, the JAG Manual states the following as it relates to the preparation of records of summary courts-martial:

> Unless otherwise prescribed by the convening authority or officer having supervisory authority, the evidence considered by a summary court-martial need not be summarized or attached to the record of trial.

The significance of this provision is this: the evidence must be summarized in a summary court *if* the commanding officer, or the officer next in the chain of command who reviews the summary courts-martial, requires it. Therefore, the instructions of the reviewing authorities should be consulted before the court is held, in order to properly prepare a record for review.

There are many publications that are published by the Army, Navy, and Air Force that are invaluable. For example, the Navy (through JAG) publishes its own trial guides and instructions for presidents and military judges of special courts-martial.

Other source materials, less frequently used, may be found in various service law libraries throughout the world.

109 The Present Military Justice System

Prior to going further, it is essential to understand the basic nature of our present military justice system. Offenses may vary from those that are very minor to those that are very serious. The type of accused may vary from the continual troublemaker to the one-time offender. Consequently, as in the civilian system of law, our military law provides a graduated response to offenses committed. As the offense and offender warrant, this response becomes more severe. The following discussion is intended as an introduction and is only a brief summary of future material.

1. *Nonpunitive Measures.*   Paragraph 128c of the MCM encourages the commanding officer to employ a broad spectrum of encouragements and discouragements without formal proceedings or safeguards. For example, oral reprimands or extra military instruction (EMI) may be utilized. See Chapter VI.

2. *Nonjudicial Punishment.*   Nonjudicial punishment is utilized to impose disciplinary punishment for minor offenses without the convening of a court-martial. It is imposed when nonpunitive measures will not

suffice. Chapter VI of this publication and Chapter XXVI of the MCM discuss nonjudicial punishment.

3. *Summary Courts-Martial.* A summary court-martial, as its name implies, is the court that can award the least punishment and furnishes the least protection to the accused. For example, a summary court-martial cannot award a bad conduct discharge, nor may it award over one month's confinement at hard labor. It consists of one commissioned officer who generally acts as judge, jury, trial and defense counsel. Objection may be made to this form of trial. In such an event, the case could be forwarded to a general or special court.

4. *Special Courts-Martial.* The special court-martial is an intermediate court and the one with which many Navy and Marine Corps officers are most familiar. The punishment that a special court can award is limited. For example, a special court-martial can only award a maximum of six months' confinement at hard labor regardless of what the maximum punishment for the offense is.

A bad conduct discharge can only be adjudged if a verbatim record of the proceedings and testimony has been made, the appointed defense counsel is a certified military lawyer, and a military judge is detailed to the trial (except when the military judge could not be detailed because of physical conditions or military exigencies). A special court-martial may consist of not fewer than three members, or a military judge and not fewer than three members, or a military judge sitting alone. A military judge need not be detailed to a special court-martial which cannot adjudge a bad conduct discharge.

However, the accused must be afforded the opportunity to be represented by a certified military lawyer even though the court cannot award a bad conduct discharge. If the accused requests such a counsel, a certified military lawyer must be furnished him unless physical conditions or military exigencies prevent it. See Chapter VIII for a complete discussion of this material.

5. *General Courts-Martial.* The general court-martial is the most "serious" of the three. For example, it can award any punishment that the MCM prescribes for an offense, including death. As the possible punishments are more severe, the rights of the accused are greater. It must be composed of at least five members and a military judge. The detailed trial and defense counsel in such a case are always certified military lawyers.

A military judge, if the accused requests and the judge consents, may sit alone (without members) in any non-capital (i.e., non-death penalty) case and determine the facts and the law and arrive at an appropriate sentence. See Chapter XII.

110 Summary

Sea law was first developed by early civilizations to protect ships and their cargoes in international commerce. Naval law developed as a branch of sea law. Custom and tradition kept it alive for centuries.

The British set the pattern for our naval law. As Congress was given the responsibility of making laws for the naval service, naval law began to reflect more and more civilian concepts of jurisprudence. Legislative enactments were beginning to take the place of the customs and traditions of the sea. Eventually, in 1951, the Uniform Code of Military Justice virtually extinguished naval law as a separate entity and put all three services under one body of law. The Military Justice Act of 1968, a major change to the Uniform Code of Military Justice, further narrowed the distinctions between a federal court and a military court-martial and expanded the rights of the accused.

The basic direct sources of military law are the U.S. Constitution, the Code, the MCM, the JAG Manual and the Court of Military Appeals.

Discussion Case

Acting Midshipman Philip Spencer, U.S. Navy, 18 years of age, must have regarded the USS *Somers* with awe when he first beheld her on 13 August 1842. The *Somers* was a beautiful new brig-of-war that had just been released from the shipyards some months ago. Although displacing 266 tons, she was so sharply built that she only carried a crew of 120. Designed for swiftness, the brig was very top-heavy and carried only ten cannons.

Anyone observing this young midshipman would hardly envision him as the principal participant in the first recorded mutiny on board a United States vessel since the founding of our country.

An indolent, dull-witted boy in many ways, Spencer attended Hobart College from 1838 to 1841, when he was withdrawn for academic failure. He next attended Union College, where he was one of the founders of Chi Psi fraternity. He especially enjoyed and originated some of the secret rituals for his fraternity. Shortly

thereafter, he obtained an appointment as an acting midshipman in the United States Navy.

His father was perhaps instrumental in his appointment, as he was then Secretary of War in President Tyler's cabinet. What the elder Spencer did not know, or chose to ignore, was that his son's highest dream was to become a famous and renowned pirate. During short tours on two previous U.S. vessels before he arrived on board the *Somers,* Spencer retained his dream—and often discussed it. However, the reasons given for Spencer's transfer from his previous ship were "drunkeness and scandalous conduct."

When Philip Spencer reported to the USS *Somers,* there was no United States Naval Academy. The Navy had begun to realize, however, that there was a need for training future officers and had chosen to do so by setting up small schools in some of the principal cities of the east and utilizing vessels as "floating academies." The USS *Somers* was the first of such training ships.

As captain of the *Somers*, the Navy had selected Commander Alexander Slidell Mackenzie, a well-known naval officer-author of his day and a man with wealth, power and influence in his own family. For example, his sister, Jane Slidell, was the wife of Commodore Matthew Calbraith Perry.

The *Somers* left on 13 September 1842 for a cruise to Africa, thence to travel to the West Indies, and finally home to New York. Spencer, for whatever reasons, was never accepted by his fellow officers and sought the comfort of the crew—many of whom he generously furnished with rum and cigars. For example, by 26 November 1842, Spencer had purchased ten pounds of tobacco and 700 cigars. Spencer had two intimate enlisted friends—Samuel Cromwell and Elisha Small.

During the voyage, it was apparent that Spencer's obsession with piracy had not ended. Outside his intimate circle, he discussed pirates and what a pirate ship the *Somers* would make. He discussed a pirate flag and what it would look like. After the captain criticized him for another matter, he stated he would like to throw the captain overboard. Whether these were just the rantings of an insubordinate dolt whose father happened to be in a position of importance, we shall never know.

However, Spencer did more than talk. He put his aspirations in writing. A list, written in Greek, indicated whom he considered would join him, whom he considered doubtful, and who would not join in an apparent takeover of the ship. Only four names were listed as "certain" and those included Spencer himself. One man was never involved and James W. Wales, who was listed as "certain," first re-ported Spencer to the captain. An "E. Andrews" was listed. No such man was aboard the ship, but Spencer insisted the name was an alias for Small.

On 25 November 1842, Midshipman Spencer approached Purser's Steward Wales, listed as "certain" on his Greek list, and asked him to join in a mutiny. Spencer reportedly told Wales that he had 20 men in his group and that he planned to take over the *Somers* and turn her into a pirate ship. All the officers were to be killed. He then threatened Wales not to divulge his plan and asked him to join the mutiny. Small was in the vicinity and appeared to be involved with Spencer in the plan, according to Wales.

Wales related the story to the captain who at first dismissed it as a joke, but as a precaution asked Lieutenant Gansevoort to investigate the matter. The lieutenant did develop that Spencer had asked another officer if he was familiar with the Isle of Pines, a well-known pirate haunt. That was the only corroborative evidence prior to the ordering of Spencer's arrest on 27 November 1842. It is worthwhile relating what occurred prior to Spencer's apprehension. At evening quarters the following transpired:

MACKENZIE: I learn, Mr. Spencer, that you aspire to the command of the *Somers*.

SPENCER: Oh, no, sir!

MACKENZIE: Did you not tell Mr. Wales, sir, that you had a plan to kill the commander, the officers, and a considerable portion of the crew of this vessel and convert her into a pirate?

SPENCER: I may have told him so, sir, but in joke.

Spencer was then searched and placed in irons.

Small and Cromwell were arrested one day later. Later, the lieutenant interviewed Spencer who admitted he had had this plot on every ship he had been attached to, but had never gone as far with it as he had aboard the *Somers*. Spencer thought it was a "mania" with him. He also stated that "E. Andrews," the name on the list, stood for Small and not Cromwell.

The captain and his officers became convinced that a mutiny was possible at any moment and that the only way to avoid it was to hang the ringleaders. In truth, the evidence to this effect was, at its best, slim. Apparently Lieutenant Gansevoort had discussed the possibility of hanging the three captives with most of the officers and had majority approval. However, they felt they needed a reason for hanging the men at this time. They told the captain that if more prisoners were taken this would obstruct navigation (the prisoners were in irons on the quarterdeck) and increase the possibility of rescue of the prisoners. Commander Mackenzie then arrested four more men for mutiny (none of whom were ever convicted of any crime regarding the mutiny). Upon this basis, the captain then asked his officers "to take into deliberate and dispassionate consideration the present condition of the vessel and the contingencies of every nature that the future may embrace, throughout the remainder of our cruise, and enlighten me with your opinion as to the best course to be pursued."

The officers heard thirteen witnesses, all of whom were sworn and their testimony written down. They then signed these statements. Lieutenant Gansevoort, who had already expressed his opinion of the guilt of the accused on several occasions and had garnered most of the evidence, was the senior man present. The prisoners were not brought before the officers, nor did they know they were being tried. The captain had already begun to prepare a watch bill for the executions; however, the council still continued to hear evidence. The inquiry did not arrive at a decision and resumed the next day. By midmorning they had reached a decision. They recommended the three accused should be put to death based upon the fact that "it would be impossible to carry them to the United States" due to the possibility of further mutinous acts. Even before they were led away, both Cromwell and Spencer asserted Cromwell's innocence.

The three were then hanged with the roll of drums and the thunder of cannon, as prescribed in the commander's watch bill.

When the *Somers* arrived in New York and the story was released, Commander Mackenzie was considered a hero. However, Secretary of War Spencer and Cromwell's widow began to raise questions about the nature of the proceedings. A court of inquiry was held and found Mackenzie blameless. Mackenzie was later tried for murder of the three men by a court-martial and acquitted.

NOTE

Many people considered Spencer, Small, and Cromwell innocent, including James Fenimore Cooper, who wrote a pamphlet in 1844 called "The Cruise of the *Somers*," in which he severely criticized the Navy and Commander Mackenzie.

Some historians contend that James Melville was contemplating the *Somers'* mutiny when he wrote *Billy Budd*.

To this day, there are many who believe Spencer was hanged because of the suspicious and unreasoning fear of Commander Mackenzie. The captain's flagrant abuse of authority and his disregard for the forms of law are the reasons why Spencer's guilt or innocence remains such an issue. Even in 1842, an accused was entitled to appear before the tribunal, make objections, plead, confront the witnesses against him, and examine them and present a defense. (Regulations for the Navy and Marine Corps, 19 February 1841.) As a man of letters, Mackenzie must have been well aware of the procedure for trial by court-martial in his day. An analysis of the case indicates that whatever "dire necessity" was present for an immediate trial, it was not of such a nature as to deny these elemental rights.

The *Somers* mutiny, by emphasizing the necessity of weeding out the likes of Midshipman Spencer and the need for developing a truly professional academy for naval officers, provided the impetus for the formation of the United States Naval Academy. Frederic F. Van de Water in his book *The Captain Called It Mutiny* expressed it thus: "George Bancroft was the father of the professional school at Annapolis, but Alexander Slidell Mackenzie, in association with Philip Spencer, were among the academy's remoter forebears."

The court of inquiry and the subsequent court-martial brought out the fact that flogging was the main instrument for enforcing discipline on the *Somers* and that it was used frequently. Partly as a result of this case, flogging as a punishment was abolished in the U.S. Navy in 1850.

The hanging, without the intervention of a court-martial or formal investigation, has affected the Navy's policy as regards the death sentence for over a hundred years. Although the Army and Air Force have executed 159 persons since 1930, the Navy has not executed anyone since 1849!

Perhaps the most important lesson of the Spencer mutiny, and why it is discussed at length here, is that it emphasizes what can transpire if the form and substance of laws are ignored or flaunted:

1. A severe and final penalty (hanging) was exacted, yet many are not sure that *all three men* were guilty.

2. The Navy suffered immeasurable damage to its reputation.

In the end, perhaps justice triumphed. The sadness of the *Somers* case is that we will never know. If a court-martial or even a fair investigation had been held, many of the doubts raised about the "mutiny" would long ago have been dispelled.

Today, the Uniform Code of Military Justice provides the following:

> Any person subject to this chapter who . . . knowingly and intentionally fails to enforce or comply with any provision of this chapter regulating the proceedings before, during, or after trial of an accused; shall be punished as a court-martial may direct.

DISCUSSION AND SELF-QUIZ*

1. You are the legal officer on board your ship. Seaman Jones has just been tried by special court-martial for larceny and acquitted (i.e., found not guilty). After the court-martial, a Seaman Doe, who has been on leave, comes to you and informs you that he *saw* Jones take the money. The trial counsel (i.e., prosecutor) tells you that this new evidence is sufficient to obtain a conviction if Jones is retried. The Fifth Amendment to the Constitution of the United States states that no person shall "be subject for the same offense to be twice put in jeopardy of life or limb. . . ." Does this constitutional provision apply to the military? See Article 44(a) of the Code.

2. As Officer of the Deck (in port), you are informed by the messenger of the watch that Seaman Roe has assaulted Seaman Apprentice Smith with a knife and has maimed him terribly. The commanding officer of your ship feels a general court-martial (the most serious type) may be warranted. The Fifth Amendment to the Constitution provides that "no person shall be held to answer for a capital or otherwise infamous crime, unless on a presentment or indictment of a Grand Jury." A grand jury in civilian law is a group of persons (12 to 23 in number) designated to examine into accusations against persons charged with a crime to determine if there is just cause to bring them to trial. Is there a similar provision in the military? See Article 32 of the Code and paragraph 34 of the MCM.

3. A special court-martial on board your ship has just awarded Seaman Doe four months' confinement at hard labor, the forfeiture of $50 per month for four months, and reduction to E–1 (seaman recruit). "Bail" is security (such as money) given to guarantee the appearance of a person in court or jail. It may be tendered prior to and after a trial (while awaiting appeal). The Eighth Amendment to the Constitution states that "excessive bail shall not be required." Does the military have a bail provision? See Article 57(d) of the Code and paragraph 89*c* (7) of the MCM.

4. Let us now examine amendments to the Constitution and determine their military equivalents. After each constitutional guarantee will follow the MCM or Code provision applicable:

a. "Speedy and public trial." This constitutional right is contained in Articles 10 and 33 of the Code and paragraphs 68*i* and 215*e* of the MCM.

b. "To be informed of the nature and cause of the accusation." This constitutional right is contained in Article 35 of the Code and paragraphs 32*f*(1) and 33*c* of the MCM.

c. "To be confronted with the witnesses against him." This constitutional right is contained in Article 39 of the Code.

d. "To have compulsory process for obtaining witnesses in his favor." This constitutional right is contained in Article 46 of the Code.

e. "To have the assistance of Counsel for his defense." This constitutional right is contained in Article 27 of the Code.

---

* Answers to Self-Quizzes begin on page 343.

NOTE

There are other rights that are constitutional in nature that apply to the serviceman such as habeas corpus, "due process," the opportunity to testify in his own behalf or remain silent, and the right not to be subject to cruel and unusual punishments. However, the serviceman is also given advantages that his civilian counterparts generally lack, such as:

1. Automatic review of the findings *and* sentence in any court-martial;

2. The assistance of a free lawyer *automatically* regardless of the financial status of the accused and in cases the seriousness of which would not warrant counsel in a civilian court;

3. A broader right against self-incrimination under Article 31 than is given in the Fifth Amendment to the Constitution;

4. The right of a hearing on the sentence and of the accused to make an unsworn statement in mitigation and extenuation.

CHAPTER II

Apprehension
and Restraint

This chapter will be devoted to those events and situations that may arise following the commission or report of an apparent offense. The Navy or Marine Corps serviceman may be required to perform more police functions than the ordinary citizen in civilian life (even when he is off duty). Therefore, it is vital that he understand the basic rules pertaining to apprehension, custody, pretrial restraint, and speedy trial.

201   Apprehension

An offender against the Code may first come into contact with the judicial processes through being apprehended. *Apprehension* in military law means the same thing as *arrest* under other criminal laws. But since arrest under military law means something else again, the reader is enjoined to adhere carefully to the terminology of the Code.

The circumstances surrounding the apprehension of offenders will vary with each situation. Sometimes the offender is apprehended, practically on the spot, by an actual witness to the offense; again he may not be apprehended except as the result of a long, tedious investigation.

Physically, the act of apprehension is simple. Informing the accused that he is being taken into custody or being apprehended will suffice, as long as the accused understands that the person apprehending him intends to detain him. Simple sentences like "I am taking you into custody," or "I am apprehending you" are considered adequate to convey that intent.

The person apprehending an accused should inform the suspect of the reason therefor and should identify himself.

In most cases, a person being taken into custody will not resist. If he does, then reasonable force may be used to take and retain custody of him.

Who may apprehend? Officers, warrant officers, noncommissioned officers, petty officers, and persons performing military police, air police, or shore patrol duties and such persons as are designated by proper authority to perform guard or police duties, including duties as criminal investigators, may apprehend anyone subject to the Code *upon reasonable belief that an offense has been committed and that the person apprehended committed it.* Noncommissioned officers and other enlisted persons performing police duties should apprehend a commissioned or warrant officer only if specifically directed by a commissioned officer, except where such action is necessary to prevent disgrace to the service, the commission of a serious offense, or the escape of one who has committed a serious offense. In all cases where an enlisted man or warrant officer apprehends a commissioned officer, he must immediately notify the officer to whom he is responsible or an officer of the shore patrol.

The military status of a person does not exempt him from arrest by civilian law enforcement officers. When a single criminal act is a violation of both the laws of a State and of the Code, the offender may either be arrested by civilian police or apprehended by the military authorities.

202 Custody

Custody is that *restraint* of free movement imposed by lawful apprehension. The restraint may be forcible, utilizing handcuffs, an armlock, or other physical means, or the restraint may consist of a submission to apprehension by the offender.

Once a person is apprehended for an offense he should be returned to his command without delay. Responsibility for the offender is then assumed by the duty officer. A shore patrol report or other written notice of the alleged offense may either accompany the offender or be forwarded to the commanding officer by other means.

203 Probable Cause for Pretrial Restraint

Once an alleged offender has been taken into custody following apprehension and he is returned to his command, a determination must be made as to whether the accused should be subjected to pretrial restraint.

The MCM states that no person may be ordered into pretrial restraint except for probable cause. No authority may order a person into pretrial restraint unless he has personal knowledge of the offense or has made inquiry into it. To constitute probable cause, full inquiry is not required, but the known or reported facts should be sufficient to furnish reasonable grounds for believing that the offense has been committed by the person to be restrained. No restraint need be imposed in cases involving minor offenses.

Pretrial restraint should not be used as a convenience to command nor should it be arbitrarily imposed. Each instance should be determined on its individual merits.

204 Who May Restrain

Only a commanding officer to whose authority the individual is subject may order a commissioned officer, warrant officer, or civilian into pretrial restraint. This authority may not be delegated.

Any commissioned officer may order an enlisted member into pretrial restraint. However, the commanding officer may delegate to warrant officers and rated men authority to place enlisted members of his command or detachment (or who are temporarily within his jurisdiction) in pretrial restraint *at the instant when restraint is necessary.*

205 Types of Pretrial Restraint

Pending disposition of his case, one of three types of pretrial restraint may be imposed upon the accused: confinement, arrest, or restriction in lieu of arrest. (It must be emphasized at this point that no restraint need be imposed in cases involving minor offenses.)

1. *Confinement.* This is the physical restraint of a person, generally in a brig or guardhouse. *It will not be imposed pending trial unless deemed necessary to insure the presence of the accused at the trial or because of the seriousness of the offense charged.*

For example, a person charged with an offense normally tried by summary court-martial or a person who surrenders following an unauthorized absence ordinarily should not be confined prior to trial.

A person is generally placed in confinement by the committing officer signing a "Confinement Order" (NAVPERS Form 1523). Information contained in the form includes the identity of the accused and the offense with which he is charged. The accused is then escorted under guard to the place of confinement and the confinement order is presented to the person in authority at the confinement facility. The prisoner should be given a physical examination prior to his confinement.

2. *Arrest.* Arrest is a moral (as distinguished from physical) restraint imposed upon either officers or enlisted men by oral or written orders of competent authority limiting the person's personal liberty pending disposition of the charges. For example, an order for a person to remain within his quarters or barracks constitutes an arrest. *United States v. Haynes,* 15 USCMA 122, 35 CMR 94 (1964) and *United States v. Williams,* 16 USCMA 589, 37 CMR 209 (1967). The restraint is not enforced by physical force but by virtue of the accused's moral and legal

obligation to obey the order. A person in arrest cannot be required to perform his full military duties. If he is placed on duty inconsistent with his status of arrest, his arrest is terminated. However, he can be required to do ordinary cleaning or policing of his personal area and to take part in routine training or duties not involving the exercise of command or the bearing of arms.

3. *Restriction in Lieu of Arrest.* This is a moral and legal pretrial restraint on the liberty of the individual imposed by an order directing him to remain within certain specified limits. Although very similar to the status of arrest, it is a lesser restraint because it involves broader geographical limits and permits the restricted person to perform his military duties. For example, restriction in lieu of arrest would generally encompass the limits of a naval or marine base, less certain prescribed areas. Restriction in lieu of arrest is imposed either because the accused's presence during an investigation of his conduct may be necessary or to prevent further exposure to the temptation of misconduct similar to that for which he is already under charges.

During pretrial restraint, no punishment (other than minor punishments for infractions of discipline while confined) may be imposed either prior to trial or until the sentence has been ordered executed after trial. If an accused is compelled to perform hard labor, work with, and receive the same treatment as sentenced prisoners, he is being punished. *United States v. Nelson,* 18 USCMA 177, 39 CMR 177 (1969).

An officer placed under arrest or confinement cannot visit his commanding officer or other superior officer except in cases of illness or emergency. In the event he desires to discuss official business with his superiors, the restrained officer must request an audience in writing. He generally is not confined to his room nor is he deprived of the proper use of any part of the ship to which he had a right before his restraint, except the quarterdeck and bridges. Similarly, an officer's confinement or restraint on a shore station should not be unduly rigorous (Article 1405, Navy Regulations).

Policy considerations and further discussion regarding pretrial restraint may be found in the Code, the MCM, the Corrections Manual (NAVPERS 15825 Revised), Navy Regulations, and BUPERS Instruction 1626.5.

206 Release from Restraint

Restraint, once imposed, may not be removed except under certain specified conditions. Arrest and restriction in lieu of arrest may be lifted by the authority ordering the restraint or by a superior in his chain of command. Once a person is confined, however, he passes from the jurisdiction of the person ordering confinement, and can only be released by order of the commanding officer of the activity where the confinement takes place.

207　Offenses Connected with Apprehension and Restraint

1. *Offenses Against Restraint.*　Article 95 of the Code provides for the punishment of a person who resists apprehension; or who, once lawfully apprehended, escapes from custody; or who breaks arrest; or who escapes from confinement. By analyzing the technical terms of these offenses it can be determined that custody and confinement are forms of physical restraint, since their violation constitutes an escape, while arrest is a form of moral restraint since its violation constitutes a breaking. There is no mention of restriction in lieu of arrest in Article 95, so its violation is charged as an offense under Article 134, "Conduct to the Prejudice of Good Order and Discipline."

2. *Unlawful Detention of Another.*　Article 97 of the Code provides that "any person subject to this Chapter who, except as provided by law, apprehends, arrests, or confines any person shall be punished as a court-martial may direct." This article is self-explanatory, and its warning is clear.

3. *Releasing a Prisoner Without Authority.*　Article 96 makes a person punishable for the negligent or intentional release of a properly detained prisoner committed to his charge.

208　Speedy Trial

The MCM states that an accused "is entitled to be tried within a reasonable time after being placed under a restraint such as restriction, arrest, or confinement or after charges are preferred." If an unreasonable delay results, an accused is entitled to a dismissal of the charges. The imposition of restraint or preferring of charges (whichever was first) starts the period of time for which the government must account in bringing the accused to trial. Paragraph 215e, MCM.

Some matters to be considered in determining "reasonableness" are:

1. Whether the accused has demanded to be brought to trial and, if so, when;

2. How much delay, if any, occurred at the defense request;

3. The amount of time required for pretrial processing, investigation, and preparation;

4. Whether the delay or any part thereof was arbitrary or oppressive;

5. Whether the accused was in pretrial restraint and, if so, the nature of that restraint.

Reasonableness of delay should also be determined in the light of the following articles in the UCMJ:

1. Article 10 provides that when any person "subject to this chapter is placed in arrest or confinement prior to trial, *immediate steps* shall be taken to inform him of the specific wrong of which he is accused and to try him or to dismiss the charges and release him." (Emphasis supplied.)

2. Article 33 requires the completion of a pretrial investigation (the prelude to a general court-martial) and its forwarding with allied papers to the officer exercising general court-martial jurisdiction within *eight days* after the accused is ordered into arrest or confinement.

3. Article 98 provides for the punishment of any person who "is responsible for unnecessary delay in the disposition of any case of a person accused of an offense under this chapter."

What if an officer is unaware of the provisions of the Code as regards the accused's right to a speedy trial? In *United States* v. *Parish,* 17 USCMA 411, 38 CMR 209 (1968) this issue was discussed. The Court of Military Appeals stated:

> As to the inexperience of the officers involved, we do not believe this is a legally or factually sufficient explanation. Whether they thought they were doing their job is irrelevant. The plain fact of the matter is that the delay occurred.

209 Summary

An officer may apprehend anyone subject to the Code if he has a reasonable belief that an offense has been committed and that the person to be apprehended committed it.

Confinement will not be imposed pending trial unless deemed necessary because of the seriousness of the offense charged or to ensure the presence of the accused at trial. A lesser criteria is provided in order to warrant restriction in lieu of arrest.

After charges are preferred, or if an accused is subject to any form of pretrial restraint, he must be brought to trial within a reasonable period of time. Reasonableness must be evaluated in terms of the Code, which discusses immediate steps in this regard.

Discussion Case

UNITED STATES, Appellee

v.

RICHARD P. ELLSEY, Private, U.S. Marine Corps, Appellant

16 USCMA 455, 37 CMR 75

(1966)

Opinion of the Court

FERGUSON, Judge:

The accused was taken from the battalion adjutant's office by a guard, who was there furnished with a written confinement order directing his incarceration in the brig. En route to the confinement facility, accused was accompanied to his barracks in order to pack his gear. While at the latter place, accused evaded his guard and disappeared. Based on these facts, the accused was, as noted above, charged with escape from custody and convicted, because of the alteration of the count, of escape from confinement. The question of variance before us thus turns on the difference between "custody" and "confinement."

Code, Article 95, under which the accused stands convicted, provides for the punishment of "any person subject to this chapter who resists apprehension or breaks arrest *or who escapes from custody or confinement.*" (Emphasis supplied.) It is urged that the emphasized portion of the statute creates but the single offense of escape which may be proven to be committed —regardless of the allegations—from either custody or confinement, both being mere forms of physical restraint. We cannot agree, for we believe the argument overlooks essential differences between the two statutes.

Confinement is defined by the Uniform Code of Military Justice as "the physical restraint of a person." Code, Article 9. It may be imposed upon an enlisted person only by a commissioned officer, and by a warrant officer, petty officer, or noncommissioned officer only when such authority is conferred upon them by a commanding officer. It may be imposed upon a commissioned or warrant officer or civilian "only by a commanding officer to whose authority he is subject." Such authority may not be delegated. Code, Article 9. It may not ordinarily be executed if an accused is charged with an offense normally tried by summary court-martial, Code, Article 10, nor may it be carried out "in immediate association with enemy prisoners or other foreign nationals." Code, Article 12. Where imposed by a court-martial, it begins to run from the date the sentence is adjudged. Code, Article 57. Confinement cannot be refused "when the committing officer furnishes a statement, signed by him, of the offense charged against the prisoner," and must be reported by the custodian, "within twenty-four hours after commitment or as soon as he is relieved," to the commanding officer. Code, Article 11.

On the other hand, custody is defined only inferentially by the Code, which declares "Apprehension is the taking of a person into custody." Code, Article 7. The Manual elaborates upon this by declaring, in paragraph 174*d*:

". . . Custody is that restraint of free locomotion which is imposed by lawful apprehension. The restraint *may be corporeal and forcible or, once there has been a submission to apprehension or a forcible taking into custody, it may consist of control exercised in the presence of the prisoner by official acts or orders.*"

Unlike confinement, "any person authorized under regulations governing the armed forces" may apprehend members of the services and thus impose the status of custody upon them. So, also, may officers, warrant officers, and noncommissioned officers quell disorders and "apprehend persons subject to this chapter who take part therein." Code, Article 7. In short, as the Manual points out, "There is a clear distinction between the authority to apprehend and the authority to arrest or confine." Manual, paragraph 19*d*. Moreover, those empowered to apprehend are only authorized "to secure the custody of an alleged offender until proper authority may be notified." Manual, paragraph 19*d*.

Thus, it will be seen that custody and confinement are entirely different in nature. The first results from apprehension and lasts "until proper authority may be notified." Manual, paragraph 19*d*. It may be imposed by any person empowered by departmental regulations. Confinement, on the other hand, absent authorization by a commanding officer, may be ordered only by a commissioned officer. Its execution before and after trial is subjected to strict control. Finally, while custody may of necessity be maintained by physical restraint, it also suffices to utilize no more than moral suasion. Hence, far from being identical to confinement, it is an altogether different condition.

Indeed, the legislative history evidences the intent of Congress to create two different types of restraint in dealing with custody and confinement. By the enactment of the pertinent Articles of the Code, a "certain duality of meaning in the words 'arrest,' 'restraint,' 'confinement,' and words of that character," was found and "we adopted this scheme to clarify the defintions [*sic*] of those words and started off with 'apprehension' in article 7." Hearings before House Armed Services Committee on H.R. 2498, 81st Congress, 1st Session, pages 901–902.

What was intended by custody was the temporary form of restraint imposed upon an individual subject to the Code by his lawful apprehension. *United States* v. *West,* 1 CMR 770. It was to continue until "proper authority may be notified." Manual, paragraph 19*d*. At that time, such authority may take cognizance of the circumstance and order the individual into confinement . . . "a screening-out process will occur here in reference to a more permanent status." Hearings, supra, at page 904. As was said in *United States* v. *West,* supra, at page 773:

". . . Such status (custody) thereafter may be altered by the arrest, confinement, restriction, or release of the individual. After confinement has been effected in a lawful manner (MCM, 1951, par 21a) (which is 'confinement' as contemplated by Article 95 and MCM, 1951, par 174c and is something more than mere restraint within a confinement facility), such confinement is not a continuation of custody but a new and different form of restraint. Nor does confinement include custody in this sense, because confinement may be imposed in cases where there has been no apprehension and resultant custody."

Applied to the facts before us, the fatal variance between the evidence and the "charge" upon which the accused was tried becomes apparent. The accused had been duly ordered into confinement. It appears he was then taken into custody for delivery to the confinement facility. Before that delivery could be effected and confinement actually imposed upon him, the accused made his escape. Hence, his offense was breach of lawful custody of his guard and not of a confinement in which he never entered. Poetically speaking, "Stone walls do not a prison make, nor iron bars a cage;" practically and legally, they do.

The findings of guilty of Additional Charge II and its specification are set aside. The decision of the board of review is reversed and the record of trial is returned to the Judge Advocate General of the Navy. The board may reassess the sentence on the remaining findings of guilty or order a rehearing on a proper charge and the penalty.

Judge KILDAY concurred.

Chief Judge QUINN dissented.

NOTE

A *dissent* is an explicit disagreement of one or more judges of a court with a decision made by the majority. The majority opinion is the law until the opinion is either expressly or implicitly overruled. At a later date, a dissent may become the basis for a majority opinion (and then becomes the law) if a majority of the judges later decide in another case to adopt the dissent as the new majority rule.

DISCUSSION AND SELF-QUIZ

1. You are the OOD-in-port of a destroyer. Seaman Jones, a member of your command, is returned to your ship by the shore patrol, following an unauthorized absence of two days. This is his first offense. The shore patrol informs you that the accused surrendered himself. What form of pretrial restraint, if any, would be appropriate in this case?

2. You are the assistant shore patrol officer in a foreign port and observe a sailor in your command commit a crime in your presence. You approach him and state, "I am taking you into custody." The sailor turns and states to you: "I haven't done anything."

   a. Is he resisting apprehension by this statement? See paragraph 174a, MCM.

   b. Assume, under your direction, he walks with you for about 30 feet, then he abruptly runs and escapes. Has he escaped from custody?

State your reason. See paragraph 174d, MCM.

3. What is the difference between *apprehension* and *arrest* as used in military law terminology?

4. On two occasions, the accused, on duty in Japan, was convicted by summary court-martial of wrongful appropriation of property. On each of these occasions he was sentenced to thirty days' confinement at hard labor. Upon completion of the second period of confinement, he was restricted to limits of his air base by his squadron commander. The squadron commander reasoned that as the accused's previous difficulties involved the sale of wrongfully appropriated property in the local community in Japan, the accused "would continue to do the same thing if the opportunity presented itself." There was no time limit on the restriction. The accused was told that if he had any business to transact off the base to see his squadron commander or First Sergeant who would restore his pass to him "to transact the business that he had to transact." On one occasion, the accused's pass was restored to him.

At the time of the order placing him on restriction the accused was not under charges, no investigation was pending against him, nor was he a suspect or a material witness in a judicial proceeding. Was the restriction lawfully imposed? See *United States* v. *Haynes*, 15 USCMA 122, 35 CMR 94 (1964) and paragraph 205 of this publication.

5. Article 10 of the Code states that when "any person subject to this chapter is placed in arrest or confinement prior to trial, immediate steps shall be taken to inform him of the specific wrong of which he is accused and to try him or to dismiss the charges and release him." Does this requirement apply to restriction in lieu of arrest? See *United States* v. *Haynes*, 15 USCMA 122, 35 CMR 94 (1964); *United States* v. *Smith*, 17 USCMA 427, 38 CMR 225 (1968) and *United States* v. *White*, 17 USCMA 462, 38 CMR 260 (1968) and paragraph 215e, MCM.

CHAPTER III

The Preliminary Inquiry, Statements, and Search and Seizure

This chapter, in order to describe events in a more or less chronological order, relates them from the viewpoint of the preliminary inquiry officer. However, a duty officer or other person in authority is often required to conduct a search or question a suspect. This chapter, as it pertains to these duties, would be equally applicable to such situations.

301 Initiation of Charges

The initial report to the proper military authorities of the known, suspected, or probable commission of an offense by a person subject to the Code is called the initiation of charges. This report is either initially presented to, or subsequently forwarded to, some person in military authority over the accused, such as the officer of the day, command duty officer, legal officer, executive officer, or discipline officer.

The initiation of charges can be done orally or in writing. Any person (military, civilian, adult, child, officer, or enlisted man) may initiate a complaint. A shore patrol report, or Naval Investigative Service report, or other official or nonofficial correspondence will suffice. If the accused is apprehended, the person making the apprehension may be the person who initiates the charges.

Although some commands utilize locally prepared report of offenses forms (see Appendix 1), the most common method of initiating charges is by the completion of the top portion of the NAVPERS 2696, "Report and Disposition of Offenses." (See Appendix 2.)

302 Duty to Initiate Charges

All persons in the naval service have an obligation to report to the proper authority all offenses committed by persons in the naval service which may come under their observation. Article 1216, Navy Regulations. Further, Article 1217 of Navy Regulations requires any Navy or Marine Corps man having knowledge of the actual commission of a felony under federal law to report same to persons in civil or military authority.

303 Action Upon Receipt of Charges

Generally, the discipline officer (a collateral duty in most small commands) would next receive the NAVPERS 2696 containing the initial charges for action, although this may vary according to local command policy.

Following consultation with appropriate superior authority, he would next draft the charges and specifications against the accused, utilizing Appendix 6 of the MCM. The "Details of Offenses" section of the NAVPERS 2696 would then be completed. (See Appendix 2.)

The "Information Concerning Accused" section must also be completed. The service record of the accused is a reliable source of information that may be utilized in completing this section of the NAVPERS 2696.

The accused is then called in for a personal interview with the discipline officer for the purpose of informing the accused of his rights under Article 31 of the Code. (See Appendix 2.)

The discipline officer will satisfy himself that the accused, in fact, understands the nature and effect of the Article 31 warning. He will then request the accused to sign the "Acknowledged" blank in the Article 31 warning block on the NAVPERS 2696. He will then sign the "Witness" blank himself. The commanding officer generally determines what individuals, other than himself, may order an enlisted man into pretrial restraint.

In many small commands, the legal officer may also serve as discipline officer. If he performs these dual functions, he should not investigate cases, but should refer all investigatory work to a preliminary inquiry officer or some other officer. Otherwise paragraph 6(c) of the Code would preclude the legal officer from performing his duties as legal adviser to the commanding officer in such a case. Article 6(c) of the Code states as follows:

> No person who has acted as member, military judge, trial counsel, assistant trial counsel, defense counsel, assistant defense counsel or investigating officer in any case may later act as a staff judge advocate or legal officer to any reviewing authority upon the same case.

304 Investigation

The MCM requires the convening authority to make or cause to be made a preliminary inquiry into the charges sufficient to enable him to make an intelligent disposition of them.

If the incident does not warrant referral to the Naval Investigative Service, the commanding officer will normally refer the responsibility for conducting the preliminary inquiry (i.e., the investigation of the case) to a junior officer attached to his command. He is the *preliminary inquiry officer*.

Some incidents are serious enough to require professional assistance from the Naval Investigative Service (NIS). Investigators from NIS are available and must be utilized in cases involving espionage, sabotage, murder, robbery, sodomy, narcotics, and other matters of gravity involving major violations. They may be requested in the investigation of such matters which require the application of professional investigative techniques. NIS agents are available at most large shore facilities and can travel to smaller commands upon request. There should be no hesitancy in requesting assistance, as NIS is a service command to the fleet in this area. SECNAVINST 5430.13 and the JAG Manual contain the guidelines as to the type of offenses which warrant recourse to the facilities of the NIS. The commanding officer may utilize the statements and information obtained in lieu of the preliminary inquiry in determining proper disposition of the case.

305 Preliminary Inquiry

The junior officer is instructed to inquire into the circumstances surrounding an accusation and to recommend disposition of the matter. He should resolve such questions as:

1. Whether the reported misconduct actually occurred;
2. Whether the misconduct constituted an offense under the Code;
3. The amount of evidence present to link the accused with the offense.

The junior officer so assigned must make his inquiry informal, but complete. Although the MCM provides that in certain cases the preliminary inquiry need only consist of an examination of the charges and a summary of the expected evidence which accompanies the charges, the preliminary inquiry officer should, as a general rule, attempt to personally interview the accused and all important witnesses. Pertinent objects, photographs, and documents should be assembled, marked, and placed under adequate security.

In conducting his inquiry the officer should be unfailing in his quest for the truth. He should remember that his job is to conduct an impartial inquiry, designed to establish the facts in the case and not to perfect a case for the government. He should collect and examine all evidence that is essential to a determination of the guilt or innocence of the accused, including evidence in mitigation and extenuation.

He should ensure that the personal data concerning the accused in the "Information Concerning Accused" block of the NAVPERS 2696 is complete and accurate. He should personally interview the division officer of the accused in order to complete the "Remarks of the Division Officer" completely and accurately.

306 Obtaining a Statement from the Accused

During the conduct of the preliminary inquiry, it may be advisable to attempt to obtain a statement from the accused and it may be necessary to conduct a search of some type. If a statement is taken it will either reflect incriminating matter or contain information that may be useful in proving the accused's innocence of the offense charged.

Incriminating statements are classified legally as either confessions or admissions. A confession is an acknowledgment of guilt. An admission is a self-incriminating statement falling short of an acknowledgment of guilt. In other words, the two terms differ in their degree of self-incrimination. Confessions and admissions are admissible against an accused as exceptions to the hearsay evidence rule (see Chapter XI) *if they are voluntary.*

307 The Voluntary Statement

The Fifth Amendment to the U.S. Constitution states that "no person . . . shall be compelled in any criminal case to be a witness against himself. . . ." The mandate of the Fifth Amendment prohibiting self-incrimination is enforced in the military via Article 31 of the Code.

In order to ensure that the statement taken from a suspect or accused is voluntary, and hence admissible into evidence, the preliminary inquiry officer *must,* prior to discussing the case with the accused, give him the warning provided by Article 31(b) of the Code. Article 31(b) provides as follows:

> No person subject to this chapter may interrogate, or request any statement from, an accused or a person suspected of an offense without first informing him of the nature of the accusation and advising him that he does not have to make any statement regarding the offense of which he is accused or suspected and that any statement made by him may be used as evidence against him in a trial by court-martial.

If the case is of a serious nature, or is considered serious enough to warrant at least a summary court-martial, the accused must also be given the warning required by the Court of Military Appeals in the case of *United States* v. *Tempia,* 16 USCMA 629, 37 CMR 249 (1967) in addition to the 31(b) warning. The requirements of the *Tempia* case, and the language contained therein, directed themselves only to trials by court-martial. Nonjudicial punishment (Captain's Mast or Office Hours in the Marine Corps) is not a trial.

The *Tempia* case requires that a suspect or an accused must be advised prior to making a statement:

1. That he has the right to consult with and obtain an attorney, either a civilian attorney at his own expense, or, if he wishes, a military lawyer will be provided for him free of charge;

2. That he has this right to consult with an attorney prior to the commencement of the interrogation;

3. That he has the right to have the attorney present during the interview.

Prior to commencing the interrogation, it must be affirmatively shown that the accused or suspect freely, knowingly, and intelligently waived his right to the assistance of counsel and to remain silent. A form, NAVJAG 5810/10, Appendix 3, contains the warning presently required and should be utilized in taking a statement. A major part of *United States* v. *Tempia* is reprinted at the end of this chapter. The accused or suspect has the right to terminate the interview at any time and for any reason.

Miranda v. *Arizona,* 384 US 436, 86 S Ct 1602 (1966), the Supreme Court decision which enunciated the principles of law accepted as the military rule in the *Tempia* decision, discussed "custodial interrogation" as a prerequisite to the requirement for a warning as to the right to counsel. However, in *United States* v. *Tempia,* the Court of Military Appeals, quoting from the *Miranda* decision, stated that the test to be applied in determining custody is either that the accused has been taken into custody or otherwise deprived of his freedom of action in any sig nificant way. For example, when the accused or suspect is summoned for questioning, he is considered to have been deprived of freedom of action and the *Miranda-Tempia* warning must be given. Later cases emphasized that the lack of freedom of movement by military personnel, especiall during normal working hours, deprives them of freedom of action Furthermore, the Supreme Court of the United States has stated tha even if the accused is in his own bunk when interrogated, the warning should be given if he is under apprehension or is otherwise deprived o freedom of action. Therefore, a preliminary inquiry officer should giv the *Tempia* warning in *every* case in which a court-martial is possible regardless of the absence of any form of pretrial restraint or custody.

A confession or admission, to be voluntary, cannot be obtained throug coercion, unlawful influence, or promises of any benefit. Threats o bodily harm, confinement, disadvantage, deprivation of privileges or necessities, or the actual carrying out of these threats in order to induce a statement all are examples of involuntary statements. A failure to comply with Article 31(b) or the rights enumerated in *United States* v. *Tempia* also makes a statement involuntary and consequently inadmissible as evidence against an accused in a court-martial.

A statement of an accused or suspect obtained from him in violation of any of the above warning requirements is considered to be involuntary, and therefore inadmissible against him, because of the violation alone, even if the accused or suspect knew that he had these rights. If an involuntary statement is admitted into evidence, the case will probably be reversed and a new trial ordered, or the charges dismissed. If the statement was made by him spontaneously (for example, without urging, interrogation, or request) it may be regarded as voluntary.

308 Search and Seizure

The preliminary inquiry officer may determine that a search may be required in order to complete his investigation. If the results of a search and seizure are to be admissible into evidence against an accused they must be the product of a lawful search and seizure. This part of the chapter discusses what constitutes such a lawful search and seizure.

The Fourth Amendment to the U.S. Constitution states that the "right of the people to be secure in their persons, houses, papers, and effects against unreasonable searches and seizures shall not be violated. . . ." This constitutional mandate applies to the military, although the term *reasonable* may have a different meaning in military law than in civilian courts. The reader should note that only *unreasonable* searches are condemned. The listing of the various kinds of searches in this part of the chapter is not all-inclusive in that other reasonable searches may be lawful in very unique situations.

309 Legal Objects of a Search

Searches of a person's house, dwelling, automobile, effects, papers, locker, or person (without his freely given consent) must be for:

1. Instrumentalities of the crime (for example, burglary tools);

2. Fruits of the crime (for example, stolen property such as a stolen watch);

3. Things which might be used to resist apprehension or to escape (for example, a weapon such as a pistol);

4. Property the possession of which is itself a crime (for example, narcotics);

5. Evidence which there is reason to believe will otherwise aid a particular apprehension or conviction. (For example, in *United States* v.

Whisenhant, 17 USCMA 117, 37 CMF 381 [1967], the Court of Military Appeals stated that bloodstained clothing belonging to the accused, which was seized at the time of his arrest on charges of assault with intent to commit murder, was properly admitted into evidence.)

Common usage blends "search and seizure" into one phrase. You might legally search and illegally seize. You might illegally search and legally seize, as in the case of contraband. However, to use evidence in a trial, it must have been legally seized in a legal search.

Contraband is property, the mere possession of which is unlawful. Narcotics, counterfeiting plates, liquor aboard ship, and false I.D. cards are examples. Since the very possession of contraband is illegal, it may be seized whenever and wherever found. Even during the course of a totally unwarranted illegal search, contraband may be seized and retained. However, to be admissible in evidence in the trial of the person from whom it was seized, the search must also be legal.

310 The Search Authorized by a Commanding Officer

Paragraph 152 of the MCM discusses lawful searches. The most common lawful search is the search authorized by the commanding officer. This search is described in the MCM as follows:

> A search of any of the following three kinds which has been authorized *upon probable cause* (emphasis supplied) by a commanding officer, including an officer in charge, having control over the place where the property or person searched is situated or found or, if that place is not under military control, having control over persons subject to military law or the law of war in that place:
>
> (1) A search of property owned, used, or occupied by, or in the possession of, a person subject to military law or the law of war, the property being situated in a military installation, encampment, or vessel or some other place under military control or situated in occupied territory or a foreign country.
>
> (2) A search of the person of anyone subject to military law or the law of war who is found in any such place, territory, or country.
>
> (3) A search of military property of the United States, or of property of nonappropriated fund activities of an armed force of the United States.

Probable cause for ordering a search exists when there is reason to believe that items properly the subject of a search are located in the place or on the person to be searched. Such a reasonable belief may be based on information which the authority requesting permission to search has received from another (i.e., an informant).

If probable cause for the search is based upon information supplied by an informer, the commanding officer must be aware of some of the facts upon which the informant relies in concluding that the items in question are where he claims they are. The commanding officer should also be aware of the basis upon which the person requesting permission to search concludes that the informant is credible or his information reliable.

No such independent, corroborative evidence is required if the informant is either an accomplice or co-actor, or a victim. *United States v. Herberg,* 15 USCMA 247, 35 CMR 219 (1965) and *United States v. Goldman,* 18 USCMA 389, 40 CMR 101 (1969). An example of an authorization for a search is contained in Appendix 4.

There is no specific formula for determining the adequacy of probable cause to support a search, as each case is factually different. Consider the probable cause factor in a situation such as larceny of a white hat. The commanding officer would be justified in ordering a search of a sailor's locker under the following circumstances: if the victim reported that someone had removed a white hat from his locker without permission; if the victim later reported that he saw a white hat with his initials on it in the suspect's locker when the latter opened it; and where the suspect occupies the same compartment as the victim. Under the circumstances, the commanding officer would have probable cause to conclude that an offense had been committed, that the suspect was the perpetrator, and that he retained the fruits of the crime in his locker. There was more than mere suspicion to justify the search. For example, if the commanding officer was only aware of the fact that the accused occupied the same compartment with the victim (with 20 other men) and was a "suspicious-looking character," he would not have had probable cause to authorize the search.

The commanding officer may delegate the general authority to order searches. *The delegation of authority to order searches must never be delegated to individuals primarily engaged in criminal investigations or police work.* Such a delegation should be limited to those persons whose rank, experience, duties, responsibilities, and temperament are such as to insure a dispassionate and impartial "judicial" determination. *United States v. Drew,* 15 USCMA 499, 35 CMR 421 (1965).

The actual search may be conducted by any person so authorized in the authorization for a search. Whenever possible, it is recommended that it be conducted by at least two persons, neither of whom is personally involved in the case. One of the two persons should, if possible, be a commissioned or petty officer experienced in conducting such searches. The preliminary inquiry officer may be authorized to conduct a search.

Personnel conducting a search will only search those areas or persons indicated in the authorization for a search. If it later becomes desirable to extend the scope of the search, the person authorizing the search should be so informed and further instructions obtained.

Property seized as the result of the search should be properly tagged or marked with the date of the search; identity of the person or property searched; location of the seized article when discovered; the name of the person authorizing the search; and the signatures of the persons conducting the search. The items seized should then be safely secured in the manner prescribed by the authorizing officer.

311 "Shakedowns" and the Area Search

Only a quest for incriminating matter is a "search" within the meaning of the Fourth Amendment. Quests or activities conducted as routine administrative acts for the purpose of preserving discipline, ensuring the operational effectiveness of the command, or maintaining security are not searches. This is a recognition of the fact that a commanding officer is responsible for the cleanliness, safety, and maintenance of his command, including the health, discipline, and welfare of his personnel. Therefore, any property seized during *routine* bag, locker, or vehicle inspections is admissible against an accused in whose possession it is found.

"Shakedowns" are general exploratory inspections within the command of all or a portion of the command. If a shakedown constitutes a search, the rules as to search and seizure apply. In each case, the purpose of the shakedown must be analyzed. If the shakedown is ordered for the purpose of carrying out the commanding officer's responsibilities for discipline, operations, and security, it is not a search. *If the purpose is the discovery of guilt of an accused, it is a search and the rules regarding a search must be complied with. The so-called fishing expedition is prohibited.*

The above rule does not prevent a search of an area such as a barracks where probable cause and awareness of the items to be sought are present and when circumstances render such an "area search" necessary.

For example, in *United States* v. *Drew* (cited above), an Air Force case, the Court of Military Appeals found a search of an entire barracks necessary and lawful under the following circumstances:

1. Over a period of approximately 45 days there had been a series of larcenies in the military police barracks;

2. When several men in the military police barracks were transferred to barracks number 132, larcenies in the military police barracks ceased and new larcenies began in barracks 132;

3. Three larcenies were committed on a Saturday and on Monday morning the executive officer was advised of two of them;

4. There was no basis for suspecting any one man over a number of other individuals;

5. The executive officer who authorized the search was aware of all the facts and circumstances of each offense including what items were missing; and

6. The search authorized was of barracks 132 and not of the personal effects of any one man.

312   Other Lawful Searches

Other searches which are lawful are:

1. *A search conducted as an incident to the lawful apprehension of a person.* This may include a search of his person, of the clothing he is wearing, of property which, at the time of apprehension, is in his immediate possession or control. The Supreme Court of the United States has ruled that such a search is limited to the area from within which a suspect might have reached either a weapon or something that could have been used as evidence against him.

For example, a search incident to an apprehension may include the individual's person and clothing, property in his immediate possession and control, a seabag he is carrying when apprehended, and his open locker if he is standing immediately adjacent to it at the time of the apprehension. As discussed in Chapter II, *the apprehension must be based upon a reasonable belief that an offense has been committed and that the person apprehended committed it. The apprehension must not be only for the purpose of creating an excuse to conduct an exploratory search. There must be probable cause for an apprehension.*

2. *A search under circumstances demanding immediate action to prevent the removal or disposal of property believed on reasonable grounds to be criminal goods.* Such a search is permitted out of necessity, but there must be "probable cause" in order for the search to be lawful. *United States* v. *Soto,* 16 USCMA 583, 37 CMR 203 (1967).

3. *A search of one's person with his freely given consent.* A search of his property may also be lawful if a person, entitled in the situation involved to waive the right to immunity from an unreasonable search (such as an owner, bailee, tenant, or occupant), freely gives consent. However, mere acquiescence in the face of authority is not "freely given consent." For example, a "request" from a superior officer or enlisted man to search a locker would not be sufficient, if the accused understood it to be an order. Therefore, it is strongly recommended that before an accused gives consent, he be informed of the following matters:

a. The specific reason for the search;

b. That the accused has the absolute right to refuse to give consent to the search;

c. That if the accused consents to the search, any evidence discovered in the search can be used against him at a criminal trial or other disciplinary proceedings.

An example of a consent to search form is contained in the JAG Manual and is reproduced in Appendix 5 of this book. Utilization of a form is not required; however, it is invaluable in the event the case is tried by court-martial because it assists in proving the existence of a lawful search.

4. *A search incident to a lawful hot pursuit of a person, including, when so incident, a search reasonably necessary to prevent his resistance or escape.*

5. *A search of open fields or woodlands, with or without the consent of the owner or tenant.*

6. *A search conducted in accordance with the authority granted by a lawful search warrant.*

A search warrant is:

> an order in writing, issued by a justice or other magistrate, in the name of the state, directed to a sheriff, constable, or other officer, commanding him to search a specified house, shop, or other premises, for personal property alleged to have been stolen, or for unlawful goods, and to bring the same, when found, before the magistrate, and usually also the body of the person occupying the premises, to be dealt with according to law. (*Black's Law Dictionary,* Fourth Edition.)

This warrant is based upon probable cause. A "magistrate" includes a city court judge, U.S. Commissioner, justice of the peace, or county court judge. *No one in the military can issue a valid search warrant, but the search authorized by the commanding officer, discussed in paragraph 310, is the equivalent to this search.*

313 "Fruit of the Poison Tree" Doctrine

The "fruit of the poison tree" doctrine applies to unlawful searches, seizures, and involuntary statements. Paragraph 152 of the MCM provides as follows:

> If a search is unlawful because conducted without probable cause and a second search is conducted based on information supplying probable cause discovered during the first search, evidence obtained by the second search is inadmissible against an accused entitled to object to the evidence even if the second search would otherwise be lawful.

In discussing involuntary statements, paragraph 140a of the MCM states that the fruit of the poison tree doctrine applies to subsequent statements unless "it clearly appears that all improper influences of the preceding interrogation had ceased to operate on the mind of the accused or suspect at the time he made the statement."

This doctrine does not apply if the government obtained its information from an independent source, as only knowledge gained from such an illegal act cannot be used.

314 Completion of the Preliminary Inquiry

Following the gathering of all the evidence, the preliminary inquiry officer should set forth a summary of the evidence in the "Comment" block of the NAVPERS 2696 and attach all statements thereto.

The investigating officer should make recommendations to the commanding officer as to the disposition of the case by filling in the "Recommendation as to Disposition" block of the NAVPERS 2696. There are several possible recommendations:

1. Dismiss the case;

2. Dispose of the case at Captain's Mast if the offense is minor;

3. Refer the case to a court-martial and attach the completed charge sheet;

4. Recommend a JAG Manual (see Chapter XIV) or Article 32 investigation be conducted.

If the preliminary inquiry officer decides to recommend referral to a court-martial, he should "prefer charges" against the accused. This is accomplished by filling out a charge sheet (DD Form 458) and includes signing, and swearing to, those charges and specifications shown by his investigation to warrant such action. A sample of a completed charge sheet may be found in Appendix 6. Appendix 7 contains directions for completion of a charge sheet. Charges can only be preferred by a person subject to the Code.

The preferring of charges should be distinguished from the initiation of charges, previously discussed in this chapter, in which the offense is first reported to military authorities.

The reason why the preliminary inquiry officer executes a charge sheet if he feels that the charges are of sufficient gravity to warrant at least a special court-martial is to prevent the commanding officer from being legally considered an accuser. If the *commanding officer directs that charges nominally be signed and sworn to by another after hearing the case at Captain's Mast he is considered to be an accuser.* An accuser is ineligible to convene a special or general court-martial. The charges would then have to be referred to a higher authority, who then could, if appropriate, convene the case. If, however, the commanding officer receives the preliminary inquiry without a charge sheet attached, this would not preclude him from returning the case to the investigating

officer, and from pointing out wherein the report is defective or incom
plete. In this event, he would not generally be considered an accuser. The
fact that the convening authority is the accuser does not invalidate a
summary court-martial.

The investigating officer swears to the charges placed upon the charge
sheet before an officer authorized to administer oaths. Article 136 of the
Code and the JAG Manual delineate who may administer such an oath

315 Final Pre-mast Screening

After the preliminary inquiry officer has completed his investigation he
generally files his report with the discipline or legal officer.

The file is next forwarded to the executive officer. The executive officer
then checks over the report. He may call the accused before him and
advise him of his rights under Article 31(b) and, if appropriate, to counsel. If the accused is *not* attached to or embarked on a naval vessel, he
has the right to refuse nonjudicial punishment. Generally, the executive
officer can afford him such an opportunity at this stage in the proceedings. The executive officer then requests the accused to sign the appropriate block of the NAVPERS 2696, the "Right to Demand Trial by Court
Martial" on page 2.

The executive officer is generally empowered by the commanding officer to dismiss any case if the charge is minor. He may possess the authority to dismiss any charge unwarranted by the evidence regardless of
whether it is a mast or court-martial offense. He may hold a screening
session complete with witnesses to assist him in making a proper determination. The term "XO's Mast" is a misnomer, however, as he has no
authority to punish nor may he legally convene a court-martial. If the
executive officer feels that the case is one which warrants trial by court-
martial and the charges have not been preferred on a charge sheet, he
may return the file at this time to the discipline officer with instructions
to draft formal charges and have them sworn to by military personnel
having knowledge of the offense.

Upon completion of his action on the case, the executive officer will
fill in the "Action of Executive Officer" block on the back of the NAV-
PERS 2696. Although not so indicated, he may, of course, recommend
trial by court-martial, if, in his opinion, the nature of the charges so
warrants.

316 Commanding Officer's Action

Upon receiving the case file (with the NAVPERS 2696, statements, and
other appropriate information relating to the accused and the offense
included therein), the commanding officer studies the case. He is not
bound by the recommendation of the officer who makes the preliminary

inquiry and may or may not follow his recommendations as contained on the NAVPERS 2696. Occasionally the commanding officer will decide that the evidence is insufficient, and will either send the records back for further inquiry or will dismiss the charges.

If the commanding officer decides that he can handle the case by non-judicial punishment at mast, he will do so. If he considers the case warrants a summary or special court-martial, or if the alleged offender does not desire nonjudicial punishment, he may, if he so desires, refer the case to a court-martial without hearing the case at Captain's Mast. In this event, he would merely execute the 1st Indorsement on page 3 of the charge sheet referring the case to a court-martial.

If the commanding officer decides that the charge is serious enough to warrant trial by general court-martial, he will refer it to a qualified officer for a pretrial investigation under the provisions of Article 32 of the Code. This is required to determine if a general court-martial should hear the case, and is the military counterpart to a grand jury in civilian law. It should be distinguished from the less formal investigation of the preliminary inquiry officer, which is reported on the NAVPERS 2696.

317 Summary

It should be evident that the duties of a preliminary inquiry officer can be tedious and require minute attention to detail in any given case. The suspect or accused must receive the Article 31(b) warning before he is asked any questions, even though he is not in custody. The *Tempia* warning need only be given when an accused or suspect is in custody or otherwise deprived of his freedom of action. However, as a rule of thumb, the Article 31(b) and *Tempia* warnings should always be given when there is any doubt or question as to their applicability. Perhaps giving these warnings may preclude the preliminary inquiry officer from obtaining a statement from the accused. Certainly, as the drafters of the India Evidence Act pithily suggested back in 1872, it "is far pleasanter to sit comfortably in the shade rubbing pepper into a poor devil's eyes than to go about in the sun hunting up evidence." The point is that a thorough investigation generally need not rely on the legal crutch of a confession.

A search authorized by a commanding officer should always be based on probable cause. If a shakedown is ordered in the interest of discipline, operations, or security, it is lawful when no particular person is suspected of an offense, no particular offense is thought to have been committed, and as far as the inspectors are concerned, they do not expect to find anything. A shakedown of all the members of a command should not be used as a screen where sufficient evidence does not exist to support a specific search of a particular service member's locker.

The area of confessions and search and seizure is an extremely complicated area even for attorneys. The past decade has witnessed convulsive changes in this area as the result of Supreme Court and Court of Military Appeals decisions. The line officer cannot be expected to be familiar with all the case law in this area, but he should know how to take a statement from an accused and conduct a proper search. In the event the case becomes complicated the assistance of a member of the Judge Advocate General's Corps should be sought.

Punishment, in order to achieve discipline, must be fair and impartial. The manner in which a preliminary inquiry is conducted will reflect not only on the officer conducting the investigation but upon the morale and discipline of the command itself.

Discussion Case

UNITED STATES, Appellee

v.

MICHAEL L. TEMPIA, Airman Third Class, U.S. Air Force, Appellant

16 USCMA 629, 37 CMR 249

(1967)

Opinion of the Court

FERGUSON, Judge:

This case, certified by the Judge Advocate General, United States Air Force, presents important questions concerning the administration of military justice. Basically, it inquires whether the principles enunciated by the Supreme Court in *Miranda* v. *Arizona*, 384 US 436, 16 L ed 2d 694, 86 S Ct 1602 (1966), apply to military interrogations of criminal suspects. We hold that they do. As to cases tried on and after June 13, 1966, the doctrine set forth in our earlier decision in *United States* v. *Wimberly*, 16 USCMA 3, 36 CMR 159, has largely been set at naught by the *Miranda* decision.

I

The accused was tried by general court-martial at Dover Air Force Base, Delaware, and convicted of taking indecent liberties with females under the age of sixteen, in violation of Uniform Code of Military Justice, Article 134. He was sentenced to bad-conduct discharge, forfeiture of all pay and allowances, confinement at hard labor for six months, and reduction. Intermediate appellate authorities affirmed, and the case was, as indicated above, certified to this Court on the question:

"Was the Board of Review correct in its determination that the accused's

pretrial statement was properly received in evidence?"

The accused's trial commenced on June 14, 1966, one day after the effective date of applying the principles set forth in *Miranda, supra.* See *Johnson v. New Jersey,* 384 US 719, 16 L ed 2d 882, 86 S Ct 1772 (1966). The testimony of the witnesses therein disclosed the following evidence.

On May 1, 1966, accused accompanied an Airman Keitel to the base library. Upon request, Keitel pointed out the location of the latrine. Accused left Keitel in the reading room and returned in five or six minutes.

From other testimony, it appears he went to the ladies' rest room, stood in its partially opened door, and made obscene proposals to three young girls. The victims left the library, returned with one of their parents and the Air Police, and pointed accused out in the reading room. Accused was asked "to come back to the office" by one of the policemen. He did so.

At the Air Police office, accused was advised by Agent Blessing that he was suspected of taking indecent liberties with children; of his rights under Code, supra, Article 31 and "that you may consult with legal counsel if you desire." Agent McQuary assisted Agent Blessing in the interview. It was immediately terminated, as Tempia stated "he wanted counsel." He was released from custody.

On May 3, 1966, Tempia was again called to the "OSI Office" where he was once more advised by Blessing, in the presence of Agent Feczer, of his rights and entitlement to consult with counsel. Accused "stated he had not yet received legal counsel." Blessing thereupon called Major Norman K.

Hogue, Base Staff Judge Advocate, and made an appointment for Tempia.

Blessing's interview with Tempia terminated at 8:50 A.M., and the latter proceeded to Major Hogue's office. Hogue informed him he was the Staff Judge Advocate and "that I could not accept an attorney-client relationship with him because if I did, it would disqualify me from acting in my capacity as Staff Judge Advocate." He further stated to Tempia that he would nevertheless "advise him of his legal rights and explained to him that this was different than acting as his defense counsel in that I did not want to hear any of his story, but I would answer any legal questions he had after I explained some rights to him."

Major Hogue also told accused he could not make a military lawyer available to him "as his defense counsel during that OSI investigation," but that he had the right to employ civilian counsel; would be given a reasonable time to do so; and that civilian counsel would be entitled to appear with him at the investigation. In addition, Hogue advised him of his rights under Code, supra, Article 31, and explained those rights to him, but:

". . . as I say, I told him no military lawyer would be appointed to represent him during the OSI investigation or any investigation by the law enforcements [sic] agents on this base. I told him that if charges are preferred—in his case, referred to trial by special court-martial or general court-martial, where it's referred to an investigation under Article 32(b)—he would be furnished a military lawyer at that time, one certified under Article 27(b) of the Uniform Code of Military Justice."

In addition, accused filled out a written form in which it was indicated he had been advised:

a. That he had the right to retain civilian counsel at his own expense;

b. That no military lawyer would be appointed to represent him while under investigation by law enforcement agents;

c. That he would be furnished military counsel if charges were preferred and referred to trial or a pretrial investigation convened;

d. Of his rights under Code, supra, Article 31;

e. Of the maximum punishment involved; and,

f. That he had not discussed his guilt or innocence or any of the facts involved with Major Hogue.

Following his session with Major Hogue, Tempia returned to the Office of Special Investigations, at 9:24 A.M. He "was then called in . . . readvised of his rights, readvised of the nature of the investigation and of his rights to seek legal counsel the second time." He stated he had consulted with Major Hogue, and did not desire further counsel as "they could not help him. . . ." He said, "They didn't do me no good." Thereafter, he was interrogated by Blessing and Feczer, to whom he began to dictate his confession.

At the trial, defense counsel sought exclusion of the statement on the basis of the Supreme Court decision in *Miranda,* supra, as he had found it reported in the press. The law officer overruled his timely objection and admitted Tempia's confession in evidence.

II

The Judge Advocate General, United States Navy, has filed a brief amicus curiae in which it is urged that military law is in nowise affected by constitutional limitations and, in consequence, that the principles enunciated in *Miranda* v. *Arizona,* supra, do not apply to the situation herein presented. The Government, however, takes a different tack. Conceding the application of the Constitution, it urges the Supreme Court has no supervisory power over military tribunals. Construing *Miranda* v. *Arizona,* supra, as announcing only procedural devices designed to enforce a Constitutional right in the exercise of the Supreme Court's supervisory power, it contends this Court is neither required to follow *Miranda,* supra, nor are its stringent formulae necessary or desirable in the administration of military justice. In this latter connection, it adverts to our decision in *United States* v. *Wimberly,* supra, and points to the safeguards erected by Congress in Code, supra, Article 31.

Counsel for the accused and other amicus curiae (who represented Miranda before the Supreme Court) disagree; point out that the decision in *Miranda,* supra, was one of constitutional dimensions; and, therefore, urge it is binding on military interrogations.

The time is long since past—as, indeed, the United States recognizes—when this Court will lend an attentive ear to the argument that members of the armed services are, by reason of their status, ipso facto deprived of all protections of the Bill of Rights.

Military jurisprudence is and has always been separated from the ordinary Federal and State judicial systems in this country. Such is the meaning of Mr. Chief Justice Vinson's language in *Burns* v. *Wilson,* 346 US 137,

97 L ed 1508, 73 S Ct 1045 (1953), at page 140:

"Military law, like state law, is a jurisprudence which exists separate and apart from the law which governs in our federal judicial establishment. This Court has played no role in its development; we have exerted no supervisory power over the courts which enforce it; the rights of men in the armed forces must perforce be conditioned to meet certain overriding demands of discipline and duty, and the civil courts are not the agencies which must determine the precise balance to be struck in this adjustment. The Framers expressly entrusted that task to Congress."

That military law exists and has developed separately from other Federal law does not mean that persons subject thereto are denied their constitutional rights. To the contrary, the very issue before the Supreme Court in *Burns* v. *Wilson,* supra, was whether such a denial had occurred. The Chief Justice, in an opinion in which three other justices concurred (two dissenting justices would have gone further and ordered additional examination of the facts below), pointed out: "The federal civil courts have jurisdiction over such applications." He then went on to state the duty of this Court and that of every other judicial body inferior to it:

"The military courts, like the state courts, have the same responsibilities as do the federal courts to protect a person from a violation of his constitutional rights."

∞

The point need not, however, be belabored. Sufficient has been said to establish our firm and unshakable conviction that Tempia, as any other member of the armed services so situated, was entitled to the protection of the Bill of Rights, insofar as we are herein concerned with it. We pass, therefore, to the Government's contention that *Miranda,* supra, involves a decision in the area of the Supreme Court's supervisory authority rather than constitutional principles.

∞

A cursory scrutiny of the opinion in *Miranda* makes crystal clear that the formulae there laid down by the Court are constitutional in nature, although the door was left open for the legislative process to innovate "other procedures which are *at least as effective* in apprising accused persons of their right of silence and in assuring a continuous opportunity to exercise it." (Emphasis supplied.) *Miranda,* supra, at page 467. Thus, the Court noted, at the outset, it had granted certiorari in these cases . . . to explore some facets of the problems, thus exposed, of applying the privilege against self-incrimination to in-custody interrogation, and to give concrete *constitutional guidelines* for law enforcement agencies and courts to follow." (Emphasis supplied.) It spoke not of the exercise of its supervisory authority over the Federal judicial system, but of the "constitutional issue"; "adequate safeguards to protect precious Fifth Amendment rights"; "whether the privilege is fully applicable during a period of custodial interrogation"; "the protection which must be given to the privilege against self-incrimination when the individual is first subjected to police interrogation"; "the issues presented are of constitutional dimensions"; and of similar matters, all indicative of the fact, hardly to be gainsaid, that the Court was laying down constitutional rules for criminal interrogation which are part and parcel of the Fifth Amendment.

∞

We turn, therefore, to the merits of the controversy before us. *Miranda* v. *Arizona,* supra, explicitly and at length lays down concrete rules which are to govern all criminal interrogations by Federal or State authorities, military or civilian, if resulting statements are to be used in trials commencing on and after June 13, 1966. We commend a reading of that opinion to all involved in the administration of military criminal law as well as the undertaking of educative measures to see that its precepts are not violated in pretrial interrogations. While we here intend no definitive treatment of the manifold questions which may arise in this connection, we quote the Supreme Court's summary of what must be done:

"Our holding will be spelled out with some specificity in the pages which follow but briefly stated it is this: the prosecution may not use statements, whether exculpatory or inculpatory, stemming from custodial interrogation of the defendant unless it demonstrates the use of procedural safeguards effective to secure the privilege against self-incrimination. By custodial interrogation, we mean questioning initiated by law enforcement officers after a person has been taken into custody or otherwise deprived of his freedom of action in any significant way. As for the procedural safeguards to be employed, unless other fully effective means are devised to inform accused persons of their right of silence and to assure a continuous opportunity to exercise it, the following measures are required. Prior to any questioning, the person must be warned that he has a right to remain silent, that any statement he does make may be used as evidence against him, and that he has a right to the presence of an attorney, either retained or appointed. The defendant may waive effectuation of these rights, provided the waiver is made voluntarily, knowingly and intelligently. If, however, he indicates in any manner and at any stage of the process that he wishes to consult with an attorney before speaking there can be no questioning. Likewise, if the individual is alone and indicates in any manner that he does not wish to be interrogated, the police may not question him. The mere fact that he may have answered some questions or volunteered some statements on his own does not deprive him of the right to refrain from answering any further inquiries until he has consulted with an attorney and thereafter consents to be questioned."

We now proceed to examine the facts presented in this record, in light of the foregoing requirements.

a. CUSTODIAL INTERROGATION.

The government urges upon us the proposition that the accused was not in custody, and, hence, the need for appropriate advice and assistance did not arise. We may at once dispose of this contention. The accused was apprehended on May 1, 1966; freed to seek counsel, and recalled for interrogation on May 3, 1966; an appointment was made for him with Major

Hogue, following which he immediately returned to the Office of Special Investigations, where his interrogation was successfully completed. The test to be applied is not whether the accused, technically, has been taken into custody, but absent that, whether he has been "otherwise deprived of his freedom of action in any significant way." *Miranda,* supra, at page 444. Here, the accused was clearly summoned for interrogation. Had he not obeyed, he would have undoubtedly subjected himself to being penalized for a failure to repair. Code, supra, Article 86; Manual for Courts-Martial, United States, 1951, paragraph 127b. In the military, unlike civil life, a subject may be required to report and submit to questioning quite without regard to warrants or other legal process. It ignores the realities of that situation to say that one ordered to appear for interrogation has not been significantly deprived of his freedom of action. See *People* v. *Kelley,* 57 West's Cal Rptr 363, 424 P2d 947 (1967). Hence, we conclude there was "custodial interrogation" in this case.

b. THE WARNING.

The accused was fully advised of his rights under Code, supra, Article 31, and of his right to consult with counsel. On indicating a desire to speak with counsel, he was initially freed and, ultimately, on May 3, was referred to Major Hogue for further advice concerning his rights. But that officer went no further than to emphasize to the accused that he could not form an attorney-client relationship with him; to advise him again of his rights under Code, supra, Article 31; and to inform him he could retain civilian counsel at his own expense, who could appear at his interrogation.

He specifically told accused no military lawyer would be appointed "to represent him during the OSI investigation or any investigation by the law enforcement agents on this base."

Miranda, supra, squarely points out "the person must be warned that he has a right to remain silent, that any statement he does make may be used as evidence against him, and that he has a right to the presence of an attorney, *either retained or appointed.*" (Emphasis supplied.) In addition, if the accused "indicates in any manner and at any stage of the process that he wishes to consult with an attorney before speaking there can be no questioning. Likewise, if the individual is alone and indicates in any manner that he does not wish to be interrogated, the police may not question him."

Undoubtedly, the advice given Tempia under Code, supra, Article 31, sufficed to inform him both of his right to remain silent and the purpose for which any statement he might make could be used. The advice as to counsel, however, was deficient.

First, accused was only warned by the agents that he was entitled to consult with counsel. When Major Hogue elaborated on this proposition, he limited the availability of counsel to private attorneys employed by the accused at his own expense. He specifically told accused no attorney would be appointed to represent him in any law enforcement investigation. This is exactly contrary to the information which, under *Miranda,* supra, must be preliminarily communicated to the accused. In the words of the Supreme Court, at page 472:

"If an individual indicates that he wishes the assistance of counsel before any interrogation occurs, the authorities cannot rationally ignore or deny his request on the basis *that the individual does not have or cannot afford a retained attorney. The financial ability of the individual has no relationship to the scope of the rights involved here.* The privilege against self-incrimination secured by the Constitution applies to all individuals. The need for counsel in order to protect the privilege exists for the indigent as well as the affluent. In fact, were we to limit these constitutional rights to those who can retain an attorney, our decisions today would be of little significance. The cases before us as well as the vast majority of confession cases with which we have dealt in the past involve those unable to retain counsel. While authorities are not required to relieve the accused of his poverty, they have the obligation not to take advantage of indigence in the administration of justice. Denial of counsel to the indigent at the time of interrogation while allowing an attorney to those who can afford one would be no more supportable by reason or logic than the similar situation at trial and on appeal struck down in *Gideon* v. *Wainwright,* 372 US 335 (1963), and *Douglas* v. *California,* 372 US 353 (1963).

"In order fully to apprise a person interrogated of the extent of his rights under this system then, *it is necessary to warn him not only that he has the right to consult with an attorney, but also that if he is indigent a lawyer will be appointed to represent him.* Without this additional warning, the admonition of the right to consult with counsel would often be understood as mean-ing only that he can consult with a lawyer if he has one or has the funds to obtain one. The warning of a right to counsel would be hollow if not couched in terms that would convey to the indigent—the person most often subjected to interrogation—the knowledge that he too has a right to have counsel present. As with the warnings of the right to remain silent and of the general right to counsel, only by effective and express explanation to the indigent of this right can there be assurance that he was truly in a position to exercise it." (Emphasis supplied.)

As accused was informed no counsel would be appointed for him it follows that the statement thereafter taken from him was inadmissable in evidence.

c. WAIVER.

The government suggests that accused knowingly and intelligently waived his rights against self-incrimination by making his statement after being repeatedly warned under Code, supra, Article 31, and subjecting himself to further interrogation following his conference with Major Hogue. In connection with the latter circumstance, it invites our attention to testimony that, on returning from Hogue's office, accused stated he did not desire further counsel, "that they could not help him. . . . They didn't do me no good."

Aside from the fact that accused was improperly advised as to his entitlement to appointed counsel, we point out that he, in fact, received no legal advice, as Major Hogue specifically declined to act as his attorney. The testimony, taken as a whole, indicates not that accused did not desire a lawyer's services but that he had been frustrated in obtaining advice on whether to exercise his rights—hence, his comment: "They didn't do me no good." There should be small wonder at his feelings, when he had just been refused the opportunity to discuss the case with Hogue, relate any of the facts to him, or to obtain any information as to a desirable course of action. "If the interrogation continues without the presence of an attorney and a statement is taken, a heavy burden rests on the government to demonstrate that the defendant knowingly and intelligently waived his privilege against self-incrimination and his right to retained or appointed counsel." *Miranda*, supra, at page 475.

Quite apart from the insufficiency of the warning as to accused's right to counsel, here the government did not carry its burden, and no waiver is made out. To the contrary, it merely shows accused's entitlement to consult with counsel was frustrated by the Staff Judge Advocate's well-meant but legally improper statements.

∽

In sum, we are not persuaded by our brother's views that we have anticipated the Supreme Court in this area, nor that the military picture is as rosy as he paints it. What does concern us is our duty to follow the interpretation by the Supreme Court of the Constitution of the United States insofar as it is not made expressly or by necessary implication inapplicable to members of the armed forces. It is well to remember that we, "like the state courts, have the same responsibilities as do the federal courts to protect a person from a violation of his constitutional rights." *Burns* v. *Wilson*, supra, at page 142. We necessarily must effectuate that mandate by holding *Miranda* v. *Arizona*, supra, applicable in military prosecutions.

The decision of the board of review is reversed, and the record of trial is returned to the Judge Advocate General of the Air Force. A rehearing may be ordered.

Judge KILDAY concurred.
Chief Judge QUINN dissented.

DISCUSSION AND SELF-QUIZ

1. You are the OOD aboard a destroyer alongside the pier at Norfolk, Virginia. Two incidents occur as follows:

a. You are making your routine 2215 "lights out" inspection throughout the ship. As you pass through the "X" Division compartment you notice the lights are still on and an enlisted man is standing in the back of the compartment facing an open locker, with his back toward you. You ask him: "Why didn't the MAA turn the lights off?" The man turns around and states, excitedly, "Sir, I'm sorry. I didn't mean to do it! I'm broke." You recognize the speaker as Seaman Brown from 1st Division, whose compartment is located several compartments from the "X" Division compartment. In his hand is a wallet with the initials "E.A.J." on it. An Edward Jones is a seaman apprentice attached to "X" Division. You take the billfold as you take Brown into custody and then place him in restriction in lieu of arrest. Would the statement made to you without an Article 31(b) warning be admissible against Brown? Could you lawfully seize the billfold? *United*

States v. *Ballard,* 17 USCMA 96, 37 CMR 360 (1967) and paragraphs 307 and 312 of this chapter.

b. Later, while standing on the quarterdeck, you observe Seaman Apprentice Doe, attached to 2nd Division, proceed up the after-brow. As he approaches you, it is evident he has been drinking for he smells of liquor. However, his speech is not slurred and his gait is steady. You know that Doe has recently been to Captain's Mast and punished for carrying a false I.D. card, which he utilized to obtain liquor. Doe is 17 and cannot legally drink. You approach Doe and state: "May I see your I.D. card?" Doe pulls out an I.D. card belonging to Seaman Apprentice I. M. Smith, attached to the 2nd Division. Smith is 22 years old. Did you violate Article 31(b)? *United States* v. *Nowling,* 9 USCMA 100, 25 CMR 362 (1958).

2. In *United States* v. *Volante,* 4 USCMA 689, 16 CMR 263 (1954) the facts were as follows: The accused was one of four Marines working in a Marine Corps exchange. The workers were required to make up any shortages. A recent inventory disclosed shortages of merchandise. A sergeant, a co-worker of the accused's, suspected him of larceny of the merchandise. The sergeant was told "You'd better do something about it, or it will be on your neck." The sergeant searched the accused's locker without permission and found some of the missing merchandise. He did this because he "didn't want to be stuck with the shortage," and have his pay checked. Was the search legal?

3. You are the legal officer on a ship homeported in Long Beach, California. Your executive officer, who has been delegated authority to order searches by the commanding officer in writing, informs you of the following:

For the past few weeks, the leading chief has been reporting missing tools from the "M" Division tool locker. Yesterday, a Seaman Roe from a nearby ship reported to him that Machinist's Mate Second Class Jones, attached to "M" Division on your ship, offered to sell him some tools. Roe noted that the tools had government markings on them and that one, a screwdriver, had the name of the ship scratched thereon. The executive officer checked with the leading chief and he confirmed that one of the missing items was a screwdriver inscribed with the ship's name. Jones had also informed Roe that some of the tools he had for sale were in his home and others in his locker on board ship.

The executive officer knows that Jones is married and has an apartment on the beach. He also has a locker in the "M" Division compartment. Would it be proper for the executive officer to order a search of Jones's apartment on the beach? Could the executive officer order a search of Jones's locker? Advise him. (See paragraph 310 of this chapter.)

4. In *United States* v. *Dollison,* 15 USCMA 595, 36 CMR 93 (1966) the following occurred: The accused's commanding officer, upon receipt of a letter questioning the accused's marital status, directed the Army Criminal Investigations Detachment (equivalent to the Naval Investigative Service) to conduct an inquiry into the matter. A telephone call was placed to accused's former station, Fort Carson, Colorado. Nothing was known there relative to the subject of inquiry, but it was learned that at about the time the

accused departed in an unauthorized absence status from Fort Carson some six months previously, a tape recorder and light meter were discovered missing from the Public Information Office where the accused worked. The accused had returned to military control after a month's absence. His return was known to the authorities at Fort Carson although he did not return there.

A search was ordered by the commanding officer. Pawn tickets for a camera and radio, other than the items missing from the old unit, were discovered. The accused confessed to taking the discovered items and was convicted of larceny. Was there probable cause for the search?

5. In *United States* v. *Coleman,* 32 CMR 522, CM 407463, a recruit reported an electric razor missing in a basic training unit.

Four days later, upon graduation from their basic training cycle, the trainees, including the accused, were required to pack their possessions and vacate the barracks so that a cleanliness inspection could be conducted prior to their leaving. Unlocked and cleaned lockers and quarters were required as they were to be utilized by other incoming trainees.

As the inspection proceeded, one of the sergeants in charge returned to the vacant barracks to inspect conditions. There he found a locked government foot locker and, upon inquiry, determined it belonged to the accused. He summoned the accused and directed the locker be unlocked. This was done. When the sergeant lifted the top tray inside the locker he observed the razor in question lying visible to view in a cardboard box resting on the bottom of the locker. The sergeant recalled the incident of four days ago. Therefore, he took the accused and the razor to his company commander. The accused confessed after appropriate warnings. Was the search and seizure lawful?

CHAPTER IV

A Study of Offenses
and Drafting Specifications:
Unauthorized Absence

Unauthorized absence and larceny are two of the most common offenses in the military. The two offenses are very diverse in their nature. Unauthorized absence is the least complex of the two, although it is far more complex than is generally recognized. A thorough understanding of these common offenses will assist the Navy and Marine Corps officer in understanding other articles of the Code, as they all have basic similarities. Further, it is difficult to understand the proper drafting of specifications and charges or the nature of a particular defense without a knowledge of the nature of the offense itself.

This material is presented before a discussion of nonjudicial punishment and courts-martial procedure in order to permit the reader to fully appreciate the fact that procedures should not be considered in a vacuum, but, in practice, are only utilized when a violation of the Code has apparently occurred. Questions 3 and 5 of the Discussion and Self-Quiz are especially important in understanding the nature of other offenses.

401 Article 86

Article 86 of the Code is by far the most often violated article in the military. *Approximately 80 percent of all offenses committed in the military fall under this article of the Code.*

Five different offenses may be charged under Article 86. They are:

1. Unauthorized absence from a unit, organization, or place of duty;
2. Failing to go to the appointed place of duty;
3. Going from the appointed place of duty;
4. Absence without leave from guard, watch, or duty station with the intent to abandon the same;

5. Unauthorized absence, with intent to avoid maneuvers or field exercises.

The first three are the most commonly violated. Of those three, unauthorized absence from a unit, organization, or place of duty is the offense this chapter will discuss.

402 Elements of Unauthorized Absence

The elements of an offense are simply the facts which must be proven—they are the essential components of the offense.

Article 86 states as follows:

> Any member of the armed forces who, without authority . . . *absents himself or remains absent from his unit, organization, or place of duty at which he is required to be at the time prescribed;* shall be punished as a court-martial may direct. (Emphasis added.)

In reading the Code and the discussion in Chapter XXVIII of the MCM, it is apparent that there are *two* elements for this common offense:

1. That at the time and place alleged in the specification, the accused *absented* himself from his unit, organization, or other place of duty;

2. That such absence was *without authority*.

In discussing the first element, the type of military command the accused absented himself from should be considered. It may be a:

1. "Unit," for example, a ship, or in the Marine Corps, a company;

2. "Organization," larger than a unit or company;

3. "Other place of duty." This refers to a *general* place of duty as distinguished from a *specific* place of duty within a command. For example, in *United States* v. *Skipper,* 1 CMR 581, 1 USCMA 581 (1951), the accused was ordered to report for duty aboard a Coast Guard vessel. He was charged under paragraph (1) of Article 86 for failure to go to his appointed place of duty. A board of review (equivalent to the Court of Military Review today) stated: "The offense of failing to go to an appointed place of duty contemplates only a specific place of duty such as muster, the number 1 fireroom, etc., and not a failure to go to his unit, his *general* place of duty." (Emphasis supplied.)

At times an issue may arise as to where an accused is attached. In general, a military man is attached to that ship or station which holds his record. If en route between duty stations on permanent change of station orders, he is considered to be attached to the activity to which he is ordered to report. If a military member is on temporary additional duty, he is considered absent from both his permanent and temporary units.

It is evident that as the Code refers to absence from a particular unit, an accused could still be present on a military installation and be an unauthorized absentee. For example, Seaman Jones would be absent from his ship the moment that he left it without authority even though he still is on a naval base or other military installation.

The second element, that the absence was "without authority," *must* be contained in the specification and must be proven. In *United States* v. *Fout,* 3 USCMA 565, 13 CMR 121 (1953), the accused pleaded guilty to three specifications of unauthorized absence. None of the three specifications stated whether or not the absence was without authority. The Court of Military Appeals stated that it "necessarily follows that a plea of guilty to a specification which alleges only an absence, without any words importing a want of authority, is a plea to an innocent act." The charges were dismissed.

It is obvious that the lack of authority is the essential factor in this offense. For example, Seaman Smith could be absent from his ship on leave, liberty, or temporary additional duty and would *not* violate Article 86.

403   Duration of the Absence

In the typical unauthorized absence case, a determination of the length of the absence is vital. If the accused is absent for not more than three days, the maximum confinement at hard labor he can be awarded at a court-martial is one month. If he is absent for more than three days but not more than 30 days, he can receive up to and including six months' confinement at hard labor. For an absence of over 30 days, he can be sentenced to confinement for a year.

Unauthorized absence commences immediately upon the leaving of the ship without authority. The length of the absence only permits the awarding of a harsher punishment. For example, in *United States* v. *Lovell,* 7 USCMA 445, 22 CMR 235 (1956), the specification alleged the accused was absent without authority from 28 October 1955 to 20 December 1955. The beginning of the absence was established by an official record of the Air Force organization to which the accused was attached. However, a second entry showing the accused's return to military control was excluded from evidence and no other evidence of termination was presented. The Court of Military Appeals stated that as termination was not proven the accused could only be convicted of an absence of less than three days.

An unauthorized absence begins either when the accused leaves his unit, organization, or place of duty without authority or when he fails to return at the proper time from authorized leave or liberty.

Generally, there are three methods by which an absence may be terminated:

1. *Surrender.* An absentee who surrenders to a military activity or organization and notifies them of his status terminates his absence.

2. *Delivery.* A *known* absentee's delivery by another person to a military activity or organization terminates his absence.

3. *Apprehension.* The unauthorized absence of a known absentee may be terminated by apprehension by military authority. It may also be terminated by civilian authority under certain circumstances. Article 3430100 of the Bureau of Naval Personnel Manual states:

> The period of absence of absentees . . . is terminated by their apprehension by civil authority if the apprehension is made at the request of competent authority of the Armed Forces, through issuance of the . . . DD Form 553 or by other means.

The DD Form 553 is a request by military authorities that civilian authorities apprehend a known absentee.

Except when it is terminated by civilian authorities at the request of the military, unauthorized absence is terminated by the return of the accused to military control regardless of the service involved. For example, a Navy man on unauthorized absence was apprehended by civilian authorities. The civilian authorities turned him over to the Air Force. He escaped from them the same day. The Court of Military Appeals stated that certainly "an unauthorized absence is legally ended by return to *military control,* regardless of whether that control be exercised temporarily by a service other than that of the offender involved." *United States* v. *Coates,* 2 USCMA 625, 10 CMR 123 (1953). The casual presence of an absentee at a military installation unknown to competent authority and for his own purposes does not terminate an absence. Sometimes even a known presence at an installation may not terminate his absence where the absentee conceals his status, and his status could not have been determined by reasonable diligence.

404 Defenses

In its broadest terms, an accused may be said to have a defense to an offense when it appears that he should not be held legally responsible for the crime charged.

In this chapter certain defenses will be discussed. Most of these defenses will also apply to many other offenses charged under the Code. However, a reader may better understand the nature of certain offenses by relating them to a specific offense than by considering them in the abstract.

Of course, an accused may defend *any* offense by pleading "not guilty" to it. While this may imply an assertion by him that he is innocent, all that he is really stating is "the obligation is upon the government to prove, beyond a reasonable doubt (i.e., to a moral certainty) that I am guilty. Let them prove it." Generally, his counsel would then attack the government's case by a contention that one or more of the elements of the offense do not meet the "beyond a reasonable doubt" standard of proof.

There are other defenses that may be raised to show why the accused should not be held legally responsible for the crime charged and there are some that are particularly applicable to unauthorized absence. However, to understand these defenses an officer must understand the nature of unauthorized absence from a unit, organization, or other general place of duty.

This type of unauthorized absence is called a "general intent" offense. Actually, intent is more or less a "fiction" as there are only *two* facts which must be proven: the absence and the fact that it was without authority. The accused does not have to intend to commit unauthorized absence to be guilty of this offense. However, in most crimes, there must be some sort of "mind at fault" on the part of the accused in order for him to be guilty of an offense and this applies to unauthorized absence as well.

Paragraph 165 of the MCM, in discussing Article 86, considers this "mind at fault" concept as it applies to unauthorized absence when it states that this "article is designed to cover every case not elsewhere provided for in which any member of the armed forces is through his own fault not at the place where he is required to be at a prescribed time. Specific intent is not an element of this offense. . . ." The MCM further states that when "a man on authorized leave is unable to return at the expiration thereof through *no fault of his own,* he has *not* committed the offense of absence without leave, there being an excuse for the absence in such a case." This is the "mind at fault" concept. Negligence or lack of foresight is therefore insufficient to warrant a finding of innocence.

405 The Defense of Impossibility

One of the defenses to unauthorized absence is the impossibility of returning. It is a defense unless the impossibility was foreseeable or due to the accused's own fault. For example, Seaman Smith is on liberty and knows it generally takes five minutes for him to return to the ship from the train station. If all the traffic lights were red and he arrived seven minutes late, impossibility would not be a defense to the unauthorized absence, as it was foreseeable that this could happen.

Acts of God, such as sudden unexpected floods, snow storms, hurricanes, etc., can constitute a defense, unless they were foreseeable. For example, in areas such as Vermont, where snow storms frequently occur during the winter, a snow storm must be anticipated and enough time reserved to return to the ship if such a storm should occur.

The acts of others may permit the assertion of the defense of impossibility. For example, if Seaman Smith is returning to the base by auto and is involved in an auto accident in which he was in no way at fault, this would be a defense to a charge of unauthorized absence. On the other hand, air travel, at certain seasons and in certain localities, can be uncertain. Therefore, a reasonable time must be allowed for possible delay when these factors are present.

Civilian police authorities, by jailing a serviceman, may prevent his return from leave or liberty. There are three situations that may arise:

1. If he is acquitted by civilian authorities, his absence is excused as the absence is not due to his fault;

2. If he is tried and convicted of the civilian offense, the absence is not excused and the accused may be tried for this absence;

3. If the accused is not tried for the civilian offense or if no determination of guilt or innocence is made, the question of fault would rely upon his actual *guilt* of the civilian offense. Consequently, if this defense is raised by an accused, the guilt or innocence of the civilian offense would have to be determined first before the unauthorized absence could be resolved.

However, a member of the armed forces who is turned over to civilian authorities by the military is not an unauthorized absentee during the period of time he is retained regardless of whether or not he is convicted by civilian authorities.

Physical disability, if not the fault of the accused, may make it impossible for the accused to return from leave or liberty at the proper time. For example, an accused who becomes too sick to travel may have a defense. However, if he stays in a bar too long and becomes intoxicated to the extent he cannot return in time, this would be due to his own fault. Each case must be decided on its own merits.

406 The Defenses of Mistake and Ignorance of Fact

A mistake or ignorance of fact, to constitute a defense to a general intent crime such as unauthorized absence from a unit, must be both honest and reasonable. For example, Seaman Smith is in the duty section, but he honestly believes that he is not. He departs the ship. He has no defense to a charge of unauthorized absence on the grounds of mistake of fact, for while his mistake was honest, it was not reasonable. He could have discovered his true status by ordinary diligence.

407 Some Rules of Thumb

These defenses are subject to a general rule of thumb, that is, "once UA, always UA." Therefore, even if the defenses of impossibility or physical disability would normally be applicable to a particular case, if the incident occurs *after* leave or liberty has ended, they are inapplicable. The reason for this is that the offense resulted because he was absent from his ship, and therefore it was his own fault.

However, the fact that a serviceman's absence was in part involuntary, for whatever the reason, should be considered in determining whether the case should be referred to nonjudicial punishment or a court-martial and the punishment to be awarded. They are factors that lessen the seriousness of the offense.

The occurrence of an unforeseen incident does not automatically furnish the accused with a defense to unauthorized absence. For example, in *United States* v. *Kessinger*, 9 CMR 261 (1952), the accused, who was returning to his command from liberty, had an auto accident. He waited until the vehicle was repaired and was late. If he had taken an available bus, he would not have been late. He was guilty of unauthorized absence as the facts indicated he delayed to suit his own convenience. The unforeseen occurrence will only constitute a defense for the length of absence caused by the occurrence. Any amount of time in excess of a reasonable period of time is unauthorized absence.

408　Defenses Barring Trial

Defenses barring trial are generally available to an accused regardless of the type of offense involved. They generally are raised by a motion (i.e., request) to the president of the court or military judge to dismiss the case. If granted, they do not resolve the issue of the guilt or innocence of the accused, but the trial ends, at least for the time being. The only exception to this is the motion raising the factual issue of the lack of mental responsibility (i.e., insanity) of the accused at the time of the commission of the offense. This must be finally resolved by the member of the court when they close to deliberate on the findings (i.e., the guilt or innocence of the accused).

A brief summary of some of the defenses which may be raised are:

1. *Insanity.* A person is not mentally responsible in a criminal sense for an offense unless he was, at the time, so far free from mental defect, disease, or derangement as to be able, concerning the particular act charged, both to distinguish right from wrong and to adhere to the right. Mere defect of character, will power, or behavior, or ungovernable passion, does not necessarily indicate insanity. See Chapter XXIV of the MCM for a further discussion of insanity.

2. *Former Jeopardy.* Generally, no person may, without his consent, be tried twice for the same offense. This constitutes the principle of "former jeopardy" commonly called "double jeopardy." However, when the accused is found guilty by a court-martial, but the case is reversed on

review and the admissible evidence is sufficient to support the findings of guilt, a rehearing of the case may be ordered.

The defense of former jeopardy is only available if the same "sovereign" attempts to try someone twice. For example, an offense against the Code may also be an offense against federal law. Our military courts, although not a part of the formal federal court system, are United States courts. Therefore, they are the *same sovereign* (i.e., the United States government) and the principle of former jeopardy would apply. However, a state trial, representing a separate sovereign would not bar trial by military courts or the federal district courts. However, the JAG Manual states that a person in the naval service who has been tried in a domestic or foreign court, whether convicted or acquitted, or whose case has been adjudicated by juvenile court authorities, shall not be tried by court-martial for the same act or acts, except in those unusual cases where trial is considered essential in the interests of justice, discipline, and proper administration within the naval service. The JAG Manual then provides the instances when this rule would apply and the procedure to be ultilized.

If a case is dismissed or terminated by the convening authority or if the prosecution withdraws the case due to lack of evidence after evidence has been presented on the issue of the guilt or innocence of the accused, this constitutes a "trial."

3. *Failure to Allege an Offense.* If a specification fails to allege an offense (for example, if "without authority" is left out in an unauthorized absence specification) the proceedings are a nullity. This rule applies whether the accused pleads guilty or not guilty, as it is a plea to an *innocent act.* Therefore, there was no *trial,* and the accused may be tried by another court. The defense of former jeopardy would not apply in such case.

4. *Former Punishment.* The awarding of punishment at Mast may also bar a trial by court-martial for the same offense, if the offense is a minor one (see Chapter VI of this publication for a further discussion of this defense in the Discussion Case at the end of that chapter).

5. *Statute of Limitations.* It becomes increasingly difficult to assure the accuracy of evidence relating to an offense after the lapse of several years. Therefore, Article 43 of the Code provides certain periods of time within which *initial* steps must be taken in the prosecution of a case or the accused cannot be tried. This period of time is called the "statute of limitations." For example, unauthorized absence has a two-year statute of limitations whereas larceny has a three-year period. Some offenses, such as desertion, unauthorized absence in time of war, or murder, have *no* limitation.

Once the initial step is taken of receiving sworn charges by the officer exercising summary court-martial jurisdiction over the accused, the accused can be tried for the offense when he returns to military control, no matter how long a period of time expires.

6. *Lack of Jurisdiction.* The jurisdiction of a court-martial is its power to try and determine a case. Therefore:

a. The court must be convened by an official empowered to convene it;

b. The membership of the court must be in accordance with the law as to membership and competency to sit on the court;

c. The court must have the power to try the person and the offense charged.

A motion to dismiss on the ground of lack of jurisdiction is ordinarily based on an assertion that the court is not properly constituted because it was not convened by an official empowered to convene it or that the offense is not service-connected. As in the case of a failure of a specification to allege an offense, if the court lacks jurisdiction, the proceedings are a nullity. This means the accused may be tried again for the same "offense" as he has never really been charged with any crime. See Chapter VIII for further discussion.

7. *Pardon and Grant of Immunity.* A pardon is an act of the President of the United States which exempts the individual upon whom it is bestowed from the punishment for the crime he has committed.

A grant of immunity is a promise of immunity for courtroom testimony in a case involving more than one participant. It is utilized when the testimony of the witness is essential and granting the immunity would be in the interest of justice.

8. *Speedy Trial.* An accused is entitled to be tried within a reasonable time after being placed under a restraint such as restriction, arrest, or confinement or after charges are preferred. See Chapter II of this publication for a further discussion of what constitutes speedy trial.

409 Drafting Charges and Specifications

Prior to drafting the charges and specifications, the facts garnered in the investigation must be analyzed with care. With this analysis as a basis, the officer should turn to the punitive articles (Articles 77 to 134) in Appendix 2 of the MCM and select the offenses that may be applicable. Next he should proceed to Chapter XXVIII of the MCM entitled "Punitive Articles." There he will find a discussion of the facts, which must be proven beyond a reasonable doubt (called the "elements") to convict the accused, and background on the particular punitive article that concerns him. Appendix 6 of the MCM contains explicit directions as to the proper method of drafting charges and specifications, and sample forms for this purpose.

The proper drafting of charges and specifications is an exacting art. It must be done carefully and with precision. Therefore, it is recommended that the sample specifications in Appendix 6 of the MCM be followed exactly as contained therein. The omission of a single, seemingly insignificant, word can result in dismissal of the specifications for failure to allege an offense. The wording of specifications is of the utmost importance in the proper administration of military justice.

Essentially, the charges and specifications reflect the violation of military law that the drafter believes the accused committed. They constitute the formal, written *accusation* that the accused committed a certain crime. As such, they consist of two parts:

1. *The Charge.* This is the article of the Code that the accused violated. For example:

Charge: Violation of the Uniform Code of Military Justice, Article 86

2. *The Specification.* This sets forth the specific *facts* that constitute the violation of the Code. For example:

Specification: In that Seaman John J. Jones, U.S. Navy, USS *Washtub,* did on or about 20 September 19___, without authority, absent himself from his unit, to wit: the USS *Washtub,* located at the U.S. Naval Base, Newport, Rhode Island, and did remain so absent until on or about 30 September 19___.

The sum total of the charges and specifications against the accused are often referred to as the "charges" against him. If there is only one charge or one specification under a charge, it is not numbered. When there is more than one, the charges should be numbered with roman numerals (I, II, III, etc.) and specifications with arabic numbers (1, 2, 3, etc.).

Every charge begins with the words "Violation of the Uniform Code of Military Justice, Article ___." The paragraph of the article charged would not be reflected. For example, paragraphs (1), (2), and (3) of Article 86 allege different offenses, but any one of the three offenses would be written in a charge simply as a violation of Article 86.

The specification *must* inform the accused of the specific facts that constitute the violation of the Code. Generally, a specification would, as a minimum, contain the following information:

1. *Rate or Rank of the Accused.* When the rate or rank of the accused has changed since the date of the offense, the accused should be designated by his present grade followed by a statement of his grade at the date of the offense. For example, "In that Seaman John A. Jones, U.S. Navy, then gunner's mate third class, U.S. Navy . . ."

2. *Name.* The accused's first name, middle initial and last name should be stated.

3. *Armed Force and Unit or Organization.*　The armed force should be stated in order to show that he is a person subject to the Code.

Generally, if the accused is a member of the regular Navy, he is subject to the Code. This would be reflected by the designation "U.S. Navy." On the other hand if the possibility exists that the accused may not have been subject to the Code, the facts that make him subject should be shown. For example, "In that Seaman John L. Jones, U.S. Naval Reserve, USS *Blue,* on active duty, did . . ."

The unit or organization further identifies the accused. It also clarifies who is the convening authority (generally the convening authority is the commanding officer of the ship). The unit is designated by simply stating the name of the ship, "the USS *Blue.*" The hull number is *not* included.

4. *Time and Place.*　The time and place of the commission of the offense should be stated with sufficient precision to enable the accused to understand what he is charged with and to prepare a defense.

Generally, in alleging an offense it is proper and advisable to allege that it occurred "on or about" a specified day. This is because an approximate time of the occurrence of the offense is sufficient, unless it is so inaccurate as to mislead the accused. This is true in alleging unauthorized absence offenses.

In unauthorized absence cases, the approximate time usually is not pleaded, unless it is necessary to show that the absence was more than 3 or more than 30 days. For example, it would be necessary to allege the time when the absence occurred "at or about 0730 on 14 October 1969" and terminated "at or about 0800 on 17 October 1969" a period of 3 days and 30 minutes. Notice that when the exact *time* is stated, it is preceded by "at or about" and that when the *date* only is given it is preceded by the words "on or about." The purpose of writing a specification in such a manner is to give the government some leeway as to proof as to when the offense was committed and at the same time inform the accused of what he is charged.

If the offense took place on board the ship or station to which the accused is attached, the specification may read "on board said ship" or "at said naval station" as they have been previously identified as the unit of the accused. For example, absence from an appointed place of duty discussed in Article 86 (1) could be written in this manner. If the offense took place elsewhere, the specification may read, for example, "on board the USS *Rock.*"

5. *The Facts Constituting the Offense.*　These facts must be contained in the specification. All elements must be either stated directly or contained therein by necessary implication.

6. *Aggravation.*　To a certain extent aggravating circumstances may be contained in the specification. If an unauthorized absentee is appre-

hended by military or civilian authorities, rather than surrendering himself, this is considered an aggravating factor that a court-martial may consider in determining an appropriate sentence.

However, it is recommended that the termination by apprehension *not* be written into the specification. In its stead, the trial counsel can utilize either an official record entry on page 13 to prove this aggravating factor or the defense may be willing to stipulate to this fact.

This permits more flexibility in the event the accused desires to plead guilty but disputes the fact that he was apprehended.

410 Proving the Unauthorized Absence

Generally, the inception, termination, and lack of authority for the absence can be proven initially by the entry into evidence of two appropriate official entries in the Administrative Remarks section (page 13) of the accused's service record (page 12 in the USMC). Appendix 8 contains examples of the Navy entries. Testimony of witnesses and other evidence may, of course, be utilized, and may be necessary to prove the accused guilty if the accused contests the case.

As a minimum, it is recommended that the chapters on evidence, the trial and defense counsel (including the *vital* check lists in Appendices 19 and 20), and trial procedure be studied prior to appearing before any court-martial for either side.

It is important to remember that each specification, together with the charge under which it is placed, constitutes a separate accusation. The accused must plead guilty or not guilty to each one and the court must determine his guilt or innocence of each.

411 Summary

The proper drafting of charges and specifications requires a thorough analysis of the facts and a study of the punitive articles in the Code and the interpretive discussion in Chapter XXVIII of the MCM. It should be evident now that even a relatively "simple" case of unauthorized absence can present a myriad of problems to the preliminary inquiry officer or counsel who does not pay attention to detail and does not research every issue that arises.

If an officer understands one or two offenses thoroughly, especially such a common one as unauthorized absence, he can develop a basic understanding of other offenses. Chapter V will discuss larceny, a common offense that is considerably more complicated and difficult than unauthorized absence.

It is not possible to discuss all the possible defenses that may arise in a typical unauthorized absence case. Defenses denying the accused actually committed the act charged, such as alibi, good character, and mistaken identity are seldom asserted in defense of this type of charge.

Discussion Case

UNITED STATES, Appellant

v.

WILLIE S. HOLDER, Private, U.S. Marine Corps, Appellee

7 USCMA 213, 22 CMR 3

(1956)

Opinion of the Court

GEORGE W. LATIMER, Judge:

Despite his plea of not guilty, the accused was convicted by a general court-martial of desertion, in violation of Article 85, Uniform Code of Military Justice, and sentenced to dishonorable discharge, total forfeitures, and confinement for three years. The convening authority approved, but the board of review, one member dissenting, held that the law officer erred in failing to give defense counsel's requested instruction on mistake of fact as a defense to the charge of desertion. The board, therefore, affirmed only a short unauthorized absence and a sentence to a bad-conduct discharge, total forfeitures, and six months' confinement. The dissenting member was of the opinion that the evidence failed to raise any issue of mistake, although he was uncertain as to whether the issue presented involved a mistake of law or of fact.

Thereafter, The Judge Advocate General of the Navy, by certificate filed under the provisions of Article 67(b)(2) of the Code, asked this Court to review the following question:

"*As a matter of law, was the issue of mistake of fact raised in this case?*"

On February 6, 1953, the accused, who was then serving a sentence ad-

judged by a previous court-martial, was restored to duty from the Retraining Command, Mare Island, California. His bad-conduct discharge was suspended for one year and he was transferred to Camp Pendleton, California, where he was told by his commanding officer that if he "didn't walk the straight and narrow way," his punitive discharge would be executed. Within a short period of time accused had furnished a reason for further disciplinary proceedings, for on March 24, 1953, he absented himself without leave. He testified that he had invited further trouble in this manner because of marital problems and because he felt he was being unfairly treated within his unit.

On April 17, 1953, the accused was arrested by civilian police in Van Nuys, California, for petty theft. He was tried, convicted, and sentenced to a short period in jail. At that time he disclosed his status as a member of the Marine Corps to the civilian authorities, and the evidence is clear that his unit commander was informed of his whereabouts through official channels. He was due to be released from jail about May 23, 1953, and he ascertained informally from persons en-ployed at his place of incarceration that the Navy Shore Patrol normally picked up the servicemen released from civilian jails. When the day of his release came the accused discovered that the military authorities had not filed a "hold" order on him, and believing that his suspended bad-conduct discharge had been executed, did not return to Camp Pendleton. Instead, he obtained civilian employment. As time went by, however, he began to wonder why a discharge had not been forwarded to him, for he knew that "when a man has not received his last discharge, there is something very wrong about it." At irregular intervals he asked the opinion of his civilian friends about his situation, but they invariably informed him the Marine Corps would eventually mail his discharge to him. In October 1954, during the course of a family argument, he informed his wife of his unauthorized absence from the Corps. She went so far as to call the Federal Bureau of Investigation, hoping they would come and get the accused, but was informed that he was no longer wanted by that service. The accused was eventually apprehended on April 6, 1955, by civil authorities and returned to military control.

It only remains to be mentioned that the accused was no novice in the ways of the Marine Corps, for his service in that armed force began in 1947, and he had received one honorable discharge and one general discharge prior to this incident. Nevertheless, he steadfastly maintained that he had never intended to desert, believing at all times that the military authorities had executed the punitive discharge and did not want him.

Turning to the problem presented by the certificate, we must mention that the phrasing of the question leaves some doubt in our minds as to how it should be answered. When this case was tried, the specification alleged that the accused had committed the offense of desertion, and thus a specific intent to remain away permanently was involved. The instruction requested by defense was directed against that intent only. However, the board of review reduced the crime to absence without authority, that offense requires only a general intent, and a different principle is at stake. We can, of course, make certain that we answer the question by discussing all facets of the issue, and so we will proceed on that basis.

In *United States* v. *Rowan*, 4 USCMA 430, 16 CMR 4, the accused was charged with larceny by check, and defended on the ground that he had made an honest mistake of fact. The issue presented was whether or not an instruction which required the mistake to be both honest and reasonable was erroneous. Because we were dealing with an offense which involved a specific intent to deprive an owner permanently of his property, we held that an instruction which required both conditions was erroneous.

The same rationale must be applied to the offense of desertion, for as previously stated, it requires a specific intent. Therefore, it follows that the defense of mistake of fact to desertion need only include a showing that it was honest, for the notion that an accused can negligently intend to remain away permanently represents as great a logical impossibility as does the theory that he may negligently intend to deprive permanently an owner of his property. . . . With the test laid down in that case as our measuring rod, we turn to the facts to ascertain whether an issue was raised.

We, like a majority of the board of review, conclude that a reasonable person could find that the accused honestly, even though negligently, believed he had been discharged from the service, and that an issue of mistake of fact was raised in so far as the offense of desertion is concerned.

∞

Surely he could have learned the truth about his discharge if he had made inquiry at any one of several military installations in the area where he lived, and a reasonable man would have sought an official determination as to his status. But the accused's testimony was not inherently improbable, his mistaken belief was supported by some independent facts, and we cannot say that, as a matter of law, it was not an honest belief. If we cannot do that, we must conclude that an issue was raised as to the offense of desertion, and that the law officer erred in failing to give the requested instruction.

We mentioned earlier that the board of review had affirmed a conviction for absence without leave; that is the offense presently before us, and the certified issue can be viewed as posing an inquiry concerning that offense, which, as previously stated, involves only a general intent.

∞

Turning to the civilian decisions, it is clear they are far from adopting a general rule that honest mistake or ignorance of fact will serve as a defense to crimes involving only a general criminal intent.

∞

In *De Forest* v. *United States,* 11 App DC 458 (1897), the defendant was convicted of keeping a bawdy house under a predecessor statute to Section 22–2722, supra. In construing the early enactment, the court said (page 463):

". . . It is enough that the acts done are contrary to law and subversive of the public morals, that the house is commonly resorted to for the commission of such acts, and that the proprietor knows, or should in reason know, the fact, and either procures it to be done, connives at it, or does not prevent it."

The court then proceeded to give its approval to the trial judge's charge to the jury, which included the statement that "every person is . . . presumed to have knowledge of that which goes on in his own house."

∞

From what has been said it must be manifest that thus far we have preferred to adopt the principle that to be a defense, in general intent cases, a mistake or ignorance of fact must be both honest and reasonable. When we apply that principle to these facts, we conclude the issue of mistake was not reasonably raised because, by the exercise of ordinary care, the accused would have known he had not been discharged. He had finished two tours of duty in the Marine Corps, and he was familiar with the fact that a certificate is issued to the individual concerned when he is discharged. He had lived for some two years near Marine Corps installations, and never once sought to ascertain, from anyone likely to know, whether or not he had been discharged from that service. The accused, had he acted reasonably, would have returned to Camp Pendleton when he was released from jail despite the absence of official transportation. Even were we to assume otherwise, an inquiry by mail to his unit commander would have elicited the necessary information. Giving to the accused every benefit of doubt, we are convinced his failure to take reasonable measures to ascertain his status was negligence of sufficient importance to render fatally defective any claim that his mistake was both honest and reasonable. We, therefore, conclude that mistake of fact was not raised as an issue as to the offense of absence without leave.

In its holding the board of review affirmed only a conviction for absence without leave for the period from March 24, 1953, to May 23, 1953, the date upon which the accused was released from the Van Nuys, California, jail. In order to reach that result the board had to conclude that the accused had reasonably raised an issue of mistake of fact as to unauthorized absence. In this it erred, and this error requires corrective measures. In the light of the rule announced herein the accused is guilty of being absent without leave for the entire period during which he was out of the hands of military authorities.

Chief Judge QUINN and Judge FERGUSON concur.

DISCUSSION AND SELF-QUIZ

1. John Smith, a seaman aboard your ship, was on authorized leave until 0730 on 10 September 19___. Shortly before his leave was to expire, he was apprehended by New York City police. He was placed in a civilian jail until 19 December 19___. At that time, after consultation with a legal aid lawyer, he pleaded "guilty" to a charge of being a "youthful offender" and was sentenced to the Elmira Reception Center for "an indefinite term not to exceed three years." However, execution of the sentence was suspended and the accused was delivered by the civilian authorities to the military. You are a member of Smith's court-martial for unauthorized absence from 0730, 10 September 19___ until on or about 19 December 19___.

Paragraph 165 of the MCM states that if "a member of the armed forces is convicted by the civil authorities, the fact that he was arrested, held, and tried does not excuse any unauthorized absence." The accused contends that his adjudication as a youthful offender is not a "conviction" and consequently cannot be the basis for a conviction of unauthorized absence.

Is the defense argument valid?

2. You have been appointed a preliminary inquiry officer in the case of John M. Doakes, seaman apprentice, U.S. Naval Reserve. He is attached to your ship, the USS Ball (DD–909), presently located at Newport, Rhode Island. Your preliminary inquiry develops that at or about 0730 on 4 September 19—, Doakes was an unauthorized absentee and that he did not return to the ship until 1500 on 15 September 19—. Draft a sample charge

and a sample specification against Doakes.

3. You are the preliminary inquiry officer investigating an alleged offense involving Seaman Joseph B. Stack, U.S. Navy, attached to your ship the USS *Pan* (DLG–509) presently alongside the pier at Long Beach, California. At 0745 on 10 April 19—, Stack was to report to relieve the quarterdeck watch at the forward gangway. He failed to report until 0900. BM3 Rogers tells you that he notified Stack two days ago about standing this watch, and the time and the place Stack was to stand it. He further states he had posted a copy of the watch bill in Stack's compartment. Stack said that he had relied on his buddy, John Smith, to wake him up but that Smith had been out drinking that night and overslept. Stack said he had an alarm clock, but two days before the incident he had broken it. He did not ask the OOD's messenger to wake him up because he was relying on Smith.

    a. On what charge and specification would you write up Stack?

    b. Does Stack have a defense?

    c. Draft the appropriate charge and specification.

See paragraphs 171*b* and 165 of the MCM and Appendix 6 of the MCM.

4. On 3 November 1964, the accused, who had more than 14 years of honorable service, absented himself without authority from his unit at Fort Polk, Louisiana. On 10 February 1967, the accused surrendered to civilian authorities and was returned to military control at Fort Campbell, Kentucky. The accused was charged and convicted of desertion. Upon review the Court of Military Review concluded that there was insufficient evidence of the accused's intent to remain away permanently from his unit, and therefore affirmed findings of guilty of only the lesser included offense of unauthorized absence. There is a two-year statute of limitations for unauthorized absence and a three-year statute for desertion.

Generally, in the Navy, after an accused is absent 30 days, his service record is forwarded to Washington, D.C., where sworn charges by an officer exercising summary court-martial jurisdiction are made, thus ending the running of the two-year statute of limitations. The U.S. Army did not terminate the statute of limitations in this manner in this case.

The Court of Military Review then determined that the offense was committed in time of war and that therefore the two-year statute of limitations did not apply.

Article 43 of the Code provides as follows:

> A person charged with desertion or absence without leave *in time of war,* or with aiding the enemy, mutiny, or murder, may be tried and punished at any time without limitation. (Emphasis supplied.)

At the time of the offense, 3 November 1964, was the United States "at war" in Vietnam?

5. On 10 March 19—, in Norfolk, Virginia, the crew of the USS *Aground* (DD–901) was informed at morning quarters that the ship was going to depart Norfolk for Newport, Rhode Island at 0800 on 15 March 19—. Seaman Jones and Roe attended morning quarters. An announcement of the impending movement was also placed in the POD (Plan of the Day).

a. Seaman Jones has met a girl in one of the local bars. She persuades him to go on unauthorized absence on 15 March 19— and remain in Norfolk, which he does.

b. Seaman Roe, knowing the ship is going to get underway, decides to celebrate the night before departure as the ship will be at sea for two weeks. He becomes intoxicated, stays overnight with a friend, and sleeps through the ship's departure the next day.

c. Assume in the foregoing example, the ship was only to move from Pier 7 in Norfolk to Pier 9 at 0800 on 15 March 19—.

What articles of the Code, if any, have Seamen Jones and Roe violated? State your reasons. See Chapter XXVIII of the MCM and Appendix 2 of the MCM.

CHAPTER V

A Study of Offenses and Drafting Specifications: Larceny

This chapter discusses an offense that is considered much more complex in its nature than unauthorized absence. The purposes of this chapter are to give the reader a basic understanding of the most common type of larceny and to prepare him for further research into other offenses when the situation arises. To do so, extensive quotes have been made from the MCM to facilitate familiarization with the phraseology used therein. To advance further into a study of offenses it is vital that question 3 of the Discussion and Self-Quiz be completed.

501 The Nature of Larceny

Larceny is one of the most common offenses tried by court-martial. It is also one of the most serious offenses because of its adverse effects upon morale.

Under the close living conditions of service life, larceny is like a disease which becomes highly contagious unless corrective action is taken quickly. For example, Seaman Apprentice Jones needs a clean white hat for inspection. Seaman Doe has laid a clean white hat on his bunk and has proceeded into the head to shave. Jones steals Doe's white hat. Doe, frustrated because he now must fail inspection, steals Smith's white hat. The spread of such "minor" larcenies can have a devastating effect on the mutual trust and confidence that is essential to an effective fighting organization.

502 Types of Larceny

Article 121 of the Code discusses both larceny and wrongful appropriation. Larceny, as presently defined in Article 121, encompasses what were once three crimes under the common law of England: larceny by taking, larceny by obtaining by false pretenses, and larceny by embezzlement.

A wrongful *obtaining* with intent permanently to defraud includes the offense formerly known as obtaining by false pretenses. Possession of property is transferred to a thief voluntarily as the result of a false representation made by the thief and relied on by the victim.

For example, if an accused obtained a loan from Navy Relief by making misrepresentations as to his name, organization, and financial condition, this would be sufficient to establish the offense of obtaining money by false pretenses. A discussion of "false pretenses" is contained in paragraph 200*a* (5) of the MCM.

A wrongful *withholding* with intent permanently to appropriate includes the offense formally known as embezzlement. A withholding may arise as a result of a failure to return, account for, or deliver property to its owner when a return, accounting, or delivery is due, even if the owner has made no demand for the property, or it may arise as a result of devoting property to a use not authorized by its owner.

> For example, if a person obtains the vehicle of another by hiring it and thereafter decides to keep the vehicle permanently, and pursuant to that decision either fails to return it at the appointed time or uses it for a purpose not authorized by the terms of the hiring, he has committed larceny, even though at the time he obtained the vehicle he fully intended to return it after using it according to the agreement of hire. (Paragraph 200*a*(6) of the MCM.)

Larceny by *taking* is the most common of the three types of larceny. It is the type of larceny we shall discuss in this chapter. Paragraph 200*a* (1) of the MCM states that:

> a person is guilty of larceny if he wrongfully takes . . . by any means, from the possession of the owner or of any other person any money, personal property, or article of value of any kind, with intent permanently to deprive or defraud another person of the use and benefit of property or to appropriate it to his own use or the use of any person other than the owner.

503 The Elements of Larceny

There are four elements that must be proved beyond a reasonable doubt in order to convict an accused of larceny:

1. *That the accused wrongfully took from the possession of the owner, or of any other person, the property described in the specification.* The "taking" type of offense is essentially an offense against possession. Therefore, any movement of the property or any exercise of dominion over it by any means is sufficient if accompanied by the requisite intent.

While this would be the general rule, there are exceptions to it. For example, consider the case of Private Jones, USMC, who attempts to steal Corporal Smith's watch. Jones reaches into Smith's locker, finds the watch, picks it up, and discovers it is attached inside the locker by means of a watch fob. As it is dark and Jones cannot determine how to release the watch, he abandons his quest. In this case, although Jones has moved the watch, he has not exercised dominion over it and no larceny has been committed. However, Jones has committed an attempted larceny. Paragraph 1304 of this book discusses attempts. The MCM discusses a *taking* without a *touching*. For example, if a person entices another's horse into his own stable this could constitute a larceny even though he does not touch the animal.

2. *That the property belonged to a certain person named or described.* To a great extent, the wording used in sub-paragraph 1 above must be related to this second paragraph as the first element really describes *who* the property belongs to. For example, *possession* includes the care, custody, management, and control of property. The term *owner* refers to a person who, at the time of the taking, had the superior right to possession of the property. For example, the renter of a car has the superior right to its possession during the period of his lease. The phrase "any other person" means *any* person—even a person who has stolen the property—as he has possession or a greater right to possession than a second thief.

In drafting a specification of larceny, the owner of the property may be any person, other than the accused, who at the time of the theft, was a general or special owner of the property. A general owner of property is a person who has title to it, whether or not he has possession of it. A special owner, such as a borrower or hirer, is one who does not have title, but who does have possession, or the right to possession of the property. The word *person* in referring to one from whose possession property has been taken, includes natural persons, a government, a corporation, an organization, or an estate. For example, a thief may steal articles of value from the U.S. Navy, a part of the U.S. Government. It need not be a legal entity (for example, incorporated in accordance with state law).

A taking must be *wrongful*. Generally, it is wrongful if done without the consent of the owner. However, if a taking is authorized by law (such as the seizure of property after obtaining a lawful authorization to search) or if done by a person who has a right to the possession of the property either equal to or greater than the right of the one from whose possession he takes, it is not larceny. For example, the true owner of an item could take back his property from a thief, as the owner has the greater right of possession.

3. *That the property was of the value alleged or of some value.* Generally, value is an essential element of larceny and must be proven. However, when the character of the property clearly appears in evidence, by exhibition to the court or otherwise, the court, from its own experience may infer that it has some value, or if the property value is obviously in excess of $100 (as in the case of an auto in good condition), the court may infer a value of over $100.

If property has *no* value, it cannot be the subject of larceny. The value of property alleged to have been stolen is significant insofar as the sentence to be awarded is concerned. For example, paragraph 127c of the MCM provides up to six months' confinement at hard labor for the larceny of property of the value of $50 or less, but up to a year for property of a value of between $50 and $100. For over $100, the period of confinement may reach five years. Paragraph 200a(7) of the MCM relates the method by which value may be determined.

4. *That the taking by the accused was with intent permanently to deprive or defraud another person of the use and benefit of property or to appropriate it to his own use or the use of any person other than the owner.*

The existence of an intent to steal must, in most cases, be inferred from the circumstances. Thus, if a person secretly takes property, hides it, and denies that he knows anything about it, an intent to steal may be inferred; but if he takes it openly, and returns it, this would tend to negative such an intent. Proof of a subsequent sale of the property may show an intent to steal, and, therefore, evidence of such a sale may be introduced to support a charge of larceny. An intent to steal may be inferred from a wrongful and intentional dealing with the property of another in a manner likely to cause him to suffer a permanent loss thereof. (Paragraph 200a(6), MCM.)

For example, if Seaman Jones throws Seaman Doe's watch in deep water where it cannot be found, he has committed larceny of that watch if he intended to deprive the owner of it permanently.

It is not larceny for a person to take from a thief in order to restore property to the true owner. In fact, the Court of Military Appeals has held that an accused is not guilty of larceny if he takes back money he has lost in a crooked gambling game. This is so because his taking is by claim of right under the bona fide belief he *is* the owner. *United States v. Brown,* 13 USCMA 485, 33 CMR 17 (1963).

An intent to pay for stolen property or to replace it with an equivalent is not a defense, although it may be considered in mitigation of the sentence if the accused is found guilty.

However, in *United States* v. *Hayes,* 8 USCMA 627, 25 CMR 131

(1958), the Court of Military Appeals stated that apart "from circumstances which may impart special value to a coin or bill as a numismatic
item, one dollar bill is the same as another. It is not larceny, for example,
to take two five-dollar bills in exchange for a ten-dollar bill without the
knowledge or consent of the owner."

504 Wrongful Appropriation

Wrongful appropriation under Article 121 is defined exactly as larceny
is—with one exception. The accused need only intend to *temporarily*
deprive another of his property to be guilty of this offense.

An example of wrongful appropriation would be taking an automobile
of another without permission or authority, with intent to drive it a short
distance and then return it or cause it to be returned (joy riding).

As in larceny, there must be a criminal intent to constitute the offense.
For example, the Court of Military Appeals has found a lack of criminal
intent where an accused borrowed property from a friend or acquain-
tance, without the owner's consent. In *United States* v. *Caid,* 13 USCMA
348, 32 CMR 348 (1962), the accused stated, under oath, that he was
without the proper uniform in which he was required to appear for trial
before summary court-martial. Unable to borrow money to redeem his
own clothing from the dry cleaner, the accused stated he sought to borrow clothing from others. He entered E's room and found it empty. He
stated he believed that E would lend him a uniform if he were there,
and took it. He left a note advising E that he had taken the uniform and
telling him it would be at the stockade in "case I didn't get back or have
a chance to give it back to him." The Court of Military Appeals stated
that if the accused's testimony was believed, he would be innocent as he
would lack criminal intent.

A charge of wrongful appropriation is necessarily included in a charge
of larceny. This means that, if an accused is charged with larceny and
the court believes beyond a reasonable doubt that he is only guilty of an
intent temporarily to deprive another—it may find him guilty of wrong
ful appropriation. This is because the intent in wrongful appropriation
is *lesser* than the intent in larceny. Paragraph 1304 of this book discusses
lesser included offenses.

505 Defenses to Larceny and Wrongful Appropriation

Both larceny and wrongful appropriation are "specific intent" crimes
That is, there must be an *intent* to deprive permanently or temporarily
It is this intent that distinguishes these crimes from a "general intent"
crime, such as unauthorized absence. That is one reason it is harder to
prove the commission of a larceny.

The "defenses barring trial" discussed in paragraph 408 of Chapter IV,
such as insanity, former jeopardy, failure to allege an offense, former

punishment, statute of limitations, lack of jurisdiction, pardon, and speedy trial, all apply to larceny as they do to most of the other punitive articles.

There are other defenses that apply to specific intent offenses, such as larceny and wrongful appropriation, some of which are as follows:

1. *Voluntary Intoxication.* This is a defense if the court believes that the accused lacked the mental capacity to entertain the required specific intent.

2. *Honest Mistake.* An honest mistake would be a valid defense to a larceny. For example, if a person takes the property of another believing he has a right to it, he lacks the criminal intent required to constitute larceny or wrongful appropriation.

3. *Teaching a Lesson.* Where the intent of the accused in taking the property is simply to teach the victim a lesson, there is no criminal intent. See the Discussion Case at the end of this chapter.

4. *Coercion.* If an accused was forced to take the article by another who threatened him with immediate death or grievous bodily harm if he did not do so, this would be a defense to a larceny or wrongful appropriation charge.

5. *Entrapment.* Entrapment is a defense which exists when the criminal design originates with government agents or persons cooperating with them. They implant in the mind of an innocent person the disposition to commit the alleged offense and thus induce its commission. "Innocent" means that the accused would not have perpetrated the crime with which he is presently charged but for the enticement of one of these persons. The fact that persons acting for the government merely afford opportunities or facilities for the commission of the offense does not constitute entrapment.

6. *Obedience to Apparently Lawful Orders.* An order requiring the performance of a military duty may be inferred to be legal. An act performed manifestly beyond the scope of authority, or pursuant to an order that a man of ordinary sense and understanding would know to be illegal, or in a wanton manner in the discharge of a lawful duty, is not excusable.

7. *Abandoned Property.* If an owner relinquishes all title, possession, or claim on property and does not vest it in another, he has abandoned it and another may take it. For example, if John Jones throws his broken watch in the Dempsey Dumpster, another could take it without committing larceny.

8. *Lost Property.* An owner who involuntarily parts with his property and cannot find or recover it, has *lost* such property.

If there is no clue to the identity of the owner, a finder does not commit larceny by retaining possession of lost property. Generally, there is some clue to the ownership of property, such as identifying marks, initials, serial numbers, the nature of the property, its value, or its location. For example, a valuable watch or a large sum of money is, in itself, a clue as to ownership. The owners will undoubtedly report such a loss to the proper authorities. Further, the fact that a pair of unstenciled dungarees is found in an isolated living compartment occupied by ten men is a clue that the dungarees may belong to one of the ten.

In order to determine the finder's intent when there is such a clue as to ownership, his conduct with respect to the property should be studied. If he made a reasonable and honest effort to restore the property, he probably lacks the intent to steal.

If an item is intentionally put in a certain place for a temporary purpose and then inadvertently left there, it is *mislaid* property.

This property always has a clue to its ownership as the owner will undoubtedly return to find the property. Therefore, any one who takes this property with an intent to keep it may commit either larceny or wrongful appropriation if he possesses the requisite criminal intent. For example, the person who leaves a package on the bus has obviously mislaid it and will return to claim it.

9. *Denial of Commission of Act Charged.*   In addition to pleading "not guilty," the defense may claim:

a. Mistaken Identity ("I was not at the scene of the crime, someone else was.")

b. Alibi ("I was with my girl friend all night.")

c. Good Character ("I know the accused and he has a good reputation for honesty in the community.")

The defenses tend to deny the commission by the accused of the objective acts charged.

506 Drafting the Larceny and Wrongful Appropriation Specifications

Some general guidelines as to drafting larceny and wrongful appropriation specifications are contained below.

1. *Ownership.*   In drafting these offenses, the ownership may be attributed to any person other than the accused, who is a special or general owner of the property. It commonly occurs that there are several owners. For example, John Doe may borrow Harry Smith's boat. Seaman Jones takes the boat from John Doe. Harry Smith is the general owner and has a superior right to possession over Seaman Jones. John Doe is the special owner and also has a superior right over Jones. When drafting a specification, it is generally better to state that the person who was last in possession before the theft (John Doe, the borrower in this case) is the owner. Otherwise, the prosecution will have to prove both the general and special ownership to prove its case.

2. *Value.* The fact that the property is of some value should be contained in the specification. However, where the specification describes property which a reasonable person would necessarily conclude had some value, the courts have generally held that the specification at least alleges an offense. *United States* v. *May*, 3 USCMA 703, 14 CMR 121 (1954). In such a case, however, the court's findings as to value would be limited to the least degree of the offense (i.e., some value).

3. *Several Offenses.* Paragraph 200a(8) of the MCM states that when "a larceny of several articles is committed at substantially the same time and place, it is a single larceny, even though the articles belong to different persons. Thus, if a thief steals a suitcase containing the property of several persons or goes into a room and takes property belonging to various persons, there is but one larceny, which should be alleged in but one specification."

The forms for drafting larceny and wrongful appropriation specifications are contained in Appendix 6c of the MCM.

507 Summary

This brief study of larceny and wrongful appropriation is intended to familiarize the student with the nature of these offenses. They are complicated and difficult. Each case must be determined on its own factual situation.

Larceny and wrongful appropriation are the two offenses under Article 121 with temporary or permanent intent distinguishing them. Not every taking violates Articles 121 as a criminal intent is required to constitute guilt of this offense.

This chapter has discussed some of the more common defenses to larceny and wrongful appropriation. Personnel concerned with the administration of military justice should be aware of those defenses that may apply to an apparent violation of the Code. Some idea of the defenses available in any particular case can be garnered from the discussion of the particular article of the Code in Chapter XXVIII of the MCM and in Chapter XXIX, relating to defenses.

An awareness of an undisputed defense that is available to the accused may prevent a time-consuming court-martial when the only verdict can be a finding of not guilty.

Discussion Case

UNITED STATES, Appellee

v.

JOHN J. O'HARA, Captain, U.S. Marine Corps Reserve, Appellant

14 USCMA 167, 33 CMR 379

(1963)

Opinion of the Court

QUINN, Chief Judge:

The accused contends his conviction for larceny from the Commissioned Officers' Mess at Camp Pendleton, California, should be reversed because the instructions are prejudicially erroneous.

It appears the accused was the Operations Officers [sic] of the Mess system, which included several units. In preparation for his release to inactive duty, he was scheduled to be detached from his station and duties on August 13, 1962. The incident which led to the Charge occurred on August 10, 1962, at the 17 Area Officers' Recreation Center, one of the units of the Mess.

On the morning of Friday, August 10, Gunnery Sergeant Dallas R. Clark, Acting Manager of the Center, was in and out of the office. One absence lasted about twenty minutes. Clark left the door of the office safe closed but unlocked. When he returned, he found the accused "standing there"; the door of the safe was ajar about an inch. Clark locked the safe. About 1:15 that afternoon he went to the safe to make change, and discovered that all the one- and five-dollar bills were missing from the cash box. He reported the loss to Major Margaret A. Brewer, the Mess Treasurer. They went over the cash account and determined the loss amounted to about $370.00.

Shortly before Major Brewer was informed of the missing money, she had had a conversation with the accused. He told her he had been in the office, and noticed the safe door was opened. He said he *"should have* taken some of the money" to teach Sergeant Clark "a lesson." (Emphasis supplied.) The following Monday morning, August 13, Major Herbert M. Lorence, of the Military Police and Guard Battalion, interrogated the accused for approximately an hour and a half. The accused said he was in the office and found the safe open. He admitted he looked into the cash drawer, but insisted "he did not take any money from the safe." About noon, the accused again talked to Major Brewer. He merely asked her how much money was missing, and whether the money had been taken from the safe. Later in the day, the accused was questioned further by Major Lorence. Once more he denied taking any money from the safe. As the questioning continued, he reversed himself. He admitted he took the money. He said he did so only "to teach Sergeant Clark a lesson." In a sworn statement, he also admitted that after he left the office he went to the bank in a nearby town and exchanged the one- and five-dollar bills for tens and twenties. He attributed the exchange to the fact that the money he took from the safe "was extremely bulky." He turned over the money, in the form of ten- and twenty-dollar bills, to the Evidence Custodian of the Criminal Investigation Section.

With some elaboration, the accused testified at trial along the lines of his pretrial statement. He said that *when* he saw the open safe in the Center office, he recalled another occasion he had found a safe open. He had then removed some money from the safe to teach the custodian that an open safe was not to be left unguarded. About an hour later and before he left the building, he returned the money to the custodian. Remembering the "salutory [sic] effect" this incident had on the person involved, he "decided at that point to do the same thing with Sergeant Clark." Referring to the bank exchange of the money, he said the larger bills were "easier to carry about and keep track of." He put the money in a bureau drawer in his home. The reason for his first denial to Major Lorence was that he "still wanted to return the money to Sergeant Clark"; he "felt" it would be "somewhat incriminating" if he gave it to the Provost Marshal. During the second interview with Major Lorence, he decided his "continual denial" was "only complicating matters," so he admitted he took the money and that he "intended [only] to teach Sergeant Clark a lesson."

Before instructing the court-martial, the law officer held an out-of-court hearing on his proposed instructions. Defense counsel indicated he examined the instructions and had no ob-

jections. On the reconvening of the court, the law officer instructed the court members on the applicable rules of law. Among other things, he advised the court-martial that it must find the accused "wrongfully took or withheld" the money with the intent to permanently deprive or defraud the Officers' Mess of its use, or to appropriate it permanently to his own use. He further instructed as follows:

"A withholding may arise either as a result of a failure to return, account for, or deliver property to its owner when a return, accounting, or delivery is due, or as a result of devoting property to a use not authorized by its owner, and this is so even though initially the property had come lawfully into the hands of the person thus withholding it.

☙

"Evidence has been introduced that the purpose of the accused in taking or withholding the money was to teach a lesson to Gunnery Sergeant Clark. Such a purpose or intent is not criminal. You are advised that not every taking or withholding of property without the consent of the owner constitutes a violation of the Uniform Code of Military Justice. In each case there must be an accompanying criminal intent either to deprive the owner permanently of the property, which is larceny, or the intent to deprive him temporarily of the property, which is wrongful appropriation. If neither of these intents is present, the taking or obtaining may be wrongful but it is not a violation of the Uniform Code of Military Justice.

"Therefore, you are advised that unless you are satisfied beyond a reasonable doubt that the accused did not intend to teach a lesson to Gunnery Sergeant Clark, then you must acquit the accused."

Instructions provide the court-martial with the legal framework within which it determines the accused's guilt or innocence. If the legal rules are not related to the evidence in the case, generalizations, although correct in the abstract, may mislead the court. See *United States* v. *Smith,* 13 USCMA 471, 33 CMR 3. We have, on occasion, called attention to the obligation of the law officer to revise the standard forms of instruction found in service pamphlets to make them more pertinent to the evidence in the case. See *United States* v. *Kitchen,* 5 USCMA 541, 547, 18 CMR 165, footnote 2. A number of cases before this Court indicate the appropriateness of such editing in a larceny prosecution.

Three separate acts denominated loosely as "larceny" are prohibited by Article 121 of the Uniform Code of Military Justice, 10 USC § 921. Under the statute, one who "wrongfully takes, obtains, or withholds" personal property of another with the designated intent commits the offense. The standard form of specification, which was utilized in this case, allows the Government to prove any one or all of these acts. *United States* v. *Sicley,* 6 USCMA 402, 408, 20 CMR 118. However, not every taking of property without the express consent of the owner or custodian constitutes a "wrongful taking" within the meaning of the Article. See *United States* v. *Hayes,* 8 USCMA 627, 629, 25 CMR 131. And, not every withholding of property known to belong to another

comes within the scope of the Article. *United States* v. *Jones,* 13 USCMA 635, 33 CMR 167. Consequently, when there is evidence in the case from which the court-martial can reasonably conclude the accused's act does not constitute a violation of the Article, an instruction in general terms may not adequately focus attention on the issues the court must decide. In the *Jones* case, for example, the accused was charged with larceny. Under one view of the evidence, the court-martial could have found the accused received from another, and thereafter withheld, property which he knew to be stolen from the Government. Such evidence would support a finding of receiving stolen property, but not a conviction for larceny. The Court, therefore, concluded the standard instruction on withholding as a basis for larceny did not adequately apprise the court-martial of the difference between the two types of withholding presented by the evidence. In the *Sicley* case, there was evidence indicating the accused had improperly received money from the Government under circumstances which imposed no obligation upon him to account for its use or to apply it to a particular use; in other words, the evidence indicated a debtor-creditor relationship between the accused and the Government. The Court held that the usual larceny instruction on withholding did not adequately inform the court-martial that nonpayment of a debt, *i.e.,* the debtor's withholding of payment from the creditor, did not constitute larceny. See also *United States* v. *Lyons,* 14 USCMA 67, 33 CMR 279.

Here, the evidence justified a finding of guilty upon either of two theories. First, the court-martial could find that when the accused took the money from the safe, he intended then and there to deprive the Mess permanently of it. Alternatively, the court-martial could find that when the accused removed the money from the safe, he intended only to teach Sergeant Clark a lesson about the danger of leaving the safe open, and then to return the money to him, but that after the money was in his possession the accused decided to appropriate it to his own use. See *United States* v. *Smith*, 11 USCMA 321, 29 CMR 137. This finding is supported by the evidence that the accused exchanged the money into bills of larger denomination; that he concealed the money in his home; that he repeatedly lied about not taking the money from the safe. The law officer's general instructions on taking and withholding covered both these theories.

Turning to the accused's defense, if the court-martial believed the whole of his testimony, it could conclude that at all times, from the original taking of the money to its return, the accused intended only to teach Sergeant Clark a lesson in safeguarding funds. That finding would require that the accused be acquitted. *United States* v. *Roark*, 12 USCMA 478, 31 CMR 64; *United States* v. *Smith*. The significance of this aspect of the evidence was recognized by the law officer; in fact, the transcript of the out-of-court hearing indicates the instructions set out above were based upon the *Roark* case.[1] Thus, the instructions in their entirety dealt directly and adequately with all issues the court-martial had to decide. The nature of the defense was clearly defined; and its legal effect on the accused's guilt or innocence was plainly delineated. We find no misstatement or inadequacy which can reasonably be said to prejudice the accused.

The decision of the board of review is affirmed.

Judges FERGUSON and KILDAY concur.

DISCUSSION AND SELF-QUIZ

1. In *United States* v. *O'Hara*, the Discussion Case, what would have been the result if the law officer (now called the military judge) had not instructed the court that "unless you are satisfied beyond a reasonable doubt that the accused did not intend to teach a lesson to Gunnery Sergeant Clark, then you must acquit the accused?" See paragraph 73a of the MCM.

2. Seaman Apprentice John T. Jones, a member of your command, has been charged with larceny. Jones is charged with taking $20 from Seaman Roe's wallet. Jones admits he took the money but states he intended to repay it on pay day. Seaman Smith is willing to testify that Jones walked up to him and stated "I took $20 from Roe's wallet to pay a bill and I'll put it back on pay day." Roe and Jones are *not* friends. Roe reports to you that on pay

[1] If anything, these instructions on accused's defense were overly favorable to him. They indicated the accused could be acquitted if his purpose in taking the money was to teach Sergeant Clark a lesson, without regard to whether he thereafter determined to appropriate the money to his own use.

day, he found $20 that someone had put into his wallet. Jones states he did it. You are the legal officer on the ship and the commanding officer requests your advice. Assuming you believe these facts and statements to be true, should Jones be charged with larceny? See paragraph 200a(6) of the MCM.

3. Utilizing Chapter XXVIII of the MCM, state what article of the Code, if any, has been violated, in each of the following incidents:

a. Seaman Recruit Jones, a compartment cleaner, has personally received an order from Petty Officer Second Class Smith, the leading petty officer in his division, to "scrub the deck of the division's living compartment." Jones does not obey the order.

b. Petty Officer Smith sees Seaman Recruit Jones the next day and again orders him to scrub the deck of the division's living compartment. Jones, tired from liberty the night before, scrubs only the passageway in the compartment and not under the bunks and sleeps the remainder of the day.

c. After taps, Seaman Recruit Jones takes out a cigarette and smokes it in his living compartment. His ship's instructions prohibit smoking in living compartments after taps. Jones is well aware of the contents of these instructions (they are read once a month at morning quarters).

d. Seaman Recruit Jones brings three quarts of rum on board ship to drink. He is unaware of any regulation that prohibits his doing so. However, paragraph 1269 of U.S. Navy Regulations prohibits the possession of alcoholic liquors on board ships for beverage purposes.

e. Seaman Recruit Jones is approached by Seaman Recruit Smith. Smith states to Jones the following: "Jones, our division officer, Lieutenant Zeal, told me to tell you that you are to report to him at once." Jones does not report.

f. Later, when asked by Seaman Roe at morning quarters in the presence of the division, why he didn't report to Lieutenant Zeal, Seaman Recruit Jones states that if "brains were ink, Lieutenant Zeal wouldn't be able to dot an *i*."

g. Seaman Roe then asks Seaman Recruit Jones why he behaved as he did. In the presence of the whole division at morning quarters, Jones says, "Petty Officer Smith, that stupid S.O.B., started the whole thing." Smith is not at quarters that morning.

h. It is then noted at morning quarters that Seaman Recruit Jones's uniform is filthy. He also has a false identification card that indicates he is 22 years of age—he is only 19. Has he violated any articles of the Code?

i. After his special court-martial and six months' confinement at hard labor, Jones has responded favorably to the Navy's retraining program and is sent back to duty. Several years later, Petty Officer Second Class Jones is sitting in Suzie Wong's bar in Hong Kong. Seaman Brown, a member of the Shore Patrol, enters the bar and orders Jones to leave, as service personnel have been "rolled" there lately. Petty Officer Jones refuses to leave stating, "I've been in enough trouble about orders, and if there's one thing I do know, it's that a seaman can give a petty officer an order." Is Jones right?

CHAPTER VI

Nonjudicial Punishment and Nonpunitive Measures

Chapter I discussed the "graduated response" present in the military justice system. The first of these responses to be considered is nonpunitive measures. A broad spectrum of encouragements and discouragements may be utilized so long as they do not constitute punishment. Consequently, in this area, military law permits a finer line to be drawn before punitive action is taken than in many civilian courts.

Nonjudicial punishment is the next step up the ladder. The commanding officer has a wide variety and combination of punishments he may impose through the utilization of nonjudicial punishment.

601 A Discussion of Nonpunitive Measures

One of the most effective methods of achieving good order and discipline in a command is not a formal method of discipline at all: this is the utilization of nonpunitive measures. Paragraph 129a of the MCM states that:

> In the great majority of instances, discipline can be maintained through effective leadership including, when required, the use of those nonpunitive measures which a commander is expected to use to further the efficiency of his command or unit and which are *not* imposed under Article 15 [the nonjudicial punishment statute of the Code]. (Emphasis supplied.)

A commanding officer may utilize "nonpunitive measures" such as administrative admonitions, reprimands, exhortations, disapprovals, criticisms, censures, reproofs and rebukes, either written or oral. These nonpunitive measures may also include, subject to any applicable regulations, administrative withholding of privileges. They are to be utilized as corrective measures, more analogous to instruction than punishment.

The question to be resolved in every case of withholding privileges would be: Does the privilege withheld bear a reasonable relationship to the deficiency sought to be corrected? For example, extra military instruction is appropriate where it bears a reasonable relationship to the deficiency sought to be corrected.

602 The Nature of Nonjudicial Punishment

A commanding officer may, under Article 15 of the Code, impose disciplinary punishments for minor offenses, without the intervention of a court-martial, upon military personnel of his command. This is called nonjudicial punishment (NJP). In the Navy and Coast Guard, nonjudicial punishment is referred to as "Captain's Mast," and in the Marine Corps, nonjudicial punishment is called "Office Hours."

Historically, the commanding officer of a ship would address his crew on the main deck near the mainmast—which was usually the widest part of the deck. There, important announcements would be made, commendations awarded, and punishments imposed and executed. The term "Captain's Mast" originated from this practice. Obviously, Mast is no longer held before the mainmast as it was in the days of sail. The executive officer now designates a space within the ship spacious enough to accommodate the necessary number of accused persons, witnesses, and other persons involved.

Today, nonjudicial punishment may only be imposed for minor offenses. Such an offense must be punishable under the Code in order for punishment to be awarded. The nature of an offense and the circumstances surrounding its commission are among the factors which must be considered in determining whether or not it is minor in nature. Generally, the term "minor" includes misconduct not involving any greater degree of criminality than is involved in the average offense tried by summary court-martial. This term ordinarily does not include misconduct of a kind which, if tried by general court-martial, could be punished by dishonorable discharge or confinement for more than one year.

Nonjudicial punishment constitutes punishments of a restrictive or monetary nature which are intended to correct and reform offenders who have not responded to less stringent methods. Nonjudicial punishment is considered less serious than a summary court-martial, but its powers of punishment are approximately the same. Captain's Mast, properly conducted, is more efficient and less time consuming than a court-martial. It can also be effectively utilized as a leadership tool. Leadership in its keenest and most polished form is required of the Captain at Mast and officers and enlisted men attending can receive a lesson in practical leadership which can point out possible past failures and future correct paths.

603 Who May Impose Nonjudicial Punishment

In the Navy, Marine Corps, and Coast Guard, authority under Article 15 may be exercised by commanding officers, officers to whom this authority has been delegated, and officers in charge of any unit of the Navy. "Commanding officer" includes a warrant officer exercising command. In the Marine Corps, a company commander is a commanding officer and may award nonjudicial punishment.

A flag or general officer in command can delegate nonjudicial punishment only to the senior officer on his staff who is eligible to succeed him in command. Otherwise, nonjudicial punishment can never be delegated, as the authority to punish resides with the office, not the individual.

The JAG Manual provides that a commissioned officer may be designated as an officer in charge of a unit by Departmental Orders, Tables of Organization, orders of a flag or general officer in command (including one in command of a multiservice command to which members of the naval service are attached), or orders of the senior officer present.

604 Persons Upon Whom Nonjudicial Punishment May Be Imposed

A commanding officer may impose nonjudicial punishment on all military personnel of his command. An officer in charge, regardless of his rank, may only impose nonjudicial punishment upon his enlisted men.

At the time nonjudicial punishment is imposed the accused must be a member of the command of the commanding officer, or of the unit of the officer in charge, who imposes the punishment. He can be either attached or assigned thereto. TAD (temporary additional duty) personnel may be punished either by the commanding officer of the unit to which they are temporarily attached or by the commanding officer of their permanent duty station.

605 Right to Demand Trial

Nonjudicial punishment may not be imposed upon any member of the armed forces who, before the imposition of punishment, demands trial by court-martial, unless he is attached to or embarked in a vessel. The right to refuse nonjudicial punishment exists up until the time the commanding officer announces the punishment. This right is not waived by the accused if he has previously signed the NAVPERS 2696 (see Appendix 2) indicating that he would accept nonjudicial punishment. Consequently, the commanding officer of a shore station should ensure that the accused is aware of his right to refuse nonjudicial punishment.

If an accused is attached to a vessel, he may *not* refuse nonjudicial punishment. A person is "attached to or embarked in" a vessel if, at the time nonjudicial punishment is imposed, he is assigned or attached to the vessel, is on board for passage, or is assigned or attached to an embarked staff, unit, detachment, squadron, team, air group, or other regularly organized body.

606 The Hearing

The executive officer has concluded his final pre-mast screening discussed in Chapter III, and the legal or discipline officer or the master-at-arms, as applicable, has assembled the witnesses, case file, and the accused's service record. The executive officer has placed his preliminary entries in the NAVPERS 2696 and advised the commanding officer of his recommendation as to disposition. We are now ready for the hearing itself.

Mast, properly conducted, is one of the most effective means of administering discipline. It should be dynamic, yet unchanging. It should be tailored to fit each individual transgression—yet its format should remain relatively the same. Each accused must be impressed with the essential fairness, impartiality, interest, and concern of his commanding officer. A sense of relationship must be developed between the offender, any witnesses, the division officer, and the commanding officer that will lead to a constant and effective state of discipline within the command. The physical setting should be as dignified and formal as the space limitations of the particular ship or shore station will allow. A typical procedure for conducting Mast, recently utilized by the School of Naval Justice, may be found at the end of this chapter.

The accused is entitled to a hearing, which shall include the following elemental requirements:

1. *Presence of the accused before the officer conducting the Mast.*

2. *Advice to the accused of the offenses of which he is suspected.*

3. *Explanation to the accused of his rights under Article 31(b) of the Uniform Code of Military Justice.*

4. *Presentation of the information against the accused.* The accused has no absolute right to confront the witnesses against him. Therefore, evidence may be introduced either by oral or written statements. Copies of written statements should be furnished the accused.

5. *Availability to the accused of all items of information in the nature of physical or documentary evidence which will be considered.* The accused has the right to inspect these.

6. *Full opportunity of the accused to present any matters in mitigation, extenuation, or defense of the suspected offenses.* For example, the accused may deny he committed the offense or he may admit the offense, but claim he acted in self-defense. It is the commanding officer's respon-

sibility to resolve the issue based upon the evidence presented. If there is not sufficient evidence, the preliminary inquiry officer can be requested to obtain more. The commanding officer *should not* refer a minor case, which he would normally punish at Captain's Mast or Office Hours, to a court-martial because he does not feel he can resolve the issue. Such action may well influence an innocent man from defending himself at Mast or force him to go through the rigors of a court-martial when he should otherwise only be punished at Mast for his offense.

The record of a court of inquiry or other fact-finding body, in which the accused was accorded the rights of a party with respect to an act or omission for which nonjudicial punishment is contemplated, may be substituted for the impartial hearing described above. Chapter XIV of this book discusses courts of inquiry and fact-finding bodies.

607 Mast Alternatives

The commanding officer has many alternatives or courses of action he may take in the event nonpunitive measures are not considered appropriate. He may:

1. *Dismiss the case.* This is normally done when the commanding officer determines that the accused is innocent of the charges or that he has not committed an offense.

2. *Dismiss with a warning.* This is normally done when the commanding officer considers the accused has committed an offense, but feels that punishment is inappropriate. To dismiss with a warning is not a "punishment."

3. *Admonish or reprimand the accused as a nonpunitive measure.*

4. *Refer the case to a superior for action.* This situation would usually arise when a commanding officer determines that his authority to punish is insufficient to make a proper disposition of the case.

5. *Postpone action pending further investigation or other "good cause."* For example, the commanding officer may determine to withhold judgment until a key defense witness returns from leave.

6. *Award one or more punishments.*

7. *Forward the case to a special or summary court-martial.* This is accomplished by filling in and signing the 1st Indorsement on page 3 of a completed charge sheet. (See Appendices 6 and 7.)

8. *Refer the case to a pretrial investigation in accordance with the provisions of Article 32 of the Code in order to determine if the case should be forwarded to a general court-martial.*

608 The Nature of Mast Punishments

The commanding officer may award one or more of nine different punishments at Mast. The commanding officer's seniority, the enlisted/officer status of the offender, and the type of punishment limits, to a certain extent, the number and amount of punishments that may be awarded. The punishments are prescribed in Chapter XXVI of the MCM. Appendices 9 and 10, publications of the U.S. Naval Justice School, contain a complete listing of the punishments and the maximum amount that may be awarded officers and enlisted men. No *particular* punishment is prescribed for any particular offense or number of offenses as in courts-martial.

1. *Reprimand or Admonishment.* These constitute adverse reflections upon, or criticisms of, an individual's character, conduct, performance, or military appearance. Reprimand is considered the more severe of the two. If it is imposed upon officers, it must be in writing. Enlisted men may receive either an oral or written reprimand or admonition.

2. *Restriction.* This is the least severe form of deprivation of liberty. It involves moral rather than physical restraint. The severity of the punishment depends on its duration and the geographical limits specified when the punishment is imposed. Unless the commanding officer provides otherwise, an individual in restriction may be required to perform his full military duties.

The restriction imposed on an officer on board ship shall not amount to confinement to the officer's room nor shall it restrict him from the use of any part of the ship to which, before his restriction, he had a "right," except the quarterdeck and bridge, *unless* more rigorous restriction is necessary for the safety of the ship or officer or to preserve good order and discipline. (For a further discussion of restriction see paragraph 205 of this book.)

3. *Arrest in Quarters.* As in restriction, the restraint involved in this punishment is enforced by a moral obligation rather than by physical means. However, it only may be imposed upon commissioned and warrant officers, by an officer exercising general court-martial jurisdiction, or a general or flag officer in command. It should be noted, however, that arrest may be imposed upon enlisted men as a form of pretrial restraint. (See paragraph 205 of this book.) The limits of the arrest are set forth by the officer imposing the punishment and may be extended beyond the officer's quarters, but if the area is *not* extended, he must remain there. The quarters may consist of his military or private residence on or off the base. The officer or warrant officer may not be required to perform duties involving the exercise of authority over any person who is otherwise subordinate to him. (See Article 1316, U.S. Navy Regulations.)

4. *Confinement on Bread and Water or Diminished Rations.* This punishment may not be awarded unless the recipient, who *must* be a non-rated enlisted man, is attached to, or embarked in, a vessel. It may

not be awarded for more than three consecutive days. A medical officer must examine both the accused and the place of confinement and certify that no serious injury to the prisoner will result. "Diminished ration" is a restricted diet set forth in the Navy Corrections Manual (NAVPERS 15825).

5. *Correctional Custody.* Correctional custody is the physical restraint of a person during duty or nonduty hours, or both, and may include extra duties, fatigue duties, or hard labor. If practicable, it should not be served in immediate association with persons awaiting trial or held in confinement pursuant to trial by court-martial. The punishment is imposable only on nonrated enlisted men (E–3 and below). SECNAV-INST 1640.7 (present series) prescribes the conditions under which correctional custody shall be served.

6. *Extra Duties.* This punishment involves the performance of duties in addition to those normally assigned the enlisted person undergoing punishment. The daily performance of the extra duties before or after routine duties are completed satisfies the punishment whether the particular daily assignment requires one, two, or more hours. The extra duties normally should not extend to more than two hours a day, or, in the case of noncommissioned or petty officers, should the work demean the person's rate.

Although the MCM states that "military duties of any kind may be assigned," Article 1410 of Navy Regulations prohibits guard duty as a punishment. Performance of extra duties on Sunday also is prohibited. Following the performance of the extra duties, the offender normally is granted liberty.

7. *Reduction in Rate.* This is one of the most severe forms of nonjudicial punishment and should be utilized with discretion. This punishment only may be imposed to the next inferior grade in the Navy and Marine Corps. It may be utilized if the grade from which demoted is within the promotion authority of the officer imposing the reduction or any officer subordinate to him. Thus, a commanding officer may reduce a First Class (E–6) to the next inferior pay grade (E–5), but he may not reduce a chief petty officer at Mast. All chief petty officers now receive initial permanent appointments. An officer in charge, designated a separate or detached command by a flag or general officer, may promote enlisted men and consequently may reduce them at Mast.

In the Marine Corps, the lowest ranking officer who can promote is a battalion commander who may promote up to and including sergeant (E–5). Therefore, only a battalion commander or higher can reduce an E–5 or below at Office Hours. Only the Commandant may reduce noncommissioned officers over pay grade E–5.

8. *Forfeiture of Pay.* This involves a permanent loss of the pay forfeited. The word "pay" refers only to the basic pay of the individual plus any sea or foreign duty pay. It does not include special pay for a special qualification, hazardous duty pay, proficiency pay, subsistance and quarters allowances, and similar types of compensation. If the punishment includes both reduction, whether or not suspended, and the forfeiture of pay, the forfeiture must be based on the grade to which reduced. E–4's or below with dependents with less than four years' service are required to make out an allotment of $40.00 in order to draw a quarters allowance (BAQ). As this is required by law, the $40.00 *must be deducted* before the net amount of pay subject to forfeiture is computed. Additionally, when an enlisted man is reduced to pay grade E–4 and he has less than four years' service, the $40.00 must be deducted before computing the net amount of pay subject to forfeiture. The amount to be forfeited per month and the number of months should be stated. Forfeiture of pay may not extend to any pay accrued before the date of its imposition.

9. *Detention of Pay.* Unlike a forfeiture of pay, a detention of pay involves only a temporary withholding of pay. The same general rules that apply to forfeiture apply to detention of pay. The period for which pay is to be detained shall, in no case, exceed one year or the expiration of the offender's term of service, whichever is earlier, and must be set forth at the time the punishment is imposed.

609 Amount, Combination, and Apportionment

The amount of punishment to be awarded varies with the authority of the officer imposing the punishment. There are three basic categories:

1. Officers exercising general court-martial jurisdiction or an officer of general or flag rank in command;

2. A commanding officer of the grade of major or lieutenant commander or above;

3. A commanding officer of the grade of lieutenant or below.

It is noteworthy that an officer in charge, regardless of rank, only may award those punishments that a lieutenant or below may award at Mast.

For example, a lieutenant can only award a maximum of seven days corrective custody whereas a lieutenant commander may award thirty days. A flag officer in command may order an officer into arrest in quarters, but a Navy captain or below in command may not. A lieutenant commander or above may award 60 days restriction; a lieutenant or below 14 days.

A complete listing of the punishments which may be awarded are found in Appendices 9 and 10.

In addition to, or in lieu of, admonition or reprimand, one or more of the disciplinary punishments may be imposed, subject to the following rules:

1. The punishments of restriction and extra duties may be combined to run concurrently (i.e., to run at the same time), but the combination may not exceed the maximum imposable for extra duties.

2. Neither restriction nor extra duties may be combined to run concurrently with correctional custody beyond the maximum duration imposable for correctional custody.

3. The punishment of restriction in the case of an officer may not be combined to run concurrently with arrest in quarters beyond the maximum duration imposable for arrest in quarters.

4. Confinement on bread and water or diminished rations may not be imposed in *combination with* correctional custody, extra duties, or restriction.

5. When it is desired to combine two or more of the punishments of correctional custody, extra duties, and restriction in the case of an enlisted person they may *not* be combined to run consecutively (i.e., to run one after the other) in the maximum amount imposable for each. All of these punishments are in the nature of deprivation of liberty and must be apportioned. For this reason, forfeiture and detention of pay must also be apportioned. Thus, when an officer desires to impose more than one kind of punishment other than admonition or reprimand, he has three main types from which to choose:

a. Restraint (extra duties, restriction, correctional custody, confinement on bread and water);

b. Deprivation of entitlement to pay (detention, forfeiture);

c. Reduction in grade.

In dealing with apportionment, utilize correctional custody as the common denominator in order to find out how much of the other punishments involving restraint may be awarded the accused. Appendices 11 and 12 are reference tables enabling quick apportionment when punishments are to run consecutively.

Tables I and II may be helpful to the student in understanding *how* to apportion consecutive punishments.

Table I

	Correctional custody (days)	Extra duties (days)	Restriction to limits (days)
LCDR or MAJOR and above	1	1½	2
Below LCDR or MAJOR	1	2	2

Table II

	Forfeiture of pay (days)	Detention of pay (days)
LCDR or MAJOR and above	1	1½
Below LCDR or MAJOR	1	2

610 Post Mast Procedures and Appeal

When he determines the course of action he desires to take, the commanding officer generally will complete the "Action of Commanding Officer" section on the NAVPERS 2696, or a yeoman will transcribe the decision and present the "smooth" for the commanding officer to sign at a later time. A sample of a NAVPERS 2696 may be found in Appendix 2. Generally, the commanding officer, if punishment is awarded, informs the accused of his right to appeal if he considers his punishment unjust or disproportionate to the offense. The appeal should be forwarded via the officer who imposed the punishment and should be addressed to the area coordinator authorized to convene general courts-martial or the officer exercising GCM authority and superior in the chain of command, as applicable. It must be in writing, must be submitted through the chain of command, and must be made within a reasonable time. In the absence of unusual circumstances, 15 days is considered a reasonable time. The time of transmission is excluded from this computation. The appeal may include the accused's reason for regarding the punishment as unjust or disproportionate to the offense. It is recommended that copies of the NAVPERS 2696 and all other related documents be forwarded along with the appeal.

If the punishment is of the kind set forth in Article 15(e) (1) through (7) of the Code, the reviewing authority must refer the record to a JAG lawyer for consideration and advice prior to acting on the appeal. However, regardless of the punishment, he may refer it to review by a JAG lawyer if he so desires. The reviewing authority may exercise the same powers with respect to the punishment imposed as the officer who originally awarded the punishment. That is, he may suspend, remit, mitigate, or set aside any punishment. He may not increase the amount of punishment or change the nature of the punishment *except* when mitigating a reduction in rate to a forfeiture or detention. After considering the appeal, the superior authority will transmit to the appellant (the accused) through appropriate channels, a written statement as to his decision on the appeal.

The "Final Administrative Action" section of the NAVPERS 2696 must be completed following the Mast. The offender generally initials the "appeal rights" section. The legal yeoman generally completes the remainder of this section.

611 Service Record Entries

Records of all punishment imposed on Navy enlisted personnel shall be entered in their service records. If no punishment is awarded, or if a court-martial is awarded, no service record entries are made, except when the service record contains absence or desertion entries. In that event, an entry on page 13 of the enlisted man's service record is required to show what action was taken in order to account for the period of absence for official record purposes. For example, the fact that the case was dismissed with a warning would even be reflected in this event.

In cases other than reduction, forfeiture, or detention of pay, entries are made on the Administrative Remarks Page (page 13). The entry is dated and sets forth (a) date of the offense; (b) nature of the offense; (c) date of the Captain's Mast; and (d) NJP awarded. (See Appendix 8.)

Punishments involving reduction, forfeiture, or detention of pay are recorded on page 6 of the service record. (See Appendix 13.)

When punishment is awarded, a special evaluation report (NAVPERS 792) may be submitted. However, the imposition of nonjudicial punishment is normally recorded as a memorandum entry on page 9, the Enlisted Performance Record. A reduction in grade also requires that an entry be made on page 4, Navy Occupation and Training History.

Marine Corps enlisted personnel have the results of nonjudicial punishment entered on page 12 of their service record, entitled "Offenses and Punishments." See paragraph 15116 of the Marine Corps Personnel Manual. Reductions are recorded on page 5, entitled "Promotion and Reduction" as discussed in paragraph 15108 of the Marine Corps Personnel Manual.

612 The Unit Punishment Book

In the Navy, each NAVPERS 2696 is placed in a binder called the "Unit Punishment Book." The Unit Punishment Book is used as an official record to reflect the results of the Mast. If the case is dismissed or dismissed with a warning, the NAVPERS 2696 shall be filed for reference in the Unit Punishment Book.

In the Marine Corps, the initial report and preliminary inquiry are completed entirely on locally prepared forms. The result of each enlisted man's Office Hours is retained on a form entitled "Unit Punishment Book" (NAVMC 10132 PD). It contains substantially the same information as the Navy's NAVPERS 2696 (Appendix 2) except that the details of the investigation are not contained on the Marine Corps form. Chapter

15 of the Marine Corps Personnel Manual contains instructions for completing this form.

613   Suspension, Mitigation, Remission, and Setting Aside

The commanding officer's authority and responsibilities do not end with the awarding of punishment at Mast. He has power to set aside, remit, mitigate, and suspend punishments which he has awarded. This power is applicable to the officer who imposed the punishment, his successor in command, and the commanding officer of a command to which the accused is transferred.

The following definitions and rules apply to the various clemency actions that may be taken:

1. *Set Aside.* This power is as its name implies. It involves setting aside in whole or in part, a punishment, whether executed or unexecuted, and restoring all rights, privileges, and property affected. It should ordinarily be exercised *only* when, under all the circumstances of the case, the punishment resulted in a clear injustice. This power exists regardless of whether the punishment has been executed or not, but if it has been executed, the power to set aside should be exercised within a reasonable time after the punishment has been executed (in the absence of unusual circumstances, four months is a reasonable time).

2. *Remit.* *Webster's New World Dictionary* defines *remit* as follows: "to refrain from inflicting a punishment." The MCM provides that the commanding officer may remit "any part or amount of the unexecuted portion of the punishment imposed." When a commanding officer remits, he stops what has not yet been served from being served, but he doesn't give anything back from that which has already been taken away.

3. *Mitigate.* This term has been defined in Webster's as "to make or become milder, less severe or less painful." A commanding officer may mitigate any part or amount of the *unexecuted* portion of the punishment imposed as follows:

   a. Arrest in quarters to restriction (applies to officers);

   b. Confinement on bread and water or diminished rations to correctional custody;

   c. Correctional custody or confinement on bread and water or diminished rations to extra duties or restriction, or both; or

   d. Extra duties to restriction.

In mitigating a punishment the commanding officer cannot increase the *quality* or *quantity* of the punishment: *a* through *d* above represent a decrease in quality. Nor should the mitigated punishment be for a greater period of time, as that would be an increase in quantity. For example, if a punishment of arrest in quarters for 15 days is to be mitigated to restriction to specified limits, the duration of the restriction may not exceed 15 days. Regardless of whether or not it is executed, reduction in grade may be mitigated to forfeiture or detention, the amount of which shall not be greater than the amount that could have been imposed initially by the officer imposing the reduction.

If reduction has been executed, then mitigation to forfeiture or detention should be accomplished within a reasonable time (four months) in the absence of unusual circumstances.

4. *Suspend.* Any part or amount of the unexecuted portion of the punishment imposed may be suspended. Unless the suspension is vacated sooner, the suspended portion of the punishment, which may be for a period up to six months in duration, is automatically remitted upon the termination of the period of suspension or the current enlistment, whichever occurs sooner.

There are two exceptions to the rule that only the unexecuted portion of the punishment imposed may be suspended. They are: (a) a forfeiture of pay may be suspended whether or not collected; and (b) a reduction in grade may be suspended whether or not executed. For example, if Seaman Jones is reduced from E–3 to E–2, but the reduction is suspended for six months, he would retain pay grade E–3. If Seaman Jones stays out of trouble during the period of suspension, the suspension would terminate at the end of six months. Seaman Jones would have retained his rate.

If executed, a reduction or forfeiture may be suspended only within a period of four months after the date of its imposition.

A vacation of a suspension may be accomplished by any commanding officer competent to impose punishment of the type involved in the vacation. This may be done at any time during the period of probation and is generally for unsatisfactory conduct. Although a formal hearing is *not* necessary to vacate a suspension, the probationer should be given an opportunity to appear before the officer considering the vacation and rebut any derogatory or adverse information upon which the proposed vacation is based. Therefore, it would be possible to vacate a suspension at Mast for a violation of the Code, and then award another punishment for that same violation, at the same Mast.

An application to have a punishment remitted, suspended, mitigated, or set aside should be made within a reasonable time, (15 days) in the absence of unusual or special circumstances.

614 Other Types of Mast

The term *Mast* does not only include disciplinary proceedings. It includes *Request Mast* and *Meritorious Mast* as well.

1. *Meritorious Mast.*

Whenever an enlisted member does anything noteworthy or commendable beyond the usual requirements of duty, or displays exceptional energy, judgment, or initiative, a report shall be made of this to his commanding officer by the senior under whose observation he has come. The commanding officer at mast shall give such reports the same formal and careful consideration given to breaches of discipline. Should he decide the circumstances warrant it, he will make an entry of the facts in the member's service record. (BUPERS Manual. See also paragraph 0709, Navy Regulations.)

2. *Request Mast.* Paragraph 3 of Article 0709 of Navy Regulations states that the commanding officer shall afford "an opportunity, with reasonable restrictions as to time and place, for the personnel under his command to make requests, reports, or statements to him, and shall insure that they understand the procedures for making such requests, reports, or statements." Additionally, paragraph 1 of Article 1244 of Navy Regulations states that the "right of any person in the naval service to communicate with the commanding officer at a proper time and place is not to be denied or restricted." These requirements are generally met by holding Request Mast.

615 Summary

Nonpunitive measures should always be considered as an alternative to nonjudicial punishment as they may be more appropriate for minor offenses. They must bear a reasonable relationship to the deficiency sought to be corrected.

Nonjudicial punishment is only appropriate for minor offenses. In only one case may the authority to impose nonjudicial punishment be delegated. An accused can refuse nonjudicial punishment, except when he is attached to or embarked in a vessel.

The accused is entitled to a hearing at Captain's Mast which complies with our fundamental concepts of justice.

The commanding officer has many alternatives at Mast as to disposition. He may dismiss the case with or without a warning; postpone the case; admonish the accused without punishing him; award punishment; refer the case to a superior for action; refer the case to a special or summary court-martial; or refer the case to an Article 32 investigating officer.

There are a great many types and combinations of punishments that may be awarded at nonjudicial punishment. The commanding officer has a wide latitude of actions he may take regarding the punishment imposed following the Mast.

Procedure for Conducting Mast

The commanding officer conducts the Mast. A location suitable to the dignity of the proceedings should be selected; the chief master at arms or another senior petty officer should be detailed to maintain order and insure that proper military etiquette is observed. The following persons should be present: legal officer; division officers of all accused; all accused; witnesses for and against all accused; mast yeoman; and chief master at arms. The following procedure is recommended:

> CMAA: (When CO arrives): Attention on deck.
> CMAA: (After CO has assumed his position): Hand salute. Two.
> CO: (To CMAA): Call the first case.

The accused will step up with his witnesses, if any. The accused's division officer should position himself in an appropriate place in the event he is asked to testify. The accused uncovers but does not salute.

> CO: (Name of accused), you are suspected of having committed (have been charged with committing) the following offenses(s): (Violations of the UCMJ). I want to hear both sides of the story so that I can intelligently decide how to dispose of your case. I must advise you, however, that you have the absolute right to refuse to make any statement or to answer any question concerning the offense(s) of which you are suspected, or which may involve you in other offenses. You must consider this right to remain silent seriously, because if you decide to make a statement or answer any questions, that statement or those answers could be used against you in the event of trial by court-martial. Do you understand fully what I have just said?
> ACC: Yes, sir.
> CO: (Name of accused), you have previously been advised by the executive officer of your right to refuse NJP and have elected to accept NJP. Do you still elect to accept NJP under the provisions of Article 15, UCMJ? *
> ACC: Yes, sir.

The commanding officer questions witnesses against the accused, and advises the accused of other information against him, such as the substance of statements of absent witnesses or results of an investigation.

The commanding officer then asks the accused for his side of the story and listens to any witnesses available on his behalf. The commanding officer may then ask for the opinion of the division officer as to the general ability and reliability of the accused.

The commanding officer then disposes of the case according to the following:

1. Dismisses with or without warning.
2. Finds guilt and imposes NJP.

---

* This assumes that the accused is at a shore command. This is inapplicable aboard ship.

3. Refers case to SCM or SPCM (if eligible to convene), or recommends trial to superior.

4. Orders formal pretrial investigation to determine appropriateness of a recommendation for trial by GCM.

5. Refers case to superior for action.

6. Postpones action pending further investigation or for other reason.

co: (If punishment is awarded, the accused is advised): If you consider this punishment either unjust or out of proportion to the offense(s) of which I have found you guilty, you may appeal under the provisions of Article 15, UCMJ. The appeal must be in writing, must set forth your reasons for appealing, must be addressed through me to (next superior in chain of command) and must be forwarded within a reasonable time, ordinarily 15 days. If you desire to forward an appeal, your division officer will assist you in preparing it.

co: You are dismissed. (To cmaa): Call the next case.

After all cases have been disposed of:

cmaa: Hand Salute. Two. (co returns salute and then departs.)

Discussion Case

UNITED STATES, Appellee

v.

JACK M. FRETWELL, Lieutenant, U.S. Navy, Appellant

11 USCMA 377, 29 CMR 193

(1960)

Opinion of the Court

GEORGE W. LATIMER, Judge:

ॐ

"Was trial of the accused barred by punishment imposed by his commanding officer under Article 15?"

The charges for which accused was tried grew out of events that occurred January 16, 1959. On that date accused was assigned as officer of the deck for the midwatch aboard the aircraft carrier USS *Hancock*. He judi-

cially confessed and there is no dispu that after having assumed and whil on such duty he was found drunk uniform, lying unconscious in a pa sageway of the ship. However, befo accused entered his plea admitting h guilt, the defense moved to dismiss t charges on the ground of former pu ishment. It was stipulated that January 23, 1959, the commandi officer of the USS *Hancock* impos nonjudicial punishment upon accus under Article 15, Uniform Code of Military Justice, for the same acts of misconduct that were the basis of the charges being tried, whereby he restricted accused to his stateroom for ten days and recommended that the commander, Fleet Air Alameda, issue accused a letter of reprimand. Accused served the imposed restriction, but the commander, Fleet Air Alameda, when the matter was referred to him for the recommended letter of reprimand, stated his belief that the nature of the alleged violations by accused more appropriately warranted trial by court-martial, for he considered the actions did not constitute minor offenses. Subsequently, charges were preferred against accused and forwarded, together with the recommendations of the commanding officer, USS *Hancock*, and the commander, Fleet Air Alameda, to the Commandant of the Twelfth Naval District, who acted as convening authority and referred them for trial to the instant general court-martial. After the government and the defense had presented their respective arguments, the law officer denied the motion to dismiss.

At the outset, we deem it worthwhile to point out that we are not here concerned with a situation where true former jeopardy is asserted as the basis for relief. A plea in bar so predicated is available in the civilian and the military communities alike, for that fundamental protection to an accused is spelled out in the Fifth Amendment to the United States Constitution and Article 44, Uniform Code of Military Justice. It is to be borne in mind, however, that the right thereby extended to an accused concerns itself solely with prior judicial proceedings, as is clear from the terms of the last-mentioned Article. And there can be

no doubt that the prior punishment visited upon accused in the case at bar is not of that nature. True it is that he was previously punished, but not judicially. To the contrary, the commanding officer of his ship undertook to discipline him under Article 15 of the Code, supra. Congress, in its wisdom recognizing the inherent necessity of administrative sanctions in the military, enacted that statute in order to permit summary disciplinary action by a commander for minor offenses committed by members of his command. The congressional intent involved is obvious from even a casual perusal of the legislative history, the wording of the Article, and its entitlement: "Commanding officer's nonjudicial punishment."

It is clear, then, that the prior punishment in the case at bar does not bring Article 44, Uniform Code of Military Justice, supra, into play. That is not to say, however, that our problem does not sound in jeopardy. Indeed, quite the contrary is true, as may be gleaned from our language in *United States* v. *Vaughan,* 3 USCMA 121, 11 CMR 121. There, in discussing a somewhat similar situation involving disciplinary punishment, this Court alluded to the "double jeopardy provisions express and implied" in Article 15(e) of the Code, supra, and paragraphs 68*g* and 128*b*, Manual for Courts-Martial, United States, 1951. Perhaps it would be more technically correct to denote the basis for such a plea in bar as "former punishment"—to use the language of the Manual—instead of "double jeopardy." But regardless of the label we place upon it, there can be no question, and the parties are agreed, that the three last cited sections of the Code and the Manual govern the certified issue.

In Article 15(e), Uniform Code of Military Justice, supra, Congress provided:

"The imposition and enforcement of disciplinary punishment under this article for any act or omission is not a bar to trial by court-martial for a serious crime or offense growing out of the same act or omission, and not properly punishable under this article; but the fact that a disciplinary punishment has been enforced may be shown by the accused upon trial, and when so shown shall be considered in determining the measure of punishment to be adjudged in the event of a finding of guilty."

Paragraph 68g of the Manual, supra, restates the codal provision as follows:

"Nonjudicial punishment previously imposed under Article 15 for a minor offense may be interposed in bar of trial for the same offense."

Our problem, then, narrows to whether the delicts charged against the accused were minor offenses, and paragraph 128b of the Manual, supra, affords us some assistance in that regard. That paragraph undertakes to set forth a yardstick to measure the gravity of offenses in these terms:

"Whether an offense may be considered 'minor' depends upon its nature, the time and place of its commission, and the person committing it. Generally speaking the term includes misconduct not involving moral turpitude or any greater degree of criminality than is involved in the average offense tried by summary court-martial. An offense for which the punitive article authorizes the death penalty or for which confinement for one year or more is authorized is not a minor offense. Offenses such as larceny forgery, maiming, and the like involve moral turpitude and are not to be treated as minor. Escape from confinement, willful disobedience of a noncommissioned officer or petty officer, and protracted absence without leave are offenses which are more serious than the average offense tried by summary courts-martial and should not ordinarily be treated as minor."

Likewise this Court, in fixing the seriousness of offenses for another purpose, has spelled out tests that are helpful. In *United States* v. *Moore,* 5 USCMA 687, 18 CMR 311, we held *inter alia,* that an offense carrying a penalty of more than one year's confinement or which permits imposition of a dishonorable discharge could be equated to a felony. See also *United States* v. *Fisher,* 22 CMR 676; cf *United States* v. *Yray,* 10 CMR 618 and *United States* v. *Mahoney,* 27 CMR 898.

∞

Here we have a more precise measuring rod, for accused's misconduct is punishable by dishonorable separation from the service aside and apart from the Article proscribing conduct unbecoming an officer. Drunk and disorderly conduct, whether by an officer or by enlisted personnel, is a much more serious offense if committed aboard ship than otherwise and will permit imposition of six months' confinement and punitive separation from the service. And drunkenness on duty is one step further up the ladder of aggravated offenses, for it may be punished by punitive discharge and nine months' incarceration.

✌

Without doubt accused's actions here constitute an even more flagrant breach of the law. Not only was he both drunk aboard ship and while on duty but, as the board of review pointed out, his duty was as officer of the deck and, as such, he was the direct representative of the commanding officer of the ship, which position carries great responsibility. Thus, even apart from the punishment that could be permissibly adjudged, there can be no doubt that the accused's misconduct in so incapacitating himself and thus endangering the ship and its crew was attended with grave consequences and shows a "greater degree of criminality than is involved in the average offense tried by summary court-martial." It would be downgrading and belittling to the responsibility placed upon an officer of the deck—whether on a ship at sea, or, as here, in drydock—to conclude otherwise.

Accordingly, we hold that the law officer properly overruled the defense motion to dismiss, and the certified question is, therefore, answered in the negative. The decision of the board of review is affirmed.

Chief Judge QUINN concurred.

Judge FERGUSON dissented.

In summary, Judge Ferguson stated as follows:

"The practical and legal conclusion which I believe should be drawn from the foregoing considerations is that we must hold that drunkenness on duty in time of peace is, as a matter of law, a 'minor offense.' While the statute is of little use to us in determining the degree of turpitude involved, the punishment prescribed for its violation established that it was to be treated as a misdemeanor. Neither a dishonorable discharge nor confinement in excess of one year is authorized for the delict."

Note

Paragraph 128*b* of the MCM now has been changed as follows:

Generally, the term "minor" includes misconduct not involving any greater degree of criminality than is involved in the average offense tried by summary court-martial. This term ordinarily does not include misconduct of a kind which, if tried by general court-martial, could be punished by dishonorable discharge or confinement for more than one year.

See paragraphs 68*d*, 215*c*, and 128*b* of the MCM and Article 15(f) of the UCMJ.

DISCUSSION AND SELF-QUIZ

1. You are the division officer aboard a destroyer. You desire to "pull" the liberty card of one of the men in your division, as your leading petty officer is continually reporting him as a "sluggard." The basis for your decision is the statement in paragraph 128c of the MCM which states that these "non-punitive measures may also include, subject to any applicable regulations, administrative withholding of privileges." May you do so? See Section 0101c of the JAG Manual.

2. You are the legal officer aboard a destroyer. Your commanding officer, a commander in the U.S. Navy, desires to reduce Petty Officer Third Class Doe to seaman apprentice, to award him 45 days extra duties and 45 days restriction to run consecutively, to forfeit two-thirds of Doe's pay per month for one month, and to admonish him at Captain's Mast. Advise him.

3. You are the executive officer aboard a mine sweeper stationed in the North Atlantic area. Your commanding officer, a lieutenant commander, has just awarded Seaman Apprentice Smith 30 days correctional custody. At a previous Mast, Smith had been awarded 60 days restriction, of which he still has 20 days to serve. Your ship has no facilities that would permit you to carry out the correctional custody sentence, but you expect to return to Norfolk, Virginia for a two-month yard period in 30 days. Normally, corrective custody, confinement on bread and water, extra duties and restriction take effect when imposed unless they are suspended. How may you implement the Captain's Mast punishment? See Section 0101e(2) of the JAG Manual.

4. You are the division officer of a navy aircraft squadron attached to a large attack carrier on deployment to WESTPAC. Who should hold Mast on the men attached to your squadron? See Section 0101b(3), JAG Manual.

CHAPTER VII

The Summary Court-Martial

The summary court-martial is one of the three types of courts-martial in the military justice system. This chapter will discuss the nature of a summary court-martial, its responsibilities, the pretrial conference, the trial, the sentence, the preparation of the record, and the review procedure.

701 The Nature of a Summary Court-Martial

A junior officer can anticipate, sometime during his first tour of duty, that he may be required to act as a summary court-martial officer. Although the MCM states that whenever "practicable, a summary court-martial should be an officer whose grade is not below that of lieutenant of the Navy" or captain of the Marine Corps, this is not always possible in a small command.

A summary court-martial consists of only one officer. No more members may be appointed. He must be on active duty and be either a commissioned officer or a commissioned warrant officer. He is, in a true sense, the judge, jury, prosecutor, and defense. If the accused is convicted and his conviction is affirmed upon review, he is considered to have been convicted of a court-martial. The junior officer should be aware of the significance of such a conviction upon the accused. The summary court-martial conviction may later permit the imposition of a bad conduct discharge or may, at the very least, be used in aggravation in the event of the commission of another future offense. It may be an adverse influence upon the type of position an offender obtains in civilian life. It is evident that the responsibility upon the junior officer assigned a summary court-martial is great and must be assumed.

702   Responsibility of a Summary Court

The summary court-martial officer has a responsibility both to the government and the accused. He must thoroughly and impartially in quire into *both sides* of the matter and will assure that the interests of both the government and the accused are safeguarded. The summary court-martial has a responsibility for conducting a thorough and im partial trial, regardless of whether the accused pleads guilty or not guilty

Although his function is to exercise justice promptly for relatively minor offenses under a simple form of procedure, the rules as to evidence including the standards for determining the guilt of the accused, are the same as required before a special or general court-martial. For example an accused person must be presumed to be innocent until his guilt i proven beyond a reasonable doubt. This rule would also apply to affirma tive defenses the accused may assert. To illustrate, in a larceny case the accused may assert that he mistakenly believed that he had the owner's permission to take the article. The burden of proof in this case would be on the government, both with respect to the elements of the offense and the issue raised by the defense evidence.

The summary court-martial has, therefore, two primary objectives: (1) he must determine the guilt or innocence of the accused utilizing the rules of evidence and standards for determining guilt provided for by the MCM; and (2) if the accused is *found* guilty, he must determine an appropriate sentence based upon the nature of the offense committed any aggravating circumstances, and evidence presented in extenuation or mitigation.

703   Convening a Summary Court-Martial

A summary court-martial must be legally convened. The JAG Manual states that those "officers who are empowered to convene general and special courts-martial may convene summary courts-martial." See Chap ter I of the JAG Manual and Article 24 of the Code for those persons authorized to convene a summary court-martial.

If only one commissioned officer is attached to a command, he will be the summary court officer. If more than one officer is attached to the command, the subordinate will be the summary court. If the convening authority is the "accuser," he cannot convene a general or special court martial. An "accuser is a person who signs and swears to charges, a person who directs that charges nominally be signed and sworn to by another, or any other person who has an interest other than an official interest in the prosecution of the accused." Article 1(9), Code. However, an accuser can convene a summary court-martial. Additionally, unlike a general or special court-martial, the summary court-martial cannot be challenged, either for cause or preemptorily. See Chapters X and XII for a discussion of challenges.

Whenever possible, it is strongly recommended that the convening authority *not* convene the court if he is the accuser and that the summary court officer be an impartial officer who has no personal interest or bias in the result of the trial. The interest of morale and discipline in the command warrants the absence of the very appearance of a conflict in motives on the part of officers exercising judicial functions.

A sample convening order is contained in Appendix 14.

A summary court-martial consists of one commissioned officer. Officers, chief warrant officers, warrant officers, cadets, aviation cadets, and midshipmen may not be tried by summary court. Consequently, only *enlisted persons* are generally tried by summary court.

A summary court has broad jurisdiction as to the offenses it may try, as it may try any noncapital offense made punishable by the Code. Therefore a capital offense (such as spying in violation of Article 106 of the UCMJ) cannot be tried by a summary court. This is purely an academic discussion, however, for as previously noted, summary courts are primarily designed to try "minor" offenses.

No person may be brought to trial before a summary court-martial if he objects thereto. *He has the absolute right to refuse summary court-martial even though he has also refused nonjudicial punishment for the same offense.* If he refuses, he may be subject to trial by a special court-martial or other appropriate legal action. Before the 1968 amendments to the Code, the accused did not always have the right to refuse a summary court-martial.

704 Examination of the Case File

When a summary court-martial officer receives the case file, he should carefully examine the charge sheet and allied papers. For example:

1. The accused's name, rate, and service number must be correct wherever they appear on the charge sheet. See Appendices 6 and 7 for sample charge sheets.

2. The stated amount of pay must be correct, taking into consideration the total amount of time which the accused has served in the armed forces.

3. If the accused has dependents, the amount of basic allowance for quarters (BAQ) must be correct. This block should indicate only the amount required by law (i.e., $40.00 for pay grade E–4 or below with less than four years service). The $40.00 must be deducted prior to computing the amount subject to forfeiture. For E–4's with more than four years of service and higher pay grades, the court may consider the amount

of any voluntary allotment by the accused to his family when he deter mines what forfeiture, if any, to award.

4. The rank or rate and armed force of the accuser must be shown The accuser must have signed the charge sheet under oath before a officer authorized to administer oaths.

5. The officer administering the oath to the accuser must have au thority to do so. (For example, a lieutenant commander or above, a JAG Corps officer, a ship's legal officer, or a summary court-martial officer ar so authorized.) See Article 136, Code and Chapter XXV of the JAG Manual. The accused may not be tried on unsworn charges if he object thereto.

6. The commanding officer (or someone directed to do so by him must have dated and signed the receipt of the charges.

7. The 1st Indorsement must refer the case to the proper summar court-martial and the commanding officer must sign the indorsement.

8. The dates in the specifications, the preparation of the charg sheet, oath of the accuser, receipt for the charges, and the 1st Indorse ment must be in proper sequence.

9. The name and description of the accused, his rate, armed forc and ship must be correct in the specification. The time and place of th offense must be stated with as much precision as possible.

10. A thorough familiarity with the elements of each offense charge and the requisites of proof is absolutely necessary. Each specification mus state an offense charged as a violation of the proper article of the Code If the specification departs from the applicable form specification (MCM Appendix 6) so as to be ambiguous or not to state an offense, the fil should be returned to the convening authority with a statement o reasons therefor.

11. Major errors in the charge sheet should be referred to the cor vening authority for correction. If trial by summary court is believed t be inadvisable for some reason, it is the summary court's duty to repor this fact to the convening authority. The summary court may correct an initial slight errors or obvious mistakes. If a change involves the inclusion of any person, offense, or matter not fairly included in the charges a preferred, new charges should be signed and sworn to.

705 The Pretrial Conference

As the hearing should be conducted without unnecessary delay, it i advisable that the summary court officer have a pretrial conference with the accused. Although such a conference is somewhat repetitious of th summary court hearing itself and is not required, it assures that th accused understands the nature of the proceeding and the charges against him and permits the summary court to determine whether or not th accused intends to consent to trial by summary court and, if so, how he intends to plead. This information may preclude much unnecessary investigation on the part of the summary court-martial officer.

Therefore, the accused should, at the pretrial conference, be informed of the following:

1. The general nature of the charges;
2. The fact that they have been referred to a summary court-martial for trial;
3. Who convened the court;
4. The name of the accuser;
5. The names of the witnesses who will probably be called;
6. The maximum sentence which the court can adjudge if the accused is found guilty of the offenses charged.

The summary court should also inform the accused that he has the following legal rights:

1. To plead "not guilty" to any or all charges and specifications and place the burden of proving his guilt upon the government;
2. To call any witnesses or produce any evidence in his own behalf;
3. The right to cross-examine any adverse witnesses or have the court ask them any questions the accused desires answered;
4. The right to testify as to his guilt or innocence;
5. The right to make a sworn or unsworn statement, or present other evidence in mitigation or extenuation if the accused is found guilty;
6. The right to refuse a summary court-martial.

The accused should then be asked:

1. "Do you intend to consent to trial by summary court-martial?"
2. "Do you intend to plead guilty or not guilty?"

The accused should have plenty of time to decide these matters for himself. The summary court should inform him that he may change his mind at any time prior to trial.

706   The Trial

All sessions will be conducted by the summary court-martial with dignity and decorum. All summary court-martial proceedings are open and spectators may attend unless classified information may be disclosed.

An example of a summary court-martial trial guide is contained in Appendix 15.

The summary court-martial has authority to subpoena witnesses, take depositions, and punish for contempt of court. He must take evidence under oath. The accused, of course, may make an unsworn statement in mitigation or extenuation, if he is convicted.

Prior to the trial all known evidence should be gathered and numbers assigned to exhibits for orderly presentation and use. The summary court has the duty of insuring that all relevant and competent evidence, both for and against the accused, is presented in court.

Even if an accused pleads guilty, a plea of not guilty must be entered for him:

1. If he desires to change his plea;

2. If the summary court is in doubt as to his understanding and desire to plead guilty; or

3. If at any time during the trial he makes a statement (either sworn or unsworn) inconsistent with his plea of guilty.

Further, the MCM provides that, in any event, the court, in the interest of justice may present evidence and if, after weighing this evidence the court believes the guilty plea of the accused to be improvident, may proceed as though he had plead not guilty.

There is no requirement that an accused being tried by summary court-martial be represented by a defense counsel. If the accused requests the convening authority to designate an officer to represent him as individual defense counsel, it is recommended that the request be granted, if the counsel is reasonably available. Similarly, the accused should be permitted by the summary court to provide civilian counsel at his own expense to act in his behalf. Counsel need not be a lawyer.

The accused and his counsel will be allowed to examine defense witnesses, to cross-examine prosecution witnesses, to object to the reception of evidence and questions asked of witnesses by the summary court-martial, to make arguments on the findings and sentence, and to otherwise properly represent the accused.

If witnesses are required, the summary court makes arrangements for their appearance. They should be excluded from the courtroom until called to testify. If evidence is presented on the merits (i.e., guilt or innocence of the accused), witnesses for the prosecution are called first. The accused may cross-examine these witnesses with the assistance of the summary court. If the accused desires, the summary court will ask questions requested by the accused. On behalf of the interests of the accused, the court will obtain the attendance of witnesses, examine them, and obtain:

1. Evidence as may tend to disprove or negate guilt (i.e., see Chapter XXIX, MCM, Matters of Defense);

2. Evidence that explains the acts or omissions charged;

3. Evidence that shows extenuating circumstances or establishes grounds for mitigation.

The principles enunciated in paragraphs 74 and 76 of the MCM relating to the findings and sentence are specifically applicable to a summary court-martial. For example, this means that:

1. Only matters properly before the court as a whole may be con-

sidered and no outside knowledge of the acts, character, or service of the accused should be utilized in making a decision;

2. In weighing evidence, a court should utilize his common sense and his knowledge of the ways of the world. In the light of all the circumstances, he should consider the inherent probability or improbability of the evidence, and consequently may believe one witness in conflict with several others.

3. He must be satisfied beyond a reasonable doubt that the accused is guilty. The MCM states that "the meaning of the rule is that the proof must be such as to exclude not every hypothesis or possibility of innocence but any fair and rational hypothesis except that of guilt; what is required is not an absolute or mathematical certainty but a moral certainty." This rule applies to every *element* of the offense, but it is not necessary that every *particular fact* advanced by the prosecution be proved beyond a reasonable doubt if, on the whole evidence, the court is satisfied beyond a reasonable doubt that the accused is guilty.

The court will announce the findings as soon as they are determined. In the event the accused is found guilty, the accused will be afforded the opportunity to present evidence in mitigation or extenuation and will be shown or read any evidence of previous convictions by court-martial to be considered. Nonjudicial punishment cannot be considered when awarding punishment, as it is not considered a previous conviction. The personal data on the charge sheet will be verified by the accused as to its accuracy and any discrepancies resolved.

707   The Sentence

A summary court-martial is limited as to the amount of certain types of punishment it may award. Thus, it may adjudge any punishment not forbidden by the Code or MCM *except* death, dismissal, dishonorable or bad conduct discharge, confinement for more than one month, hard labor without confinement for more than 45 days, restriction to certain specified limits for more than two months, or forfeiture of more than two-thirds of one month's pay. Article 20, Code.

A petty officer second class (E–5) or above may not be awarded confinement, hard labor without confinement, or reduction (except to the next inferior grade). For example, an E–5 may be sentenced to reduction to E–4, but an E–4 could be sentenced to reduction to E–1.

As the Code only states what punishments a summary court may not give, a court-martial is not limited to those types of punishment set forth in Article 20. Thus, a summary court may award admonition or reprimand, detention of pay (up to two-thirds of one month's pay), fine (up to permitted amount of forfeiture), or confinement on bread and water.

The maximum amount of confinement and forfeiture may be adjudged in one sentence. But, as restriction and confinement are both forms of deprivation of liberty, they must be apportioned. The punishment for a particular offense as listed in the Table of Maximum Punishments in the MCM may be apportioned so long as the limitations on a court's jurisdiction and on particular types of punishment are observed. See Chapter XXV, MCM.

The summary court officer must remember, however, that the Table of Maximum Punishments (Section B) provides for reduction in addition to the punishments otherwise authorized in the Table. *Therefore, reduction in rate may always be awarded, with the limitation that an E–5 or above may only be reduced one grade.*

The court will advise the accused of the sentence following determination. If the sentence includes confinement, he will advise the accused of his right to apply to the commanding officer for deferment of the service of the confinement (the military equivalent of "bail" in civilian life) as provided for in paragraph 88*f* of the MCM.

708   The Court-Martial Record

The summary court need only fill in page 4 of the charge sheet (see Appendix 7) to complete the record of trial, unless the commanding officer or a higher reviewing authority requires a summarization of evidence. If this is required, the summary court must summarize the evidence and attach this information to the charge sheet. However, if the accused has been found not guilty of all the charges and specifications, a summarization of evidence is not required. Section 0120, JAG Manual.

The record of trial (page 4 of the charge sheet) should be completely filled in. It is imperative that the question which reads "was the accused advised in accordance with paragraph 79*d*, MCM?" be answered. Upon completion, the record of trial will be forwarded to the convening authority.

The summary court-martial should cross out on the charge sheet those witnesses who were listed but not called, and should add the witnesses not listed but who actually testified at the trial. He should authenticate the record by signing each copy of the charge sheet—after assuring all portions relating to the trial are correct and accurate.

709   Review of Summary Courts-Martial

Summary courts-martial are first reviewed by the convening authority. Although it is not required that any other officer in his command review the case, the convening authority will generally refer the case for a legal review to his legal officer (a nonlawyer) or his command judge advocate (a certified military lawyer).

However, the convening authority should *not* refer the case to a legal officer or command judge advocate who has previously acted as the summary court officer, defense counsel, assistant defense counsel, accuser, or investigating officer on the case. If the summary court officer is the only officer present with the command, he may so indicate in the record of trial and may review the record and sign the convening authority's action.

The ultimate responsibility for the convening authority's action rests with him. He cannot delegate the responsibility and only *he* or his successor in command can sign the convening authority's action on the charge sheet. After the convening authority acts, the legal yeoman types a page 6 service record entry (Appendix 16) reflecting the results of his review, unless the charges are dismissed or disapproved, in which event no service record entry will be made except when the offense involves unauthorized absence or desertion.

Following the convening authority's action, the case must be forwarded to the supervisory authority, who will be either the area coordinator authorized to convene general courts-martial or the officer who is superior in the chain of command authorized to convene general courts-martial. The record must be forwarded to the area coordinator unless the superior in the chain of command directs otherwise. As a general practice, the superior in the chain of command has so directed. It is logical to assume that many superiors in the chain of command consider they have an immediate and direct interest in the disciplinary problems arising in their subordinate commands and consequently desire to retain their authority to review courts convened within their chain of command.

The supervisory authority must refer all summary courts-martial to a judge advocate to review. If no corrective or mitigating action by the supervisory authority is required or recommended, no supervisory action need be taken. In its place, the staff judge advocate may make appropriate notations on the record of trial reciting the name of the command taking the action, the date, the result of the review, and the action thereon. If corrective or mitigative action is required or recommended, action will be placed on the record over the signature of the supervisory authority. The results of the supervisory review will be forwarded to the convening authority and the command where the accused is presently attached. The latter command will require that the action of the supervisory authority be transcribed on page 6 of the accused's record. The accused must be notified of the result of the trial.

The scope of the convening and supervisory authority's reviews will vary with their requirements as to what should be contained in the record of trial. If they require a summarized record in every case in which the accused has been found guilty, the review will obviously cover more facets of the case.

The Military Justice Act of 1968 provided one more area of review for any court not reviewed by the Court of Military Review. This review would, as a general rule, include all summary and non-BCD special courts. Article 69 now provides that the accused may petition the Judge Advocate General of the Navy to review his case in the event of fraud on the court, newly discovered evidence, lack of jurisdiction over the accused or the offense, *or error prejudicial to the substantial rights of the accused.* The result of this provision is to give the accused another legal review if he considers the summary court and the reviewing authorities erred.

Paragraph 94a(2) of the MCM discusses the scope of review of the summary court-martial. The JAG Manual contains procedures for filing court-martial records.

710 Summary

Although the technical protections present in summary courts are not as great as those in general and special courts, the accused must be afforded the basic rights guaranteed by the greater tribunals. For example, the admissible evidence considered by the summary court must be sufficient to prove the accused guilty beyond a reasonable doubt *or* the summary court *must* find him not guilty.

The accused, under the Military Justice Act of 1968, has the absolute right to refuse a summary court. He may well elect this tribunal if the experiences of others indicate that his trial will be fair and impartial.

Conviction by a summary court-martial constitutes permanent blemishes upon an enlisted man's service record. If the accused is later tried for another offense by a special court-martial, two previous summary courts-martial may accelerate the permissible punishment to include a bad conduct discharge. The summary court must serve both the accused and the society which suspects the accused of a crime and must use the legal standards guaranteed to every man in uniform who appears before a judicial proceeding.

DISCUSSION AND SELF-QUIZ

1. You are the summary court-martial officer in the case of Seaman Yeo, U.S. Navy. After finding the accused guilty, you desire to restrict Yeo to the limits of the ship for 60 days and award him 45 days hard labor without confinement. Can you do so? See paragraphs 16b, 127c (2) and 131d of the MCM.

2. Petty Officer Third Class Smith, attached to your squadron, has committed a series of offenses which, while they do not warrant a special court-martial, are sufficiently serious to warrant punitive measures. Your commanding officer wants to know whether he should handle the case at Mast or

refer the case to a summary court-martial. He is of the opinion that if the accused is found guilty, the offenses committed may justify reduction to pay grade E–1. He seeks your advice as legal officer. Advise him.

3. If nonjudicial punishments and a summary court-martial are both designed to punish minor offenses, upon what basis do we determine what action to take in a particular case?

4. You are the summary court officer in the unauthorized absence case of Seaman Apprentice Richard Roe, who is charged with two unauthorized absences. The accused pleads not guilty to both offenses. After a consideration of all the evidence, you are convinced that the accused was, in fact, an unauthorized absentee on both occasions. However, he has presented for your consideration proof that he was arrested prior to one of his absences and held, tried, and acquitted by civilian authorities.. He presents no evidence as to the other offense. You believe these facts are true. What must you do? See paragraph 165, MCM.

5. You are the summary court-martial officer who has just found an enlisted man (E–5) guilty of unauthorized absence for a period of two days. He is a repeat offender. What punishments may you properly consider awarding him? See Section A of paragraph 127c of the MCM.

CHAPTER **VIII**

The Convening
Authority

A study of military law would not be complete without a discussion o
some of the basic responsibilities and problems of those military person
nel who have official duties and responsibilities in almost every specia
and general court-martial case. Therefore, the next three chapters wil
discuss the convening authority, the legal officer, the trial counsel, th
defense counsel, the members, the president, and the military judge.

The person who creates a court is called the *convening authority*. Th
creation of a court-martial and the forwarding of a case to trial are judi
cial functions. As such, these responsibilities are exercised in an impartia
manner with due consideration given to both the interest of the accuse
and the government.

801   The Authority to Convene

Articles 22, 23, and 24 of the Code and applicable provisions in th
JAG Manual state who can convene a general, special, or summary cour
Some of the principal general court-martial authorities are the Presider
of the United States, the Secretary of the Navy, all flag officers in con
mand, and the commanding officers of naval stations or larger sho
activities *beyond the United States*.

Some of the principal special and summary court-martial authoriti
are commanding officers of ships, shipyards, bases or stations; comman
ing officers of Marine brigades, regiments, or any battalion or correspon
ing unit; the commanding officer of any Marine barracks, wing, grou
squadron, station, base, auxiliary airfield, or other places where membe
of the Marine Corps are on duty; commanding officers of all battalior
squadrons and units and activities of the Navy; the commanding offic

116

or officer in charge of a separate or detached command if designated by a flag or general officer in command; and any commanding officer whose subordinates in the tactical or administrative chain of command have authority to convene special courts-martial. Any person who can convene a general court can convene a special or summary court.

Unless an officer who convenes a court is authorized to create a court, he may not do so. A court is created by a written convening order issued by the convening authority. See Appendices 14, 17, and 18 for sample convening orders. Paragraph 36b of the MCM discusses the contents of such an order.

The authority to convene courts-martial cannot be delegated or transferred to another. For example, the commanding officer could not permit the executive officer or any other officer to sign a convening order or sign the 1st Indorsement on the charge sheet referring the case to trial. (Appendices 6 and 7 are sample charge sheets.) The authority of a commanding officer to convene a court-martial is retained as long as he continues to be the commanding officer.

On board a ship, the next line officer eligible for command at sea upon the incapacity, death, relief from duty, or absence of the commanding officer may convene courts-martial as he is the successor to command of the ship. Paragraph 1373, Navy Regulations. He could then sign the referral to trial or convening order as "Acting Commanding Officer." Chapter 13 of Navy Regulations provides further guidance as to the succession to command within the naval service.

If the commanding officer is an accuser, he is ineligible to convene a special or general court-martial. An accuser is "a person who signs and swears to charges, any person who directs that charges nominally be signed and sworn to by another, and any other person who has an interest other than an official interest in the prosecution of the accused." Article 1(9), Code. Although it is clear that the person who signs and swears to charges on the charge sheet (see Appendix 7) is always an accuser, other situations are not so clear-cut. (See Chapter III, paragraph 314, where this situation is discussed.)

The convening authority of a special court-martial has various factors to consider in determining the proper disposition of a case. He should be aware of the jurisdictional aspects relating to courts-martial. Consideration should be given to the qualifications and eligibility of members to be detailed to a court-martial. He must be aware of the requirements relating to the detailing of certified military lawyers and military judges.

802 Jurisdiction

The jurisdiction of a court-martial may be defined as its power to try and determine a case. In order for a court-martial to have jurisdiction in any particular case, it must meet the following requirements:

1. *The court must be convened by an official empowered to convene it.* Paragraph 801 discusses who may convene a court.

2. *The court must be properly constituted as to the number of members.* For example, if the number of members hearing a special court-martial case falls to less than three during the course of a trial, the court cannot proceed until at least three members are detailed and present in court to hear the case. Article 16, Code.

3. *The members of the court must be legally competent to sit on the court.* For example, an accuser, a witness for the prosecution, or an investigating officer would be ineligible to serve as members. Paragraph 1001 discusses in detail who may serve as a member.

4. *The court must have the power to try the accused.* For example, a summary court-martial cannot try officers, cadets, aviation cadets, or midshipmen. Consequently, only enlisted men may be tried by summary court-martial.

5. *The court-martial must have the power to try the offense charged.* For example, courts-martial cannot try servicemen for crimes which are in no way "service-connected." This aspect of jurisdiction was determined by the U.S. Supreme Court on 2 June 1969 in the case of *O'Callahan* v. *Parker,* 395 US 258.

In discussing the constitutional basis for its decision, the Supreme Court relates the following:

> The Fifth Amendment specifically exempts "cases arising in the land and naval forces or in the militia, when in actual service *in time of war or public danger*" from the requirement of prosecution by indictment and from the right to trial by jury. (Emphasis supplied.)

The Court further cites Section 2 of Article 3 of the Constitution which states:

> . . . trial of all Crimes, except in Cases of impeachment, shall be by jury, and such trial shall be held in the State where the said Crimes shall have been committed; but when not committed within any State, the Trial shall be at such Place or places, as the Congress may by Law have directed.

Justice Douglas, who wrote the opinion, stated that military law does not provide the equivalent of a civilian jury or the grand jury nor does it have a completely independent judiciary. He also discussed command influence as a "pervasive one in military law."

In this case the following factors were present:

    a. The accused was on leave or liberty, and;

    b. The accused was in civilian clothes, and;

    c. There was no connection between his military duty and the crime in general, and;

    d. The victim was not performing any military duties relating to the military, and;

    e. The incident occurred within U.S. territorial limits (not in the occupied zone of a foreign country), and;

    f. The incident occurred during peacetime, and;

    g. There was no question of flouting military authority, the security of a military post, or the integrity of military property.

The *O'Callahan* case is a landmark decision. The complete ramifications of this major decision will be determined by future U.S. Court of Military Appeals and Supreme Court decisions.

    6. *The court-martial must have the power to award the sentence adjudged.* Although summary and special courts may have the power to try and determine a particular case, they are limited as to the amount of punishment they may award. For example, a special court-martial cannot award:

    a. The death penalty;

    b. A dishonorable discharge (however, the court may award a bad conduct discharge);

    c. Dismissal of an officer (this is the equivalent to a dishonorable discharge of an enlisted man);

    d. Confinement for more than six months;

    e. Forfeiture of pay in excess of two-thirds pay per month for a period of six months.

803 The Detailing of Members

The commanding officer, as part of his duties as convening authority, details the members of the court-martial. He should select those officers best qualified by reason of age, education, training, experience, length of service, and judicial temperament to serve as members on his courts.

The convening authority can make changes in the members, counsel, or the military judge of any court-martial convened by him by issuance of an amendment to the convening order. Permanent changes are generally made by formal written orders but, if necessary, can be made orally, by message, or by signal. They should be confirmed subsequently by written orders. However, the convening authority may not make changes in the membership after the court has assembled to hear a case, except under certain limited circumstances. See paragraph 1002 of this book.

The convening authority should designate no more members than those who are expected to be present for the trial. For example, in *United States* v. *McLaughlin,* 18 USCMA 61, 39 CMR 61 (1968) a convening authority designated twelve officers as members of a special court-martial. On the trial date, only three appeared. The reason was that the convening authority set up a schedule of court sessions, with only three members detailed to attend each session. All others were excused. The Court of Military Appeals stated that such a practice deprived the president of his right to act as such due to his seniority. Further, the court pointed out that under this system it was possible the court could be split into two or more separate parts:

> . . . each sitting on the same date for the trial of different accused. Congress never intended a court-martial to be so fragmented. . . . Apparently the convening authority desired to apportion the court-martial work load by a system of case assignments. Such a system may be proper where there are separate courts, and the assignment of a case to a particular court is effected by appropriate means.

The court added, in dismissing the charges, that:

> . . . the system of assignment must leave each court-martial free to function as provided by the Uniform Code. . . .

Changes may be advisable at times to provide the maximum opport unity for eligible, well-qualified personnel to gain experience in th administration of military justice.

However, amendments to the convening order should be kept to minimum. It is recommended that a new convening order be drafte rather than promulgate several amendments to the original one. Th convening authority should never, in creating a new court, dissolve th old court or rescind or revoke the old convening order, as it may b necessary to reassemble the old court at some later time, such as whe it is necessary for the court to clarify an apparent error or omissio in a previous record of trial or when a previous record reflects imprope or inconsistent action by the court-martial.

804 Defense Counsel and Military Judge Requirements for a BC Special Court-Martial

The Military Justice Act of 1968 provides that certain personnel mu have certain legal qualifications before a special court-martial may awai a bad conduct discharge (BCD). Paragraph 15b of the MCM states tha

A bad-conduct discharge may not be adjudged by a special court-martial unless (1) a military judge was detailed to the trial, except in any case in which a military judge could not be detailed because of physical conditions or military exigencies, (2) counsel qualified under Article 27(b) (a certified military lawyer) was detailed to represent the accused, and (3) a complete and verbatim record of the proceedings and testimony was made.

Therefore, the convening authority must first determine whether a bad conduct discharge is a possible punishment that the court can award. A bad conduct discharge can be awarded if the offenses themselves or a combination of them so warrant or the accused has a number of previous convictions. For example:

1. An accused is charged with one violation of Article 86 in that he was an unauthorized absentee from his unit for 70 days. A search of the Table of Maximum Punishments (Section A, Chapter XXV, MCM) discloses that one of the punishments that may be awarded upon conviction for this offense is a dishonorable discharge. A bad conduct discharge, as the lesser punishment of the two, may be awarded in any case where a dishonorable discharge is authorized. Paragraph 127c(4), MCM. Therefore, in this case, the offense itself makes this a BCD special court-martial.

2. An accused is charged with two offenses, neither of which, as a separate offense, authorizes the imposition of a bad conduct discharge. However, if the amount of confinement that may be awarded upon conviction of these two offenses totals six months or more, a bad conduct discharge may be awarded as a permissible additional punishment. Section B, Chapter XXV, MCM. Consequently, the combination of the two offenses makes this case a BCD special court-martial. See question 4 of the Discussion and Self-Quiz.

3. An accused has been convicted by court-martial twice previously within the past three years. The three-year period is measured from the date of the commission of the present offense. In order to be considered a "conviction," the review of the case must have been fully completed. A bad conduct discharge may be awarded as a permissible additional punishment under these circumstances. Section B, Chapter XXV, MCM. Consequently, previous convictions make this a BCD special court-martial.

If a bad conduct discharge is a possible punishment for the offenses charged, the MCM (paragraph 15b) states that it "may not be adjudged" unless a military judge is detailed to the court. *There is one exception: "if physical conditions or military exigencies" prevent detailing a military judge to the court, a bad conduct discharge may be awarded.* This is an important standard, as it is also utilized when lawyer counsel for a non-BCD (bad conduct discharge) case cannot be obtained. See paragraph 805.

Even if a military judge is available, or the conditions for his absence can be met, under no circumstances may a special court-martial award a bad conduct discharge unless the accused is represented by a qualified military lawyer who has been detailed and made available. The accused may choose not to utilize or cooperate with such detailed counsel, but such counsel must still be initially detailed. Only a certified military lawyer or a civilian lawyer may represent an accused before a BCD special. For example, the accused may *not* be represented by his division officer unless the officer is a certified military lawyer or qualified as a lawyer in civilian life, even if the accused insists. The accused does have the right to be represented by a certified military lawyer of his own selection, if such a lawyer is reasonably available. He would serve free of charge, as would the detailed military lawyer. The accused would have to pay for any civilian lawyer he desires to utilize in his defense.

However, the accused may conduct his own defense without assistance of counsel. In any event, the accused may have a nonlawyer present and may consult with him, if the presiding officer approves.

Therefore, if a commanding officer cannot justify the absence of a military judge or cannot detail a certified military lawyer for the accused after trying diligently to obtain one, he has three alternatives:

1. He may transfer the accused to a naval activity, such as a law center that can furnish the required personnel. This may present a problem if there are witnesses who must remain aboard ship.

2. He can wait until he comes into port. There, either the ship, the naval activity, or a law center can try him. In this event there must be complete written documentation as to the reasons for the delay. See Chapter II regarding speedy trial.

3. He can, in the 1st Indorsement on the charge sheet (see Appendix 6) after "subject to the following instructions," direct that "the authorized maximum punishment does not include a bad conduct discharge." The trial may then proceed without a military judge, however, a military lawyer will probably still be required (see the next paragraph).

805 Defense Counsel Requirements for a Non-BCD Special Court Martial

A military judge is only required to be present when the special court martial can award a bad conduct discharge. However, it is recommended that a military judge, when available, be detailed in non-BCD cases. The case might involve many complicated legal issues which a military judge might resolve more easily than the president of a court-martial.

A nonlawyer may be detailed initially by the convening authority to defend an accused before a non-BCD special court-martial.

The rule as to the presence of a certified military lawyer in a non-BCD special court-martial is the same as the rule relating to the presence of a military judge in a BCD special court. This is because of the fact that the MCM requires that in *all* special courts-martial, the accused must be afforded the opportunity to be represented by a certified military lawyer.

If the accused requests that a certified military lawyer defend him, one must be detailed to represent him, unless one cannot be obtained because of physical conditions or military exigencies. If the standards as to physical conditions or military exigencies are not met, and the trial proceeds, the case will be reversed on review.

If the accused elects to retain his nonlawyer detailed counsel, he may defend the accused. If the accused requests individual counsel, such counsel may defend him, if reasonably available, without regard to whether he is a certified military lawyer or not. For example, an accused may desire to be defended by his division officer, a nonlawyer, vice his appointed counsel. His division officer, if reasonably available, could then defend him.

There is no requirement that the trial counsel in any special court-martial be a military lawyer. Any commissioned officer may serve as trial counsel unless he has acted as investigating officer, military judge, court member, or for the defense in any manner, in which case he would be ineligible to prosecute the case. However, if the trial counsel, or his assistant trial counsel, is a certified military lawyer or a member of a bar of a federal or state court, or is qualified to act as counsel before a general court-martial, the detailed defense counsel must be similarly qualified. For example, in a non-BCD special court-martial case, the accused would be entitled to be represented by a certified military lawyer if the trial counsel was a certified military lawyer.

If the accused is represented by a certified military lawyer or civilian attorney, the convening authority should consider obtaining a similarly qualified trial counsel. If a naval officer on board his ship has considerable experience or has attended law school, it may be advisable to detail him as trial counsel if he is eligible. Otherwise, it is strongly recommended that a certified military lawyer be obtained to prosecute the case.

806 Physical Conditions or Military Exigencies

As discussed previously, this standard is applied in two cases:

1. In a BCD special court when a military judge cannot be obtained; *and*

2. In a non-BCD special court-martial case when the accused requests that a certified military lawyer represent him.

*Physical conditions or military exigencies "may exist under rare cir-
cumstances, such as on an isolated ship on the high seas or in a unit in
an inaccessible area, provided compelling reasons exist why trial must be
held at that time and at that place.* Mere inconvenience does not constitute a physical condition or military exigency and does not excuse a failure" to detail a military judge or furnish the accused qualified counsel.*
(Emphasis supplied) (Paragraphs 6c and 15b, MCM.)

If, in the opinion of the convening authority, physical conditions or
military exigencies do exist which preclude the detailing of a military
judge in a BCD case or the furnishing of a certified military lawyer for
an accused in a non-BCD case, he must, prior to trial, make a written
statement to be submitted at trial as an appellate exhibit. This statement must set forth, in detail, not only the reasons why either the military judge or the certified military lawyer, as applicable, could not be
obtained, but also why the trial had to be held at that time and at that
place.

807　Command Influence

The court-martial is an independent court of law. Although the commanding officer retains general power over, and responsibility for, discipline within his command, Congress, through the Code, has removed the
court-martial as an instrument of the commanding officer's desires in any
particular case. The commanding officer has a wide variety of punitive
and nonpunitive measures he can utilize, but once he refers a case to
a court-martial, he cannot influence the proceeding to the accused's detri-
ment. The question of the guilt or innocence of the accused and the
sentence to be awarded in the event the accused is found guilty is the
independent decision of the court.

Article 37 of the Code states as follows:

> No authority convening a general, special, or summary court-
> martial, nor any other commanding officer, may censure, repri-
> mand, or admonish the court or any member, military judge, or
> counsel thereof, with respect to the findings or sentence adjudged
> by the court, or with respect to any other exercise of its or his
> functions in the conduct of the proceedings. No person . . . may
> attempt to coerce or, by any unauthorized means, influence the
> action of a court-martial or any other military tribunal or any
> member thereof, in reaching the findings or sentence in any case,
> or the action of any convening, approving, or reviewing authority
> with respect to his judicial acts.

General instruction or informational courses are only permitted if
"such courses are designed *solely* for the purpose of instructing members

of a command in the *substantive and procedural aspects of courts-martial.*" (Emphasis supplied.) Consequently, it is proper for the members to understand the operation of court-martial proceedings and their duties as court-martial members. For example, such information as is contained in this publication relating to the basic duties of personnel and the trial procedure to be followed in court would be appropriate lecture material. However, the lecture material should *never* be delivered to court-martial members assembled for the trial of a case. Nor should the personal beliefs or the special value judgments of the drafter of the lecture material or the lecturer himself be given to attendees. *United States* v. *Wright,* 17 USCMA 110, 37 CMR 374 (1967).

The convening authority's expression of his personal views may constitute command control. For example, a general policy directive that repeat offenders should be awarded a punitive discharge and that "this letter will be brought to the attention of every member of every general court-martial hereafter appointed" was held to constitute command influence in *United States* v. *Hawthorne,* 7 USCMA 293, 22 CMR 83 (1956). In this regard, see *United States* v. *Cole,* the Discussion Case at the end of this chapter.

In order to further assure that the court-martial reacts as an independent body, the MCM provides the following:

1. The performance of a member of a court-martial may *not* be considered in fitness reports, or in determining whether he should be advanced in grade, retained on active duty, or assigned elsewhere.

2. No *defense* counsel may receive a less favorable fitness report because of the "zeal" with which he performs before a court-martial.

3. The convening authority cannot prepare or review the fitness report of a military judge detailed to a special court-martial which relates to his performance of duty as a military judge.

Article 98 of the Code provides that any person who knowingly "and intentionally fails to enforce or comply with any provision of this chapter regulating the proceedings before, during, or after trial of an accused . . . shall be punished as a court-martial may direct."

Consequently, not only will the exercise or the appearance of command influence result in the dismissal of the charges or their return for a rehearing, but it conceivably could result in disciplinary action against the person exercising such control.

It should be noted that it is proper for a commanding officer, in the interest of good order and discipline, to take normal measures for the prevention of misconduct, such as lectures discussing the improvement of discipline by other than judicial processes. *United States* v. *Carter,* 9 USCMA 108, 25 CMR 370 (1958).

808 The Legal Officer

Article 6(b) of the Code provides the following:

Convening authorities shall at all times communicate directly with their staff judge advocates or legal officers in matters relating to the administration of military justice; and the staff judge advocate or legal officer of any command is entitled to communicate directly with the staff judge advocate or legal officer of a superior or subordinate command, or with the Judge Advocate General.

However, Chapter 8 of Navy Regulations requires the executive officer to keep the commanding officer "informed of all significant matters pertaining to the command." The executive officer is also responsible, "under the commanding officer, for the organization, performance of duty, and good order and discipline of the entire command."

Navy Regulations further states that the discipline "of the individuals of the command shall be a chief concern of the executive officer, and he shall, to the extent of his authority, insure that these and related matters are administered in a just and uniform manner."

For these reasons, the legal officer, although a special assistant in the chain of command with direct access to the commanding officer, must keep the executive officer fully informed of all matters related to discipline on board the ship, with the reservation that he still has the right to direct access.

As the officer primarily responsible for the technical aspects and efficiency of the administration of military justice in the command, and as the principal adviser to the commanding officer on military law, the legal officer has many duties and responsibilities.

For example, he may be responsible for:

1. Advising the preliminary inquiry officer as to the scope and nature of his duties and the law applicable;

2. Properly preparing the NAVPERS 2696 (Report and Disposition of Offenses);

3. Furnishing assistance to the trial counsel in the proper preparation of court-martial records;

4. Preparing convening orders, legal documents, and legal correspondence for the commanding officer;

5. Assisting the preliminary inquiry officer in the proper preparation of a charge sheet;

6. Supervising the general preparation for Captain's Mast, attending Mast, and advising the commanding officer as to any legal matter that may arise;

7. Advising, if requested, defense and trial counsel of a court-martial as to the applicable law;

8. Reviewing and advising the commanding officer as to all courts-martial convened by him and all appeals from nonjudicial punishment;

9. Preparing properly the service record entries relating to punishment awarded at Captain's Mast or as the result of courts-martial;

10. Advising the commanding officer as to any other issue that may be related to legal matters.

This brief listing is not all-inclusive. The legal officer's training may, to a certain extent, limit the scope of his advice. For example, if he is a graduate of justice school or a JAG lawyer, he should have, at least, certain research tools not available to the average line officer. However, regardless of the extent of his qualifications, the legal officer should not hesitate to request advice from either the staff judge advocate in the chain of command or other available military lawyers.

See paragraph 303 for a discussion of the relationship between the discipline and legal officer.

809 Summary

The person who creates a court-martial is the convening authority. He does so through issuance of a convening order. He must possess the authority to convene a court and cannot delegate it within his command.

The convening authority has certain factors to consider in determining whether to refer the case to trial and in drafting a convening order: (1) jurisdiction, (2) membership, (3) qualifications of the defense counsel, and (4) the military judge. It may be advisable to detail a qualified trial counsel, defense counsel, and a military judge, even though not required, if they are available. In a difficult case, this will reduce the possibility of error.

Command influence is specifically prohibited by the Code. The court-martial is an independent court of law. Those who are detailed as defense counsel, military judge, and members are required to be guided by the law and the facts of the case and not by outside influences in the performance of their judicial duties.

The legal officer is the officer most concerned with the day to day administration of military justice at his command. His duties may vary according to his training, qualifications, and the size of the command. Generally, he supervises the great bulk of the actual paper work related to the administration of military justice and advises those concerned with its implementation.

This chapter discusses some of the convening authority's pretrial responsibilities. Later chapters relate some of his other vital functions in the judicial process. For example, his responsibilities as a reviewing authority are discussed in Chapter XIII.

Discussion Case

UNITED STATES, Appellee

v.

GEORGE W. COLE, Fireman Recruit, U.S. Navy, Appellant

17 USCMA 296, 38 CMR 94

(1967)

Opinion of the Court

QUINN, Chief Judge:

The accused was arraigned before a special court-martial convened by the Commanding Officer, United States Naval Station, Washington, D. C., on two charges in violation of the Uniform Code of Military Justice. One charge alleged the larceny of clothing belonging to another sailor; the other set out a violation of Navy regulations. The accused pleaded not guilty to the first and guilty to the second, but was convicted of both charges, and sentenced to a bad-conduct discharge, confinement at hard labor for six months, and partial forfeiture of pay. The convening authority affirmed the findings of guilty and the sentence. The supervisory authority also affirmed the findings, but modified the sentence by reducing the confinement to four months.

For the first time in the proceedings against him, the accused contends the court members were subject to command control. His contention is predicated upon the command's Plan of the Day for August 31, 1966, and a Memorandum by the convening authority, dated August 26, 1966. The Government concedes these documents were "posted on various bulletin boards and circulated in certain of-

fices" within the Naval Station. Post trial statements by four of the five court members who heard the case indicate two of them had read the Plan of the Day before trial.[1]

Among other things, the Plan of the Day contained a notice about the actions taken by the commander at mast on August 25. One of these action related to the accused. It indicated he was charged with larceny, and that the charge had been referred to a special court-martial for trial. The Plan was apparently accompanied by the Memorandum, which is titled "Petty Thievery." Part of the Memorandum patently absurd. For example, referring to a story about a thief aboard "an old coal burning battleship which was told the commander when he "was a young sailor," it observed that the thief was thrown by his shipmates into the boiler of the ship, and it implies this might still be a valid form of punishment. Other parts the Memorandum stamp the commander as unreconciled to the Un

---

[1] The Government informs us the fifth member is on duty in the Pacific area and efforts to obtain a statement from him have been unsuccessful.

form Code's endeavor to correct the abuses of earlier court-martial practice by shielding court members from command directives calculated to pressure them in their deliberations. Although not mentioned by name, the Memorandum refers to the accused's case as one in which the commander "determined to use all the means at . . . [his] disposal to deter and to punish thieves." The reference leaves the reader convinced that, in the opinion of the commander, the accused was guilty of the larceny charge and deserved more than "minor punishment."

Although not separately recited, the accused's allegation of command control has two aspects. The first is concerned with the impact of the Plan of the Day and the Memorandum on the court members; the second is concerned with their effect on the propriety of review of the case by the commander. See *United States* v. *Plummer* 7 USCMA 630, 23 CMR 94.

∾

One of the basic objectives of the Uniform Code of Military Justice is to eradicate this misuse of command power, but unfortunately total success has not yet been realized. Perhaps it never will be because of the vagaries of human nature. This Court, however, is dedicated to the Code's objective to protect the court-martial processes from improper command influence.

Government counsel contend that neither the fact nor the shadow of command control is present in this case. They point to the *voir dire* of the court members by defense counsel as clearly demonstrating that the court members were not influenced by the Plan of the Day and the Memorandum. They also refer to the disclaimers of influence in the statements of the two court members who read the documents as proof of the absence of command influence. If the statements dispel doubts in this area, one of them raises doubt as to the correctness of the member's response on the *voir dire*. Defense counsel asked the court members whether they had any "knowledge" of an "official notice" such as the Plan of the Day which "may have any bearing on this case." There was no response by any court member. However, in his post-trial statement, one member admitted he saw the Memorandum before trial and "probably saw" the Plan of the Day. He is silent as to whether he recalled his reading of either or both documents at the time of the *voir dire*. See *United States* v. *Schuller*, 5 USCMA 101, 105, 17 CMR 101. It is also noted that none of the government's argument reaches the question of the convening authority's disqualification to review the record of trial because of bias.

Neither the issue of command control, nor the other assignments of error, impugn the validity of the accused's plea of guilty to the charge alleging the violation of a Navy regulation. This circumstance, and the fact that the period of confinement has long since expired, make it unnecessary for us to examine each of the assignments of error. In our opinion, the interests of justice in this case can be best advanced by setting aside the larceny findings and reassessing the sentence.

The findings of guilty of Charge I and its specification are set aside, and the charge is ordered dismissed. The record of the trial is returned to the

Judge Advocate General of the Navy for submission to the board of review to reassess the sentence on the basis of Charge II and its specification, to which the accused pleaded guilty, and in light of the assignment of error dealing with the effect of the disclosure of uncharged misconduct. See *United States* v. *Rodriguez,* 17 USCMA 54, 37 CMR 318.

Judges FERGUSON and KILDAY concur.

DISCUSSION AND SELF-QUIZ

1. You are the legal officer on board your ship. Seaman Brown, a member of "B" Division has assaulted his leading petty officer, who was not in the execution of his office at the time. After a study of the preliminary inquiry, the commanding officer has decided to refer the case to a special court-martial but has decided that a BCD will not be included as part of the maximum authorized punishment. He requests that you submit a proposed list of members and counsel for the court-martial.

On board your ship is a Lieutenant Jones who, while he is not a member of a bar, has received a B.A. degree from New York University and a law degree from Johns Hopkins Law School. He is not a member of the JAG Corps as he has not passed his bar examination. You would like to recommend Lieutenant Jones, who is experienced in trial work and enthusiastic, to be appointed trial counsel. As defense counsel, you would like to recommend appointment of Ensign Smith, a high school graduate with no higher education, relatively little legal experience, and an aversion to court work. Would you violate Article 27(c) (2) of the Code or paragraph 6c of the MCM?

2. You are the legal officer of the USS *Sled* (DD–109). Your commanding officer desires to excuse Ensign John Jones, SC, USN, from sitting as a member of a court-martial. Ensign Jones is the supply officer on board the ship and is responsible for supervising the on-loading of foodstuffs. The court-martial *has assembled* for the special court-martial. Paragraph 37c(2) states

> . . . if the convening authority excuse a member or counsel from attendance at future session of a general or special court-martial in a particular case or series of cases, but does not desire to relieve him permanently as a member or counsel he may do this by oral order, message or signal and need not confirm the action by a written order.

What would you advise your commanding officer? See paragraph 37 MCM.

3. Seaman Richard Roe, U.S. Navy, attached to your ship located in Long Beach, California. On 20 June 19— he and a friend departed on authorized liberty. Roe changed into civilian clothes in a local fleet club. After a few beers in the bar of a hotel, Roe entered the residential part of the hotel. He then broke into the room of a young girl, and assaulted and attempted to rape her. He was apprehended by a hotel security officer who turned him over to the Long Beach police. The police have turned the accused over to military authorities

You are the legal officer on board your ship. The commanding officer would like to forward this case to an Article 32 investigation which would recommend whether or not to refer the case to a general court-martial. The charges would be attempted rape in violation of Article 80, housebreaking in violation of Article 130, and assault with intent to rape in violation of Article 134 of the Code. In such a case, would the military have jurisdiction to try the accused for this offense? Advise your commanding officer. (See paragraph 802, *Military Law.*)

4. John Jones, a seaman attached to your command, has just returned from the second of two periods of unauthorized absence. The first absence was for a period of ten days and the latter for a period of five days.

a. What is the maximum punishment that may be adjudged if Jones's case is referred to a special court-martial? See Chapter XXV of the MCM.

b. Will this case require a military judge if referred to a special court-martial?

c. Will the accused require a certified military lawyer if the case is referred to a special court?

5. Applying the principles in the *O'Callahan* v. *Parker* case discussed in paragraph 802, would the military have jurisdiction in the following cases?

a. An accused is charged with the following crimes:

1. Importing, concealing, and transporting marijuana into the United States from Mexico;

2. Wrongful possession of marijuana on board a military base;

3. Wrongful use of marijuana off-base;

4. Wrongful use of marijuana on a military base.

b. An accused steals an auto from an off-base automobile parking lot. He drives the stolen vehicle for about one day and then parks it on a military base.

c. An accused steals a truck. The truck is owned by a civilian. The only service connection is that the theft occurs on a military base.

d. An accused cashes two bad checks at a military exchange and one bad check at a local civilian grocery store off the base.

e. An accused is in an auto accident. He is taken to a military hospital. There it is discovered he possesses a concealed weapon. This violates both state and military law.

Note

The Court of Military Appeals has also determined:

1. Military authorities have jurisdiction over offenses committed off-base against active duty servicemen. The opposite would apply when the victim is a retired serviceman.

2. Military authorities have jurisdiction over *minor* offenses committed off-base, such as, drunk and disorderly conduct in uniform in a public place. The court reasoned that the *O'Callahan* case was designed to ensure the right to trial by jury and indictment by grand jury and that since a civilian tried for a petty offense would be entitled to neither of these rights, *O'Callahan* was not applicable.

3. Military authorities have jurisdiction as to off-base offenses where a military uniform or military status facilitates commission of the crime. For example, the off-base writing of a forged check was considered service connected where its cashing was facilitated by reliance on the accused's military status. The accused's endorsement on the back of the check included his military address.

4. The Court of Military Appeals stated that military authorities have jurisdiction for off-base offenses involving the possession and transfer of marijuana in Germany. The court held that the *O'Callahan* case was not applicable because the offenses were committed in a foreign country and the offenses were "not contrary to American civil penal statutes having effect in Germany."

CHAPTER **IX**

The Trial and
Defense Counsel

A *counsel* is a person who represents one of the sides in our adversary system of courts-martial. The *trial counsel* prosecutes the case in the name of the government. The *defense counsel* defends the accused. Each defense counsel may have one or more assistants; however, the number of assistant trial counsel should not be greater than the number of assistant defense counsel. In addition to his detailed defense counsel, the accused is entitled to be represented by civilian counsel of his own choice (at his own expense) or by military counsel of his own selection if reasonably available.

The legal qualifications that are required of the defense counsel will vary with the type of court that will try the accused, and, in the case of a special court-martial, the maximum punishment that may be awarded.

The same standards of performance, conduct, and ethics that apply to a certified military lawyer are required of a detailed nonlawyer counsel. This chapter will discuss these standards as they relate to a special court-martial.

A junior officer may be detailed to act as either a trial or defense counsel with either a military judge or a president without a military judge presiding.

901 Trial Counsel's Ethics and Conduct

The trial counsel and defense counsel have different and unique responsibilities. These responsibilities govern their relationship with each other. They are both officers of the court in the broadest sense. However, the duty of the defense counsel is to his client and his client's best inter-

ests are paramount. For example, if the trial counsel omits to present
evidence of previous convictions that could be considered by the court in
aggravation of the offense, it is not the responsibility of the defense coun
sel to remind the trial counsel of this matter. An analysis of such an
event from the *accused's* point of view should suffice to explain why the
defense counsel must be a partisan advocate.

However, the trial counsel's primary duty is *not* to convict. It is to
see that justice is done. In *United States* v. *Valencia,* 1 USCMA 415, 4
CMR 7 (1952), the Court of Military Appeals stated that:

> . . . we have no desire to quell the natural desire of counsel to
> win a case with which he is associated. However, in the case of
> the trial counsel, this quite commendable zeal must be tempered
> with a realization of his responsibility for insuring a fair and
> impartial trial, conducted in accordance with proper legal
> procedures.

The Supreme Court of the United States stated as regards the
prosecutor:

> He may prosecute with earnestness and vigor, indeed, he
> should do so. But while he may strike hard blows, he is not at
> liberty to strike foul ones. It is as much his duty to refrain from
> improper methods calculated to produce a wrongful conviction
> as it is to use every legitimate means to bring about a just one.

For example, the trial counsel cannot:

1. Comment on the failure of the accused to testify as to his guilt
or innocence;

2. State as fact in argument matters as to which there has been no
evidence;

3. Argue that he hasn't presented all of the accused's misdeeds to
the court;

4. Imply that his views are those of the convening authority with
respect to an appropriate sentence;

5. Make references to the fact that the Table of Maximum Punishments provides for a maximum punishment for the offense that is beyond
the jurisdictional limitations of the court.

902 Defense Counsel's Ethics and Conduct

The circumstance which most often confronts the legally untrained
officer is a request for his services as defense counsel from a man in his
own division who has confidence in the fairness and loyalty of his division officer. This is natural and proper, and most certainly is not to be

discouraged, since "loyalty up and loyalty down" is a traditional service relationship for which there is no adequate substitute.

The officer, when confronted with such a request, usually has many misgivings and doubts as to his ability and the propriety of his under-taking the defense.

Initially, if the officer has any personal motives or other considerations which might prevent his giving his best efforts in the case, he should so inform the client and immediately refuse to participate.

This does not mean, however, that he should withdraw solely because he believes that his client is guilty.

A novice in military law often poses to himself a hypothetical case such as the following: "The investigation indicates that he is guilty, and I, myself, believe he is guilty. How then, can I, in good conscience, defend this man?"

More often than not, this moral dilemma is rendered more perplexing by an admission of guilt made by accused to his counsel or even by a written confession of the accused.

There need be no problem or question of conscience here for the young officer, for his duty is plain, since the MCM specifically states that it is the duty of the defense counsel "to undertake the defense regardless of his personal opinion as to the guilt of the accused." This duty to de-fend is unchanged by either the source or certainty of counsel's belief in the guilt of the accused.

At the very base of American criminal law, both civil and military, lies the presumption that every accused person is innocent until his or her guilt is proved beyond a reasonable doubt in court, and it is the legal and moral right of the accused to enter a plea of not guilty, even when guilty. This is so because his plea of not guilty amounts to nothing more than an exercise of his right to cast upon the prosecution the burden of proving his guilt. Of course, the defense counsel cannot permit the accused to testify that he is innocent if counsel *knows* that the accused is not telling the truth.

If an accused has a moral right to plead not guilty when he knows himself guilty, then it logically follows that the defense counsel has not only a moral right, but a moral duty, to defend the accused, regardless of his own belief or disbelief in the accused's guilt.

It is not within the province of the defense counsel to judge the guilt or innocence of his client. That is the duty of the court-martial alone.

The reason for this is that if the government is permitted to short cut the requirements of the law in the case of a guilty man, the same may happen to a man who is innocent. Therefore, the law requires that the trial counsel prove every case referred to him for trial.

The defending officer's duty requires him faithfully to perform the

duties of a defense counsel and he takes an oath to this effect in cour
This sometimes poses a highly practical problem to the officer. On th
one hand, he is primarily an officer, steeped in the traditions and nee
of discipline, and is appreciative of the effect on the ship's personnel (
seeing an "obviously guilty" person acquitted by the proceedings of
court-martial. On the other hand, the officer has taken a basic oath 1
support and defend the Constitution, and subsequent oath to perfor
the duties of defense counsel.

In addition, the officer often is aware of a defense or knows that the
will be certain fatal technicalities involved. Should he assist the pros
cution? It is the duty of the defense counsel to make the case of his clie
his own, and although he may not indulge in trickery or fraud, it is ne
his province to assist in the proof of his client's guilt. He is, within ho
esty's limits, his client's "alter ego." He has the ethical duty to prese
all claims or defenses of his client unless he knows them to be false. Th
defense counsel must take every advantage that the law provides to pr
tect his client.

That is why it is so important for the naval officer acting as defens
counsel to think, and think carefully, in all his words and actions invol
ing his client.

The conscientious officer may well take comfort in the maxim of a
democratic societies, that it is far better for the morale of a comman
that a guilty individual go unpunished than to convict an innocent ma
Experienced defense counsel generally take this view.

It is the duty of the defense counsel to guard the interests of th
accused by all honorable and legitimate means known to the law and t
represent him with undivided fidelity. Nor do the defense counsel
duties end with the findings. His fidelity to the accused must extend int
the hearing before the court as to the sentence to be awarded (mitiga
tion and extenuation).

In *United States* v. *Huff*, 11 USCMA 397, 29 CMR 213 (1960), th
accused was convicted of desertion for a period of approximately 1
months following his plea of guilty. The defense counsel in his argumer
on the sentence emphasized the fact that his client had once held a highe
rate and showed that the accused's economic position was enhanced du
ing his absence by civilian employment. He did not mention the rea
reason for the accused's absence—the denial of the accused's request t
re-enlist. The court commented as follows: "As if to add the capstone t
his performance, counsel then in ringing language called for special cor
sideration for his client because of his 'high standing in the militar
community' attained by virtue of his status as a noncommissioned officer-
'an office not to be taken lightly, an office of honor that demands respect
It would be impossible to conjure up a less attractive argument for pre

entation to men whose lives are devoted to 'Duty, Honor, Country.' Rather than afford the court a reason for extending clemency, the evidence presented and the argument advanced were calculated to assure imposition of the severest of penalties. And it took but eleven minutes for this court-martial to deliberate, vote, reduce the sentence to writing, and announce in open court that the maximum penalty had been adjudged." The case was reversed and a retrial ordered.

However, it is not true that the trial counsel is bound to a high standard of ethics and conduct while the defense counsel has no bounds. Paragraph 15 of the Canons of Professional Ethics of the American Bar Association states that it is not true "that it is the duty of the lawyer to do what ever may enable him to succeed in winning his client's cause." It states further that the "office of attorney does not permit, much less does it demand of him for any client, violation of law or any manner of fraud or chicane. He must obey his own conscience and not that of his client."

903 Trial Counsel's Preparation

Thorough preparation is essential to a proper presentation of a court-martial case. It is well recognized that pretrial preparation is 95 percent of a counsel's case and that the other 5 percent may be attributed to his in-court performance.

It is beyond the scope of this book to discuss in detail all of the duties and problems that may face a trial counsel in any particular case. However, it is possible to discuss some of those situations that are most apt to arise in the preparation of a court-martial case.

The following material for both the trial and defense counsel preparation is based upon the excellent manuscript of Chapter 3 of the *Military Justice Handbook: The Trial and Defense Counsel* (DA Pam 27–10) of 1 August 1969. It has been edited to apply to the naval service.

1. *Examination of the Charge Sheet.* After the trial counsel has received the charge sheet and allied papers, he should check the charges and allied papers to assure that the file is complete. He must ascertain from the endorsement on the charge sheet and the order convening the court whether the charges are in the hands of the trial counsel of the proper court. By examining the charges and allied papers he may be able to determine whether any member of the prosecution or defense is disqualified because of prior participation in the same case or otherwise. If so, the disqualified counsel may not act in the case, and the matter should be reported to the command judge advocate or legal officer.

The trial counsel then should make certain that the data on the charge sheet are free from errors of substance or form. He should compare the name and description of the accused in each specification with the corresponding data on page one of the charge sheet and determine whether the charges and specifications set out on the charge sheet are in accord with the requirements of Appendix 6c of the MCM.

Trial counsel should note any discrepancies in the orders convening the court. He should examine the convening order, the charge sheet, and the accompanying papers to determine whether the military judge (if detailed) and counsel for the prosecution and the defense have the necessary legal qualifications.

If the trial counsel discovers a minor error in the charge sheet, for example, a misspelled word, a transposition of words, or an error of similar nature, he should correct it and initial the charge sheet adjacent to the correction. Thus, if he finds that the accused is described by one name on page one of the charge sheet and by another name in the specification, the trial counsel should reconcile and correct this discrepancy after conducting the necessary inquiry. Errors of a substantial nature in the charges and specifications, in the orders convening the court, or in the accompanying papers should be reported immediately to the command judge advocate or legal officer of the convening authority. For example, a specification which varies materially from the approved form in Appendix 6 of the MCM should be called to the attention of the above authorities immediately, so that the specification may be amended, if necessary, and required additional pretrial procedures conducted.

The trial counsel should then examine the record of previous convictions for completeness, admissibility, and freedom from errors of form and substance.

2. *Service of Charges.* After insuring that the charge sheet is in proper form, the trial counsel will cause a copy of it to be served on the accused. Prompt service of the charges is important since the accused must be given a reasonable period of time in which to prepare his defense. Service of charges is accomplished by the trial counsel or one of his assistants personally delivering a copy of the charge sheet to the accused and reading the charges and specifications to him. Normally this should be accomplished in the presence of the defense counsel. If this cannot be done, the trial counsel should advise the accused of the name of the detailed defense counsel and inform the accused that the defense counsel will communicate with him in the near future concerning the case. Trial counsel then completes and signs the statement of service on page three of the original and all copies of the charge sheet. Under no circumstances should trial counsel interrogate or otherwise discuss any matters concerning the facts of the case with the accused.

After a copy of the charge sheet has been served on the accused, the detailed defense counsel, if he was not present, should be notified that charges have been served on the accused and he should be furnished with copies of the charge sheet and all accompanying papers. The date of service begins the running of the three-day period for special courts-martial within which the accused may not be brought to trial if he objects.

After the trial counsel has served the charges on the accused, neither the trial counsel nor any other government official or agent will thereafter communicate with the accused concerning the case. All subsequent communications with the accused will be made through and with any counsel the accused may have.

The trial counsel should advise the defense of the probable witnesses to be called by the prosecution. The failure to do so may be a ground for a continuance (i.e., a request for a delay).

3. *Initial Preparation.* After serving the charges on the accused, the trial counsel should determine from defense counsel whether the data shown on the first page of the charge sheet are correct. He should then study the charges and specifications contained in the charge sheet and become familiar with the basic elements of proof required for each offense charged. In most cases, this information can be found under the discussion of the punitive articles in Chapter XXVIII of the MCM. He then is ready to plan the prosecution's case: that is, he can determine exactly how he is going to prove that the accused committed each of the offenses charged. The trial counsel should indicate by appropriate notation in his trial notes under each element of the offense the evidence which he intends to introduce in support of that element. Except to the extent that this burden may be relieved by a plea of guilty, the burden is on the trial counsel to present competent evidence showing beyond a reasonable doubt that:

    a. The offense was committed;

    b. The accused committed it;

    c. The accused had the requisite criminal intent.

Trial counsel must be prepared to establish jurisdiction over the offense, in a doubtful case, even though no attack on such jurisdiction is reasonably expected. (See Chapter VIII, *Military Law.*) Likewise, the trial counsel must be prepared to present evidence establishing the chronology of events from the date the charges were preferred or the date the accused was placed in pretrial restraint of any kind, whichever is earlier, to the date of the Article 39(a) session or trial, if it appears that a speedy trial issue will be raised. The prosecution has the burden of accounting for the time it took to bring the accused to trial. (See paragraph 208, *Military Law.*)

Counsel should undertake the trial of a case only after proper preparation and knowledge of the facts and law applicable to the case. This encompasses among other things a plan for thorough presentation of the facts. The proper preparation for the presentation of the facts includes a detailed outlining of the essential elements of each offense charged; a careful investigation of the facts surrounding each offense charged to include interviewing all available witnesses for the prosecution and the defense; and analyzing and anticipating the opposition case.

To be prepared on the law of the case requires:

a. Consulting any discussion of the offenses alleged which may be found in the MCM, making sure that later case law has not overruled or modified such discussion, or consulting other appropriate authorities in the event the offense is not one discussed in the MCM;

b. Becoming familiar with the elements of proof of each offense alleged and lesser included offenses;

c. Anticipating the defenses of intoxication, lack of intent, mistake, unlawful search and seizure, and knowing the legal requirements thereof;

d. Knowing the rules of evidence and the relevant case law pertaining to points of evidence which may be raised. See Chapter XI, *Military Law,* and Chapter XXVII, MCM. It is recommended that a nonlawyer trial counsel seek advice from a JAG lawyer whenever he is unsure of the law.

It is the responsibility of trial counsel to anticipate and be fully prepared to meet the objections which the defense might raise by motions to dismiss or motions for appropriate relief. See Chapter XII, *Military Law.* He must be prepared to introduce pertinent evidence and to present arguments.

4. *Withdrawal of Charges.* When the trial counsel is preparing a case for trial, he may discover information that causes him to conclude that trial of the case is inadvisable. Such information may have been unknown to the convening authority at the time he referred the case for trial and, therefore, should be brought to his attention with appropriate recommendations. Some matters which affect the desirability of proceeding with the trial of a case are insanity of the accused at the time of the offense, at the time of the investigation, or at the time the case is ready to be tried; the disappearance or nonavailability of a material witness or his repudiation of previous statements concerning the offense; and the discovery of evidence of an offense not charged.

Other matters which may not preclude trial but should be reported to the convening authority or his representative include discovery of substantial evidence favorable to the accused; and a substantial variance between the allegations in the specifications and the proof of such allegations. As an example of the latter, assume that the accused is charged with wrongful appropriation of nine items. The available evidence supports the wrongful taking of only four of the nine items. The trial counsel should report this fact to the convening authority so that the specifications may be amended to conform to the expected proof.

When matters such as those discussed above are referred to the convening authority, the trial counsel may make such recommendations as he deems proper. Thus, when the circumstances require it, he should not hesitate to recommend that all or certain charges or specifications be withdrawn, dismissed, or amended. Only the convening authority can withdraw a charge or specification from trial. When withdrawal of a specification is ordered before trial, the trial counsel will cross out and initial the withdrawn specification on the charge sheet, will renumber the remaining charges and specifications as appropriate and will have the copies of the charges and specifications retyped for presentation to the court at trial.

5. *Administrative Duties.* The trial counsel is responsible for the physical arrangements for the trial. It is his duty to locate an appropriate and convenient place to be used as a courtroom. He should see that suitable furniture is provided, as well as other items, such as stationery and pencils. Prior to the opening of court, he should prepare a typewritten copy of the charges and specifications on which the accused will be arraigned for each member of the court, the military judge (if detailed), and the accused.

Trial counsel should furnish the military judge with a copy of the charges and specifications as soon as copies are made. This will enable the military judge to analyze the charges and specifications in advance of trial and to prepare tentative instructions. This practice should not be followed in special courts-martial without a military judge, as the president of the court should not be given a copy of the charges and specifications prior to arraignment.

In trials by special court-martial without a military judge, the trial counsel must insure that no member of the court except the president has access to legal authorities during open sessions of the court.

The trial counsel should coordinate with the military judge, or the president of a special court-martial without a military judge, the time and place of trial. He should ascertain from the president of the court the uniform to be worn at all sessions with members. A court-martial should not meet at unusual hours except under extraordinary circumstances. As a practical matter, the trial counsel must coordinate the desires of the defense counsel, the military judge (if detailed), and the president in fixing a trial date which will be acceptable, feasible, and otherwise agreeable. While both sides must be allowed a reasonable time to prepare for trial, it usually is possible to arrange a date for trial even though either or both counsel have not fully prepared their cases if it appears that such preparation will be completed before the date set. If either side will require an unusually long period of time to prepare for trial, the trial counsel should report the matter to the convening authority, setting forth the reasons for the delay. The defense counsel may request a postponement of the time for assembly of the court in order to secure the attendance of a witness, to take depositions, or for any other proper reason. The trial counsel should require that each request on accused's behalf for any delay or continuance be in writing and attached to the record of trial so that accused cannot thereafter claim that he was prejudiced by the delay or that the trial counsel was negligent in failing to bring the case to trial promptly. When the date of trial is finally agreed upon, the trial counsel must notify the members of the court and the other parties to the trial of the time and place of trial and the uniform to be worn. The notice may be written or oral, depending upon the circumstances.

The trial counsel should make arrangements to insure the presence of the accused at any Article 39(a) session and the trial. If the accused is not in confinement, notice to his commanding officer is all that is necessary; however, if the accused is in confinement, the officer in charge of the confinement facility must be notified. The trial counsel should inform the officer who is responsible for the attendance of the accused of the uniform which has been prescribed for the court. An accused will wear the insignia of his rate and should wear any decorations, ribbons, or emblems to which he is entitled.

Prior to the assembly of the court for the trial of a particular case, the trial counsel should insure that all members not properly excused by the convening authority will be present so that the court will not be reduced below a quorum in the event some of the members are excused by challenge. If excusals will affect the legal constitution of the court, the trial counsel will make an immediate report of such absences to the convening authority.

In the event a member of the court asks the trial counsel's permission to be excused from attendance at a particular trial, the trial counsel should advise the member that his request to be excused from attendance must be addressed to the convening authority. The trial counsel has no authority to excuse a member from attendance and such authority may not be delegated to him by the convening authority. In some cases, the trial counsel and the defense counsel can reach an agreement, prior to the convening of the court, that meritorious grounds exist for challenging a particular member of the court for cause. Where such is the case, the trial counsel can save considerable trial time by recommending to the convening authority that the questioned member be excused from attendance at the trial.

The trial counsel supervises the keeping of the record of the proceedings on behalf of the court. In special courts-martial in which a bad conduct discharge is adjudged, the record must contain a verbatim transcript of all proceedings held in open session and all sessions and hearings held by the military judge out of the presence of the members. The convening order should not contain any reference to a reporter. As a practical matter, a reporter is present in every special court-martial case. The trial counsel is responsible for obtaining him.

6. *Witnesses.* Each party to a trial has the same basic right to obtain witnesses and other evidence. The trial counsel has the duty to insure the presence of all witnesses who are necessary to a determination of the issues involved in the case. Thus, the trial counsel has the power to compel witnesses to appear and testify before courts-martial including any Article 39(a) sessions by use of subpoenas. Before subpoenaing a witness who is not readily available, the trial counsel should determine whether the expected testimony of the witness can be presented by a stipulation or deposition. Generally speaking, the testimony of a witness who appears in person before a court is more effective than testimony presented by deposition or by stipulation because it usually makes a stronger impression on the court members.

When the trial counsel first receives the charges in a case, he should check the file to determine what witnesses—defense and prosecution— probably will be needed at the trial. He should communicate with these witnesses, by telephone if possible, and advise them of the probable date of the Article 39(a) session, if one is to be held, and the trial. He should inform them that their presence as witnesses probably will be required. At the same time, the trial counsel should submit the same information in writing to the commanding officer of any military witness with the request that he notify trial counsel if it becomes necessary for the prospective witness to leave the area prior to the Article 39(a) session or trial date. Where travel expense is involved, the commanding officer of the witness should be requested to have travel orders issued containing a fund citation supplied by the command of the convening authority. Additionally, trial counsel should notify defense counsel of the probable witnesses. If the trial counsel follows this procedure, he will avoid unnecessary and embarrassing delays which may result when a witness goes on leave or is transferred before the case can be brought to trial.

It is the duty of the trial counsel to take timely and appropriate action to secure the attendance of all necessary witnesses requested by the defense. In order to perform this duty and to avoid the possibility of error, trial counsel should, if possible, honor every reasonable request from the defense. If there is a disagreement between the trial counsel and the defense counsel as to whether the testimony of the requested witness will be necessary, the matter should be referred for decision to the convening authority or to the court, depending upon whether the question is raised prior to or during the trial. In such cases, the defense counsel must submit to the convening authority or the court, as appropriate, a written request for the attendance of the witness, together with a signed statement containing (1) a summary of the testimony expected from the witness, (2) the reasons why the personal appearance of the witness is necessary, and (3) any additional matters showing that the expected testimony is necessary to the ends of justice. Where a requested defense witness is an essential witness, and within the reach of process, his presence at the trial may not be denied to the accused on the basis that the trial counsel is willing to stipulate his testimony or to take his deposition. Every effort should be made to assist. This is also true of witnesses requested by the accused in extenuation and mitigation.

7. *Final Review of the Case.* When the trial counsel has carefully investigated the facts surrounding every offense charged, has interviewed all available witnesses both for the prosecution and the defense (other than the accused), has become fully acquainted with the appearance, mannerisms, intelligence, and attitude of each witness, has become familiar with the scene of the crime, if possible, and has examined thoroughly the documentary and other evidence, he is ready to consider the best method of placing it before the court. He again should carefully review the essential elements of each offense charged and determine what testimony or other evidence will prove each element. This review will enable him to prepare trial notes for use at the trial.

8. *Trial Notes.* Trial notes, which are sometimes referred to as a "trial brief" or a "trial memorandum," are nothing more than an outline of the plan to be followed by the trial counsel in presenting his case to the court. As a minimum, the trial notes should include a list of the elements of each offense charged, an outline of the evidence which will be presented to prove these elements, and a concise statement of the law applicable to both of these matters. Properly prepared trial notes will enable the trial counsel to present his case in a clear and logical manner without inadvertent omissions of evidence pertaining to material issues in the case.

In preparing for trial the trial counsel should always utilize a checklist. Appendix 19 is such an optional checklist. It is based upon the *Military Justice Handbook: The Trial and Defense Counsel* (cited previously). It has been edited in order to be applicable to the naval service.

Even though a trial counsel prepares his case thoroughly, it will all be for naught if, in the heat of passion, or in the desire to "win his case," he forgets, or does not realize, that he is subject to certain rules of conduct and ethics that apply both within and without the courtroom.

904 Defense Counsel's Preparation

Although the burden of proof is upon the government to prove the accused guilty beyond a reasonable doubt, pretrial preparation is just as essential to the defense counsel as it is to the trial counsel (and sometimes more so). Appendix 20 contains a complete checklist of duties of the defense counsel.

1. *Initial Interview.* Upon receipt of notice (usually accompanied by copies of all papers allied to the charges) that he has been detailed to represent an accused, the defense counsel will inform the accused that he has been detailed to defend him at the trial and will explain his general duties.

If the defense counsel has any personal interest, bias, or prejudice concerning the accused or his case, he should inform the accused, who may then wish to obtain other counsel. When the defense counsel lacks the requisite legal qualifications, has previously acted for the prosecution in the same case, or when his personal interest, bias, or prejudice is so strong as to affect his ability to defend the accused in a conscientious, capable, and fair manner, he must ask the convening authority to relieve him from duty as defense counsel in that case. He should not, however, request relief for the sole reason that he believes the accused to be guilty or doesn't wish to be associated with the type of case being tried.

The defense counsel must advise the accused of any previous connection with the case or a related case and give the accused the choice either of continuing the relationship with him or of securing other counsel. If the defense counsel has previously acted for the prosecution, however, he may not act for the defense, even though the accused expresses a desire for his services. If the defense counsel is an accuser or has acted as a court member, military judge, or investigating officer in the case, he may serve as counsel for the accused only if the latter expressly requests his services.

The accused must be detailed a certified military lawyer in all special courts-martial in which a bad conduct discharge may be imposed. He must be afforded the opportunity to be represented by such counsel in all special courts-martial. If a special court-martial's detailed defense counsel is not a certified military lawyer, he must inform the accused of his right to request legally qualified counsel to represent him.

Additionally, in all cases, the defense counsel will advise the accused of his right to be defended by individual counsel (i.e., counsel of his own selection) either civilian at his own expense, or military if reasonably available, in addition to detailed defense counsel. If the accused indicates that he desires to accept the services of the detailed defense counsel, the latter will immediately commence the preparation of the case for trial. In those cases in which the accused desires individual civilian or military counsel, the detailed defense counsel will aid the accused in obtaining such counsel. If the accused requests civilian counsel, the detailed defense counsel must advise the accused that such counsel cannot be retained at government expense. If the accused desires individual military counsel to represent him at the trial, the detailed counsel will notify the convening authority. Unless disqualified, the detailed defense counsel will continue to represent the accused unless the accused desires otherwise. If the accused obtains individual counsel, detailed defense counsel will act as associate counsel if the accused so desires.

In all cases the detailed defense counsel will carefully advise the accused of his right to counsel.

There are no hard and fast rules determining whether or not the special court-martial accused should request a lawyer. There are cases where the most able certified military lawyer could do little, if anything, to help. In such cases—unauthorized absence is an example—the non-lawyer detailed counsel or an individual counsel from the accused's command known to the court members could be of greater benefit to the accused. There is something to be said for not making a "federal case" out of a reasonably small matter, particularly where conviction appears certain and punishment is not likely to include confinement. These decisions must be made on a case by case basis. (See paragraphs 804 and 805 of *Military Law*.)

The accused should be informed of the confidential relationship that exists between himself and the defense counsel—that nothing the accused tells the defense counsel relating to the case will be divulged, no matter how incriminating it may be. Knowing of this confidential relationship, the accused can feel free to make a complete disclosure of all of the facts in the case as far as they are known to him.

The accused should be advised not to talk to anyone about the facts of the alleged offense or offenses except in the presence of and on advice of his defense counsel.

2. *Initial Preparation.* Before the case is discussed further with the accused, the defense counsel should analyze carefully the charges and specifications, the allied papers, and the report of the pretrial investigation or preliminary inquiry. It is essential that the defense counsel consider the facts of the case, the offenses, and the various elements of proof of those offenses and ascertain whether any defenses may be available to the accused. For discussions of various offenses under the Uniform Code of Military Justice, see Chapter XXVIII of the MCM and Chapters IV and V of *Military Law*.

When the defense counsel completes his consideration of the foregoing matters, he should endeavor to learn the accused's version of the facts. He should question the accused about the existence of any defense or objection, such as former punishment, lack of jurisdiction, alibi, and other like matters which might be asserted. See Chapters XII and XXIX of the MCM and Chapters IV and V of *Military Law*. As the accused tells his story of the facts surrounding the offense, complete notes should be taken. If the accused's recital is unbelievable, improbable, or indicates that he is withholding portions of the story, the defense counsel may inform the accused that proper advice can be given and adequate preparation for the trial can be made *only* if the accused makes a full and complete disclosure of all facts. Counsel may also advise the accused of his opinion of the effect on the court should the accused's testimony be patently unbelievable, improbable, or evasive.

The accused should then be informed of the witnesses, both for and against him, as shown on page one of the charge sheet (Appendix 6) together with the names of any other witnesses who are mentioned in the allied papers. The statements of these witnesses should be carefully reviewed with the accused, and his comments about the statement of each witness should be noted. The defense counsel should obtain from the accused the names and addresses of any other witnesses who may be helpful in the presentation of his case and any information concerning the existence and location of any pertinent documentary or real evidence which should be considered for use at the trial.

To fully develop his case, it is imperative that counsel conduct a thorough examination of *all* prospective witnesses. The defense counsel must know the limitations of his witnesses, the possible personal interest of each witness in the case, and the nature of previous associations which any witness may have had with the accused or with an alleged victim of the accused's misconduct. Witnesses should be questioned concerning the possibility of any previously undisclosed witnesses.

3. *Advising the Accused of His Rights Under the Code.* An accused has certain fundamental rights under the Code. It is the duty of the defense counsel to explain each of these rights to the accused at the appropriate time and to advise him with respect to the exercise of his rights. Some of these rights are:

a. *Right to Trial by Military Judge Alone.* Before a court-martial to which a military judge has been detailed is assembled, the accused may request in writing that his case be decided by the military judge alone. Before making such a request, the accused is entitled to know the identity of the military judge. In explaining this right, counsel should advise the accused that the request is subject to approval by the military judge and may be made prior to trial, at an Article 39(a) session, or after the court has been called to order but prior to assembly.

b. *Right to Have Enlisted Persons on the Court.* If accused is an enlisted person, he should be advised of his right to request the presence of enlisted personnel on the court convened to try the charges against him. Whether an accused should be advised by his defense counsel to request enlisted members on the court will depend upon an appraisal of all the facts and circumstances bearing on this question. If the accused decides that he wants enlisted persons on the court, a written request signed by him should be forwarded by the defense counsel, through the trial counsel, to the convening authority.

c. *Right to Challenge.* The accused has the right to challenge the military judge and each member of the court for cause on any of the applicable grounds enumerated in paragraph 62*f* of the MCM. The accused also has the right to exercise one peremptory challenge against any member of the court, but the military judge shall not be challenged except for cause. (See paragraphs 1004 and 1210 of *Military Law.*)

The defense counsel should ask the accused to examine the orders convening the court to ascertain whether he knows of any facts which may constitute a ground of challenge for cause against any of the persons listed. Interrogation of the accused by the defense counsel, concerning any objection the accused may have to each of the persons listed, may bring out facts constituting proper grounds of challenge for cause. When a proper ground exists, it should be noted by the defense counsel so that it will not be overlooked at the trial. If the accused objects to a member as to whom no ground for challenge exists, that member ordinarily should be challenged peremptorily. In this respect, however, the defense counsel should bear in mind that a challenge for cause may not be sustained by the court, and it may be advisable to use the peremptory challenge against a member who has been unsuccessfully challenged for cause. Although all challenges ordinarily should be made at an Article 39(a) session or immediately prior to arraignment, challenges for cause may be made at any stage of the proceedings if the ground for such challenge was previously unknown to the defense.

d. *Right to Assert Defenses.* The defense counsel should explain to the accused his right to assert any proper defense or objection, such as the statute of limitations, in an appropriate case.

e. *Pleas and Pretrial Agreements.* The accused has the absolute right to plead not guilty and thus require the prosecution to prove his guilt beyond a reasonable doubt. Before trial, however, counsel should consider all of the facts and circumstances surrounding the case to determine whether it is appropriate and desirable for the accused to enter a plea of guilty. If the case against the accused is clear, a plea of guilty coupled with evidence in extenuation and mitigation and/or with a pretrial agreement with the convening authority, may serve the best interests of the accused. The plea of guilty may encourage the court to adjudge a lighter sentence and, in the absence of a pretrial agreement with the convening authority, influence the latter to reduce the sentence or to suspend the execution of all or part of it.

Pretrial agreements with the convening authority are of various types, the more common of which are the following: (1) where it is agreed that the offense charged will be reduced to a lesser offense to which the accused will plead guilty and then will submit to the judgment of the court the question of the appropriate punishment; (2) where it is agreed that if the accused pleads guilty and is sentenced by the court, the convening authority will approve a sentence not in excess of that agreed upon by the parties concerned; and (3) where it is agreed that if the accused pleads guilty to certain specifications, the convening authority will withdraw the remaining specifications. A pretrial agreement has the effect of obviating the necessity on the part of the government of introducing evidence on the issue of guilt or innocence and of permitting the accused to know in advance of trial one or more of the following: (1) that he will be found guilty of an offense of a less serious nature than that initially charged; (2) the maximum punishment that will be approved by the convening authority for the offense to which the accused agrees to plead guilty; (3) that he will be found guilty of fewer offenses than originally charged. Thus, in an appropriate case, a pretrial agreement may benefit the accused by resulting in punishment less than that which might be adjudged in the event of trial on a plea of not guilty. The accused should be advised that while the convening authority may be willing to make such an agreement in a proper case, the offer to enter such an agreement must be initiated by the accused and his counsel.

After he has explained to the accused the meaning and effect of a plea of guilty and has advised him with respect to pretrial agreements, the defense counsel may make such recommendations to the accused as appear to be reasonable and proper in view of all the facts and circumstances surrounding the case. While the defense counsel should not urge the accused to attempt to procure a pretrial agreement or to plead guilty without such an agreement, a full performance by the defense counsel of his duty to safeguard the interests of the accused may, in a particular case, require him to recommend that one or the other of such courses of action be taken. However, in no instance should an accused who indicates that he believes himself innocent of the offenses charged be permitted to enter a plea of guilty thereto. See Section 0114 of the JAG Manual.

f. *Rights of the Accused as a Witness.* Prior to the trial, the defense counsel should advise the accused of his right, in an appropriate instance, to testify for a limited purpose upon certain interlocutory questions, his right (as to each offense charged) to remain silent or to testify under oath in his own behalf, and his right, if he is convicted, to testify and to make an unsworn statement as to matters in extenuation or mitigation prior to being sentenced. Explanations of these rights will be found in Appendix 8b of the MCM. For a discussion of the alternatives available to the accused, see paragraphs 75c, 140a, 148e, and 149b of the MCM and paragraph 1106 of *Military Law*.

If findings of guilty have been reached and formally announced, the defense has the opportunity to present matters in extenuation and mitigation of any offense of which the accused has been found guilty. (See paragraph 1305 of this book for a detailed discussion of extenuating and mitigating circumstances.) In many cases, especially those in which the accused has pleaded guilty, the defense counsel can render his most valuable service to the accused at this stage of the trial. There should never be an occasion, however, for presenting at this time matters which amount to a legal defense for an offense, as such matters should have been presented prior to the findings if the defense counsel has properly discharged his responsibilities to the accused. Matters in extenuation and mitigation may be introduced into evidence in the regular manner or by means of affidavits or other written statements. (See paragraphs 75c, (1), 146b, MCM.) The accused may testify under oath, make an unsworn statement, or do both. The unsworn statement may be made by the accused personally or through his counsel, or it may be presented in part by the accused and in part by his counsel. The statement may be oral, in writing, or both. The prosecution will not be permitted to cross-examine the accused on an unsworn statement, but it may rebut by evidence any assertions of fact contained in the statement. The accused may not file an affidavit executed by himself. See paragraph 75c (2), MCM.

When the accused testifies or makes an unsworn statement in extenuation or mitigation, he does not risk the possibility that he may supply an item of proof missing from the prosecution's case, for his testimony or unsworn statement may not be considered by reviewing authorities in affirming the correctness of the findings of guilty.

The defense counsel should explain to the accused his rights in this respect, and plans should be made for presenting matters in extenuation and mitigation, if any, in the event of a conviction. No matter how diligent the defense counsel has been in protecting the accused's rights prior to findings of guilty, he will have failed to fulfill his duty, not only to the accused but to the court as well, if he does not present all available and admissible matter in mitigation and extenuation. In every case, therefore, the defense counsel should determine whether extenuating and mitigating circumstances exist and, if so, how they may best be presented to the court. After considering the accused's veracity, capabilities, appearance, and attitude, the defense counsel should recommend to the accused whether he should take the witness stand and testify under oath, make an unsworn statement personally or through counsel, or remain silent.

4. *Final Preparations for Trial.* The essential elements of the offenses charged should be studied carefully once more to determine the proof necessary to establish each offense. The defense counsel must determine at this point what his "theory" of defense will be, bearing in mind the right of the accused to make the final decision in this matter. This "theory" will be reflected in his opening statement, his cross-examination of opposing witnesses, his presentation of the defense case, and in his closing argument. It will involve a determination of what defense witnesses are to be called, the order in which they will appear, and the matters about which they should testify. Based on the pretrial interviews, a tentative decision must be made as to which prosecution witness or witnesses will be cross-examined. In addition, the defense counsel should decide tentatively whether any motions are to be made, whether the case is sufficiently complex to warrant an opening statement, and whether a final argument appears to be advisable.

The defense counsel now will be ready to prepare his trial notes. These are nothing more than a simple outline of his plan of procedure. In these notes, the defense counsel should outline in proper sequence those things he will do as the trial progresses, as far as it is possible for him to anticipate them prior to trial. For example, when the defense counsel interviews the witnesses for the prosecution, he will have tentatively concluded which witnesses should be cross-examined and, to some extent at least, will have decided the subject of such cross-examination. Consequently, the trial notes should contain the names of the witnesses, what, in general, their testimony on direct examination will be, and a brief resume of the proposed subject of cross-examination.

5. *Instructions to Accused.* Prior to trial, the accused should be instructed carefully by the defense counsel concerning the manner in which he should conduct himself during the trial. This instruction is particularly important if the accused is to take the stand to testify or to make an unsworn statement. He should be cautioned to exhibit a respectful attitude toward the court and to maintain a military bearing at all times. It is not difficult to visualize the favorable impression this will create in contrast to that made by an accused who presents a sloppy, indifferent, or insolent attitude toward the court and the proceedings.

The defense counsel should assure himself by conferring with the accused, his commanding officer, and/or the confinement officer, if appropriate, that the accused will present a good personal appearance in court. The accused should have a haircut, his shoes should be polished, and his uniform should be pressed. Any decorations or service ribbons which he may have been awarded should be worn at the trial.

If the accused is to testify, he should be instructed carefully about the proper method of answering questions asked by either the defense counsel, the trial counsel, the military judge, or members of the court. He should be cautioned to "think before he speaks." The accused should avoid creating the erroneous impression that he is being prompted by the defense counsel. He is on his own when he is on the witness stand. Care in conducting a pretrial practice cross-examination of the accused will prevent his being surprised by the questions asked him during trial. In addition to the foregoing instructions, the accused should be impressed with the importance of answering only those questions that are put to him. He should neither volunteer information nor give the court the impression that he is trying to avoid giving full and truthful answers to each question.

The defense counsel should advise the accused as to his courtroom behavior. When the court enters and leaves, he should come to attention with his counsel. When he is addressed by the court, he should again rise. He should be respectful and courteous in his response to proper questions asked him.

905   Counsel's Relationship with the Judge, Members, and Opposing Counsel

> Counsel should maintain a courteous and respectful attitude toward the military judge, the members of the court, and opposing counsel, and should treat adverse witnesses and the accused with fairness and due consideration. Personal colloquies between counsel which cause delay or promote unseemly wrangling should be carefully avoided. The conduct of counsel before the court and with each other should be characterized by candor and fairness. Counsel should not knowingly misquote the contents of a paper, the testimony of a witness, the language or argument of opposing counsel, or the language of a decision or a textbook; nor, with knowledge of its invalidity, should counsel cite as authority a decision that has been reversed or an official directive that has been changed or rescinded. (Paragraph 42b, MCM.)

Counsel must scrupulously abstain from all acts, comments, or attitudes calculated to influence the members of the court or the military judge in their favor. For example, flattery or solicitude for their comfort is improper. It is error to discuss the case with a court member before or during the trial, except as military necessity dictates. During argument, neither counsel should refer to individual court members by name.

The trial or defense counsel may be personally acquainted with some or all of the members of the court. Neither counsel may take advantage of this relationship prior to or during the hearing of the case. They must abstain from any remark or mannerism designed to take advantage of such a situation.

On the other hand, loss of temper or threats addressed to the court members are highly improper and may harm the accused's interests. In *United States* v. *DeAngelis,* 3 USCMA 298, 12 CMR 54 (1953), a civilian lawyer stated to the court that if they pronounced judgment on the accused each member would "be held civilly liable." The officer accused was sentenced to dismissal, total forfeitures, confinement at hard labor for five years, and a fine of $10,000. The Court of Military Appeals stated that:

> . . . we cannot ignore such deliberately contemptuous tirades, nor permit a course of conduct designed solely to delay and hinder the completion of trial to pass unnoticed. Our review of the record of trial, consisting of approximately two thousand pages, impels the conclusion that the obstructive and abusive actions of counsel flouted the authority of the law member [military judge], made a mockery of the requirement of decorous behavior, and impeded the expeditious, orderly, and dispassionate conduct of the trial. Although counsel unquestionably has a right to press his arguments vigorously, and explore freely all avenues favorable to his client, there is a limit beyond which he may go without incurring punitive action.

While the court is in session, neither counsel should remove his coat, unless the presiding officer so permits. Counsel should not smoke, assume undignified postures, or otherwise conduct themselves improperly.

In their relationship with each other, paragraph 17 of the Canons of Professional Ethics states:

> Clients, not lawyers, are the litigants. Whatever may be the ill-feeling between clients, it should not be allowed to influence counsel in their conduct and demeanor toward each other . . . all personalities between counsel should be scrupulously avoided. In the trial of a cause it is indecent to allude to the personal history or the personal peculiarities and idiosyncrasies of counsel on the other side.

906   Arguments of Counsel

Counsel are permitted to argue the merits of any motions or objections. They also are permitted to argue on the findings (the guilt or innocence of the accused) and the sentence (following evidence in aggravation, mitigation, or extenuation).

A reasonable latitude is allowed counsel in presenting their arguments. They may make a reasonable comment on the evidence and may draw such inferences from the testimony as will support their theories of the case. The testimony, conduct, motives, and any evidence of bias, prejudice, or malice on the part of witnesses may, so far as disclosed by the evidence, be commented upon. It is improper to state in an argument any matter of fact as to which there has been no admissable evidence presented. However, a counsel may argue as though the testimony of his witnesses conclusively established the facts they related.

907 Summary

Thorough preparation is essential to the proper presentation of a court-martial case. The trial counsel not only has to equip himself for an adversary proceeding, but at the same time must make all preliminary trial arrangements. He must also guard against the commission of prejudicial error that may warrant reversal of the case.

The defense counsel must advise an accused of all the rights guaranteed him under the Code. He must seek to assure the accused a fair and just trial within our military justice system.

Discussion Case

UNITED STATES, Appellee

v.

FREDERICK W. LEWIS, JR., Airman Second Class, U.S. Air Force, Appellant

16 USCMA 145, 36 CMR 301

(1966)

Opinion of the Court

FERGUSON, Judge:

Arraigned and tried before a general court-martial convened at McChord Air Force Base, Washington, the accused was found guilty of four specifications of forgery and three specifications of larceny, in violation of Uniform Code of Military Justice, Articles 123 and 121, 10 USC §§ 923, 921, respectively. He was sentenced to bad-conduct discharge, total forfeitures, confinement at hard labor for two years, and reduction. The Board of review [Court of Military Review] set aside the findings of guilty of one of the forgery counts and one of the larceny counts and ameliorated the adjudged confinement to eighteen months. Otherwise, it affirmed. We granted accused's petition for review on the issues whether the law officer erred in denying a motion for mistrial and whether he should have ordered an out-of-court hearing to consider matters presented concerning a defense motion to dismiss the charges. Both questions revolve around the same unfortunate portion of the trial, and we consider them together.

From the outset of the trial, it became apparent that personal antagonism existed between accused's individual counsel, Colonel J____, a retired Army Judge advocate officer, and trial counsel, Lieutenant Colonel B____, a senior Air Force judge advocate who was also the staff judge advocate of accused's base, albeit not of the officer exercising general court-martial jurisdiction. The matter seems to have arisen from the fact accused was originally arraigned on one of the charges against him in the local civil courts,[1] and was there assigned the defense counsel who also represented him during his court-martial. J____ originally pleaded accused guilty, but represented to the trial judge that, although the latter suspended sentence, the Air Force intended to discharge accused administratively on account of the civil conviction rather than further to prosecute him. After some colloquy, the judge suggested withdrawal of the plea and, with the consent of the prosecutor, dismissal of the charge. This procedure was followed, and accused was returned to his unit.

From the record, it may be fairly said that Lieutenant Colonel B____ became somewhat upset at this turn in events. Accused was placed in pretrial confinement. Over B____'s objections, as staff judge advocate, Colonel J____ secured his release through the

local commander. Charges were preferred and drafted with B____'s assistance. One of B____'s subordinates was appointed pretrial investigating officer. B____ accompanied him in a successful effort to obtain the voluntary appearance of a material witness and gave him advice concerning the conduct of the investigation. When the charges were forwarded with a recommendation for trial by general court-martial, B____ volunteered his services as trial counsel.

Throughout these proceedings, it is clear that ill feelings had continued to grow between B____ and J____, who had remained as accused's counsel in the military prosecution. They came to a head at the trial when defense counsel sought a dismissal of the charges and removal of B____ on the grounds of his personal injection into the case and hostility towards the accused. A sense of charity dictates that we note the antagonism existed between counsel and if directed at all towards accused, such resulted only from the fact that he, incidentally, was J____'s client.

We need not detail the bitter exchanges between these mature members of the bar, whose experience should have taught them better. Many of these took place in the presence of the court, others in brief out-of-court conferences. On one occasion, trial counsel referred, before the court members, to the fact that, had he been biased, "I could easily have added another 20 or 25 years worth of charges to this charge sheet." A motion for mistrial, based on this comment, was overruled. Both counsel testified with respect to their pretrial activities. Accused's previous plea of guilty in the civil courts was paraded before the members. Defense counsel also in-

---

[1] This is the forgery count dismissed by the board of review.

formed them of his unsuccessful attempt to negotiate a plea of guilty with Colonel B_____ as to the charges on which accused was now being tried.

During a recess and in the courtroom, trial counsel allegedly referred to defense counsel as a "two-bit piece of cat meat" who "came out here with a crawling Army negotiation deal and when . . . I would not agree . . . threatened to smear me from one end of the Air Force to the other." The record is unclear as to whether this occurred in the presence of the members of the court. Trial counsel conceded he used "substantially the language that the gentleman charges," but claimed he, at the same time, was called "a damn liar."

In open court and while testifying, trial counsel charged defense counsel with an attempt "to smear me as an individual and the Air Force in general." In turn, he accused Colonel J_____ of unethical and improper pretrial conduct. We must say that defense counsel, not to be outdone, repeatedly made similar allegations concerning the trial counsel.

Additional instances might be cited *ad infinitum*. Suffice it to say the foregoing are a fair sampling of a controversy which occupies almost fifty pages of the transcript. Accused's naive declaration in a post-trial interview that, while he was well satisfied with his attorney, "he thought the defense counsel and trial counsel at times became more concerned with 'hammering' at each other than with his behalf" is a classic understatement of the picture presented to us.

The board of review was likewise concerned by the raging exchanges between counsel and whether the disclosures involved denied the accused a fair trial, but thought any prejudice

therefrom was limited to the charge of forgery involved in the civil court proceedings. It accordingly dismissed this count. We believe it misapprehended the extent and depth of the matter.

An accused has no more basic right than that of a fair trial. *United States v. Shepherd,* 9 USCMA 90, 25 CMR 352. The guarantee of such a hearing is the whole purpose of the Uniform Code. And when unbridled outbursts and exchanges establish a complete lack of judiciousness, they serve "to deprive the court-martial of that judicial caliber demanded by the Code." *United States v. Lynch,* 9 USCMA 523, 526, 26 CMR 303, 306. It is the law officer's duty to prevent such misconduct, see that the trial is conducted in an orderly manner, and that irrelevant and prejudicial matter is kept from the attention of the fact finders. *United States v. Burse,* 16 USCMA 62, 36 CMR 218; *United States v. Lynch,* supra. As was said in *United States v. Jackson,* 3 USCMA 646, 14 CMR 64, at page 652:

". . . The law officer is not a mere figurehead in the courtroom drama. He must direct the trial along paths of recognized procedure in a manner reasonably calculated to bring an end to the hearing without prejudice to either party. . . . A law officer must exercise control. . . ."

Here, the law officer failed to keep counsel within proper limits. He suggested an out-of-court hearing from time to time; he admonished the court to disregard some of the material it heard; but, though it was plainly apparent that both attorneys had far exceeded the bounds of propriety, he did not act positively to end the matter, keep them in proper bounds, or above all, to prevent the court members from hearing a mass of information which could only serve to deprive the accused of a fair hearing. Cf. *United States* v. *Lynch,* supra; *United States* v. *Dicario,* 8 USCMA 353, 24 CMR 163; *United States* v. *Lock,* 13 USCMA 611, 33 CMR 143. Under the circumstances here presented, the like of which we hope not to see again, we believe it an abuse of his discretion to have permitted these matters to be so lengthily aired in open court.

In like manner, neither he nor counsel for either side can escape our censure for permitting certain of the occurrences, which we have particularized above. Thus, counsel, without withdrawing from the case, were permitted to testify at length concerning matters with which the court members had no concern. We have condemned the practice repeatedly. *United States* v. *Stone,* 13 USCMA 52, 32 CMA 52, and cases cited therein. See also Canon 19, Canons of Professional Ethics, American Bar Association. References were made to accused's attempted negotiation of a plea of guilty to the charges for which he was being tried, though our cases make it clear such matters should not be brought to the attention of the fact finders. *United States* v. *Robinson,* 13 USCMA 674, 33 CMR 206; *United States* v. *Butler,* 9 USCMA 618, 26 CMR 398; *United States* v. *Palacios,* 9 USCMA 621, 26 CMR 401. And see *United States* v.

McFarlane, 8 USCMA 96, 23 CMR 320. We have also condemned adduction of evidence of misconduct not charged. *United States* v. *Back,* 13 USCMA 568, 33 CMR 100; *United States* v. *Bryant,* 12 USCMA 111, 30 CMR 111; *United States* v. *Hoy,* 12 USCMA 554, 31 CMR 140. Yet, it was here shown in the course of the controversy between counsel.

Indeed, all these things occurred, and more. Together, they not only justify accused's observation that counsel, in their zeal to attack each other, somehow overlooked him, but severally constitute the denial to him of a fair hearing. *United States* v. *Lynch, United States* v. *Shepherd,* both supra. We cannot condemn too severely the acrimonious exchanges in this record in counsel's effort to blacken each other's reputation before court members who had not the slightest official interest therein. The law officer should have acted immediately and firmly to control the matter. His failure to do so led inevitably to the disclosures we have mentioned, and, in turn, to this reversal. *United States* v. *Lynch,* supra; *United States* v. *Burse,* supra.

The decision of the board of review is reversed, and the record of trial returned to The Judge Advocate General of the Air Force. A rehearing may be ordered.

Chief Judge QUINN and Judge KILDAY concur.

Discussion Case

UNITED STATES, Appellee

v.

MALCOLM ROBERT GARDNER, Airman Apprentice, U.S. Navy, Appellant
9 USCMA 48, 25 CMR 310

(1958)

Opinion of the Court

ROBERT E. QUINN, Chief Judge:

This appeal challenges the effectiveness of the accused's representation by his appointed counsel.

The accused was brought to trial before a special court-martial on three specifications of larceny, in violation of Article 121, Uniform Code of Military Justice, 10 USC § 921 (Charge I), and one specification of failing to obey an order, in violation of Article 92, 10 USC § 892 (Charge II). He was represented by two officers who were appointed defense counsel and assistant defense counsel, respectively. They were not lawyers in the sense of Article 27 of the Uniform Code.

After arraignment, defense counsel entered a plea of guilty to each of the specifications of Charge I and a plea of not guilty to Charge II and its specification. As soon as he announced the pleas, he requested a "short recess." The request was granted and the court recessed for five minutes. On reconvening, defense counsel asked to change the plea to accord with what "the accused desires." The new plea changed the plea of guilty to specification 1, Charge I, to not guilty; in other respects it was the same as the original.

The president of the court thereupon reiterated the pleas, and explained the effect of a plea of guilty to the accused. He also advised the accused that he was entitled to plead not guilty and have the Government prove his guilt. In response to questions put to him by the president, the accused indicated that he understood the meaning and effect of a plea of guilty and that he desired to adhere to his plea.

To prove the two offenses to which the accused pleaded not guilty, the prosecution called two witnesses. One testified in connection with Charge II; the other, Lieutenant T. G. Harty, testified to a pretrial statement made by the accused regarding the circumstances of specification 1, Charge I, which alleges that the accused stole an allotment check belonging to Lora Butt, the wife of a Navy Aviation Machinist.

In the statement to Lieutenant Harty, the accused said that Mrs. Butt roomed with his wife and himself. When she moved, she asked the accused to forward her mail to her new home. Several weeks later, the accused picked up her allotment check at the

Foley (Alabama) Post Office. He signed and cashed the check. Some of the proceeds were used to pay his bills and the remainder was spent on what "was more or less a honeymoon" for his wife. He maintained that he did not think that he would have "gone so far" in using the money "if it wasn't that my wife had her heart set on a vacation and cried" when it appeared that they would not have enough money. "I want," said the accused, "to pay back the money to Lora Butt and hope to make some kind of arrangement with her."

When the prosecution rested, defense counsel made a brief statement in which he indicated that he intended to prove certain facts in regard to Charge II. He further indicated that "after consulting" Article 121 of the Uniform Code he was going to try "to answer the question" of whether the accused wanted to keep the money "in a permanent fashion." He called the accused and his wife as witnesses. The accused testified initially only on Charge II, of which he was ultimately acquitted. Defense counsel then asked permission to "renew an examination" in regard to the larceny specification. By appropriate questions he had the accused review his acquaintanceship with Mrs. Butt, and led him through a restatement of the substance of his pretrial confession. The only material questions which bear upon the "permanency" of the accused's taking, which counsel said he would try to answer, are as follows:

"Q. Upon taking this money to the bank, what was your purpose?

"A. Well, I have $500.00 up home in bonds and we owed a lot of bills and we were going home on leave to get the money, and I did not see anything wrong with taking the money to her.

"Q. Your intentions were to do so?

"A. Yes, sir.

"Q. You have sent $91.30 to Mrs. Butts.

"A. I have, sir."

Most of Mrs. Gardner's testimony is irrelevant to the issues. Asked whether she knew to what use the accused had put the proceeds of the check, she replied that she "only found out the other day," and that it went "to pay gas bills and to finance" a trip to Lansing, Michigan.

Unquestionably skilled counsel would not have allowed the accused and his wife to testify in regard to specification 1. The prosecution's case consisted only of a pretrial statement by the accused. Without independent evidence that the offense charged had probably been committed, this showing did not establish a *prima facie* case of guilt. *United States* v. *Mims,* 8 USCMA 316, 24 CMR 126. However, with the accused's judicial admissions the evidence is clearly sufficient to support the finding of guilty. *United States* v. *Shell,* 7 USCMA 646, 23 CMR 110; *United States* v. *Rushlow,* 2 USCMA 641, 10 CMR 139. This raises the question whether defense counsel's conduct in the case was "so tainted with negligence" (*United States* v. *Hunter,* 2 USCMA 37, 41, 6 CMR 37), or demonstrates such "palpable inexperience" (*United States* v. *Dupree,* 1 USCMA 665, 670, 5 CMR 93), as to amount to a denial of the effective assistance of counsel. The matter is not one which lends itself to an easy solution. Each case must be decided upon its own facts. *United States* v. *Allen,* 8 USCMA 504, 25 CMR 8. Here, the facts divided the board of review below.

The Government describes the alleged inadequacies of defense counsel as "tactical indiscretions." Among other things, it argues that the change in plea might have resulted simply from a "sudden change in tactics at the whim of the accused." It is distinctly possible that the change in plea resulted from the sudden disposition of the accused, but even if we attribute the change to him we must still consider counsel's actions in the later stages of the trial. What makes the problem particularly difficult is that we are dealing with both sophisticated aspects of the law and persons who are untrained in the law. Considerable training and experience in the conduct of a trial is necessary to learn that a confession is not ordinarily admissible until independent evidence of the probable commission of the offense has been introduced, Manual for Courts-Martial, United States, 1951, paragraph 140a; *United States* v. *April*, 7 USCMA 594, 23 CMR 58; that a motion for a finding of not guilty is appropriate when the prosecution has failed to make out a *prima facie* case; and that evidence presented by the defense can be used to fill in gaps in the prosecution's case. *United States* v. *Shell*, supra. In reading this record of trial, we are convinced that the appointed defense counsel did as well as they could, but their knowledge of the law relating to the case on trial was so deficient as to result in inadequate representation of the accused on specification 1.

In *United States* v. *Best*, 6 USCMA

39, 19 CMR 165, we pointed out that under ordinary conditions a denial of the effective assistance of counsel affects the entire proceedings. However, we also noted that "different factual settings . . . may have different effects." *Ibid*, page 45. The accused pleaded guilty to two specifications alleging thefts which were entirely unrelated to the contested issues. He does not contend that he entered the plea of guilty upon the mistaken advice of counsel; nor does he say that he has any valid defense to those charges. The record of trial shows that he had explained to him the meaning and effect of the plea by the president of the court, and he persisted in it. And he was sufficiently well-defended on Charge II to obtain an acquittal. These circumstances, coupled with the nature of counsel's deficiency, demonstrate that counsel's lack of assistance was confined to his representation of the accused on specification 1. Consequently, the interests of justice do not require that we set aside the findings of guilty as to which the accused entered a plea of guilty.

The findings of guilty of specification 1 of Charge I and the sentence are set aside. The record of trial is returned to The Judge Advocate General of the Navy for resubmission to the board of review. In its discretion, the board of review may dismiss specification 1 and reassess the sentence upon the basis of the remaining findings of guilty, or order a rehearing on the specification and the sentence.

Judge FERGUSON concurs.
Judge LATIMER dissented.

DISCUSSION AND SELF-QUIZ

1. The accused was charged with attempted rape. He denied the charge under oath and attributed the dispute to an argument over money. The trial counsel cross-examined the accused and brought out the fact that he had relied on his Article 31 rights and had chosen not to make a statement when questioned after the incident. Later two investigators testified that the accused "did not wish to talk about it anymore" after he had been advised of his Article 31 rights. You are the legal officer reviewing this case. Was there any error committed?

2. The accused was charged with assault with a dangerous weapon in violation of Article 128 of the Code. One of the defense contentions was that the weapon was not loaded. To support this contention, the accused called an expert on firearms as a witness. He had apparently conducted an experiment with the weapon involved. He testified that a round of ammunition could not have been placed in the chamber of the rifle and then extracted without being marked. He explained that the mark would be a scratch on the copper jacket and that the round of ammunition that was in evidence had never been extracted from the rifle because he had examined it closely with a magnifying glass and there were no markings. His testimony contradicted a prosecution witness who stated he saw the particular round thrown from the chamber when the witness retracted the bolt.

The trial counsel himself then testified for the prosecution that he had taken the same cartridge and rifle and had loaded and unloaded the weapon. This testimony was a direct challenge to the expert's testimony that marking would be on the cartridge if such had transpired. In his argument on the findings, the trial counsel argued that his testimony rebutted that of the defense expert. Was such a procedure proper?

3. Why is it important for the trial counsel to serve a copy of the charges on the accused and to sign the statement of service on the bottom of page 3 of the charge sheet?

4. What is a pretrial agreement and when may it be used? See section 904 of *Military Law* and Chapter I of the JAG Manual.

5. What paragraph in the Checklist for the Defense in the appendices might have prevented the counsel in the second discussion case from being regarded as inadequate?

CHAPTER X

Members, President, and Military Judge

Early in his career, the junior officer can expect to be detailed to sit as a member of a court-martial. This assignment will require him to assume the equivalent responsibilities of an impartial juror in civilian life. The close living conditions of service life require that the detailed member be extremely circumspect as to any forthcoming case prior to, during, and even after, assembly. In essence, he should avoid any conduct which may create any appearance of prejudice or bias for either side in the case.

Later in his career, an officer may be detailed as the president of a court-martial. The president of a court-martial for a particular case is the member most senior in rank who is present at the trial. The nature and scope of a president's duties vary, as they are governed by the presence or absence of a military judge.

1001 Who May Serve as Members

Members are detailed by the convening authority by the promulgation of a convening order. See Appendix 17. Any commissioned officer on active duty is initially eligible to serve on courts-martial as a member. A warrant officer on active duty is initially eligible to serve on courts for the trial of any person other than a commissioned officer. Enlisted men are initially eligible to serve on a court-martial upon the written request of the accused and if they are not attached to the same ship or unit as the accused. The only exception to this latter rule is if physical conditions or military exigencies preclude the obtaining of eligible enlisted members; then none need be assigned. See paragraphs 4c and 36c (2), MCM.

The status of a court member in relation to the accused (i.e., whether he is a commissioned officer, warrant officer, or enlisted member) governs his qualifications to sit on a court-martial. For example, a warrant officer can sit in the case of another warrant officer or in the case of an enlisted man, but he may not sit in the case of a commissioned officer.

An enlisted accused should not be tried by an enlisted member that is junior to him in pay grade. An officer should not be tried by another officer who is either junior to him in rank or date of rank.

Those officers best qualified by reason of age, education, training, experience, length of service, and judicial temperament, should be selected to serve on courts.

The following are ineligible and must not be detailed as court members (even though they are initially eligible):

1. Accusers;

2. Witnesses for the prosecution;

3. Those who have investigated the case either as preliminary inquiry officer or otherwise;

4. Those who have acted as trial or defense counsel for any of the present offenses charged;

5. Those who have previously served on the same case as court members when the case has been returned for a rehearing or another trial;

6. Enlisted members who are members of the same unit as the accused.

The convening authority should not detail members who have expressed opinions as to the guilt or innocence of the accused.

Any other facts that would indicate the prospective member should not sit as a member of the court should be considered. See 62*f*, MCM.

If during the trial a member of the court is called as a prosecution witness or any of his documents or declarations are utilized by the prosecution during the trial, he shall be excused. For example, if the prosecution in a "not guilty" plea unauthorized absence case utilizes a page 13 of the accused's service record (see Appendix 8), which was signed by a member of the court, as part of the evidence to prove his case, the member must be excused.

1002 Absence of Members

Special courts-martial may consist of any number of members but *not less than three*. If the members sitting become less than a quorum (i.e., less than three), the trial may not proceed.

The absence of a member of a special court-martial prior to the assembly of the court does not prevent the court from proceeding with the trial if a quorum is present. A court is "assembled" when, after the members have gathered in the courtroom, the presiding officer announces it is assembled. This announcement is made following the preliminary organization of the court. If a military judge is detailed, he will accomplish the preliminary organizing of the court in a procedure called an Article 39(a) session. The members are not present at an Article 39(a) session.

If a member is present at the assembly of the court but absent thereafter, the court may proceed only if a quorum remains and the absence is the result of a challenge, physical disability, or the order of the convening authority for good cause. Paragraph 37*b* of the MCM states that "good cause contemplates a critical situation such as emergency leave or military exigencies, as distinguished from the normal conditions of military life." The record of trial must reflect the reasons for an absence of a court member after assembly. The trial counsel has a responsibility to make an informal inquiry into the absence of any member and report his findings to the court. See 41*d*(4), MCM.

The convening authority may not detail additional members to a special court-martial after assembly unless the court is reduced below a quorum or for other good cause.

1003 Responsibilities Prior to Assembly

A member of a court-martial will first be notified of his appointment as a member by receipt of a copy of the convening order (Appendix 17). For example, a convening order may state that the court will convene "at 1400 hours on 20 November 1970 or as soon thereafter as practicable, for the trial of such persons as may properly be brought before it." The words "as soon thereafter as practicable" permit leeway as to when the court will first meet. In the example above, the court could first meet on 20 January 1971 or any other time.

It is recommended that the member detailed to a court contact the senior member to ascertain if there are any plans to assemble the court in the near future.

A court-martial may hold sessions at any hour of the day, but it should not meet at unusual hours. The duration of the sittings should not be unusually protracted, unless the case is one of extraordinary urgency.

The officer selected to serve as a member of a court-martial has certain standards of conduct he must adhere to even before the court assembles for the first time. As the member of the military equivalent of a "jury," the member must have no preconceived or fixed opinions as to the guilt or innocence of the accused prior to trial. *Both* the government and the accused are entitled to an impartial court, unbiased either for or against them.

It is also essential that no remarks, gestures, or witticisms, whether made in jest or otherwise, either prior to, during, or after trial, be made by the court member regarding his duties. Statements such as "let's hang the guy" while generally said in jest, do more to destroy military discipline and morale in a command then any possible ultimate result in the trial or review of the case itself. Such an offhand remark may result in the case being retried or the charges dismissed.

While the temptation may be great, a member should not inquire into the facts of any particular case that he may be called to sit on, nor should he research the law as to the case. He should not discuss any case that he may be detailed to sit on as a member.

If, before the meeting of the court, it appears to a member that he should not sit on the court, either at all, or in a particular case, he should notify the convening authority of his reasons and ask to be relieved.

1004   Duties After Assembly

There are certain attitudes a good member should possess as relates to his duties.

A court member's first obligation is to be fair and impartial. Therefore, he should determine to wait until all the evidence is in, the trial and defense counsel have argued, and he has been instructed as to the law he must apply to the facts before he judges the case. For example, the government presents its evidence first. If a member concludes that the accused is guilty at this point, he will not have given the accused the opportunity to show where the prosecution has failed to prove his guilt.

The reason why this is so is because the law is far more subtle and complex than many realize. Thus, the significance of certain prosecution or defense evidence may not be clear before the presiding officer explains the applicable law. As an example, the value of a particular item of evidence may not become clear until the trial is almost complete.

The member may not bring any MCM's, cases, or other reference material into court as he is *absolutely prohibited from utilizing them either when the court is in open session or when it is closed to determine the guilt or innocence or the sentence of the accused.* This prohibition may even include pocket books that may relate to the subject matter of the trial.

For example, in a narcotics trial one of the members purchased a book, *Narcotics, U.S.A.,* and examined it during the trial prior to the findings. The use he made of the book was unknown. The Court of Military Appeals, in reversing the conviction because of this error, stated that it:

. . . is basic legal learning that court-martial members are not allowed to seek facts or opinions from outside sources which will control or influence their findings on issues being tried before them. During such time, they are to be insulated, so far as is reasonably possible, from receiving testimony not produced in court. The rule as to military court members is no different in that regard from the one controlling their civilian counterparts, the jurymen. . . . *United States* v. *Webb,* 8 USCMA 70, 23 CMR 294 (1957).

A president of a court, if he is presiding, may utilize an MCM and trial guide during open sessions of the court.

The members are seated with the president in the center and other members alternately to the right and left according to rank. For example in a five-member court, the junior member would sit to the far left of the president. (Remember that the president *is* a member.)

The oath for a court member reads as follows:

You ————— do swear (or affirm) that you will faithfully perform all the duties incumbent upon you as a member of this
court, that you will faithfully and impartially try, according to
the evidence, your conscience, and the laws applicable to trials
by courts-martial, the case of the accused now before this court;
and that you will not disclose or discover the vote or opinion
of any particular member of the court upon a challenge or upon
the findings or sentence unless required to do so in due course
of law. So help you God.

After the court assembles, the member will be asked to disclose in open session every ground for challenge believed by him to exist.

The requirement for the member to actually *disclose* grounds for challenge is stricter than the rule in most civilian courts as civilian courts
require a counsel to uncover grounds for challenge by questioning the
jurors. This stricter rule is considered necessary because military members of a court-martial have more opportunity to become officially or
unofficially involved in the case due to the "closeness" of the military
community. For example, the member in question may have been duty
officer and investigated the incident.

In disclosing grounds for challenge, members should state only the
ultimate nature of the circumstances which might make them subject
to challenge. They *must refrain from making any derogatory remark
or from revealing information prejudicial to the accused in making such
disclosures.*

A member may be excused from serving on the court. This may be
accomplished by the exercise of either peremptory challenges or challenges for cause. The peremptory challenge is a "free" challenge by
which either counsel may remove one member, but no more than one.
No reason need be given for this challenge. It sometimes is utilized only
to achieve a given court balance or number. Some challenges for cause

are those challenges based upon some disqualifying circumstance recognized by the law. Some of the grounds for challenge are listed in paragraph 62*f*, MCM.

The procedure for the first eight grounds for challenge is the same as for any other ground listed in paragraph 62*f* of the MCM, even though the MCM states that the member must be "excused forthwith." This is because paragraph 62*h* of the MCM requires that each challenge for cause be passed upon. In the case of a special court-martial where a president is presiding, this means that the other members must vote as to the challenge on these first eight grounds, and if the facts are undisputed, but the challenge is not sustained, the case will be reversed upon appeal. Therefore, if a member is not initially eligible to serve as a member; or has not been appointed as a member; or is an accuser, prosecution witness, investigating officer, or enlisted man who is a member of the same unit as the accused; or if he has served as trial or defense counsel or as a member in a previous trial as to any of the present offenses charged; he *must* be excused by a vote of the members.

Some other factors which may disqualify a member are definite opinions as to the guilt or innocence of the accused or any other matter which would raise a substantial doubt as to the legality, fairness and impartiality of the trial. See paragraph 62*f* of the MCM.

In order to determine any basis for a challenge, counsel at times question members of the court to determine if they hold any biases or should be precluded from sitting on the court. This questioning is called "voir dire." It is not intended to cast doubt upon the honor and capability of the member questioned. Each individual has his own personal predispositions and fixed attitudes that may be contrary to the interest of the accused or the prosecution. Voir dire is simply a natural selection process designed to obtain a panel of jurors free of inclination toward either side of the case.

During the trial of the case, members must be dignified and attentive. If a member becomes drowsy, he should request a recess to refresh himself. He should disregard those matters the president or military judge instructs him to disregard (when the military judge is detailed, he presides; if absent, the president presides).

Members should not fraternize with the military judge, the witnesses, the accused, the trial counsel, or defense counsel during the trial or any recess or adjournment other than their relationships require. Although absolute segregation may be impossible in small commands in the naval service, there should be no justification for unusual gestures of friendliness during the conduct of the trial. *In essence, a member should avoid any conduct which may create any appearance of prejudice to the accused.*

During the course of the trial, the member must remember that t
trial and the defense counsel have the duty of presenting the eviden
in court. Members may ask any question of a witness that either si
properly may ask him. However, during this questioning they "must
careful not to depart from an impartial role." Paragraph 149c(3), MC
For example, in *United States* v. *Blankenship,* 7 USCMA 328, 22 CM
118 (1956) a court member questioned witnesses in a murder trial in su
a manner as to become an advocate for the prosecution. In examining
defense witness who had testified for the defense as to the victim's rep
tation for becoming involved in quarrels and in acts of violence, he ask
such scornful questions as: "Did Sergeant Argyle [the victim] pay l
bills promptly?" "Did he beat small children and dogs?" He also
tempted to discredit another defense witness who testified as to t
accused's alleged amnesia. The Court of Military Appeals held that t
court member thus departed from his role as an impartial fact find
and became a champion for the prosecution. The case was reversed.

In order to avoid a situation such as arose in the Blankenship case, t
presiding officer may require members to submit their questions to hi
orally or in writing (writing is preferred), so that a ruling may be ma
on the propriety of the question before it is asked. The question may
rephrased. The presiding officer or the trial counsel then asks the qu
tion. *This procedure is strongly recommended.*

1005   Determining Guilt or Innocence

When the prosecution and defense have completed their presentatio
of evidence and their arguments in a "not guilty" plea case, the presidi
officer will instruct the members as to the law they should apply to t
facts they have observed in determining the guilt or innocence of t
accused.

For example, a member will be informed of the elements (the fac
which must be proven) of the offense and any lesser included offen
and must be advised:

1. That the accused must be presumed to be innocent until his gu
is established by legal and competent evidence beyond a reasonab
doubt;

2. That if there is a reasonable doubt as to the guilt of the accuse
the doubt must be resolved in favor of the accused and he must l
acquitted;

3. That, if there is a reasonable doubt as to the degree of guilt, tl
finding must be in a lower degree as to which there is no reasonab
doubt;

4. That the burden of proof to establish the guilt of the accuse
beyond a reasonable doubt is upon the United States.

Paragraph 73 of the MCM and Chapter XIII of *Military Law* discuss some of the instructions the president must give.

Normally, written instructions are not taken into closed session, but any copy which is taken into closed session must be appended to the record of trial as an appellate exhibit. In any event, the presiding officer should not direct a court member to write down the instructions for use of all the members during a closed session. *United States* v. *Caldwell*, 11 USCMA 257, 29 CMR 73 (1960).

The members may always take the convening order and copies of the charges and specifications, (but *not* the charge sheet) into closed session with them. With the military judge's or president's permission, the member can also take his personal notes and items of documentary or real evidence into such sessions. *United States* v. *Hurt*, 9 USCMA 735, 27 CMR 3 (1958) and *United States* v. *Christensen*, 30 CMR 959 (1961). However, the court cannot take depositions, stipulations, or portions of the record of trial into closed session as they might place too much emphasis on that portion which is written down.

Paragraph 74, MCM, cites the following principles as they relate to the findings:

> Only matters properly before the court as a whole may be considered. A member should not, for instance, be influenced by any knowledge of the acts, character, or service of the accused not based on the evidence or other proper matter before the court; by any opinions not properly in evidence; or by motives of partiality, favor, or affection. Matters as to which comment in argument is prohibited cannot be considered.
>
> In weighing the evidence, a member is expected to utilize his common sense and his knowledge of human nature and of the ways of the world. In the light of all the circumstances of the case, he should consider the inherent probability or improbability of the evidence, and, with this in mind, he may properly believe one witness and disbelieve several witnesses whose testimony is in conflict with that of the one.
>
> In order to convict of an offense, the court must be satisfied beyond a reasonable doubt that the accused is guilty thereof. By "reasonable doubt" is intended not a fanciful or ingenious doubt or conjecture but substantial, honest, conscientious doubt suggested by the material evidence, or lack of it, in the case. It is an honest, substantial misgiving, generated by insufficiency of proof of guilt. It is not a captious doubt, nor a doubt suggested by the ingenuity of counsel or court and unwarranted by the testimony, nor a doubt born of a merciful inclination to permit the accused to escape conviction, nor a doubt prompted by sympathy for him or those connected with him. *The meaning of the rule is that the proof must be such as to exclude not every hypothesis or possibility of innocence but any fair and rational*

hypothesis except that of guilt; what is required is not an abso-
lute or mathematical certainty but a moral certainty. (Emphasis
supplied.)

The rule as to reasonable doubt extends to every element of
the offense. If, in a trial for desertion with intent to remain
away permanently, a reasonable doubt exists as to that intent,
the accused cannot properly be convicted as charged, although
he might be convicted of the lesser included offense of absence
without proper authority. . . . *It is not necessary that each par-*
ticular fact advanced by the prosecution be proved beyond a
reasonable doubt; it is sufficient to warrant conviction if, on the
whole evidence, the court is satisfied beyond a reasonable doubt
that the accused is guilty. (Emphasis supplied.)

A close reading of the above paragraphs should emphasize that "guilt
beyond a reasonable doubt" is not equivalent to a "mathematical cer
tainty" but can be established by only a "moral certainty" of guilt.

For example, a member who was questioned as to his competency to
sit on a court-martial, summed up his position by saying that if a close
question was presented, he would resolve his doubts in favor of the
government. The Court of Military Appeals, in sustaining the member'
challenge from the court, stated in *United States* v. *Carver,* 6 USCMA
258, 19 CMR 384 (1955) that this "concept, of course, does violence to al
that we know of the principles of reasonable doubt and the presumption
of innocence. Far from beginning his deliberations with the premise
that an accused is innocent until proven guilty beyond a reasonable
doubt," the member "expounded, in essence, the theory that deliberation
should be undertaken with the scales of justice weighted for the prosecu
tion. Adherence to this erroneous precept is enough to justify the imputa
tion of a forbidden bias to the member, and it adequately supports the
action taken by the court-martial."

Although there may be many other factors to weigh in any particula
court-martial, the member *must* be aware of the fact that circumstantia
evidence is *not* an inferior kind of evidence. It may be admitted eve
when there is direct evidence. Paragraph 138*b* of the MCM states in thi
regard that:

The assertion of an eyewitness may be more convincing than
contrary inferences that may be drawn from certain circumstances. *Conversely, an inference drawn from one or more*
circumstances may be more convincing than a contrary asser-
tion of an eyewitness. (Emphasis supplied.) (See paragraph 1101
of *Military Law.*)

1006   Voting on Findings

Although there may be free and full discussion before voting in th
closed session on the findings, each member must individually resolv

the ultimate issue of the guilt or innocence of the accused. Each member must determine the facts of the case, apply the law to these facts, and determine the guilt or innocence of the accused in accordance with his own conscience. Paragraph 62h(3) of the MCM states that the *"influence of superiority in rank will not be employed in any manner in an attempt to control the independence of members in the exercise of their judgment."*

The following standard instructions given by the presiding officer accurately describe the closed hearing procedure on the findings:

> The court is advised that deliberations on findings include full and free discussion of all questions pertaining to the guilt or innocence of the accused, all members having equal rights on such matters. Voting on the findings is accomplished by secret, written ballot and all members are required to vote. Voting on the specification shall precede voting on the charge. The junior member of the court shall in each case collect and count the votes; the count shall be checked by the president, who shall forthwith announce the results of the ballot to members of the court.
>
> The concurrence of two-thirds of the members present at the time the vote is taken is required to find the accused guilty of any offense. If, in computing the number of votes required a fraction results, such fraction shall be counted as one, thus, if all ——— members now present are present at the time the vote is taken, the requirement that two-thirds concur will not be met unless ——— members concur. A finding of not guilty results as to any specification or charge if no other valid finding is reached thereon; however, the court may reconsider any finding before it is announced in open court. The court may reconsider any finding of guilty on its own motion at any time before the president announces the sentence in the case.
>
> As soon as the court has determined the findings, the president will announce them in open court in the presence of the accused and counsel. Only the required fraction of members concurring in findings of guilty will be announced. If findings of not guilty result, no reference will be made to the fraction of vote for or against such findings.

The court-martial member's determination on the findings (or on the sentence, for that matter) *must not* be based upon factors outside the issues and matter presented in the court. For example, the fact that a member has a personal friendship with the defense counsel and a coolness toward the trial counsel should not be a factor in his decision. Nor should the fact that the defense counsel is flawless in his presentation of a case and the trial counsel is hesitant be a determining factor if the prosecution evidence proves the accused guilty of the crime charged. The fact that another may not have been prosecuted for the same offense should not be the basis for acquitting the accused, although it might have some weight as to the punishment to be awarded in the event the accused is convicted.

1007   Determining the Sentence

If the accused is found guilty, there is a required hearing on the sentence which will include aggravating, mitigating, and extenuating factors regarding the offense and the accused.

A standard instruction to members as to their duties would include the following:

> When the court closes to deliberate and vote upon the sentence to be adjudged, only the members of the court will be present. Deliberation may properly include full and free discussion. The influence of superiority in rank shall not be employed in any manner in an attempt to control the independence of members in the exercise of their judgment.
>
> When the court has completed its discussion, any member who desires to propose a sentence will write his proposal on a slip of paper. The junior member will collect the proposed sentences and submit them to the president. The court will then vote by secret written ballot on the proposed sentences, beginning with the lightest sentence, until a sentence is adopted by the concurrence of the required number of members. The junior member shall in each case collect and count the votes; the count shall be checked by the president who shall forthwith announce the result of the ballot to the members of the court.
>
> Any sentence adjudged in this case must be determined by the concurrence of two-thirds of the members present at the time the vote is taken. If, in computing the number of votes required, a fraction results, such fraction will be counted as one; thus, if all ——— members now present are present when the vote is taken, the requirement that two-thirds concur will not be met unless ——— members concur.
>
> As soon as the court has determined the sentence, the president will announce it in open court in the presence of the accused and the counsel for both sides. In announcing the sentence, only the required percentage of members who concurred in the sentence will be announced.
>
> The court is advised that these instructions must not be interpreted as indicating an opinion as to the kind or amount of punishment which should be adjudged, for each member of the court has the independent responsibility of making this determination. In arriving at your determination of an appropriate sentence in this case you should select, based upon the evidence presented in this case and your own experience and general knowledge, the kind and amount of punishment which will best serve the ends of good order and discipline within the [Navy]

[Marine Corps], the needs of the accused, and the welfare of society. In this connection you are advised that it is within your prerogative and authority to award no punishment at all. Further, you should not adjudge an excessive sentence in reliance upon possible mitigating action by the convening or higher authority.

The court is advised that each member has an independent responsibility for determining an appropriate sentence which may include a sentence to "no punishment" at all. Each member has the right to conscientiously disagree with the other members. However, each member, during deliberations, should pay proper respect to each other member's opinions and arguments and should listen with a disposition to be convinced of such opinions and arguments. If, however, after patient and mature deliberation the requisite number [two-thirds] of members are unable to agree on a proper sentence the president will announce this fact in open court in the presence of counsel for both sides, the accused and the reporter.

It is noted that paragraph 76*b*(2) of the MCM states that "it is the duty of each member to vote for a proper sentence for the offense or offenses of which the accused has been found guilty, *without regard to his opinion or vote as to the guilt or innocence of the accused.*"

Improper conduct by a member, such as a refusal or failure to vote or properly to discharge any other duty under his oath, may be a military offense.

1008 Duties of the Non-presiding President

In a court-martial with a military judge, the president has the duties, powers, and privileges of a member. However, he has the following additional powers and duties:

1. He consults with a military judge as to the time of assembly;

2. He prescribes the uniform to be worn at sessions attended by the members;

3. As authorized in the JAG Manual, he shall administer oaths to such counsel as have not been previously sworn;

4. He presides over closed sessions of the court;

5. He speaks for the court in announcing the findings and sentence and the result of a vote upon a matter properly presented to the court members for decision;

6. He speaks for the members in conferring with or requesting instructions from the military judge upon any question of law or procedure.

He does not preside; the military judge does. He has many of the aspects of the foreman of a jury. Paragraph 40 of the MCM states that "except for his right as a member to object to" a contempt citation by the military judge, "he shall not interfere with those rulings of the military judge which affect the legality of the proceedings."

1009　Duties of the Presiding President

In a special court-martial without a military judge, the president presides. He is responsible for the fair and orderly conduct of the trial and for ensuring that it is conducted in a dignified, military manner. In fulfilling these responsibilities, he has the following additional duties and responsibilities:

1. He sets the time of trial after consultation with the trial counsel
2. He prescribes the uniform to be worn.
3. He administers oaths to counsel not previously sworn in accordance with secretarial directives (see the JAG Manual).
4. He presides over closed sessions of the court and speaks for the court in announcing the findings and sentence and the result of any vote upon a matter presented to the court members for decision.
5. His rulings on questions of law, other than motions for a finding of not guilty, are final. This means that his decision is not subject to objection by any member (although either counsel could present an argument for ruling in his favor). Questions of law and questions of fact must be distinguished because the president's ruling is final regarding the former and subject to objection by any court member regarding the latter (if interlocutory).

In general, a question of fact raises an issue concerning what occurred while a question of law raises an issue of what the law is, concerning that which occurred. For example, if the facts are undisputed, the legality of an order when disobedience of an order is charged would generally be a question of law, and not of fact. It is possible, however, for such questions to be decided solely upon some factual issue, in which case they would be questions of fact.

An example is a question of whether the person who issued the order, *in fact* actually occupied a position which would authorize him to issue it. Paragraph 57*b*, MCM. Another example of a question of law would be the instructions that the president gives to the other members as to what the law is as regards the findings and sentence.

6. The president's ultimate ruling on a motion for a finding of not guilty, although generally a question of law, is not final, and is subject to the objection of any member of the court. This also applies to any question concerning the factual issue of the accused's mental responsibility.

7. The president may rule on interlocutory questions of fact. The president's rulings on interlocutory questions of fact are subject to objection by any court member. A question is interlocutory unless it would

terminate the case by deciding guilt or innocence. In other words, questions that go to the ultimate issue of guilt or innocence of the accused, are *not* interlocutory. These non-interlocutory questions can only be determined by the members of the court when they go into closed session to determine the accused's guilt or innocence.

Such matters as the admissibility of evidence offered during the trial, competency of the witnesses, adjournments, recesses, the order of introduction of witnesses, and the propriety of any argument or statement of the trial or defense counsel are generally interlocutory questions.

8. The presiding president does *not* rule upon challenges for cause. The members vote on such challenges.

9. Before he admits an offered item of evidence, the presiding president, when practicable, will not expose it to the risk of inadvertent examination by members of the court.

10. He should instruct the court members to disregard evidence which, once having been admitted, is subsequently excluded.

11. He should advise the court members of any limitations upon evidence that is admitted for a limited purpose.

If the president makes a ruling which may be, and is, objected to by any member of the court, the court will be closed. The members of the court will then vote orally. The question shall be decided by a majority vote. A tie vote on a motion for a finding of not guilty or on a question relating to the sanity of the accused is a determination against the accused. A tie vote on any other question is a determination in favor of the accused.

A ruling may sometimes require both a factual and legal determination. Assume that there is an issue as to the admissibility of an accused's out-of-court statement. If there is a dispute regarding whether Article 31 advice was given, then the question is one of fact. Suppose that the defense contends that no advice was given, and even if the alleged advice was given, it was inadequate. In this case, a ruling concerning whether a warning was given at all would be subject to objection. On the other hand, a ruling on the adequacy of the warning that was actually given is one of law.

1010 Duties of the Military Judge

The military judge's duties are the same whether he is detailed to a general or a special court-martial. He presides over each open session of the court-martial to which he has been detailed. In doing so, he assures that the proceedings are conducted in a dignified and military manner. He is responsible for the fair and orderly conduct of the proceedings in accordance with law.

The military judge rules finally, not only on all questions of law but on *all* interlocutory questions, including questions of fact, with one exception: if the factual issue of the mental responsibility of the accused is raised as an interlocutory question, he rules subject to objection by any member of the court. Unlike the president of a special court-martial, he rules finally on motions for a finding of not guilty. Whereas the members rule on all challenges when the president is presiding, the military judge rules finally on all challenges. The military judge does not rule on questions of fact that go to the ultimate issue of the guilt or innocence of the accused.

Military judges of general courts-martial must be members of an independent judiciary (the U.S. Navy-Marine Corps Judiciary Activity). These military judges will preside at all general courts-martial. They will also preside at special courts-martial to the extent they are available for such duties. Rating the performance of these judges and writing their fitness reports will be the responsibility of the head of the judiciary, never of a commander in the field.

In addition to the "full-time" military judges of the Judiciary Activity, officers who have been certified as military judges will be available to preside over special courts-martial.

The convening authority shall not prepare or review any report concerning the effectiveness, fitness, or efficiency of a military judge detailed to a special court-martial which relates to his performance as a military judge.

1011 Summary

One of the guiding principles underlying the conduct of any trial is that the court's actions and deliberations must not only be untainted, but must also avoid the very appearance of impurity. This is a high standard and what may appear to be an "impurity" by others may be a sincere act of an impartial member attempting to obtain justice for the accused and the government.

The court member should judge a case as he sees it—and without regard to bias, friendships, or self-interest. He should apply the facts to the law furnished him by the presiding officer.

When a military judge is present in a special court-martial, the president's responsibilities are roughly equivalent to those of the senior member of a jury. However, when he presides (i.e., a military judge is not detailed to the court), the president has most of the duties and responsibilities of the military judge and almost as much authority when he makes rulings.

Discussion Case

UNITED STATES, Appellee

v.

ROBERT H. LYNCH, Lieutenant Colonel, U.S. Army, Appellant

9 USCMA 523, 26 CMR 303

(1958)

Opinion of the Court

HOMER FERGUSON, Judge:

Accused pleaded guilty to and was found guilty of being absent without leave, in violation of Article 86, Uniform Code of Military Justice, 10 USC § 886; larceny of $12,058.07, property of the Fort Chaffee Officers' Open Mess, in violation of Article 121, 10 USC § 921; of signing a false official statement with intent to deceive, in violation of Article 107, 10 USC § 907; and of uttering a forged check in the amount of $798.84, with intent to defraud, in violation of Article 123, 10 USC § 923. He was sentenced to dismissal from the service, total forfeitures, and confinement at hard labor for three years. The board of review reduced the period of the sentence to two years because the court-martial failed to sustain a challenge addressed to its president. However, the board was of the opinion that in view of the accused's pleas of guilty to all of the offenses charged, the error could only affect the sentence and that reassessment thereof would purge such error. During the trial the president of the court-martial objected to taking a *voir dire* oath. Thereafter, the following colloquy occurred during defense counsel's *voir dire* of the president:

DC: . . . Assuming that an officer has been tried for the offenses of absence without leave, larceny of approximately $12,000.00, making a false official statement and uttering a check and has been convicted of those offenses and you are deliberating on a proper sentence in his case, would you feel compelled to vote for his dismissal from the service regardless of the mitigation offered by the defense?

The president: I certainly would. The law officer sustained an objection to the question upon the ground that it was hypothetical. Thereafter, the defense counsel tried unsuccessfully several times to rephrase it to the satisfaction of the law officer. Further, in the *voir dire* examination, the president testified that during a recess he had commented to other members of the court-martial upon the question addressed to him by defense counsel. The defense counsel then asked, "Do you feel like they were influenced by your comments?" The president replied, "I don't know. I think they were probably influenced by your question." He also stated he had said to other court-martial members during the recess that he regarded having been placed under separate oath as an implication against his honor. He then addressed individual civilian defense counsel as follows:

> You, as a civilian lawyer, may not be aware that an officer of the United States Army is bound to tell the truth.

∞

> Possibly, in civilian courts, you do not trust the witnesses or the members of the jury. This is not a jury. This is a court—it's a military court. It is a custom of the service—from all usage of the military courts—that those members of the court are officers and—I'm running out of words. I think you know what I mean. There is a difference between civilian trials and military trials.

Defense counsel challenged the president for cause. The court-martial voted adversely to his challenge and defense counsel thereupon peremptorily challenged the president. The law officer instructed the court-martial they should not be prejudiced by the in-and-out-of court remarks of its president. The court-martial members gave silent acquiescence to this instruction. The defense then moved for a mistrial. The motion was overruled.

We granted the accused's petition for review to determine three issues.

I

The first issue with which we are concerned questions whether the president of the court so inflamed the membership thereof that the court was incapable of sitting in judgment of the accused.

"It is the right of a defendant accused of crime to have nothing reach the mind of the jury concerning the case except strictly legal evidence admitted according to law, and if facts prejudicial to him reach the jury otherwise, it is the duty of the trial judge to withdraw a juror and grant a new trial." *Griffin* v. *United States*, 295 Fed 437 (CA 3d Cir) (1924).

"It is the duty of the trial judge to maintain the integrity of trials by jury, and if it appears at any stage of the trial before the verdict that misconduct of any juror or other person has tainted the panel with any sort of corruption, or intimidation, or coercion, the trial should be stopped and a mistrial granted." *Klose* v. *United States*, 49 F 2d 177 (CA 8th Cir) (1931).

"To be sure, the jury should pass upon each case free from external causes tending to disturb the exercise of deliberate and unbiased judgment." *United States* v. *Sorcey*, 151 F 2d 895 (CA 7th Cir) (1945). See also *Smith* v *United States*, 238 F 2d 925 (CA 5th Cir) (1956).

In the present case it does not appear open to question but that the actions of the president improperly influenced the other members of the court-martial. We note his intemperate language addressed to individual civilian defense counsel, the mistake inherent in his statement that "There is a difference between civilian trials and military trials," and also the impropriety of his conversation with the other court-martial members during court recess on the subject of impugnment of his military honor. His unbridled outburst demonstrated so completely his lack of judiciousness as to deprive the court-martial of that judicial

cial caliber demanded by the Code. In short, as a result of his course of conduct, the court-martial became incapable of receiving a plea of either guilty or not guilty.

In *United States* v. *Richard,* 7 USCMA 46, 21 CMR 172, we held it to be an abuse of discretion to deny a defense motion for mistrial when the accused had been improperly and grievously injured by the actions of a court-martial member. In the present case the defense motion for a mistrial should have been granted.

II

The second issue puts into inquiry whether the accused was prejudged by the law officer's curtailment of the *voir dire* examination. In *United States* v. *Parker,* 6 USCMA 274, 19 CMR 400, we said:

When a member is examined with a view to challenge, it is to be remembered that he may be asked any pertinent question tending to establish a disqualification for duty on the court. Statutory disqualifications, implied bias, actual bias, or other matters which have some substantial and direct bearing on an accused's right to an impartial court, are all proper subjects of inquiry. The accused should be allowed considerable latitude in examining members so as to be in a position intelligently and wisely to exercise a challenge for cause or a peremptory challenge. Accordingly, when there is a fair doubt as to the propriety of any question, it is better to allow it to be answered. While materiality and relevancy must always be considered to keep the examination within

bounds, they should be interpreted in a light favorable to the accused.

In *United States* v. *McMahan,* 6 USCMA 709, 21 CMR 31, we stressed the importance of a *voir dire* examination in acceptable trial strategy. See also *Morford* v. *United States,* 339 US 258, 70 S Ct 586, 94 L ed 815.

The question put to the president of the court-martial by the defense, far from being hypothetical, in effect summed up the offenses of which the accused stood charged.

Consequently, we hold that the law officer committed prejudical error by his curtailment of the *voir dire* examination.

III

The last issue questions, in the event the second is answered in the affirmative, whether the error was cured by the action of the board of review.

It is obvious that when we are confronted with a prejudiced court, there is no way to cure its action with regard to sentence except by wiping it out entirely. It is so because it is impossible to say at what sentence an unprejudiced court would have arrived. While we have condoned boards of review curing prejudice within limitation, it is obvious that those bodies cannot impose sentences *de novo.*

We hold that the board of review failed to purge the error in the present case. Consequently, the decision of the board of review is reversed. The record of trial is returned to The Judge Advocate General of the Army for action consistent with this opinion. A rehearing may be ordered.

Chief Judge QUINN concurs.

LATIMER, Judge (concurring in part and dissenting in part):

I concur in part and dissent in part.

This opinion leaves me confused because I do not understand what disposition is being ordered. While I believe a rehearing on the sentence will better serve the ends of justice, I cannot concur with the concept that the court-martial was without jurisdicion to accept a plea of guilty. The guilt of the accused was never placed in issue, and the ill-advised conduct and comments of the president could affect only the sentence.

I would, therefore, limit the rehearing to the imposition of sentence.

DISCUSSION AND SELF-QUIZ

1. You are a member of a court-martial in the case of Seaman John R. Brown, U.S. Navy. Seaman Brown pleaded not guilty to, but was convicted of, failure to go at the time prescribed to his appointed place of duty in violation of Article 86, UCMJ. After the findings of guilty were announced, the trial counsel offered a record of a previous conviction to be considered by the court when awarding an appropriate sentence. (See Appendix 16.) The defense counsel then noted that you had signed the page 6 entry when you had previously served as legal officer.

He challenges you for cause. You take the stand and state that you signed many documents in the course of your official duties and that you had no independent recollection of this document. You further state that you knew nothing about the accused other than had been presented in court.

Should the challenge be sustained? See paragraph 63, MCM.

2. You are a member of a special court-martial. There is no military judge detailed to the court. The trial counsel has several extra "trial guides" and MCMs and distributes them to some of the members of the court. Has any error been committed? See paragraph 53*d* of the MCM.

3. You are sitting as a member of a court-martial. The members are now in closed session and are determining the findings. This is a four-member court. Three of the four members must vote to convict in order to properly find the accused guilty by the required two-thirds of the members present. One member is positive the accused has not been proven guilty. Two members are positive he is guilty. You are not sure. The president, who is one of the two who is positive of the accused's guilt, says to you "if you vote for conviction of the offense, I'll vote for lighter sentence." Is this proper? Why or why not?

4. You have been assigned as a member of a special court-martial. The accused has been awarded the maximum sentence which, in this case, includes a bad conduct discharge. Several days later, the defense counsel shows you a letter from the accused's mother. It states that his father had developed a heart attack and died upon hearing of his son's receipt of the punitive discharge. The accused is remorseful and now desires to remain in the service. As a member of the court, what, if anything, can you do to reduce the sentence in this case if you believe that such is warranted? See paragraph 77 of the MCM.

CHAPTER XI

Basic Rules of Evidence

What is evidence? Evidence is the system of rules and standards by which the admission of proof at a court-martial is regulated. It is a study in admissibility; that is, what evidence the court members may or may not properly consider in arriving at their conclusions. The court members cannot utilize inadmissible evidence in arriving at these conclusions.

If the accused pleads "not guilty" to any offense, evidence is then presented on the question of the guilt or innocence of the accused and other issues. Of course, as the trial counsel has the burden of proving the accused guilty beyond a reasonable doubt, he *must* present sufficient evidence to convince the court on that issue.

The rules of evidence in our military law are the end product of the English common law.

Primitive man used many unsatisfactory methods to "determine" the guilt or innocence of an accused. Most of the methods utilized in earlier periods, such as trial by ordeal or by battle, placed the burden on the accused to prove his "innocence" in a very primitive way. If the accused survived the ordeal or won the battle, he was "innocent." Gradually, the methods of proving guilt or innocence changed in England. A form of trial developed in which questions of fact were decided by people untrained in legal matters. This developed into the civilian jury system.

The incorporation of civilian concepts of jurisprudence into our present military law has already been discussed. Under the Code, military court members perform the same function that the jury still performs under the common law—determining what the facts are. As a jury lacks legal training, certain rules must be developed to determine what matters it should, in fairness to the accused, consider.

1101 Direct and Circumstantial Evidence

There are two types of evidence: direct and circumstantial.

Direct evidence is evidence which tends directly to prove or disprove a fact in issue. For example, if Seaman Smith sees the accused take Roe's hat out of Roe's locker, Smith's testimony to that effect would be direct evidence as to the taking.

Circumstantial evidence is evidence tending to establish a fact from which a fact in issue may be inferred. For example, assume Ensign Doe, the officer of the day, after obtaining a lawful search authorization, searches the accused's locker and finds Roe's missing hat. Ensign Doe's testimony on this matter would be circumstantial evidence that the accused took the hat. Another witness may have seen the accused in the vicinity of Roe's locker immediately before the theft occurred. This, too, would constitute circumstantial evidence that the accused took Roe's hat.

Circumstantial evidence is not inferior to direct evidence in military law. There is no rule for weighing one against the other. Circumstantial facts may, at times, be more convincing than an eyewitness.

In many situations no direct evidence will be available on an element, such as, intent to steal in a larceny case, or knowledge in a failure to obey a lawful order case.

In *United States* v. *Wilson,* 13 USCMA 670, 33 CMR 202 (1963), the Court of Military Appeals upheld a larceny conviction based almost entirely on circumstantial evidence. In this case, the court said there was sufficient evidence to permit the court members to find, beyond a reasonable doubt, that the accused entered the victim's room in a barracks and stole a record player. The court stated:

> Thus, the record demonstrates that the item had in fact been taken; that accused was seen at the approximate time of the theft in the very barracks from which it was taken; that he was seen leaving the building by the fire escape carrying an item resembling a record player . . .

and that an individual had given a similar name and identical address to that used by the accused in pawning another record player.

> True it is that there is little or no direct evidence of accused's guilt, but the web of circumstances here depicted suffices as well to establish his culpability, and scrutiny of this record leads inevitably to the conclusion that there was a substantial basis for the fact finders' conclusion.

1102 The Purposes of the Rules of Evidence

The rules of evidence serve certain purposes. They are:

1. To ensure that the case is presented in an orderly manner;

2. To ensure the reliability of evidence before the members hear it;

3. To avoid the waste of time and eliminate confusion as to the issues;

4. To exclude certain evidence which is unduly prejudicial, unreliable or which public policy demands be excluded.

The next four topics will discuss examples of the manner in which the rules of evidence achieve these purposes.

1103   An Orderly Presentation

The prosecution first presents its case, which is called the "Prosecution Case in Chief." The trial counsel and his assistants must prove all the elements of each offense charged. After the prosecution closes his case by stating the "prosecution rests," the defense may present evidence.

However, the defense is not required to present any evidence at all, as the prosecution has the burden of proving guilt. The defense may have achieved its objective by cross-examination of prosecution witnesses or by otherwise illustrating where the trial counsel has failed to prove the accused guilty beyond a reasonable doubt.

If the defense has any evidence of persuasive value that coincides with his theory of how to defend this case, he should present evidence. This presentation is called the "Defense Case in Chief." His case may consist of any of the defenses discussed in Chapters IV and V of this book, or of witnesses who rebut the matters presented by the prosecution's witnesses or any other matter that would aid the accused in proving his innocence. The defense would then "rest."

The prosecution may then present his "Prosecution Case in Rebuttal," which should be limited to rebutting any matters raised during the defense case. The defense can then rebut these matters by a "Defense Case in Rebuttal."

The court may then, if it wishes, call witnesses. Extreme caution should be utilized if the court calls witnesses, in order to avoid even the appearance of the members perfecting a case for either side. See Chapter X of this publication as to the duties of members.

Generally, in a contested case, the prosecution and defense may present, as part of their cases, the testimony of some witnesses. There is an order for presentation of such testimony and certain rules as to how a counsel may question these witnesses.

Regardless of which side calls the witness, the trial counsel administers the oath.

> TC: You swear or affirm that the evidence you shall give in the case now in hearing shall be the truth, the whole truth, and nothing but the truth. So help you God.
> Witness: I do.

(Then, although some counsel prefer to handle their own case from this point, the trial counsel generally asks a few introductory questions.)

> TC: State your full name, grade, organization, station, and armed force.
>
> Witness: _____.

(Then, the trial counsel will state:)

> TC: Do you know the accused?
>
> Witness: _____.

(The witness may then be asked to point to the accused unless he states he knows the accused and the accused's identity has already been established.)

Following this introductory material, the side calling the witness will ask the witness questions. The party calling the witness seeks to establish all the information, which the witness is testifying to, that is favorable to his side of the case. Generally, a counsel knows what response a witness will make, as he has interviewed him beforehand.

The initial examination of a witness is called "Direct Examination." The general rule is that on direct examination the counsel calling the witness cannot ask leading questions. A "leading question" is one which either suggests the answer it is desired the witness shall make or which, embodying a material fact, is susceptible of being answered by a simple yes or no.

The reason for the rule is that the court is interested in hearing the witness' story, *not* the counsel's. Additionally, since the witness usually is cooperative, suggestive answers may supply a "false memory" for the witness.

Leading questions are subject to objection. Constant objections reduce the effectiveness of the side calling the witness. Therefore, leading questions should be avoided.

A rule of thumb would be to begin questions with "who, what, where, when, and how." Generally, if it appears that the counsel is "putting words in the witness' mouth," or that the counsel is testifying, the chances are the question is leading.

There are exceptions to the rule prohibiting the asking of leading questions on direct examination. For example, a witness hostile to the interests of the prosecution and desirous of acquitting the accused may be asked such questions, as the reason for restricting counsel to nonleading questions is not present in such a case. Paragraph 149b of the MCM relates other exceptions.

Here are some examples of leading questions:

1. On a charge of desertion, the trial counsel asks a prosecution witness: "You heard Jones state I'm going UA tonight and I'm never coming back to this ship, before he went over the hill, didn't you?"

2. On a charge of larceny of a watch, the trial counsel asks a prosecution witness: "Isn't it true that you saw Smith with his hands in Doe's locker after taps?"

3. On a charge of missing movement through neglect, the defense counsel asks a defense witness: "Isn't it true that you never saw the accused at quarters when the announcement of the ship getting under way was made?"

Here are some examples of how the same questions could have properly been asked on direct examination:

1. *The Desertion.*

TC: Where were you at or about 2000 on 30 October 19——?
Witness: I was on the afterbrow.
TC: Who was present?
Witness: Myself and Seaman Jones, the accused.
TC: State whether or not you had any conversations with him at that time.
Witness: I did.
TC: What were those conversations?
Witness: Jones told me "I'm going UA tonight and I'm never coming back to the ship."

2. *The Larceny.*

TC: Where were you at or about 2300 on 10 June 19——?
Witness: I was in my rack in the 1st Division compartment.
TC: What were you doing?
Witness: I was trying to sleep after taps and I heard a noise.
TC: What sort of noise?
Witness: A clank.
TC: State whether or not you could see anything.
Witness: A small light was lit in the passageway and I could see the lockers alongside.
TC: State whether or not you saw anything.
Witness: I saw Smith with his hand in Doe's locker.

3. *The Missing Movement through Design.*

DC: How did you know when the ship was getting under way on 10 August 19__?
Witness: It was announced at muster on 8 August 19__.
DC: State whether or not the accused was present for the muster on 8 August 19.__
Witness: No sir. He was not.

Following the direct examination of a witness, the opposing party has a right of cross-examination. It is a matter of *right*. To deny the right is prejudicial to the rights of the accused and warrants reversal of the case. The side cross-examining a witness can ask leading questions.

In general, cross-examination is limited to the issues which the witness has testified to on direct examination *and* the question of his credibility. For example, a defense witness may be a close friend of the accused, and the trial counsel could question him about that relationship. Or a prosecution witness may, in a case where he has positively identified the accused, be questioned as to visual powers. In short, a witness' interests, motives, way of life, misconduct, powers of discernment and other characteristics which are relevant to the issue of whether he should be believed are subjects of cross-examination, as these factors may influence the weight the members give the witness' testimony.

However, there is nothing to prevent believing a man who is biased. Who is more biased as regards the outcome of the case than the accused himself, if he chooses to testify as to his innocence?

Following cross-examination, there is redirect examination that is conducted by the side initially calling the witness. Its purpose is to rehabilitate a witness if his testimony has been damaged on cross-examination or to explain away apparent inconsistencies in his testimony. Recross examination by the other counsel follows. It should be limited to matters covered in redirect examination.

The court is then permitted to examine witnesses. This questioning must be done cautiously. See Chapter X as it relates to the responsibilities of members in this regard.

In any examination by either side, ambiguous, misleading, and unfair questions should never be permitted. A counsel should not misstate the evidence in asking a question, or assume a fact not in evidence, or argue with or harass a witness.

A counsel on direct examination cannot repeat a question which has already been answered. However, a cross-examiner may go over the same ground several times so long as the privilege is not abused.

1104 Ensuring Reliability of Evidence—Authenticity

Prior to the admittance of evidence, it must first be shown that what is offered *is* what it purports to be and that it is genuine (i.e., authentic). For example, the presiding officer in an aggravated assault case might require that the trial counsel show that the knife in court is the very knife found at the scene of the alleged crime, and not some other.

Evidence may be in several forms (oral, real, or documentary):

1. *Oral Evidence.* Oral evidence is the sworn testimony given by a witness. Oral evidence is authenticated by the oath administered to the witness. The religious nature of the oath (so help you, God), the possi

bility of prosecution for perjury, and the public nature of the trial tend to ensure that the witness tells the truth.

2. *Real Evidence.* Real evidence is any physical object, such as a stolen watch, jewelry, or a weapon used in an assault.

Real evidence is authenticated by two methods: chain of custody and identification. *Chain of custody* is generally established by the testimony of one or more witnesses concerning the actual possession of the object from the time it was first discovered until it is offered into evidence in the courtroom.

Identification is the process of having a witness testify that he recognizes the object. A witness can identify real evidence by such methods as inscriptions, marks, scratches, etc., appearing on the piece of real evidence.

3. *Documentary Evidence.* Documentary evidence includes anything in writing which is offered into evidence, such as a page from the accused's service record, a letter, or a forged check. It is more difficult to authenticate documentary evidence. Generally, the *original* of a document may be authenticated by one of several methods:

a. A witness who saw the execution of the document may testify as to its authenticity.

b. Judicial notice may be taken by the presiding officer of the signature of the custodian of military personnel records and their deputies and assistants. Paragraph 147a, MCM and paragraph 1105, *Military Law.*

c. The trial and defense counsel, with the express consent of the accused, may agree that the document is authentic. This is called a stipulation of fact. See paragraph 1105, *Military Law.*

d. Letters can be authenticated by showing that the letter being offered was written in reply to a previous letter.

e. An official custodian may, by testimony, authenticate a service record entry; or testimony of one or more witnesses may show a chain of custody from the origin of the document to its appearance in court.

f. Opinion evidence may be used to identify the handwriting on a document.

g. An attesting certificate may authenticate an original document. This type of certificate is a certificate or statement, signed by the custodian of the record or his deputy or assistant, which states that the attested writing is an original, and that the signer of the attesting certificate is acting in an official capacity as the person having custody of the record or his deputy or assistant. Paragraph 143b (2), MCM.

If an original document is used and authenticated by one of the methods above, certified copies of the original may be substituted in the record of trial.

The following illustrates one of the methods for introducing a page 13 entry from the accused's service record. See Appendix 8 of this book for a copy of such an entry.

> TC: As personnel officer of the USS *Awash,* are you the custodian of the service record book of the accused?
> Witness: I am.
> TC: Will you produce it, please?
> Witness: Here it is.

(Absence entries should be introduced to show each specification in sequence. Where there is more than one specification of UA, the following guide should be followed with respect to each specification.)

> TC: Directing your attention to page 13 of the service record, do you find thereon one or more entries pertaining to the offense of unauthorized absence charged by specification 1 of charge II?
> Witness: I find two such entries.
> TC: I now offer into evidence the two entries as prosecution exhibits 1 and 2, respectively, and show them to the defense for inspection, interrogation of the witness, and possible objection. I request permission to withdraw them at the conclusion of the trial and to substitute true copies therefor.

(Opposing counsel now inspects the document for admissibility, questions the witness, when appropriate, and states his objection or lack of objection as follows:)

> DC: ( ) Defense counsel has no objection.
> or
>   ( ) Defense counsel objects to the admission of _____
>
>   upon the following grounds _____ _____.

(If objection is raised, counsel may argue the issue and then the court rules.)

> Pres: The two entries on page 13 of the service record of the accused offered into evidence by the prosecution will be admitted into evidence as prosecution exhibits 1 and 2, respectively. Certified copies of the exhibits may be substituted in the record of trial in lieu of the originals.
> TC: Please read prosecution exhibits 1 and 2.
> Witness: (Read.)

Three methods of authenticating a *copy* of an official record are as follows:

1. Prior to trial, counsel obtains a true *copy* of the official record (for example, a page 6 entry of a previous conviction similar to the one in Appendix 16 of this publication). He then attaches an attesting certificate with the custodian's signature. In the case of a page 6 entry, the personnel officer on board a ship would be such a custodian. It would look like this:

ATTESTING CERTIFICATE

A true copy of the original is on file in the office of the

USS GRANGER (DD–19)
_____
(*name of command where record is filed*)

/s/ John Doakes
John Doakes, LT, USN, Personnel Officer, USS GRANGER
_____
(*name, grade and title of officer having official custody of the record*)

10 June 19___
_____
(*date certificate executed*)

In court, the counsel has the document marked for identification by the reporter, states the essential facts apparent on the face of the document showing its relevancy, and asks the court to take judicial notice of the signature of the officer who executed the attesting certificate affixed to the document, and to take judicial notice of his duties as custodian of the official record. He then offers the exhibit into evidence. If no objection is made, the exhibit is then received into evidence and read to the court. This method is the most common means of authenticating copies of official military records.

2. The seal, inked stamp, or other identification mark of a "department, agency, bureau, branch, force, command, or unit" may authenticate a copy of an official military record.

3. The trial and defense counsel, with the express consent of the accused, may stipulate to the authenticity of a copy.

There is one basic replacement for real and documentary evidence. It is called *demonstrative evidence*. Sometimes members have a difficult time visualizing the scene of an incident. Maps, charts, diagrams, photographs, or scale models may assist them in their determination of what the facts are in a particular case. Any witness who is familiar with the object or area portrayed can authenticate it simply by testifying that the object is a true and accurate representation of the area or object in question.

1105   Wasting Time and Confusing the Issues—Relevancy

The rules of evidence are also designed to avoid wasting time and confusing the issues. The requirement that evidence be relevant to be admissible is the principal means of accomplishing these objectives. *Evidence is relevant when the fact which it tends to prove is part of any issue in the case.* The question to be determined is "Does the evidence aid the court in answering the questions before it?" In and of itself, it need not be sufficient to establish the proposition but need only, when considering all other evidence presented, render the proposition more probable. If the evidence is too remote to have any appreciable value in proving any issue, it is *not* relevant.

For example, evidence *is* relevant if it tends to establish:

1. An element of one of the offenses charged;
2. A defense;
3. The identity of the perpetrator;
4. A collateral issue such as the admissibility of a confession or admission of the accused;
5. The credibility of a witness' testimony.

Evidence which appears to be irrelevant may be admitted provisionally by the presiding officer if the party offering such evidence states that other evidence will show its relevancy. Paragraph 137 of the MCM states that "it is generally more desirable, however, to require the party offering the evidence first to prove the facts showing its relevancy."

Some other rules of evidence that facilitate the trial are judicial notice and stipulations. These are two substitutes for evidence.

1. *Stipulations.* Stipulations are agreements between the trial and defense counsel with the express consent of the accused as to the existence or nonexistence of any fact (a stipulation of fact) or the content of the testimony that an absent witness would give if he were present in court (a stipulation of testimony).

As regards stipulations, paragraph 48*d* of the MCM, in discussing the duties of the defense counsel, states that "with a view to saving time, labor, and expense, he should cooperate with the trial counsel in the preparation of depositions and in appropriate stipulations as to unimportant or uncontested matters." A party may withdraw from a stipulation agreement at any time before the stipulation is received into evidence. As a matter of discretion, the presiding officer may permit the withdrawal of a stipulation once accepted.

However, a stipulation of fact in a contested case, which practically amounts to a confession, should not be accepted nor should a stipulation which, if true, would operate as a complete defense.

As to whether a party can contradict a stipulation, see *United States v. Gerlach,* the Discussion Case at the end of this chapter. Stipulations of fact may also be made as to the contents of a written document.

A stipulation of testimony does not admit the truth of the testimony nor does it add anything to its weight. It may be attacked by the counsel not offering it in the same manner as the testimony of any other witness.

The net result of a stipulation is that counsel does not have to present the witness whose testimony is stipulated or to present evidence as to the facts stipulated.

Stipulations of fact or testimony may be oral or written. An example of an oral stipulation would be:

> TC: The trial and defense counsel, with the express consent of the accused, stipulate that Prosecution Exhibit 1 for Identification is what it purports to be, page 13 of the accused's official service record.

This type of stipulation eliminates the need to prove the authenticity of the document.

A written stipulation of fact or testimony should never be taken into closed session as there is a danger of the members attaching undue weight to it.

2. *Judicial Notice.* Judicial notice is the formal recognition by a court of the existence of certain kinds of facts without the formal presentation of evidence. It has been discussed previously in this chapter as a method of expeditious authentication of documents. Paragraph 147 of the MCM discusses the principal matters of which judicial notice may be taken, such as general facts of history; the ordinary divisions of time into years, months, weeks, and other periods; the laws of the U.S.; the organization of the departments; and the signature of the Judge Advocate General and his deputies.

A more common example would be "the signatures of custodians of personnel . . . records of an armed force of the United States and their deputies and assistants." Thus, to prove an unauthorized absence, a trial counsel could authenticate an original official service record entry by requesting the presiding officer to take judicial notice of the "signature of the custodian."

Judicial notice may also be taken of the actual "duties of a person who has signed a writing in a capacity which would allow judicial notice" to be taken of his signature. Paragraph 147*a*, MCM.

1106 The Exclusionary Rules of Evidence—Competency

Competent evidence is evidence which is authentic and relevant and is *not* excluded from the court's consideration because of one or more of the recognized "exclusionary rules of evidence." In other words it is authentic, relevant, and *legally permitted to be used as evidence.*

The exclusionary rules are generally based upon the unreliability of certain evidence, public policy, or undue prejudice to the accused if such information were brought before the members.

1. *Unreliability.* Hearsay evidence, opinion evidence, and the best evidence rule are the basic examples of rules that concern themselves with "reliability."

a. *Hearsay Evidence.* Hearsay evidence is a statement made out of the courtroom, which is offered in evidence to prove the *truth* of the matters stated therein. Such evidence generally is inadmissible, since in a criminal prosecution any witness who has made a pertinent statement should, himself, be in court under oath, and subject to cross-examination, and the scrutiny of the court. Further, it is a fundamental principle that the accused has the right to be confronted by his accusers. Another reason for the hearsay rule is the presumptive inherent unreliability of twice-told tales.

The word "statement" means not only an oral or written expression, but also non-verbal conduct of a person intended by him as a substitute for words in expressing the matter stated. For example, a nod of the head signifying "yes" might constitute such a statement.

An example of hearsay evidence is related in paragraph 139 of the MCM as follows:

> The accused is being tried for the larceny of clothes from a locker. A is able to testify that B told A that he, B, saw the accused leave the quarters in which the locker was located with a bundle resembling clothes about the same time the clothes were stolen. This testimony from A would not be admissible to prove the facts stated by B.

What about a statement *that is not offered in evidence to prove the truth of the matters stated therein?* Such a statement is admissible, as it is simply evidence *that a statement was made.* It is *not* hearsay evidence and the Navy has coined the phrase "original evidence" in discussing it. The MCM gives several examples of non-hearsay evidence in paragraph 139:

> A is being tried for assaulting B. The defense presents the testimony of C that just before the assault C heard B say to A that he was about to kill him with his knife. The testimony of C is not hearsay, for it is offered to show that A acted in self-defense because B made the statement and not to prove the truth of B's statement.

Private A is being tried for disobedience of a certain order given him orally by Lieutenant B. C is able to testify that he heard Lieutenant B give the order to A. *This testimony, including testimony of C as to the terms of the order, would not be hearsay.* (Emphasis supplied.)

The above two examples are *not* exceptions to the hearsay evidence rule because they do not meet the initial definition of hearsay (i.e., the evidence is not being offered to prove the *truth* of the matters therein.) The distinction is important because there are exceptions to the hearsay evidence rule—and very important ones. Confessions and admissions of an accused are such important exceptions. See Chapter III for a discussion of these out-of-court statements. They are considered reliable because of the assumption that a person would not make a voluntary statement against his best interest unless it were true.

Dying declarations, statements of accomplices, fresh complaint in sexual offenses, business entries, past recollections recorded, depositions and former testimony are exceptions that are seldom seen by the average Navy or Marine Corps officer and will not be discussed in this publication. Chapter XXVII of the MCM discusses them in detail.

However, there are certain exceptions that do warrant further discussion, such as official records, spontaneous exclamations, and statements of motive, intent, or state of mind or body.

A spontaneous exclamation is an "utterance concerning the circumstances of a startling event made by a person while he was in such a condition of excitement, shock, or surprise, caused by his participation in or observation of the event, as to warrant a reasonable inference that he made the utterance as an impulsive and instinctive outcome of the event, and not as the result of deliberation or design. . . ." See paragraph 142*b*, MCM. Such statements are admissible as an exception to the hearsay rule because the spontaneity of the incident ensures its reliability. Any witness who heard the statement may testify. It is not necessary to have seen the offense.

The MCM cites the following example: in "a prosecution for assault by stabbing, the testimony of a person who did not see the attack, but who came upon the alleged victim thereafter, that the victim, while visibly in agony as a result of the wounds received, cried out, 'John Drew stabbed me!' is admissible" to prove the exclamation *and* that John Drew stabbed the victim.

Statements of *motive, intent, state of mind or body* are exceptions to the hearsay evidence rule. The MCM states that "if a statement made under circumstances not indicative of insincerity discloses a relevant and then existing motive, intent, or state of mind or body of the person who made the statement, evidence of the statement is admissible for the purpose of proving the motive, intent, or state of mind or body so disclosed."

In other words, a statement which directly tends to prove a motive, intent, or state of mind or body is admissible as an exception. This rule exists for the purpose of making available what frequently is the most credible evidence of the condition at issue; hence the "reliability factor" is present.

Indeed, proof of the state of mind of the accused is essential in any specific intent offense such as larceny or desertion. It could be essential to show the fear of the defendant in establishing a defense to an assault case (self-defense) or consent in a rape case.

However, evidence of the statement of someone other than the accused cannot be received into evidence when the statement amounts to an accusation that the act charged had been committed by the accused or that the act charged had been committed, even though it would reveal a relevant motive, intent, or state of mind.

The authentication of *official records* has already been discussed in great detail. It is obvious that a page 13 entry out of the service record book of the accused is hearsay, for it is a statement made out of court, offered in court to prove the truth of its contents. However, it is admissible if the person who makes the entry has an official duty to know or to ascertain through appropriate and trustworthy channels, the truth of the fact or event and to record such fact or event. This is the reliability factor that makes official records an exception to the hearsay evidence rule.

For example, the personnel or legal officer who signs a page 13 entry in the accused's service record regarding the inception and termination of an unauthorized absence (Appendix 8) has such a responsibility.

The MCM cites other examples of official records, such as enlistment papers, physical examination papers, records of court-martial convictions, logs, etc.

An official record made "principally with a view to prosecution, or other disciplinary or legal action, as a record of, or during the course of an investigation into, alleged unlawful or improper conduct" is inadmissible. Paragraph 144d, MCM. In *United States* v. *Wooten,* 13 USCMA 71, 32 CMR 71 (1962), a special court-martial at Camp Pendleton, California, admitted a shore patrol report into evidence against the accused. Terming this report "patently erroneous and highly prejudicial to the accused," the Court of Military Appeals reversed the conviction.

Entries in morning reports, service records, etc., as to absence without leave are admissible because these entries are made for the legitimate purpose of personnel accounting. The fact that they may also be used as evidence before a court-martial does not render them inadmissible. A confession or admission is admissible as it comes under another exception to the hearsay evidence rule.

b. *Best Evidence Rule.* An official record is not subject to objection on the ground that it was copied or compiled from notes, a memorandum, official records or other writings. However, the fact that the evidence was gathered from one source that is not as reliable as another source may affect the weight the courts should give these records in determining the findings. Nor is it subject to objection on the grounds that it is secondary evidence and not the "best evidence." The best evidence rule provides that in proving the contents of a document, the best evidence of its content is the "original" of the writing and must be offered unless counsel can show it is lost, destroyed, infeasible to produce, etc. However, a copy of an official record, otherwise classed as secondary evidence, may be admissible without first proving that the original has been lost or destroyed or accounting for the original, if the copy is properly authenticated.

Paragraph 143 of the MCM states that the term "original" can mean a complete carbon copy (including signatures) or an identical copy made by a photographic or other duplicating process for use as an original or as one of a number of originals. These are called duplicate originals and are admissible as originals. All others are secondary evidence.

c. *Opinion Evidence.* As a general rule, opinion evidence is inadmissible. Ordinarily, a witness may testify only as to matters of which he personally has had sensory perception: the facts.

Assume that the accused is charged with the larceny of a Navy tool box belonging to the USS *Awash* in San Diego, California.

The accused had been attached to the *Awash* for two years. He had been transferred recently to the naval base at Norfolk, Virginia. The tool box had a serial number (100902) and other Navy markings thereon. The tool box was reported missing from the accused's division the day after he left the ship. The tool box was found in the accused's possession in Norfolk.

These are facts that a witness may testify to in court. However, the court must make its own opinions based upon the facts. In this case, the court may be justified in reaching the following opinions: the accused removed the tool box from the USS *Awash*; the accused took it to Norfolk, Virginia; and the accused is guilty of larceny.

The principal exception to this basic rule is that any witness may state his opinion, if it results from his personal observation of certain facts, and is of a kind commonly experienced, and cannot adequately be conveyed to the court by a mere recitation of the observed facts.

The reason for the exception is that sometimes facts cannot be described in sufficient detail to enable the court to form a conclusion without the opinion of the witness.

The exception permits a witness to testify as to such matters as drunkenness; smells (i.e., it smelled like lighter fluid); facial features (i.e., the accused looked surprised); color; weight; size; or the speed of a vehicle (i.e., he was going at least 60 miles per hour).

The counsel questioning a witness as to his opinion should first show that the witness was in a position to observe, smell, or taste what he states he did. Then, if possible, his prior experience with these matters should be related. For example, the witness may state, "I picked up the can, put it near my nose, and smelled the contents. I have been smoking for 20 years, utilizing lighter fluid, and in my opinion the can contained lighter fluid."

Opinions may also be expressed by expert witnesses. An expert witness is a person who is qualified as an expert in a technical field requiring specialized training and knowledge. His opinions are admissible if the technical matters in issue require highly specialized knowledge not generally possessed by the average court member. His qualifications to testify must be demonstrated to the court before he may do so.

As a general rule, no witness may be permitted to give his opinion as to the ultimate issue in the case: the guilt or innocence of the accused. For example, the victim in a larceny case could not testify that "the accused stole my watch." Nor could a witness testify, as regards the disobedience of an order that "the accused disobeyed my order."

2. *Public Policy.* Exclusionary rules of evidence may also be based upon public policy. Public policy can be defined as our society's attitude on a given subject, expressed either in the Constitution of the United States, laws passed by Congress or a state, and judicial decisions. It is a principle of law by virtue of which acts contrary to the public good are held invalid.

a. *Illegal Search and Seizure.* The rules against illegal search and seizure and self-incrimination (as it relates to the taking of the statement of a suspect) have already been discussed in Chapter III. However, the rules against self-incrimination apply to in-court statements as well as to out-of-court statements.

b. *Self-incrimination.* The Fifth Amendment to the U.S. Constitution states that "no person . . . shall be compelled in any criminal case to be a witness against himself . . ." Article 31(a) of the Code provides that "no person subject to this code shall compel any person to incriminate himself or to answer any question the answer to which may tend to incriminate him."

This means that the accused has an absolute right not to testify at his own trial and that the trial counsel cannot comment on this decision.

either directly or by implication. Nor can the prosecution call the accused as a witness in his trial. If a person is called to testify as a witness in the trial of another, he may then refuse to respond to any question if the answer would tend to incriminate him.

However, if the accused, at his trial, elects to testify as to an offense, he loses his right to refuse to answer questions on the grounds it may incriminate him as to *that* offense. For example, if the accused is on trial for two or more offenses and on direct examination testifies concerning his guilt or innocence of only one, or some of them, he may not be cross-examined with respect to the issue of his guilt or innocence of the offenses about which he has not testified. If the accused does testify as to one offense, he may be cross-examined on *all* aspects of that one offense.

The accused may elect to testify as to matters not bearing upon the issue of his guilt or innocence of any offense for which he is being tried. If he does, he may only be cross-examined on that issue. For example, the accused may testify that he was not advised of his right to have a military lawyer represent him free of charge prior to his confessing to the crime. He could testify to this collateral (interlocutory) issue and could not be cross-examined on the crime itself.

c. *Husband-Wife Communications.* Certain other public policy rules of evidence are worth a brief discussion. Generally, one spouse may not testify as to confidential communications made by the other while they were husband and wife and not living in separation under a judicial decree.

d. *Marital Privilege.* However, not only is there a privilege relating to confidential communications between husband and wife, but one spouse cannot take the stand and testify against the other regardless of the nature of the communication. The reason for these rules is the necessity of protection of the marital relationship. There are certain exceptions to these rules. For example, if a wife is assaulted by her husband and he is tried by a court-martial, she may testify against him as regards the assault. Paragraph 148e of the MCM discusses other exceptions to this rule.

e. *Attorney-Client Communications.* Generally, communications between a client (or agent of the client) and his attorney (or his agent, such as a yeoman) are privileged when made if the relationship of attorney and client existed. The attorney cannot reveal them under these circumstances. Military or civilian counsel detailed, assigned, or otherwise engaged to defend or represent a person in a court-martial case or in any military investigation are considered to be "attorneys" for this purpose. *Therefore, the Navy and Marine Corps officer is bound by this privilege, even though he is not a lawyer.*

f. *Priest-Penitent Communications.* A chaplain, priest, clergyman or their assistants or agents cannot reveal communications of a penitent revealed either as a formal act of religion or concerning a matter of conscience. There are various exceptions to these rules which are discussed in paragraph 151b(2) of the MCM.

3. *Undue Prejudice.* Some facts may be authentic and relevant and still not be admissible as competent evidence if their admission would cause undue prejudice to the accused.

a. *Inflammatory Matters.* The rule prohibiting unduly "inflammatory" matter from being considered by the members of a court is one example. If real or demonstrative evidence is offered solely to appeal to the emotions or passions of the members or to distract their attention, it is inadmissible. A general principle of the law of evidence is that evidence may be held inadmissible where its legitimate probative value is slight and the danger of misuse is great.

For example, in *United States* v. *Bennett,* 7 USCMA 97, 21 CMR 223 (1956), the accused was charged and convicted of rape and attempted murder of a child and awarded the death penalty. The defense argued that a sketch drawn by one of the medical witnesses showing certain anatomical features of the female body and the more important physical injuries suffered by the victim inflamed the minds of the court members "to the prejudice of the accused." The defense argued that the document served no instructional purpose and was of no probative value.

The Court of Military Appeals disagreed, stating as follows:

> The sketch no doubt rendered the medical testimony intelligible, and to that extent it served a legitimate purpose. . . . So far as the exhibit is concerned, it was not prepared in a manner calculated to magnify the more odious features of this criminal attack, and we cannot conclude the law officer erred in permitting its receipt in evidence.

The court approved the conviction and sentence.

b. *Bad Moral Character.* Generally, evidence that the accused has a *bad moral character* may not be used initially by the prosecution to prove the guilt of the accused of the offense charged. This prohibition does not apply if the defense first introduces evidence of the good character of the accused. For example, to show the probability of his innocence, the accused may introduce evidence of his military record and standing as shown by authenticated copies of efficiency or fitness reports or evidence of his general character as a moral, well-behaved law-abiding citizen or both.

The prosecution may *then* rebut this evidence, but it must *first* have been presented by the defense in order for him to do so. Paragraph 138*f* of the MCM discusses character evidence in detail.

The reason for the rules regarding bad moral character is that if the prosecution is allowed initially to introduce such evidence, the court might improperly base its findings on the character of the accused, and not on whether he has been proven guilty of the offense charged.

c. *Prior Offenses.* This same rationale applies to prior offenses or acts of misconduct of the accused. Generally, evidence of other offenses or acts of misconduct of the accused are not admissible as tending to prove his guilt. "However, if evidence of other offenses or acts of misconduct of the accused has substantial value as tending to prove something other than a fact to be inferred from the disposition of the accused or is offered in proper rebuttal of matters raised by the defense, the reason for excluding the evidence is not applicable." Paragraph 138*g*, MCM. For example, the MCM lists seven circumstances when such evidence might be admissible:

1. When it tends to identify the accused as the perpetrator of the offense charged;

2. When it tends to prove a plan or design of the accused;

3. When it tends to prove knowledge or guilty intent in a case in which these matters are in issue;

4. When it tends to show the accused's consciousness of guilt of the offense charged;

5. When it tends to prove motive;

6. When it tends to rebut a contention, express or implicit, made by the accused that his participation in the offense charged was the result of accident or mistake or that he was entrapped;

7. When it tends to rebut any issue raised by the defense (see 138*f* (2) of the MCM for one minor exception).

For example, the accused is charged with larceny of property belonging to X. Evidence that the accused sold the property is admissible, even if the sale is itself an offense—since this evidence would tend to prove that he intended to deprive X of the property permanently. (Case "3" above.)

1107 Summary

Admissible evidence must be authentic, relevant, and competent. The rules of evidence are complicated and varied and, as a rule of thumb, "the exceptions make the rule."

The hearsay evidence rule appears to exclude as incompetent everything except the testimony of a witness on the stand—and it appears to even restrict that testimony to a great degree. However, because of the "reliability" factor, evidence that would otherwise be excluded may be admitted into evidence as an exception.

This chapter has not covered all of the rules of evidence nor even related all the exceptions to the rules discussed, except in those areas where the officer would be most concerned. It is intended to explain some of the more common experiences to be encountered in the courtroom.

The MCM should always be consulted when any question arises and a JAG lawyer consulted if the answer is not clear.

The discussion and self-quiz at the end of this chapter has been utilized at the School of Naval Justice in Newport, Rhode Island. It has been slightly modified by the author to incorporate the Military Justice Act of 1968. It is an excellent example of the application of the rules of evidence to a factual situation.

Discussion Case

UNITED STATES, Appellee

v.

ROGER T. GERLACH, Lance Corporal, U.S. Marine Corps, Appellant
16 USCMA 383, 37 CMR 3

(1966)

Opinion of the Court

QUINN, Chief Judge:

Appellant was brought from Vietnam to Okinawa to stand trial before a general court-martial on a charge of committing an assault, in which grievous bodily harm was intentionally inflicted upon a fellow Marine, in violation of Article 128, Uniform Code of Military Justice, 10 USC § 928. He pleaded guilty, and was sentenced to suffer punishment extending to confinement at hard labor for two years and a bad-conduct discharge. With provision for a limited suspension of part of the punishment, the convening authority approved the sentence. His action was affirmed by the board of review. The accused then appealed to this Court, contending that he was prejudiced by trial counsel's argument as to the sentence.

At trial, a stipulation of facts was introduced in evidence, with the consent of the accused and trial counsel. In pertinent part, it reads as follows:

". . . Lance Corporal Roger T. Gerlach, on the evening of 11 November 1965, *was involved in a scuffle* with an unknown Marine, *at which time he was kicked in the groin.* He then went from the scene of the assault to his squad bay area, secured a K-bar knife and returned to the scene of the assault. *Seeing Lance Corporal Helus, and believing him to be the man who kicked him in the groin,* he cut Lance Corporal Helus in the abdomen, on the left side, and on the back of the neck." [Emphasis supplied.]

In addition, the accused testified in his own behalf during the sentence proceedings. He reviewed his Marine Corps background, which included duty in the Dominican Republic, and revealed that he had volunteered for service in Vietnam. He also related circumstances about the offense which were not set out in the stipulation of facts. Among other things, he said that he had been drinking, but admitted he was not too drunk to know what he was doing at the time of the assault. He maintained he had never before "pulled a knife on anyone," and he could not "understand" why he had done so on this occasion.

Lance Corporal Wallace L. Helus, the victim of the accused's assault, testified for both the prosecution and the accused. For the government, he identified two photographs of the knife wounds. These were admitted into evidence as "matters in aggravation." He also testified that "to the best of . . . [his] knowledge" he had not kicked the accused. On behalf of the accused, Helus testified that previous to the incident he had done so much drinking his recollection of the incident was "hazy." He could not recall the immediate circumstances of the assault, but admitted that when he had "too many drinks" he sometimes got "rowdy." He did not know how the incident "started" or "whose fault it was," so he could not "bear a grudge" against the accused.

Trial counsel argued passionately for the maximum penalty. Referring to the evidence that the accused had been kicked in the groin by an "unknown Marine" in a "scuffle" moments before the accused went for his knife, he argued as follows:

". . . [F]rom evidence here we have seen today there's been nobody that kicked him. Lance Corporal Helus is the only one that possibly could have, and the first time he saw Gerlach was when he came downstairs. Gerlach himself said he was kicked in the groin at a prior time, then he went up the stairs, got the K-bar and came back, so it would be impossible for Helus to kick Gerlach in the groin."

At the end of trial counsel's argument, defense counsel called attention to the recitals in the stipulation of facts, and asked whether the Government was "now refuting" the stipulation by questioning "what really happened there." He was interrupted in the middle of his remarks by the law officer [military judge] who summarily directed him to "proceed with . . . [his] argument." Thereafter, the law officer gave no instructions to the court members to disregard trial counsel's assertion that the evidence demonstrated that "nobody . . . kicked" the accused.

Evidence may properly be presented by way of stipulation between the Government and the accused. Manual for Courts-Martial, United States, 1951, paragraph 154*b; United States* v. *Cambridge,* 3 USCMA 377, 12 CMR 133. Two broad categories of stipulation are generally recognized. One is a stipulation as to the testimony that an absent person would give if called as a witness; the other is a stipulation as to the existence or nonexistence of an agreed fact. The difference between the two classes is material. The usual stipulation of expected testimony does not admit the truth of the testimony; consequently, the party adversely affected by the testimony may introduce other evidence inconsistent with, or contradictory of, the stipulated testimony. A stipulation of fact, however, is usually conclusive. See *United States* v. *Cambridge,* supra. It has been compared to a judicial admission, "so that the one party need offer no evidence to prove it, and the other is not allowed to disprove it." Wigmore, Evidence, 3d ed, § 2588. However, the Manual for Courts-Martial seems to accord the stipulation of fact less effect. It provides that the "court is not bound by a stipulation [of fact] even if received," where "other evidence" before the court convinces it "that the stipulated fact is not true." Manual for Courts-Martial, supra, paragraph 154*b* (1). Except possibly for a fact that may be judicially noticed (see *Attorney General* v. *Rice,* 64 Mich 385, 391, 31 NW 203 (1887)), it is difficult to see how other evidence contradictory of a stipulated fact may come before the court, without a direction that the stipulation be disregarded. In this case, we need not consider the extent or the conditions, if any, under which the court may properly disregard a stipulation of fact. Unless, and until, the stipulation is withdrawn or stricken from the record, the parties are bound by it. *United States* v. *Cambridge,* supra. Consequently, trial counsel should not have contended, as he did, that the evidence demonstrated that "nobody . . . kicked" the accused. Furthermore, when defense counsel challenged the propriety of counsel's argument, the law officer should have in-structed the court members to disregard trial counsel's remarks.

Improper argument by trial counsel does not necessarily require corrective action by an appellate court. *United States* v. *Carpenter,* 11 USCMA 418, 29 CMR 234. Also to be considered is whether there is a fair risk that the argument had any effect upon the court members. *United States* v. *Simpson,* 10 USCMA 229, 27 CMR 303. The government contends that the seriousness of the victim's injuries and the leniency of the sentence compared to the permissible maximum punishment of five years' confinement and a dishonorable discharge, which could have been adjudged, compellingly indicate that the court members were not influenced by the prosecutor's argument. These factors are indeed relevant to assessment of the probable impact of the error, but they are not determinative of the issue. From the record of trial it is clear the parties attached importance to the evidence that the accused was kicked in the groin. That circumstance was included in the stipulation of facts, and trial counsel expended considerable effort in attempting to discredit it as an ameliorative factor. It cannot, therefore, be said that trial counsel's argument was so insignificant as to be entirely devoid of persuasiveness. *United States* v. *Anderson,* 8 USCMA 603, 25 CMR 107.

The decision of the board of review as to the sentence is reversed. The record of trial is returned to the Judge Advocate General of the Navy for resubmission to the board of review. In its discretion, the board of review may reassess the accused's punishment in light of the error or direct a rehearing on the sentence.

Judges FERGUSON and KILDAY concur.

DISCUSSION AND SELF-QUIZ

You are the legal officer of the USS *Schmidt* (DD–111). A special court-martial aboard your ship has convicted Jones, Robert A., Seaman, U.S. Navy, of one offense of missing movement through design on 3 January 19___ and has sentenced him to confinement at hard labor for six months, reduction to seaman recruit, and forfeiture of $60.00 per month for six months. The record of trial has been submitted to you, and you are reviewing it prior to advising your commanding officer concerning his action in the case.

Quoted below are excerpts from that record of trial. Read it carefully and decide what, if any, errors were made by the president in his rulings during the trial.

Ensign Joe Worth, U.S. Naval Reserve, was called as a witness for the prosecution, was sworn, and testified as follows:

DIRECT EXAMINATION

Questions by the prosecution:

Q. State your full name, grade, organization and armed force.
A. My name is Joe Worth, Ensign, U.S. Naval Reserve, personnel officer aboard this ship.
Q. Do you know the accused?
A. Yes, that is he sitting right over there.
TC: Let the record show that the witness pointed to the accused.
PRES: The record may so show.
Q. Are you the legal custodian of the accused's service record book?
A. I am. Here it is.
Q. Does that service record book contain page 13 entries regarding a period of unauthorized absence commencing on 2 January 19___?
DC: Now, just a minute. I object to that. The accused is not on trial for unauthorized absence, and evidence of such an absence would be irrelevant.
TC: If it please the court, one of the elements of missing movement through design is that the accused was not aboard his ship when it moved. The prosecution feels that this evidence is relevant to show that fact.
PRES: The objection is overruled. The witness may answer that question.

1. The President's Ruling was (CORRECT) (INCORRECT). *Reason:*

A. Yes, sir, the accused's service record book does contain such entries. Here it is.
Q. Do those entries purport to bear a signature?
A. Yes, sir. They bear my signature as Personnel Officer, By direction of the Commanding Officer.
TC: Request that the reporter mark this exhibit for identification.
REPORTER: This will be Prosecution Exhibit 1 for identification.
Q. I now show you Prosecution Exhibit 1 for identification and ask you what it is.
A. This is the page 13 from the accused's service record which I previously identified.
TC: I now offer Prosecution Exhibit 1 for identification into evidence as Prosecution Exhibit 1, and show it to the defense for

inspection and possible objection.
DC: I object to this document on the grounds that it has not been properly authenticated. The witness has not shown that the contents of this document are true.
TC: Well, Mr. President, we have shown that this document came from the official service record of the accused; and we have shown that it was executed by the personnel officer, whose duty it is to prepare such entries. I don't really believe that we need show that its contents are true, but only need to show that it is a genuine service record entry.
PRES: The objection is overruled.

2. The President's Ruling was (CORRECT) (INCORRECT). *Reasons:*

TC: I have no further question. Does the defense desire to cross-examine this witness?
DC: The defense does not.
TC: Does the court have any question of this witness?
PRES: The court does not.

Robert (n) Brown, Seaman, U.S. Navy, was called as a witness for the prosecution, was sworn, and testified as follows:

DIRECT EXAMINATION

Questions by the prosecution:

Q. State your name, rate, and duty station.
A. Robert Brown, Seaman, U.S. Navy, USS *Schmidt* (DD–111).
Q. Do you know the accused in this case?
A. Yes, sir. That's him.

TC: Let the record show that the witness pointed to the accused.
PRES: The record may so show.
Q. What division are you in aboard the *Schmidt?*
A. 1st Division, sir.
Q. What division is the accused in?
A. 1st Division, also, sir.
Q. Where was your ship on 3 January 19___?
A. We were in Norfolk, sir, but that's the day we got under way for Newport, Rhode Island. We had been planning this trip for over two weeks.
Q. How did you know your ship was going to leave on 3 January?
A. Well, the ship's plan of the day carried the word for about two weeks before we left, and, also, Lieutenant (junior grade) Hatten, our division officer, announced it at quarters every morning during the last week before we left.
Q. State whether or not the accused was in attendance at those musters.
A. Yes, sir, he was at almost all of them.
Q. Directing your attention to the morning muster on 27 December, was he there at that time?
A. Yes, sir, he was.
Q. State whether or not you had any conversations with him at that time.
A. I did.
Q. What were those conversations?
A. Jones told me at that time that he sure was glad that we were going to Newport. He said that he knew the girl who worked down at the Blue Moon, and that he was anxious to renew their friendship.

Q. State whether or not the accused was aboard the *Schmidt* when she departed Norfolk for Newport?

A. No, sir.

TC: No further questions. Does the defense desire to cross-examine?

DC: The defense does.

CROSS-EXAMINATION

Questions by the defense:

Q. Brown, do you know why the accused wasn't aboard when you left for Newport?

A. Yes, sir. You see, he's got this girl down in Norfolk, and I had gone over to her place with him for a New Year's Eve party. . . .

TC: Just a minute. I object to this. We aren't interested about any party on New Year's Eve. We just want to know why the accused wasn't on board on 3 January.

DC: I'm trying to show that, Mr. President. I think that the accused's activities on the two days preceding the movement may shed some light on his intention to move with his ship.

PRES: The objection is sustained.

3. The President's Ruling was (CORRECT) (INCORRECT). *Reason:*

Q. Now, Brown, when was the last time you saw the accused before you left for Newport?

A. That was about noon on 1 January, sir, but he was in a bad way.

Q. What do you mean by that?

A. Well, sir, he was drunk.

TC: Now, I object to that answer, and move that it be stricken. The accused is not on trial for drunkenness, and this would be irrelevant.

PRES: Motion is denied.

4. The President's Ruling was (CORRECT) (INCORRECT). *Reason:*

Q. Did you have any conversation with him at that time?

A. Yes, sir, he asked me to hold his wallet and money for him until the ship left, as he was so drunk that he was afraid to keep it himself.

DC: I request this object be marked for identification.

REPORTER: This will be Defense Exhibit A for identification.

Q. Brown, I show you Defense Exhibit A for identification and ask you what it is.

A. Sir, that is the accused's wallet that he gave me on 1 January 19—.

Q. How do you recognize it as such?

A. Well, it is black, has the same inscription on it that it had when he gave it to me—"To Bob from Suzie"—and it has the accused's I.D. card in it still.

DC: I now offer this into evidence as Defense Exhibit A, and show it to the Trial Counsel for his inspection and possible objection.

TC: I object to this on the grounds that the Defense Counsel has not adequately shown the chain of custody of this real evidence.

DC: Mr. President . . .

PRES: Objection sustained.

5. The President's Ruling was (CORRECT) (INCORRECT). *Reasons:*

CHAPTER XII

Trial Procedure

The procedures utilized in courts-martial have changed dramatically i the past twenty years, as discussed in Chapter I. It is essential that th Navy and Marine Corps officer possess a concept of the basic procedur utilized before courts-martial in order to understand what is tran piring.

All courts-martial, including a summary court-martial, should be co ducted with the formality warranting such important proceedings. Th manner in which an accused may be apprehended, and the duties of th preliminary inquiry officer, the convening authority, the trial counsel, th defense counsel, the members, the military judge, and the president of court-martial have been discussed.

1201 The General Court-Martial

There are few differences in procedure between the general and th special court-martial in which a military judge is detailed. Howeve there are some differences in the personnel authorized to appear befo such courts and the punishments that can be awarded. For example, a general court the detailed trial and defense counsel are always certifi military lawyers and there is always a detailed military judge. The speci court does not always require a military judge and a certified defen counsel be detailed to the court.

A special court-martial is somewhat limited as to the punishments may award, whereas a general court-martial can adjudge *any* punishme that military law permits for a particular offense.

In general courts-martial, the president of the court is never the p siding officer. In special courts-martial, the president is the presidi officer whenever a military judge is not detailed to the court. (See Chapter X.)

1202 Setting the Trial Date

After consultation with the trial counsel, the presiding officer (either the military judge or president, as appropriate) sets the time of trial. If the defense counsel request a delay, they should furnish the trial counsel with a written statement requesting such delay and stating that a subsequent written notification will be furnished by the defense when they are ready to proceed to trial. Any valid and reasonable request for a reasonable delay should generally be honored.

1203 The Article 39(a) Session

The Article 39(a) session is an integral part of the trial.

It is conducted outside the presence of the members. *Article 39(a) sessions may only be held when a military judge is detailed to the court. The military judge presides.* A president of a special court-martial may never conduct an Article 39(a) session.

Immediately after an Article 39(a) session begins, the military judge ensures that the court is properly constituted. He accomplishes this by following the same preliminary procedures utilized in a court-martial with members. For example, the announcing, introducing, and swearing of personnel present will generally be covered at this time.

The military judge may conduct Article 39(a) sessions for the following reasons:

1. To hold the arraignment (see paragraph 1212), receive pleas, and enter findings of guilty, if accepted;

2. To hear defenses and objections;

3. To dispose of interlocutory matters;

4. To rule upon the admittance of evidence;

5. To determine whether the accused desires to be tried by a court composed of at least one-third enlisted members or by a court composed of a military judge without members;

6. To perform other procedural functions which do not require the presence of court members.

Unless the defense waives it, the session cannot be held within five days after the service of charges for a general court-martial and within three days after such service for a special court.

Article 39(a) sessions are not confined strictly to matters arising before assembly. They may be held either before, during, or after the formal assembly of the court. However, they are generally held before assembly. They eliminate much of the "dead time" that a member formerly wasted by sitting through preliminary proceedings or by retiring to a separate

room while an interlocutory question (such as a motion to dismiss fo
lack of speedy trial) was resolved.

1204 Trial Before a Military Judge Alone

In a case in which a military judge is detailed, an accused may reque
that a military judge hear his case without the members. This is th
military equivalent to a judge without a jury in civilian law. The mi
tary judge would then determine the guilt or innocence of the accuse
and when appropriate, award an appropriate sentence. He would ru
finally on all questions of law and fact.

A military judge alone has jurisdiction to try any case except or
which has been referred to trial as a capital (possible death penalty) ca:

The accused may request trial by a military judge alone either pri
to an Article 39(a) session, during such a session, or prior to assemb
with the members. The accused has a right to know who the milita
judge is and to consult with his defense counsel before making a decisio

His request should be in writing. The military judge may then appro
or disapprove the request. Generally, the request should initially be ma
no later than the Article 39(a) session.

1205 Initial Informal Inquiry

Paragraphs 1203 and 1204 have discussed matters that apply only wh
a military judge has been detailed to a court-martial. The remainder
this chapter and Chapter XIII will be generally applicable to cou:
martial convened with either a military judge or president presidi
except where stated otherwise.

After court personnel have gathered for the trial, but prior to calli
the court to order, the presiding officer should accomplish the followir

1. Examine the convening order and determine if a quorum of t
members are present (no *less* than three in a special court);

2. Determine that the accused is present for trial;

3. Determine that the members of the prosecution and defense
apparently qualified. For example, the defense counsel should be a ce
fied military lawyer if the punishment a special court could award
cludes a bad conduct discharge;

4. Determine whether the accused has made a request for enlis
men and if so, one-third of the members present must be enlisted n
of a unit other than the accused's;

5. Determine if the accused requests trial by a military judge alo

1206 Calling the Court to Order

The members are seated with the president in the center and ot
members alternately to the right and left of him according to rank. 7

iilitary judge sits apart from the court. The presiding officer determines
here other personnel will sit (generally this is prearranged). Appendix
b of the MCM has a suggested courtroom arrangement.

When the court is ready to proceed, the presiding officer (either the
iilitary judge or the president without a military judge) calls the court
) order.

207 Announcing the Personnel of the Court

The trial counsel states by what order the court is convened.

Then, the trial counsel announces the name of the military judge, if
etailed, and the names of the members and counsel who are present
nd those who are absent. There is a strict accountability rule relating
) the absence of detailed members. (See Chapter X of this publication.)
imilar announcements are made when there is a change of personnel.
'he trial counsel then announces the name of the accused and the fact
iat he is present in court.

The trial counsel will next swear in the reporter (unless previously
vorn) and the interpreter, if any. Chapter XXII of the MCM contains
ie forms for the various oaths.

208 The Qualifications of Counsel

The trial counsel next announces whether the legal qualifications of
ie members of the prosecution are other than as stated in the convening
rder and whether any member of the prosecution has acted as investi-
iting officer, military judge, court member, or a member of the defense
1 the same case, or has acted as counsel for the accused at a pretrial
ivestigation or other proceedings involving the same general matter.
'he court-martial must avoid even the appearance of unfairness. Conse-
uently, such dual roles are absolutely prohibited. See paragraph 61e,
ICM, for the action to be taken if a trial counsel appears to be dis-
ualified.

In a non-BCD special court-martial, the presiding officer would then
iquire of the accused whether he has been afforded the opportunity to
e represented by a certified military lawyer (counsel qualified under
rticle 27 (b)). If not, a special court-martial is not legally constituted un-
·ss physical conditions or military exigencies prevented such detailing. A
:rtified military lawyer must be initially detailed to represent an accused
i a BCD special court-martial.

The accused must also be advised by the presiding officer that he has
ie right to individual counsel. This may be a civilian lawyer employed
: the accused's own expense. It may be a certified military lawyer or
onlawyer (in certain cases) if the requested service member is reasonably
vailable.

In a non-BCD special court-martial, if the accused has been off[
certified counsel and declines to be represented by him, the accused]
be represented by a detailed nonlawyer counsel, represent himself
utilize an individual counsel, who need not be a lawyer. (See Cha
VIII for a further discussion of this matter.)

However, if the special court-martial can adjudge a BCD and the
cused has been offered and refused a certified military lawyer, he]
not be represented by an individual counsel who is not qualified]
lawyer, although he may represent himself.

Regardless of the legal qualifications of the individual counsel,
detailed defense counsel (military lawyers or otherwise) shall act as]
ciate counsel unless expressly excused by the accused.

If the trial counsel has certain legal qualifications, the defense cou
must have them also. See paragraph 805 of this publication and p
graph 61*f* of the MCM for further details in this regard.

In any special court-martial, the presiding officer will adjourn the c[
and report to the convening authority if the accused has not been g[
the opportunity to be represented by a certified military lawyer c
either the trial counsel or assistant trial counsel has greater legal qu[
cations than the defense counsel.

After the court has ascertained the qualifications of the member
the prosecution, the trial counsel will ask the accused whom he de[
to introduce as counsel. Counsel representing the accused will then
asked to state whether the legal qualifications of the detailed mem
of the defense are other than as stated in the order convening the co

If the accused introduces individual counsel and his legal qualificat[
are not reflected in the convening order, he will state what qualificat
he does possess.

After the court has determined that the defense counsel has the re
site legal qualifications, the trial counsel will ask the defense to sta[
any member of the defense is the accuser, has acted for the prosecut
or as the investigating officer, military judge, or court member in
same case. A member of the defense who has acted for the prosecu[
must be excused as he cannot, under *any* circumstances, act for
defense. The others may act if the accused *expressly* requests their serv

1209　Oaths of the Military Judge, Counsel, and Members

It will then be established whether the military judge, counsel,
the members have been sworn previously, and if not, they shall be sw[
The JAG Manual provides that the military judge and the cert[
military lawyers need only be sworn in once during their careers;
is, at the time they are originally certified to perform such duties.

Court members may be given a single oath for the duration of convening order that detailed them. However, civilian and noncertified military counsel must be sworn at each trial.

In a case in which a military judge is presiding, the proceedings up until the announcement of the assembly of the court generally would have been already accomplished in the Article 39(a) session. In such case, there is no need to repeat these procedures and the proceedings could begin at this point. However, if the president is the presiding officer, no Article 39(a) session is permitted and these procedures would be consummated before the members who would be present in court.

The presiding officer then announces that the court is "assembled."

1210 Challenges

The presiding officer then requires all persons who expect to be called as witnesses to depart the courtroom.

The trial counsel then relates the general nature of, and who forwarded and investigated, the charges. For example:

> The general nature of the charges in this case is two violations of the Uniform Code of Military Justice, Article 86, unauthorized absence for 6 and 20 days; forwarded with recommendations as to disposition by Captain J. P. Jones, USN, the convening authority; and investigated by Ensign J. D. Smith, USN.

The trial counsel will next disclose the name of any court member or military judge who participated in any proceeding already held. He will then disclose every ground for challenge he is aware of and will request that the military judge and each member do likewise.

If the defense counsel consents, the trial counsel may, at this time, present copies of the charges and specifications to the members. This will furnish them with some information upon which to refresh their memory, as *they are required to state any grounds for challenge they are aware of either regarding themselves or others involved in the proceedings.* (See Chapter X for a discussion of challenges of members.) Each accused and the trial counsel are entitled to one peremptory challenge of a member, but the military judge may only be challenged for cause.

Challenges for cause should be made at this time but, in his discretion, the presiding officer may allow a challenge for cause at any stage of the proceedings. Such challenges may also be renewed, even though once overruled, if for good cause. For example, newly discovered evidence could constitute "good cause."

The trial counsel and then the defense counsel announce whether they have any challenges for cause or peremptory challenges.

If a challenge for cause is made, both sides have an opportunity to question the person challenged, to introduce evidence, and to argue the case.

The military judge determines all challenges. He may do so either in the hearing of the court or in an out-of-court session. The president of a special court-martial without a military judge cannot make this determination. All members must vote on the challenge, except for the challenged member who will be excluded. A simple majority vote determines the issue. A tie vote disqualifies the member. Paragraph 1004 discusses challenges from a member's point of view.

The trial counsel must remember that after every adjournment, recess or closing of the court, he must state for the record whether all parties to the trial who were present before the court adjourned or recessed or closed are again present. This procedure ensures that the record of trial always reflects *who* was present in court.

An adjournment generally puts off the trial until a stated time or indefinitely. For example, the court would adjourn until the next day. A recess generally is for a relatively short period of time (i.e., a lunch period). A court is "closed" whenever its members are required to consult either on the findings or sentence or some other matter. No one other than a member is permitted to be present when a court is closed.

1211 Withdrawal of Charges and Specifications

The convening authority may, technically, withdraw any specification or a whole case from court at any time. Withdrawal after the introduction of evidence bearing on the guilt or innocence of the accused may preclude retrial of the accused for that offense. See paragraph 56 of the MCM for a discussion of this procedure.

1212 The Arraignment

If the accused has not been arraigned at an Article 39(a) session, the presiding officer will announce that "the accused will now be arraigned."

The arraignment consists of the following:

1. Distribution to the court of copies of the charges and specifications (unless distributed earlier with the consent of the defense counsel);

2. The trial counsel then reads the charges and specifications or the accused waives their reading (waiver is most frequently used);

3. The trial counsel then states the name of the accuser, states that the charges are properly sworn to before an officer authorized to administer oaths, and relates the name of the convening authority who referred the charges to trial;

4. The trial counsel then relates the day the charges were served on the accused. Except in time of war, unless three days prior to the trial date in a special court have elapsed or five days prior to the trial date in a general court-martial have elapsed, the trial may not proceed if the defense objects;

5. Thereafter, the accused is asked how he pleads.

This procedure constitutes the arraignment. Neither the plea itself nor any motions are part of the arraignment.

There is no need for another arraignment if one has been conducted by the military judge at an Article 39(a) session. If there has been an Article 39(a) arraignment, the trial counsel should present to the members copies of those charges and specifications upon which the accused has been arraigned and should inform the court of the date of arraignment.

The arraignment is significant to the accused, for if he absents himself without authority after such a proceeding, the trial may continue in his absence. He loses his right to confront the witnesses against him by his own wrongful act.

1213 Motions

A motion is a request to the court, by either counsel, for particular relief. It asks the court to take some desired action or to grant some form of relief. Motions are generally made by counsel and may be oral or in writing. The motion should clearly set forth the nature of the motion and the grounds for it. Each side is given the opportunity to introduce evidence and to argue. There are three basic categories of motions: the motion to dismiss, the motion to grant appropriate relief, and the motion for a finding of not guilty.

1. *Motion to Dismiss.* The motion to dismiss generally raises any defense or objection in bar of trial. If the motion is granted, the trial stops as to those specifications to which the motion relates. For example, if there has been an unreasonable denial of speedy trial such an assertion could be raised by a motion to dismiss. See Chapter II for a discussion of speedy trial. Some other motions which may be raised are lack of jurisdiction, failure of the charges to allege an offense, expiration of the statute of limitations, former jeopardy, pardon, and former punishment. Chapter IV of this publication discusses these defenses.

Paragraph 67*f* of the MCM states the following:

> If a specification before a court-martial has been dismissed on motion and the ruling does not amount to a finding of not guilty, the convening authority may return the record to the court for reconsideration of the ruling and any further appropriate action. Article 62(a). This action should be taken only on application by the prosecution, with notice to the defense, after affording both sides an opportunity to be heard.

However, the convening authority may not return a record for reconsideration if it amounts to a finding of not guilty. For example, the granting of motions for a finding of not guilty or because of a lack of mental responsibility of the accused at the time of the offense could not be

returned for reconsideration. Additionally, the convening authority ma
not direct the military judge or special court-martial to reconsider
ruling on a motion to grant appropriate relief or a ruling granting
request for a continuance.

2. *Motion to Grant Appropriate Relief.* The motion to gran
appropriate relief is made to cure a defect of form or substance whicl
impedes the accused in properly preparing his defense. The effect o
granting this motion is generally to postpone the trial. This motion neve
relates to the jurisdiction of the court or the question of whether the
accused is guilty or innocent. For example, a specification might alleg
an offense, but be poorly drawn, or indefinite, or redundant, or migh
misname the accused. If it appears that the accused is not misled by the
specifications, they may be amended in court. Otherwise, they may be
stricken or the presiding officer may postpone (adjourn) the case to cor
rect the defects. See paragraph 69, MCM, for a discussion of othe
motions to grant appropriate relief.

3. *Motion for a Finding of Not Guilty.* The motion for a finding
of not guilty is a request to the court to return a finding of not guilt
as to one or more of the offenses charged on the basis that the evidence
is insufficient to sustain a conviction of that offense.

This motion is generally made *after* the prosecution completes its case
and before the defense offers any evidence, although it may also be made
at the end of the defense case.

If there is any evidence which, together with all inferences which car
properly be drawn therefrom and all applicable presumptions, could
reasonably tend to establish every essential element of an offense charged
or included in any specification to which the motion is directed, the
motion should not be granted.

The presiding officer may defer action on any such motion and permi
the trial counsel to present any further evidence prior to his ruling on the
motion.

A military judge would rule finally on any such motion. A president
without a military judge would rule subject to the objection of any
member of the court. If the motion is granted as to any specification, this
is equivalent to a finding of not guilty. In this event, the convening
authority could not return such a case to the court for reconsideration.

1214 The Plea

The plea is the accused's response to each charge and each specification.
Generally, he pleads either "guilty" or "not guilty" as to each specification, or not guilty of the offense charged but guilty of a lesser included
offense. The pleas follow disposition of any motions. Paragraph 1304
discusses lesser included offenses.

If the pleas were received at an Article 39(a) session, the trial counsel should state the following:

> TC: At a session of this trial held on _____ the accused entered the following pleas: _____.

If a plea of guilty to a lesser included offense is entered, the trial counsel shall proceed with the prosecution of the offense charged. Generally, this relieves him of the burden of proving those elements of the major offense which are included within the lesser included offense.

However, if an accused charged with desertion pleads guilty to unauthorized absence, the trial counsel may wish to prove the absence to assist him in proving the element of intent to remain away permanently. If the trial counsel does not prove the unauthorized absence, the court can only infer the intent to desert from other circumstantial evidence.

1215 The Guilty Plea

If the accused pleads guilty, the court must determine if he understands what acts or neglects he is pleading guilty to (the elements of the offense), what the consequences of his guilty plea are, and what advantages there are in pleading not guilty. This procedure is called a hearing to test the providency of the accused's plea of guilty.

An accused who defends himself cannot plead guilty. A plea of not guilty will be entered for him. An accused cannot plead guilty to an offense for which the court may adjudge the death penalty—he must plead not guilty.

The accused may, of course, plead guilty to one specification, not guilty to another, and not guilty to a third, but guilty of a lesser included offense.

If a military judge is detailed, he holds the hearing out of the presence of the members and may hold it as part of the Article 39(a) session even before the court assembles. If the president is presiding, he conducts the hearing in the presence of the members.

During the hearing on the providency of the plea, the following must be accomplished:

1. The plea of guilty will not be received unless the accused has had sufficient time to consult his defense counsel;

2. The meaning and effect of his plea should be explained, that is, he should be informed of:

a. The elements of the offense;

b. The fact that a guilty plea admits every element charged and every act or omission alleged and authorizes conviction of the offense without further proof;

c. The maximum authorized punishment and the fact that it may be adjudged upon conviction. If the maximum punishment for the offense is less than the maximum punishment a special court-martial can give, the accused should also be advised that other factors may warrant a more severe sentence. For example, in *United States* v. *Zemartis,* 10 USCMA 353, 27 CMR 427 (1959), the accused pleaded guilty to a 26-day unauthorized absence. The president of the special court-martial, in ascertaining that the accused understood his plea, advised him correctly that the maximum punishment for the offense was confinement at hard labor for six months, the forfeiture of two-thirds pay per month for six months, and reduction to pay grade E–1 (in this case fireman recruit).

However, after the accused was found guilty, the trial counsel presented evidence of three previous convictions. As it relates to this issue section B of paragraph 127c of the MCM provides that if an accused is found guilty of an offense or offenses for none of which a bad conduct discharge is authorized, "proof of two or more previous convictions" during the three years immediately preceding the commission of the offense will authorize a bad conduct discharge.

The Court of Military Appeals stated that the accused should have been informed of this acceleration clause as otherwise he would not fully appreciate the consequences of pleading guilty.

    3. The accused must be personally questioned by the presiding officer about what he did or did not do and what he intended as regard the offenses to which he is pleading guilty.

    4. The accused must be personally advised and understand that his plea waives his right against self-incrimination, his right to a trial of the facts by a court-martial, and his right to be confronted by the witnesses against him.

    5. The presiding officer must, based upon the foregoing inquiries and such additional information as he deems necessary, then make a finding that there is a knowing, intelligent, and conscious waiver on the part of the accused before he can accept the guilty plea. *United States* v. *Care,* 18 USCMA 535, 40 CMR 247 (1969).

Even though an accused pleads guilty, aggravating and mitigating circumstances surrounding the commission of the offenses may still be presented to the court.

For example, in an unauthorized absence case, the fact that the absence was terminated by apprehension may be presented by the prosecution the court as an aggravating circumstance. Generally this is done when the court is hearing evidence as to an appropriate sentence to award.

1216 The Not Guilty Plea

A not guilty plea means nothing more than that the accused stands upon his right to require the prosecution to prove his guilt. The accused has both a legal and moral right to enter a not guilty plea even if he knows that he *is* guilty as the issue is: can I be proven guilty? *A court-martial can never refuse to accept a not guilty plea, but it can always refuse to accept a guilty plea.*

1217 Opening Statements

The trial counsel may, if he wishes, make an opening statement immediately after a not guilty plea and prior to the presentation of the prosecution's initial presentation of evidence (called his "Case in Chief").

The statement consists of a brief recitation of the issues to be tried and what he expects to prove. He may *not* discuss facts as to which there is no admissible evidence.

The trial counsel usually makes an opening statement when the facts are complicated or unusual, or there are many witnesses or charges against the accused, although he may make one in any case.

The defense counsel may make his opening statement either after the trial counsel's or after the presentation of the prosecution's case.

1218 Summary

In a special court-martial case, in which a president is presiding, the procedure up until the presentation of the prosecution's evidence would be as follows:

1. The president would set the time for trial.

2. Prior to calling the court to order, the president would determine if a quorum of the members and the accused are present; if at least one-third of the members are enlisted men if the accused requested enlisted members; and if the counsel are qualified.

3. The court is called to order after the members and counsel have seated themselves.

4. The trial counsel announces the names of the members and the accused, and swears in the reporter.

5. The qualifications of counsel are then related.

6. The members, if not already sworn under the convening order in a previous case, and nonlawyer counsel would then be sworn.

7. The trial counsel then relates the general nature of the charges and discloses any ground for challenge he is aware of and requests the members to do the same. Challenges for cause and peremptory challenges generally are made at this time.

8. The accused is then arraigned on the charges. Essentially, the arraignment consists of distributing and reading copies of the charges and specifications, establishing the identity of the accuser and convening authority, stating the date the charges were served on the accused and asking the accused how he pleads.

9. Either counsel may then request the court to take some desired action through a motion to dismiss or a motion for appropriate relief.

10. The pleas as to each charge and specification are then made. The three basic types of pleas are guilty, not guilty, or not guilty of the offense charged but guilty of a lesser included offense.

11. If the accused pleads guilty, the president must determine if the accused understands what acts or neglects he is pleading guilty to, what the consequences of his plea are and what advantages there are in pleading not guilty.

12. The trial counsel and the defense counsel may then make opening statements to the court. The statements generally consist of a brief recitation of the issues to be tried and what each counsel expects to prove

If a military judge is detailed to the court, he can eliminate many of the preliminary matters relating to the trial and test the providency of the accused's plea of guilty prior to the members meeting for the first time. A president who is presiding cannot conduct an Article 39(a) session.

In a noncapital case, the accused has the right to request trial by the military judge alone. In such a case, the military judge would then determine the findings and award an appropriate sentence. The members would not participate in the case.

This chapter has related the procedure before the court-martial itself from the setting of the trial date to the presentation of the prosecution's case in chief. If the accused pleads not guilty, evidence is next presented by the prosecution and sometimes by the defense.

Discussion Case

UNITED STATES, Appellee

v.

ARLON R. CHANCELOR, Airman Second Class, U.S. Air Force, Appellant

16 USCMA 297, 36 CMR 453

(1966)

Opinion of the Court

FERGUSON, Judge:

Tried before an Air Force special court-martial, the accused pleaded guilty to charges of wrongful cohabitation, in violation of Uniform Code of Military Justice, Article 134, 10 USC § 934, and issuing a worthless check, in violation of Code, supra, Article 123a, 10 USC § 923a. In accordance with his plea, he was found guilty and sentenced to bad-conduct discharge, partial forfeitures of his pay for a stated period, and confinement at ha labor. Except as hereinafter noted, intermediate appellate authorities have finally affirmed his conviction, and the case is before us on the granted issue whether accused's plea of guilty to the bad check count was improvidently made. Our inquiry therein requires a recital of the following circumstances.

Upon accused's pleading guilty at his trial, the president's inquiry into its providence was limited to the formula advice suggested by the Manual for Courts-Martial, United States, 1951, Appendix 8a, page 509, including a statement of the maximum punishment which might be imposed. In answer, the accused indicated he understood the meaning and effect of his plea and persisted therein. By means of a stipulation of facts, the prosecution, in accordance with Air Force practice, established a *prima facie* case as to the bad check offense. Thus, it was demonstrated that accused, on November 10, 1964, drew a check on Terre Haute First National Bank in the amount of $5.00, and cashed it at Bunker Hill Air Force Base. On November 30, 1964, the check was returned unpaid through normal banking channels on account of insufficient funds. On December 1, 1964, and December 31, 1964, letters were written to accused concerning the nonpayment of the check. No reply was received; however, the check was finally paid on March 22, 1965. The case, however, was submitted to the court on the accused's plea, as well as the stipulation.

During a post-trial clemency interview, accused declared that he thought he had sufficient funds in the bank to pay the check when he drew it. The staff judge advocate conceded the comment appeared inconsistent with the guilty plea but, in light of the president's *pro forma* explanation of the plea's effect, the accused's representation by certified counsel, and failure to present any evidence *at the trial* which indicated improvidence, he concluded the post-trial comment to be of no moment.

The board of review returned the record of trial to the supervisory authority for inquiry into the providence of the accused's plea in light of his post-trial declaration, and a new post-trial review. The inquiry involved obtaining affidavits from the accused, his counsel, his first sergeant, and the manager of the bank on which the check was drawn.

Accused maintained his statement that he believed he had sufficient funds in the bank to meet payment of the check on presentment. He indicated his financial difficulties arose from an earlier overpayment by the Air Force, which resulted in receipt of either no pay or minimal partial payments from October 1964 through March 1965. In consequence, although counseled by his first sergeant and notified by the bank of the check's return, he did not redeem it until March. Indeed, his financial difficulties were so great that he "forgot" about the check until charges were preferred against him. He specifically denied any intent to defraud, an essential element of the offense.

Accused conceded his counsel had properly advised him regarding the weight of the evidence against him; pointed out the alternatives of pleading guilty or not guilty; and that he had, on counsel's recommendation, freely chosen the former course, although he maintained his innocence. He considered counsel to have competently represented him.

Counsel confirmed accused's statement. He declared he pointed out the alternatives to the accused; that he was entitled to plead not guilty; that he, for good and sufficient reasons, recommended a guilty plea in spite of accused's protestations of innocence; and that he fully explained Chancelor's rights in the premises, emphasizing that the decision as to what plea to enter was his alone to make.

Following this inquiry, the supervisory authority, acting on the case pursuant to the recommendation of his staff judge advocate, found accused's plea of guilty to have been fully provident and again approved the sentence.

We reverse. The accused has from the outset of these proceedings maintained his innocence, except upon the actual entry of his plea. That, indeed, was made with no more than the usual *pro forma* explanation of its meaning and effect. Particularly, there was no explanation of the elements of the offense to him, or that he admitted he wrote the check with intent to defraud. *United States* v. *Richardson*, 15 USCMA 400, 35 CMR 372. Just as in that case, the plea was followed by a post-trial assertion that accused wrote the check in question believing in good faith that funds were present in the account to pay it upon presentment. And we long ago stated in *United States* v. *Lemieux*, 10 USCMA 10, 27 CMR 84, at page 12:

> "Had the facts which the accused disclosed to the staff judge advocate . . . [been inconsistent with his plea], we would have no hesitancy in holding accused's guilty plea to be improvident."

We reiterated that injunction in *United States* v. *Richardson*, supra, in setting aside a conviction on the same basis as presented here. See also separate opinion, *United States* v. *Brown*,

11 USCMA 207, 29 CMR 23, at page 214; *United States* v. *Henn*, 13 USCMA 124, 32 CMR 124; and *United States* v. *Williams*, 15 USCMA 65, 35 CMR 37.

By our action, we do not, as the government urges, permit the accused to plead guilty in all cases and thereafter, at his pleasure, negate its effect by simple post-trial declarations of innocence if he is ultimately displeased at the result. In neither *Richardson*, *Henn*, both supra, nor in this case, did such occur. Rather, the accused maintained his innocence throughout and, in the trial itself, no examination into the matter was made other than use of a rote formula which offered no real opportunity for disclosure of his motivation to confess guilt or whether he had any genuine understanding of the admissions expressed in his plea, as to the elements of the offense charged.

During the hearings on the Uniform Code of Military Justice, there was considerable concern expressed regarding the entry of guilty pleas in courts-martial, and Congress made clear the nature of the safeguards which they intended to surround the receiving of such a judicial confession. See Hearings before House Armed Services Committee on H. R. 2498, 81st Congress, First Session, pages 1052–1057.

Thus, it provided in Code, supra, Article 45, 10 USC § 345, "If an accused . . . after a plea of guilty *sets up matter inconsistent with the plea*, . . . a plea of not guilty shall be entered in the record, and the court shall proceed as though he had pleaded not guilty." (Emphasis supplied.) In addition, the Congress pointed out that the "provisions of this article will be supplemented by regulations issued by the President." House Report No. 491,

81st Congress, First Session, page 23. These regulations were to set forth the procedure to be followed in all guilty plea cases and were to include the following:

"(1) In general and special court-martial cases, the plea should be received only after the accused has had an opportunity to consult with counsel appointed for or selected by him. If the accused has refused counsel, the plea should not be received.

"(2) In every case the meaning and effect of a plea of guilty should be explained to the accused (by the law officer of a general court-martial; by the president of a special court-martial; by the summary court), *such explanation to include the following:*

(a) That the plea admits the offense as charged (or in a lesser degree, if so pleaded) and makes conviction mandatory.

(b) The sentence which may be imposed.

(c) *That unless the accused admits doing the acts charged, a plea of guilty will not be accepted.*

"(3) The question whether the plea will be received will be treated as an interlocutory question.

"(4) The explanation made and the accused's reply thereto should be set forth in the record of trial exactly as given." [Emphasis supplied.] [House Report, supra, pages 23–24.]

In testimony before the Armed Services Committee, Mr. Felix Larkin, Assistant General Counsel, Department of Defense, in proposing the foregoing inquiry on the record into every guilty plea, declared:

"We feel that is a procedure which will give an added amount of protection to the innumerable cases where pleas of guilty are taken, particularly among the younger men.

"I think it would have the added advantage of settling once and for all that he is the man who did what he is charged with doing and we would be relieved thereafter of the continually [sic] complaint of accused that they did not understand what they were doing when they took their plea.

"In addition to that, we would have the colloquy between the court and the accused at the taking of the plea and the record transcribed verbatim *and not just have a form which is printed and says the accused was informed of his rights."* [Emphasis supplied.] [House Hearings, supra, page 1054.]

Regulations embodying the foregoing requirements were promulgated by the President, including the fact accused's plea "admits every act or omission alleged and every element of the offense charged." Manual, supra, paragraph 70*b*. Unfortunately, an attempt was also made to codify the necessary inquiry into a *pro forma* advice to the accused in the Manual's Trial Procedure Guide. See Manual, supra, Appendix 8*a*, page 509. The result has been that, as in this case, accused is not advised of the elements of the offense and his guilt in fact is not always established on the record. In consequence, after the trial is concluded, the Government is faced with appellate avowals of innocence and the boards of review and this Court with the necessity to make important and binding determinations on the basis of a veritable blizzard of conflicting affidavits. If, however, the procedure understood by the Congress to be instituted and adopted by the President in the Manual, supra, paragraph 70*b*, had been followed, there would have been a delineation of the elements of the offense and an express admission of factual guilt on the record. Thus, the accused's later, post-trial protestations of innocence would have fallen on deaf ears. Such regulations by the President—here so clearly recommended by the Congress—have the force and effect of law. *United States* v. *Smith*, 13 USCMA 105, 32 CMR 105. We have heretofore suggested they be followed in addition to or in lieu of the formula advice in the Trial Procedure Guide. See separate opinion, *United States* v. *Brown*, supra; *United States* v. *Williams*, supra; *United States* v. *Richardson*, supra. Under the facts of this case, the failure to make such inquiry—where the accused has throughout his subjection to disciplinary proceedings, except for the actual entry of his plea, insisted on his innocence—leads to reversal. We, therefore, strongly urge the services to take remedial action and insure compliance with the statutory and regulatory inquiry to be made into guilt in fact. From records before us, we note that such is done, almost without exception, in Army and Navy cases. Should the procedure be adopted throughout all the services, we believe the haunting issue of improvident pleas would become rare indeed and, as Mr. Larkin declared, "would have the added advantage of settling once and for all that he [the accused] is the man who did what he is charged with doing." House Hearings, supra, at page 1054.

That is the purpose of taking a guilty plea in a criminal trial. Neither the government nor the accused derives any advantage in so establishing guilt unless it has in fact been brought home to the proper person. The procedure so cogently outlined in House Report No. 491, supra, " 'insures providence upon the record and gives the lie to . . . later claims of impropriety.' " *United States* v. *Richardson*, supra, at page 404. As it was not done here and as accused has maintained his innocence even in face of full post-trial inquiry, we find error prejudicial to his rights.

The decision of the board of review is reversed, and the record of trial is returned to the Judge Advocate General of the Air Force. A rehearing may be ordered, or the board of review may reassess the sentence on the basis of the remaining findings of guilty.

Judge KILDAY concurs.

QUINN, Chief Judge, dissented.

NOTE

A later case, *United States* v. *Care*, cited in paragraph 1215, now requires an in-depth inquiry by the presiding officer in *every* guilty plea case. Paragraph 1215 enumerates the present law in this area.

DISCUSSION AND SELF-QUIZ

1. You are the trial counsel in a special court-martial. The president of the court has granted a defense request that the charges be dismissed on the grounds that they do not allege an offense. The question is one of law. As trial counsel you believe the court has made a mistake and that the specification does allege an offense. What can be done? See paragraph 67*f* of the MCM.

2. In relation to the basic issue in the case of *United States* v. *Chancelor,* what does the MCM 1969 now require in order to test the providency of a guilty plea?

3. Answer the following questions:

a. May the president of a special court-martial without a military judge be requested to hear a case without the members and determine the guilt or innocence of the accused and an appropriate sentence?

b. May the president of a special court-martial without a military judge ever hold an Article 39(a) session?

c. Do the members need to be sworn every time they hear a new case?

d. Can a president, who is presiding, rule alone upon a challenge for cause?

e. May a president, who is presiding, hold a "hearing" outside the presence of the members to determine the providency of the accused's plea of guilty?

f. Is the president a member of the court?

g. Is the military judge a member of the court?

CHAPTER **XIII**

Trial Procedure
and Review

This is the final chapter pertaining to the military judicial system. It is considered that a discussion of trial procedure would be more cohesive to the reader if it is uninterrupted by a chapter relating to evidence. Therefore, the rules of evidence and the order of presentation of evidence have already been discussed in Chapter XI. In order to thoroughly cover other areas of vital importance to the Navy and Marine Corps officer, some aspects of trial procedure have been discussed in other chapters in this book. Generally, the more significant areas have either been cross-referenced or repeated.

This chapter discusses the instructions that the members must receive prior to their determination of the guilt or innocence of the accused (the findings), the deliberations on the findings, pre-sentencing procedure, instructions on the sentence, punishments, clemency, the record of trial, review procedures, and extraordinary relief under Articles 69 and 73 of the Code.

Instructions supply the law that applies to a particular court-martial case. The members must apply the law as furnished them by the instructions of the presiding officer in their resolution of the factual issue of the guilt or innocence of the accused. If the accused is convicted, further instructions by the presiding officer will furnish the guidelines to be utilized in determining an appropriate sentence.

1301 Proposed Instructions

After both sides present their evidence, they announce that they "rest" their cases.

If a military judge is presiding, he would next commence an Article

224

39 (a) session. At the session, he would inform each counsel of the instructions he intends to give the court. He would then permit counsel to submit proposed instructions and to argue the merit of any particular proposal.

If a president presides, he cannot hold an out-of-court hearing. Therefore, he should either furnish both counsel with a copy of his proposed instructions or refer to standard printed instructions. These standard printed instructions are prepared by the Judge Advocate General and published by the Bureau of Naval Personnel in instructional guides. Counsel may then propose additional or modified instructions by written draft. The determination of the presiding officer as to the instructions that are ultimately given is final. The purpose of resolving the instructional issue in this manner is to shield the court members from hearing arguments that might improperly affect them in their deliberations on the findings.

1302 Arguments

The arguments of counsel follow resolution of the instructional issue. These arguments furnish counsel the opportunity to present to the court, by way of oral argument, the facts, circumstances, and inferences of the case in the light most favorable to their side.

The trial counsel has the right to make the first argument (i.e., the "opening argument"). The defense counsel then makes his "defense argument." If any argument is made by the defense counsel, the trial counsel may make a "closing argument." This argument is generally limited to a discussion of propositions or matters argued by the defense. See Chapter IX for a discussion of a counsel's duties and responsibilities and the permissible scope of his argument.

1303 Instructions

After closing arguments, the presiding officer will instruct the court as to those matters it should consider in determining the guilt or innocence of the accused. The instructions given vary with the facts of the case, the nature of the offense, and what has transpired during the trial. The following are some of these instructions:

1. *Reasonable Doubt.*

That the accused must be presumed to be innocent until his guilt is established by legal and competent evidence beyond a reasonable doubt;

That, in the case being considered, if there is a reasonable doubt as to the guilt of the accused, the doubt must be resolved in favor of the accused and he must be acquitted;

That if there is a reasonable doubt as to the degree of guilt, the finding must be in a lower degree as to which there is no reasonable doubt; and

That the burden of proof to establish the guilt of the accused beyond "reasonable doubt" is upon the United States.

2. *The Elements of the Offenses Charged.* The elements of the offense are those issues of fact related to the offense which must be determined by the members of the court on the question of the guilt or innocence of the accused.

Paragraph 73*a* of the MCM states that a "mere reading of the elements of proof from applicable subparagraphs will not, however, in most cases be sufficient to apprise the court of what must be proved to warrant a conviction, nor will it provide other necessary instructions, such as those on affirmative defenses in issue. Instructions should be tailored to fit the circumstances of the individual case."

For example, the presiding officer of a special court-martial in the case of Seaman Apprentice John J. Doe (see Appendix 6 of *Military Law*) would inform the court of the following as it relates to specification 1 of charge I—unauthorized absence:

> The court is advised that to find the accused guilty of charge I and specification 1 thereunder, alleging the unauthorized absence from a unit in violation of Article 86, UCMJ, it must be satisfied by legal and competent evidence beyond a reasonable doubt:
>
> (1) That on or about 4 April 19__, at the Naval Station, Norfolk, Virginia, the accused absented himself from the USS *Glory,* and did remain so absent until on or about 30 April 19__.
>
> (2) That such absence was without authority from anyone competent to give him leave.

3. *The Elements of Each Lesser Included Offense in Issue.* See paragraph 1304 of this publication for a discussion of lesser included offenses.

4. *The Law Governing Each Defense in Issue.* The law governing each defense reasonably in issue must be explained to the court. For example, if the accused is charged with larceny, a specific intent crime, there must be an instruction on the possible effect of intoxication when that issue is reasonably raised by the evidence. See Chapters IV and V of this publication for a discussion of defenses.

5. *Words of Art.* "Words of art" must be defined. Words of art are words or phrases that are employed in the instructions that have some special legal meaning or connotation.

As an illustration, the word "steal" would be utilized in a specification alleging larceny. Steal would be defined by the presiding officer's instructions on the elements of taking and the intent to deprive permanently. Other words of art require a special definition and a reading of the elements will not suffice.

6. *Evidence Admitted for Limited Purpose.* If any evidence has been admitted for a limited purpose, the court must be instructed to consider the evidence only for that purpose. For example, the accused may have taken the stand and testified only as to the involuntariness of a confession or admission. As long as he successfully limits his testimony to that issue, his statements cannot be considered as to his guilt or innocence.

7. *Voluntariness of Statement.* If the voluntariness of a statement of the accused is raised, but the presiding officer admits the statement, the court members must be instructed that they must be convinced beyond a reasonable doubt that the confession or admission was voluntary before they may consider it in determining guilt or innocence.

8. *Members' Responsibilities.* Instructions as to members' responsibilities when voting should be given. See paragraph 1006 of this publication for a description of those responsibilities.

9. *Military Judge's Statement.* In an appropriate case, the military judge may make an orderly statement of the issues of fact and summarize and comment upon the evidence and law on each side of those issues. This procedure is seldom used, but when it is, an accurate, fair, and dispassionate statement is mandatory. A presiding president may not make such a summarization.

1304 Findings

After receiving their instructions from the presiding officer, the court closes for the purpose of determining the guilt or innocence of the accused. When the court closes, the members meet alone. Paragraphs 1005 and 1006 of this publication discuss, in detail, the basis for the findings, the weighing of evidence, reasonable doubt, the members' responsibilities, and the procedure to be utilized while the court is determining the findings.

During their deliberations as to the findings, the members of a court-martial may desire further information. They may wish to clarify a point of law or ascertain whether they may make a finding of guilty of a specification by exceptions and substitutions.

In this event, if a military judge is detailed to the court, the court would open and request that the members be furnished with additional instructions. If the special court-martial is without a military judge, the court may open and request counsel for both sides to present legal authorities on the question or direct the trial counsel to obtain the information.

The court may believe, beyond a reasonable doubt, that the accused is not guilty of the crime charged but is guilty of a lesser included offense.

A lesser included offense is an offense contained, either expressly or by fair implication, within the offense charged. The basic specification must be worded in such a manner as to put the defense on notice that he must be prepared to defend against such a lesser offense. However, the notice requirement can be met when the elements of the included offense are necessary elements of the offense charged. For example, to be found guilty of desertion (Article 85) the accused must intend to remain away permanently from his unit, whereas to be guilty of unauthorized absence he only has to have been absent without authority. Therefore, if the court believes the accused to be only guilty of unauthorized absence, it may announce its findings as follows:

> Of the specification of the Charge: Guilty, except the words, "and with intent to remain away therefrom permanently," and "in desertion," of the excepted words, not guilty.
> Of the Charge: Not guilty, but guilty of a violation of Article 86.

If the court convicts the accused of a lesser included offense under the same article of the Code—such as missing movement by neglect instead of by design in violation of Article 87 of the Code, the findings would be announced as follows:

> Of the specification of the Charge: Guilty, except the word "design" substituting therefor the word "neglect;" of the excepted word, not guilty, of the substituted word, guilty.
> Of the Charge: Guilty.

An accused may be found guilty of either an attempt to commit the offense charged or of an attempt to commit a lesser included offense.

An attempt is a crime. If committed, it occurs on the threshold of completion of the crime. It is a separate crime and is, generally, although not always, charged under Article 80 of the Code. If the accused is charged with committing the completed act, an attempt is a possible lesser included offense.

Paragraph 159 of the MCM describes an attempt as an "act, done with the specific intent to commit an offense, amounting to more than mere preparation and tending, even though failing to effect its commission." An accused may be convicted of an attempt even though the proof shows that he actually completed the crime.

Therefore, if a court believes beyond a reasonable doubt that an accused charged with desertion is guilty of neither desertion nor unauthorized absence, but is guilty of an attempted unauthorized absence, their findings would be as follows:

> Of the specification of the Charge: Guilty, except the words, "and with intent to remain away therefrom permanently," and substituting the words "attempt to" before "absent," of the excepted words, not guilty, of the substituted words, guilty.
> Of the Charge: Not guilty, but guilty of violation of Article 80.

Therefore, the findings as to the charges may be *guilty; not guilty; or not guilty, but guilty of a violation of a different article*. As to the specifications, the findings may be *guilty; not guilty, or guilty with exceptions and/or substitutions*.

Each finding of guilty must be with the concurrence of *two-thirds* of the members present at the time the vote was taken. The only exception is: a finding of guilty to a charge which calls for a mandatory death penalty requires the concurrence of *all* members present at the time the vote is taken. "If, in computing the number of votes required, a fraction results, the fraction will be counted as one; thus, if five members are to vote, a requirement that two-thirds concur is not met unless four concur." Paragraph 74d (3), MCM.

The court may utilize a findings worksheet, properly marked as an appellate exhibit, to record the findings.

After the court has determined its findings, the court opens. The military judge may then assist the court in putting their findings into proper form in the presence of all parties to the trial. The findings are then read to the accused by the president. If the findings are not guilty to all the offenses charged, the trial ends. A finding of not guilty results as to any specification or charge if no other valid finding is reached thereon; however, a court may reconsider any finding before the same is formally announced in open session. The court also may reconsider any finding of guilty on its own motion at any time before it has first announced the sentence in the case. See paragraph 74d (3) of the MCM.

As soon as the court has determined its findings in a case, it will announce them in open session in the presence of the military judge, counsel and the accused.

In the event John J. Doe, the hypothetical accused in the charge sheet in Appendix 6 of this book, is found guilty of all charges and specifications, the president of the court could state as follows:

> PRES: John J. Doe, it is my duty as president of this court to inform you that the court in closed session and upon secret written ballot, two-thirds of the members present at the time the vote was taken concurring in each finding of guilty, finds you:
> Of all the specifications and charges: Guilty.

The President only states the required fraction of votes necessary to convict (two-thirds) not the actual number of members who concurred in the findings of guilty.

1305   Pre-sentencing Procedure

If the court has announced findings of guilty, the prosecution and defense may present appropriate matter to aid the court in determining the kind and amount of punishment to be imposed.

1. *Matters Presented by the Prosecution.*

a. *Data as to Service.* The trial counsel will read the data as to age, pay and length of service of the accused and the duration and nature of any pretrial restraint. (See page 1 of Appendices 6 and 7.)

b. *Evidence of Previous Convictions.* The trial counsel may next present evidence of any previous convictions. The conviction must relate to offenses committed during the six years preceding the commission of any offense of which the accused stands convicted. No "proceeding in which an accused has been found guilty by a court-martial upon any charge or specification shall, as to that charge or specification, be admissible as a previous conviction until the finding of guilty has become final after review of the case has been fully completed." Paragraph 75b(2), MCM.

c. *Conduct and Character.* The court may be furnished with further information as to the conduct and character of the accused if a military judge is detailed to the court. Section 0117 of the JAG Manual provides that the trial counsel may, prior to sentencing, obtain and present to the military judge, for use by either the members or the judge (if sitting alone), personnel records of the accused or copies or summaries thereof. These include all those records made or maintained in accordance with departmental regulations which reflect the past conduct and performance of the accused. Records of nonjudicial punishment must relate to offenses committed prior to trial and during the current enlistment of the accused. The offense must have been committed within two years from the date of the commission of the present offense. Periods of unauthorized absence are excluded in computing the two-year period.

d. *Aggravating Circumstances.* "If a finding of guilty of an offense is based upon a plea of guilty and available and admissible evidence as to any aggravating circumstances was not introduced before the findings, the prosecution may introduce that evidence after the findings are announced." Paragraph 75b(3) of the MCM. For example, if an unauthorized absentee is apprehended by military or civilian authorities, rather than surrendering himself, this is considered an aggravating factor that a court-martial may consider in determining the sentence.

2. *Matters Presented by the Defense.* The defense must, after find-

ings of guilty are announced and before the court closes to vote on the sentence, introduce matter in extenuation or mitigation. (Paragraph 904 of *Military Law*.) *Matter in extenuation* of an offense serves to explain the circumstances surrounding the commission of the offense. This may include the reasons that motivated the accused to commit the crime.

Matter in mitigation has for its purpose the lessening of the punishment to be assigned by the court or the furnishing of grounds for a recommendation for clemency. For example, the fact that the accused has a wife and child to support, or has a good reputation in the civilian or military community all may be considered in determining the amount and kind of punishment, if any, to be awarded the accused.

Matter in extenuation and mitigation is normally received by the court with considerable relaxation of the rules of evidence. Character witnesses, affidavits, letters from friends or associates of the person convicted—all may be introduced at the discretion of the court. The accused may make a sworn or unsworn statement, written or oral, as to these matters. If the statement is unsworn, he cannot be cross-examined. Other witnesses may be called to testify on behalf of the person convicted and they may be cross-examined by the prosecution. The prosecution may call its own witnesses to rebut matter introduced in extenuation or mitigation. However, the rules of evidence are not relaxed for this rebuttal evidence.

Assume the accused does not desire to present any evidence in mitigation or extenuation and requests his counsel to remain silent. If his defense counsel cannot persuade the accused to do otherwise, he must adhere to the accused's desires. In this case, the accused should be requested to sign a statement containing the advice he has received from his counsel and declaring that he, the accused, insisted that his defense counsel remain silent. The court will *not* be informed of this statement. It will be retained by the defense counsel in the event the adequacy of his representation of the accused is raised as an issue upon appeal. *United States v. Blunk*, 17 USCMA 158, 37 CMR 422 (1967).

After introduction of matters relating to the sentence, counsel for each side may make an argument for an appropriate sentence. The presiding officer may determine the order of argument on the sentence. (See paragraphs 905 and 906 of *Military Law*.)

1306 Instructions on Sentence

Before the court-martial closes to deliberate and vote on the sentence, the presiding officer must furnish the members with appropriate instructions on the punishment. He must inform them:

1. Of the maximum authorized punishment which may be imposed;
2. Of their responsibility for selecting an appropriate sentence;
3. That they may consider all matters in extenuation or mitigation

as well as those in aggravation whether introduced before or after the findings;

4. That they may consider evidence presented by the prosecution and defense as to the background and character of the accused; and the reputation or record of the accused in the service for good conduct, efficiency, fidelity, courage, bravery, or other traits of good character. Of course, such an instruction would *only* be given if evidence has been presented as to these traits. However, each matter in mitigation *must* be mentioned, if presented.

5. If two or more offenses are "multiplicious" (i.e., they really are not two completely separate offenses) the court must be advised that they should not consider these offenses as separate for punishment purposes. The prescribed punishment for the more severe offense is the maximum punishment which can be awarded. See paragraph 76*a* (5) of the MCM.

6. If a bad conduct discharge may be awarded only because of the permissible additional punishments provided for in Section B of paragraph 127*c* of the MCM, the court must be advised of this fact. *United States* v. *Hutton,* 14 USCMA 366, 34 CMR 146 (1964) and *United States* v. *Yocom,* 17 USCMA 270, 38 CMR 68 (1967). Paragraph 76*b*, MCM.

7. The court must be advised of the procedure for voting as to the sentence including the fact that the court must begin the voting with the lightest proposed sentence and continuing in severity until a sentence is adopted by the concurrence of the required number of members. (See paragraph 1007 of *Military Law.*)

A court must not be advised as to the reason why a sentence limitation is imposed in any particular case. Assume that the maximum punishment for an offense is one year's confinement at hard labor. The accused is being tried by a special court-martial. The jurisdictional limit for all special courts-martial is six months' confinement at hard labor. The court should not be advised that the only reason the accused cannot be given a year is because a special court can only award six months' confinement.

If the president is presiding, he may request that the trial and defense counsel obtain information concerning the maximum punishment that may be adjudged if he has any question relating thereto.

In summary, the presiding officer must tailor his instructions to fit the facts and circumstances of the individual case.

Paragraph 1007 of this publication discusses the members' responsibilities when voting.

1307 Punishments

Some of the more common punishments awarded as the result of a court-martial are as follows:

1. *Bad Conduct Discharge.* This is a separation from the service

under conditions other than honorable. An accused who has been convicted repeatedly of minor offenses and whose punitive separation from the service appears to be necessary may be awarded a BCD. Only enlisted persons can receive a bad conduct discharge. A general court-martial can always award a bad conduct discharge. Generally, a special court-martial can only award a bad conduct discharge if certain legally qualified personnel are present. (See paragraph 804 of this publication.) A court-martial cannot award administrative discharges (such as general or undesirable discharges).

2. *Confinement at Hard Labor.* This is the physical restraint of a person in a brig, disciplinary command, or other place of confinement with the imposition of *hard labor* as a part thereof. If the offense so warrants, a special court-martial can award up to six months' confinement at hard labor. The period of confinement starts on the day the sentence is adjudged by the court. A court-martial cannot suspend a sentence or defer confinement.

3. *Forfeiture of Pay.* This is the permanent deprivation of a specified amount of an accused's pay for a stated number of months or days. For example, a court may award, among other punishments, the forfeiture "of $60.00 per month for six months." The specific amount of forfeiture should be stated. It is essential that the number of months be specified.

For example, in *United States v. Johnson,* 13 USCMA 127, 32 CMR 127, (1962), a court-martial awarded six months' confinement at hard labor and "$70.00 forfeiture of pay for six months." The Court of Military Appeals held that only $70.00 forfeiture could be awarded—and that would be spread over six months. If the court had stated "$70.00 forfeiture of pay *per month* for six months" their apparent intent when they awarded the punishment would have been accomplished.

A special court-martial may only adjudge a forfeiture up to two-thirds pay per month for six months. A general court-martial may adjudge total forfeitures.

Paragraph 126*h* (2) of the MCM states as follows:

The maximum amount of a partial forfeiture . . . is computed by using the basic pay authorized for the cumulative years of service of the accused and, if no confinement is adjudged, any sea or foreign duty pay. When a sentence includes a reduction of an enlisted member, . . . and whether or not suspended, the forfeiture must be based on the pay for the reduced grade. Additionally, any monthly contribution which an enlisted member is required to make, or will be required to make as the result of a sentence including a reduction, in order to entitle him to a basic allowance for quarters must be deducted before the amount of pay subject to forfeiture is computed. However, other allotments need not be deducted. The term "basic pay" includes no element of pay other than the basic pay of the grade or class within grade as fixed by statute and does not include special pay for a special qualification such as diving pay, or incentive pay for the performance of hazardous duties such as flying, parachute jumping, or duty on board a submarine.

In the naval service, enlisted men in pay grades E–1 through E–4 with four years of service or less are required to make out the "monthly contribution" discussed above. Therefore, this BAQ (basic allowance for quarters) contribution is not subject to forfeiture. The voluntary BAQ of higher rated enlisted men, or those in pay grade E–4 with more than four years, is subject to forfeiture. Consequently, this amount may be computed in their base pay in determining the total amount of pay subject to possible forfeiture by a court. However, court members in determining an appropriate sentence should consider the welfare of the accused's dependents in determining the sentence to be awarded. Section 0119, JAG Manual.

4. *Reduction in Rate.* "If an enlisted member of other than the lowest enlisted grade is convicted by a court-martial the court may, in its discretion, adjudge reduction to any inferior grade in addition to the punishments otherwise authorized." Section B of paragraph 127c of the MCM. This means that either a special or general court-martial can reduce an enlisted man to pay grade E–1, regardless of the other punishments that may be prescribed for an offense. See paragraph 707 as it relates to the summary court-martial.

Other punishments that may be awarded by court-martial, such as dishonorable discharge, dismissal, reprimand, admonition, restriction, fine, detention of pay, and hard labor without confinement, are not discussed in this chapter. See Chapter XXV of the MCM.

The number of votes required for various punishments are:

1. Death: All members present.
2. More than ten years' confinement: Three-fourths of the members present.
3. All other: Two-thirds of the members present.

After arriving at the sentence, the court is opened and the accused is informed of the sentence. Appendix 13 of the MCM contains forms for the sentence announcement. For example, a typical special court-martial announcement of sentence might be as follows:

PRES: John J. Doe, it is my duty as president of this court to inform you that the court in closed session and upon secret written ballot, two-thirds of the members present at the time the vote was taken concurring, sentences you:

To be confined at hard labor for three months, to forfeit $60.00 per month for six months, and to be reduced to pay grade E-1.

The court then asks the trial counsel if he has any other cases to present. If not, the court is adjourned.

1308 Recommendation for Clemency

If the accused is found guilty and sentenced, the defense counsel may submit to the convening authority a *recommendation for clemency* in which (all or some) members of the court may join. It is prepared as a letter to the convening authority concerning those matters which would justify the convening authority's taking requested clemency action, such as showing that collection of the forfeitures adjudged by the court would cause undue hardship on the dependents of the accused. In addition to the basis for the requested clemency, the recommendation should state what form of clemency is desired. This might be a recommendation that the convening authority suspend the sentence when the sentence includes a punitive discharge or a recommendation that the convening authority reduce the period of confinement or the amount of forfeiture adjudged. This recommendation should not constitute a review of the trial, but should relate only to matter arising after the trial.

Those members of a court who desire to recommend clemency sign the recommendation stating their reasons for signing, taking care *not* to divulge their vote on the findings or sentence. If no members desire to join in the recommendation, it is proper for the defense counsel to sign the petition alone and forward it to the trial counsel for attachment to the record of trial before it is submitted to the convening authority.

1309 The Record of Trial

The record of trial is prepared by the trial counsel under the direction of the court. Appendices 9 and 10 of the MCM are guides that may be utilized for the preparation of records of trial. The preparation of the record includes responsibility for accuracy and form, as well as for the required number of copies and their distribution. Paragraph 49*b* (2) of the MCM and 0120 of the JAG Manual discuss the preparation of records of trial.

After completion of the record, the trial counsel should furnish the defense counsel an opportunity to examine it. The defense counsel's acknowledgment of this opportunity will be reflected in the record.

The record of trial is then forwarded to the presiding officer, who "authenticates" the record. Authentication is a signed certification that the record is true and accurate.

The trial counsel will then arrange for the furnishing to the accused of a copy of the record of trial and all documentary exhibits received into evidence as soon as the record is authenticated. The receipt of the accused for this copy will be attached to the original record of trial. If the personal receipt of the accused cannot be obtained, the trial counsel will forward a copy of the record to him and attach a certificate reflecting the action taken. In this case, the receipt of the accused will be forwarded to the convening authority as soon as it is obtained.

1310   Initial Review

After every court-martial trial, the record must be forwarded to the convening authority for initial review and action. No sentence can be executed until he has "acted" on the record. He has complete power to approve or disapprove all or any part of the findings or sentence of any court-martial that comes to him for review.

In a typical case, the commanding officer of a ship would designate one of his officers (generally the legal officer) to review the record of trial and submit advice thereon.

However, the final responsibility for the action taken on the record is the convening authority's. He must sign the convening authority's action personally.

The convening authority may not permit any of the parties involved in the trial, or who have acted for either side, to act as his legal adviser as to the record. Nor should an investigating officer, court member, accuser, or military judge who has participated in the case review it for the convening authority.

1. *Initial Action of the Convening Authority.* If the trial resulted in findings of not guilty, or a ruling to that effect, as to all charges and specifications, the convening authority only determines whether or not the court-martial had jurisdiction. If it *had* jurisdiction, he takes the action discussed later in this chapter. If there was no jurisdiction, the trial was a nullity and he may order another trial, if the jurisdictional defect is capable of correction. If the convening authority finds errors which he wants corrected prior to his detailed review of the record, he may direct the court-martial to take appropriate action depending on the type of error. These actions are to accomplish:

a. *Certificate of Correction.* This is a certificate authenticated by the presiding officer stating that a certain material action *not* appearing in the completed record actually took place. This certificate is made without reconvening the court and it is used when a material error is evidenced by an *omission* from the record of some action that actually took place, such as swearing a witness or the members of the court. It may not be used to correct a material error *actually made* at the trial.

b. *Proceedings in Revision.* When there is an apparent error or omission in the record or when the record shows improper or inconsistent action by a court-martial with respect to a finding or sentence which can be rectified without material prejudice to the substantial rights of the accused, the convening authority may return the record to the court for appropriate action.

The convening authority sends the record back to the trial counsel, informing him of the error or omission. The court is reconvened with the defendant, counsel, and the members present who participated in the determination of the findings and sentence. Corrective action is then taken. Proceedings in revision may *not* be used to reconsider a "not guilty" finding or to increase the severity of a sentence imposed unless the greater sentence is made mandatory by the Code.

2. *Review by the Convening Authority.* When the convening authority commences his actual review of the complete record of a trial, his primary concern is whether or not any error may have materially prejudiced the substantial rights of the accused, either as to the findings or the sentence. If it appears that an error or errors *have* materially prejudiced the rights of the accused, the convening authority must take one of several courses of action. In every instance, his action may not add to or increase the severity of punishment, except where mandatory punishments are provided for by the Code. The various forms of action authorized for convening authorities are shown in Appendix 14 of the MCM.

a. *Disapproval of the Sentence and Dismissal of the Charge(s).* This action is taken when there is insufficient evidence in the record to support the findings of the court. It is accomplished by disapproving the sentence and stating the reasons for the disapproval. In this case jeopardy *does* attach since there has been a valid trial. The accused may not be retried.

b. *Disapproval of the Sentence and Order for Another Trial.* This is the action taken when the court lacked jurisdiction either because it was improperly convened, or constituted, or if a specification did not allege an offense. Before ordering another trial, the convening authority must feel that the jurisdictional defect is capable of correction at the new trial. The new trial must be before a court-martial, none of whose members sat as members in the original trial. The effect of this action is as if a trial had never occurred and jeopardy does *not* attach.

c. *Disapproval of the Sentence and Order for a Rehearing.* This action is taken when there has been sufficient evidence to support the findings of guilty, but there has been some other error in the proceedings which has materially prejudiced the substantial rights of the accused. Such an error occurs, for example, in the introduction of incompetent evidence, such as a confession which is illegally obtained. A rehearing is a new trial before a court-martial, all of whose members must be different from the members who participated in the first trial. The *president or military judge* of the court-martial holding the rehearing may look at the record of the first trial to avoid the same error at the rehearing. A convening authority must disapprove the entire original sentence before ordering a rehearing. No jeopardy attaches because of the first trial, since final review of the case has not been completed. The effect of this action is a setting aside of the first trial's finding and sentence, and commencing anew with another court-martial, subject to the maximum punishment imposed at the first trial and as further reduced by reviewing authorities.

d. *Approval of the Sentence.* The convening authority approves the sentence; this includes approval of the findings which he has not otherwise specifically disapproved. As part of approving the sentence, he orders it executed. If a bad conduct discharge has been adjudged and approved, it cannot be executed until the completion of appellate review.

e. *Approval of the Sentence but Suspension of All or Part of the Sentence.* When the convening authority desires to grant a probationary period so the defendant may show his worth to the service, he approves the sentence and suspends all or a part of it. Generally, suspensions do not exceed a six-month period. If a sentence imposed by a special court includes a bad conduct discharge, and it has been suspended, or in any general court sentence, certain steps must be taken before the suspension can be vacated and the sentence put into effect. The form for proceedings to vacate suspension is contained in Appendix 16 of the MCM.

f. *Approval of the Findings but Only a Part of a Sentence.* When there are no errors which materially prejudice the substantial rights of the accused, the convening authority may approve only a part of the sentence for one, or a combination of the following reasons:

> 1. The sentence is in excess of the legal limits, so the convening authority reduces it to conform to the legal limits. This amounts to a reduction in the amount of punishment imposed.
> 2. For reasons of *clemency,* the convening authority may mitigate or commute the punishment imposed. In mitigating, the convening authority reduces in quantity or quality the punishment imposed by the court-martial. Forfeiture may be mitigated to detention of pay for a like or lesser period, and confinement at hard labor may be mitigated to restriction again for a like or lesser period. In commuting, the convening authority changes the nature of the punishment imposed by the court-martial. For example, a bad conduct discharge may be commuted to a less severe punishment of a different nature, such as confinement or forfeiture.

3. A convening authority may find the evidence not sufficient to sustain a guilty finding for the offense charged. He may find that it will only support a guilty finding for a *lesser included offense*. Only as much of the sentence as is authorized for a guilty finding as to such a lesser offense may then be approved.

1311 Subsequent Review

The Code provides for an automatic appeal to higher authority from the convening authority's action on every court-martial. This automatic review of both the findings and sentence in every court-martial case is unique, as few civilian courts give an accused such broad rights.

1. *Summary Court-Martial or Non-BCD Special Court-Martial.*

a. *Navy.* The "area coordinator" (in the absence of specific direction to the contrary by an officer authorized to convene general courts-martial and superior in the chain of command to the convening authority) will review all such records. He is termed the "supervisory authority." As a practical matter, the general court-martial convening authority so directs in most cases. If the superior authority does not have a certified military lawyer who can review the case, it will be forwarded to any appropriate superior general court-martial authority for the supervisory authority's review.

b. *Marine Corps.* In the Marine Corps the review will be accomplished within the chain of command, if practicable. If the convening authority has general court-martial jurisdiction, the record will be forwarded to a superior general court-martial authority in the chain of command who will act as supervisory authority.

In both the Navy and Marine Corps if the record of trial is approved and no mitigative or corrective action taken, the staff judge advocate may note the decision on the record of trial and notify the convening authority of the results. Otherwise, action will be taken over the signature of the supervisory authority. Section 0125a(5), JAG Manual. Paragraph 709 discusses the review procedure for a summary court-martial.

When this action is completed, the proceedings are considered final.

2. *Special Court-Martial Involving a Bad Conduct Discharge.* Generally, the supervisory authority would be the same regardless of whether the case is a BCD or non-BCD special court-martial. However, if the convening authority is a general court-martial authority and approves of the bad conduct discharge, the record would be forwarded directly to JAG for review by a Court of Military Review. The case is then final unless reviewed by COMA.

Prior to taking action on the record, the supervisory authority must have the record reviewed by a judge advocate. If the BCD is approved, or suspended, the record is then forwarded to JAG for review by a Court of Military Review.

After review by a Court of Military Review, the case would go to th
U.S. Court of Military Appeals for review if:

    a. Certified to the Court of Military Appeals by JAG (i.e., JAG
requests a review);

    b. The accused petitions for review and his request is granted;

    c. The case affects a general or flag officer.

The scope of the review by the supervisory authority and the Court
of Military Review is generally the same as that of the convening author
ity (except the Court of Military Review cannot suspend a sentence o
any part thereof). However, the U.S. Court of Military Appeals has au
thority to act only in regards to matters of "law." For example, it canno
weigh the evidence, judge the credibility of witnesses, or make new find
ings of fact.

    3. *General Courts-Martial.* The general court-martial is generall
convened at a higher level in the chain of command than a special court
martial. Usually a flag or general officer in command convenes such ;
court. Following review by his Staff Judge Advocate, the case is forwarde
to the Judge Advocate General of the Navy.

The level of review the case receives once it is forwarded to the Judg
Advocate General varies with the severity of the sentence imposed, th
rank of the accused, or the desires of the Judge Advocate General
Articles 69, 66(b) of the Code and paragraph 103 of the MCM.

1312   Deferment of Confinement

The convening authority may defer the service of confinement awarde
the accused by a court-martial. The accused must request such a defer
ment. If granted, the deferment remains in effect until rescinded by th
convening authority or until the sentence is approved and ordere
executed, whichever occurs sooner. The deferment does not reduce th
amount of confinement that has been awarded—it merely postpones th
serving of the confinement.

Both the interests of the government and the accused should be con
sidered by the convening authority in granting a deferment. For example
it should not be granted when the accused may be dangerous, may com
mit the same crime again, or may flee if his sentence is deferred.

1313   Article 69 Relief and New Trial Petitions

The rights given an accused do not necessarily end when a court
martial conviction becomes "final."

Even though review of a case is completed and the accused is con
sidered legally convicted, Article 69 of the Code provides that in an
court-martial case which has not been reviewed by the Court of Militar

eview, the accused has the right to petition the Judge Advocate General of the Navy for further consideration of his case on the grounds of:

1. Newly discovered evidence;
2. Fraud on the court;
3. Lack of jurisdiction over the accused or the offense;
4. Error prejudicial to the substantial rights of the accused.

The relief under Article 69 would be principally applicable to summary and non-BCD special courts-martial as they have not previously een reviewed by a Court of Military Review. This is a significant additonal right for an accused tried by these courts. There is no limitation s to the number of times relief may be requested under Article 69 nor there any time limitation within which an application for relief may e submitted. See Section 0144 of the JAG Manual.

However, regardless of the scope of previous reviews, any person conicted under the Code may petition the Judge Advocate General of the Iavy for a *new trial* under Article 73 of the Code. This article permits ich a petition on two grounds: newly discovered evidence and fraud on ie court.

The petition may be submitted even if the accused is out of the service nd even if his case has been finally reviewed. It must be submitted ithin two years after approval by the convening authority of the senence. See Section 0143 of the JAG Manual.

314   Court-Martial Orders

The results of trial in all special and general court cases are published promulgating orders called *court-martial orders*. These are issued by ie officer who has the authority to order the sentence executed. This ould be the convening authority in a special court-martial case not djudging a bad conduct discharge, or in a bad conduct discharge case hich he has disapproved. If the sentence includes a bad conduct disiarge, the supervisory authority issues the promulgating order. A bad onduct discharge may not be executed until it is approved by the Court f Military Review, and, in cases reviewed by it, the U.S. Court of Miliry Appeals.

315   Summary

After the trial and defense counsel present their evidence, they anounce that they "rest" their cases. The presiding officer then determines hat instructions he will utilize after affording the trial and defense ounsel an opportunity to present proposed instructions. The trial counl then makes an "opening" argument on the findings. This is followed y a defense argument. As the trial counsel has the burden of proof, he granted the opportunity to make a "closing" argument. The presiding fficer then instructs the court as to the law it must apply to the facts.

The court then goes into closed session. During the session, the members may not be convinced beyond a reasonable doubt that the accused is guilty of the principal offense charged, but may believe he is guilty of a lesser included offense. They may then find him guilty of this lesser included offense.

The court then opens in the presence of the military judge, counsel, the reporter and the accused. If a military judge is present, he may assist them in putting their findings in proper order.

If the accused is found guilty of one or more specifications, the prosecution and defense may present appropriate matter to aid the court in determining the punishment to be imposed. The prosecution would present information as to the service history of the accused as reflected on page 1 of the charge sheet, prior convictions of the accused, aggravating circumstances in the event of a guilty plea, and information as to the accused's conduct and character (if a military judge is presiding). The defense should then present evidence in mitigation or extenuation.

Each counsel may then make an argument as to an appropriate sentence. The presiding officer will then instruct the members as to matters relating to the sentence. Some of the punishments that a special court-martial may award, if the offense so warrants, include a bad conduct discharge, confinement at hard labor, forfeiture of pay, and reduction in rate.

Following the announcement of the sentence, the court is adjourned or proceeds to other cases. Following the trial, the members may sign a petition for clemency, but in doing so they must *not* divulge their vote on the findings or sentence.

The trial counsel prepares the record of trial. The presiding officer authenticates the record and the defense counsel reviews and signs it. Every court-martial must be reviewed by the convening authority.

The convening authority's primary concern is whether any error may have materially prejudiced the rights of the accused. Some of the alternatives the convening authority has are dismissal of the charges, ordering another trial or a rehearing, suspension of all or part of the sentence, or approval of only a part of the sentence.

There is an automatic review beyond the convening authority in every court-martial case. The extent of the review is basically determined by the type of court and the sentence imposed. At his discretion, the convening authority may defer the service of confinement awarded the accused for any length of time up until the sentence is ordered executed. The rights given an accused do not necessarily end when a court-martial conviction becomes "final." Articles 69 and 73 provide extraordinary relief under certain circumstances. The procedure for appeal under these provisions is contained in the JAG Manual.

Discussion Case

UNITED STATES, Appellee
v.
EARL F. WHEELER, Private, U.S. Army, Appellant
17 USCMA 274, 38 CMR 72

(1967)

Opinion of the Court

FERGUSON, Judge:

Tried by general court-martial convened by the Commanding General, 1st Infantry Division, the accused, upon his plea of guilty, was convicted of absence without leave, in violation of Uniform Code of Military Justice, Article 86, 10 USC § 886, and sentenced to bad-conduct discharge, forfeiture of all pay and allowances, and confinement at hard labor for one year. With a reduction in the period of confinement to nine months, intermediate appellate authorities affirmed. We granted accused's petition for review on issues dealing with the law officer's instructions on sentence and trial counsel's argument for imposition of a severe sentence. As these assignments are intermeshed, we will discuss them together.

I

Accused absented himself without leave for a period of approximately seventeen weeks. Evidence of two previous convictions was introduced. One involved two brief absences and the other an absence of eight days and one of slightly over nine weeks. All the offenses, including that of which accused now stands guilty, occurred in 1965 and 1966. During the fourteen-month period extending from June 2, 1965, to October 8, 1966, Wheeler was absent without leave a total of 207 days. In addition, he served confinement as a result of his last previous conviction from April 9, 1966, to May 24, 1966. One week after returning to duty, he absented himself for the period here involved. Hence, in fourteen months, accused was only available for duty less than half that time.

Contrasting with this harsh portrait of a recidivistic absentee, however, is the evidence relating to his prior military service between September 15, 1947, and the day in June 1965 on which his first recorded delict occurred. During that period, he rose to the grade of Sergeant First Class E-6. He served as a combat medic, first sergeant, and operations sergeant in Korea in four campaigns. Until June 1965, his conduct and efficiency ratings were uniformly excellent. He was thrice awarded the Good Conduct Medal and holds numerous campaign ribbons. In addition, he was wounded in action in Vietnam, for which he received the Purple Heart medal.

Asked to explain what happened to effect such a great change in his military career at a stage when he was approaching the possibility of retirement, the accused attributed his downfall to compulsive drinking, commencing with detecting his wife in unfaithfulness while stationed at Fort Riley, Kansas, and thereafter losing both her and their children. In addition, he blamed himself for the untimely death of a young assistant during the operation in Vietnam in which he was wounded. After ending his final unauthorized absence, he had apparently obtained psychiatric assistance from Army medical authorities and alleged to the court:

> ". . . I know I have ruined my last eighteen months. I haven't been worth while to the Army or to anyone else, but I do understand my faults and I'd like to have another chance to finish up my service. I am willing to accept everything you sentence, to go to jail or whatever it is. I would like to finish up my duty."

Defense counsel made a lengthy and vehement argument in which he referred at length to accused's long and honorable prior service; his difficulties; that psychiatric help had now been provided him; and, even though stiff confinement was adjudged, pleaded for the accused that a punitive discharge not be included in the sentence.

In reply, trial counsel emphasized accused's more recent record and referred to his previous failure to rehabilitate himself. He argued that the "court is not trying the accused for his previous record of service," invited it to disregard such, and contended "this accused should receive the maximum penalty . . . which you are authorized to impose."

Thereafter the law officer instructed the court on the maximum sentence. Except for matter relating to the mechanics of voting on a penalty, his entire advice consisted of the following statement:

> "Gentlemen, of the court. You are advised that the maximum punishment which may be imposed for the offense of which the accused stands convicted is dishonorable discharge, total forfeitures, reduction to the grade of E–1 and confinement at hard labor for one year."

Not a word was said about the evidence in mitigation or aggravation, nor was any information imparted concerning the respective contentions of counsel, the effect of a guilty plea, the possibility of lesser punishments, or any other matter.

II

The Government contends the only positive requirement for sentence instructions by the law officer is to inform the court-martial of the maximum penalty or, in the case of previous convictions affecting that maximum, the role which they play in authorizing a punitive discharge. Relying primarily on *United States* v. *Turner*, 9 USCMA 124, 25 CMR 386, it urges that any additional advice is confided solely to the law officer's discretion and, absent a request by defense counsel, it cannot be held that discretion was abused. On the other hand, the defense points out that this Court has never precisely delineated the scope of the law officer's responsibility in this area and urges that the circumstances, including the trial counsel's argument, are such as to require the law officer to give further instructions in this area. We believe the importance of the question presented called for a definitive approach to the issue of the law officer's responsibility.

Our inquiry must of necessity begin with the Uniform Code of Military Justice and the nature of court-martial sentences. With the exception of specified instances of mandatory punishments of death or life imprisonment, almost every offense under the Code is left to be punished "as a court-martial may direct." The only restrictions to be found on that power are in the codal prohibition against cruel and unusual punishment and in the authority granted the President to prescribe maximum limitations on the discretion thus conferred upon the court-martial. Code, supra, Articles 55, 56, 10 USC §§ 855, 856. The President, of course, has prescribed such limitations with respect to most offenses. See Manual for Courts-Martial, United States, 1951, paragraph 127c.

Still, a vast discretion is vested in the court members and, unlike their civilian counterparts, they have a variety of punishments from which to choose. Thus, while a judge or jury, as the case may be, normally imposes only a sentence to confinement or fine, military tribunals go beyond these ordinary punishments and, for example, are permitted also to reduce an individual to the lowest enlisted grade, exact forfeitures from him over a period of time, reprimand him, or direct his punitive separation from the service.

The severity of these penalties, unknown to civil life as they are, cannot be denied. In the present days of military economy, to deprive a noncommissioned officer of his rank alone is, in essence, to effect financial retribution of the immense sum he would otherwise have accrued during the years it may take him to regain his former position. In like manner, the ordering of a punitive discharge so characterizes an individual that his whole future is utterly destroyed. He is marked far beyond the civilian felon, hampered as he may be by the sneering term "ex-con," for, justifiedly or not, the punitive discharge so dishonors and disgraces an accused that he finds employment virtually impossible; is subjected to many legal deprivations; and is regarded with horror by his fellow citizens. Truly, it has come to be the modern equivalent of the ancient practice of branding felons, and the stain it leaves is as ineradicable. And, in the case of a soldier with extended service, the discharge can be even more severe, for, as the Chief Judge wisely noted in *United States* v. *Prow,* 13 USCMA 63, 32 CMR 63, at page 64, "an executed punitive discharge terminates military status as completely as an executed death penalty ends mortal life."

Contrary to the government's argument that the law officer need only instruct the court-martial on the maximum sentence, this Court has always insisted the members be furnished with adequate guidance regarding the exercise of their discretion in reaching an appropriate punishment. As early as *United States* v. *Linder,* 6 USCMA 669, 20 CMR 385, Chief Judge Quinn declared, at page 674:

". . . The law officer must provide the court members with appropriate instructions on the law which applies to all matters to be decided by them. He should not require or expect the court members to consult other sources for the law. See *United States* v. *Lowry,* 4 USCMA 448, 16 CMR 22. And his responsibility in that regard does not end with the findings. In *United States* v. *Strand,* 6 USCMA 297, 306, 20 CMR 13, we said: 'Until the sentence proceedings are complete, the trial is not ended.' Until the trial ends the law officer must supply the court members with adequate legal assistance."

And, while the question then before us was one of inconsistency in the sentence, the Chief Judge again noted in his separate opinion in *United States* v. *Cleckley,* 8 USCMA 83, 23 CMR 307, at page 87, that, without adequate instructions, the court-martial "cannot make an intelligent determination of an appropriate sentence."

In *Turner,* supra, on which the government relies here, we dealt only with the total absence of any instructions, including advice on the maximum sentence. As we have since stated, we there decided only the question then before us, and the decision is no authority for the proposition that the law officer may, with impunity, so limit his instructions in every case. See *United States* v. *Hutton,* 14 USCMA 366, 34 CMR 146, and *United States* v. *Yocom,* 17 USCMA 270, 38 CMR 68. The last cited cases, indeed, epitomize the subject on which we now dwell. In each of those cases, advice was given as to the maximum sentence, but in neither was the court-martial informed that the punitive discharge therein was only a permissible additional punishment, based, in the one instance, on evidence of previous convictions, and, in the other, on the fact that charges permitting confinement in excess of six months were tried together. In each, we pointed out the need for enlightenment of the court-martial in order that it might be led to adjudge an appropriate sentence. As

the Court said in *United States* v *Rake,* 11 USCMA 159, 28 CMR 38. at page 160:

"So far as instruction on the sen tence is concerned, the basic require ment is that the court-martial b properly advised of the legal limit; tions of punishment. That is not al Since the court-martial is not boun except in certain cases, to adjudg a maximum sentence, it is appr priate for the law officer to provid 'general guides governing the ma ters to be considered in determinin the appropriateness of the particula sentence.' *United States* v. *Mamalu)* 10 USCMA 102, 106, 27 CMR 176.

See also *United States* v. *Cook,* 1 USCMA 579, 29 CMR 395.

Summed up, then, the whole thrus of this Court's opinions regarding pr sentence instructions has been to r quire the law officer to delineate th matters which the court-martial shoul consider in its deliberations. While th law officer has some discretion in thi regard, we have expressly noted tha such "ought not to have the same r straining effect during the sentenc procedure." *United States* v. *Cook* supra, at page 581. This is particularl true in light of the range of punish ments to which a military accused ma be subjected under the Code—"as court-martial may direct"—when com pared to those imposable by a civi court. In short, we reiterate here th duty of the law officer to tailor his in structions on the sentence to the la\ and the evidence, just as in the case o his prefindings advice. *United State* v. *Yocom, United States* v. *Hutton* both supra.

Under the circumstances of this case we are not satisfied that this standar\

is met by a mere rote instruction on the maximum imposable sentence. Here, the accused presented evidence of extensive honorable service to his country as a career noncommissioned officer. All his offenses were of a military nature and had occurred in the fourteen months prior to his trial. It is apparent they resulted from his alcoholism, said to have been motivated, in turn, by his serious domestic problems. It further appeared that he had, for the first time, received medical aid in connection with his difficulties and sought an opportunity to finish out his service and rehabilitate himself. Trial counsel, however, argued to the court that these matters should not be considered, as it was "not trying the accused for his previous record of service," and demanded the maximum penalty. Both he and defense counsel were acting as advocates, and their inherently opposed views as to what the court-martial could consider should have alerted the law officer to the need to instruct the court-martial on its responsibilities, particularly with respect to the exercise of its sentencing discretion in light of the evidence in mitigation and extenuation. At the same time, the government was likewise entitled to have advice presented regarding the other side of the coin, namely, that the retention of the accused was totally unjustified in light of his inexcusable failure to remain present for duty. We take no sides on the issue. We merely emphasize the duty of the law officer to advise the court-martial of the nature of its sole responsibility for the sentence; the exercise of its duty; and what it was entitled to consider.

In this respect, we call attention to the decision in *United States* v. *Cook*, supra, which involves almost identical circumstances. There, as here, the accused had long and honorable service. There, as here, extensive evidence was presented in extenuation and mitigation. While the particular matter in that case related to accused's mental state as opposed to Wheeler's domestic difficulties and their result, the same conclusion must obtain, namely, that the failure to give advice to the court-martial was erroneous and, in light of the near-maximum sentence adjudged, prejudicially so.

Of course, there will be many cases in which the situation will be such that either there is nothing for the law officer to embody in his advice to the court or in which the accused's own evidence leaves nothing to be said. In such instances, though omission of the full advice as to the court's discretion is erroneous, the limitation of his instructions may not be prejudicial. See *United States* v. *Mabry,* 17 USCMA 285, 38 CMR 83, this day decided. Nevertheless, to avoid the possibility of prejudice and consequent reversal, we urge law officers carefully to shape their instructions on the sentence to the evidence presented and to inform the court members fully as to their responsibilities. The Army has long provided suggested instructions fulfilling the latter function. See Appendices XXXII, XXXIII, Department of the Army Pamphlet No. 27–9, Military Justice Handbook: The Law Officer, April 1958, paragraph 89. Indeed those instructions would have been peculiarly appropriate here, for they refer to the need to consider "the background and character of the accused; . . . the . . . record of the accused in the service for good conduct, . . . [and] other traits which characterize a good soldier;" the plea of guilty; and other matters which the court should consider. In addition, they place emphasis on its sole responsibility to select an appropriate sentence within the limits prescribed by law. *Id.,* Appendix XXXIII. We have seen similar instructions in nearly every Army case before us. In light of our prior decisions, we wonder at their absence here.

The decision of the board of review is reversed and the record of trial is returned to the Judge-Advocate General of the Army. As the lack of instructions principally went to the question of a punitive discharge, the board may either disapprove that portion of the sentence or order a rehearing thereon.

Judge KILDAY concurs.

QUINN, Chief Judge, concurred in the result.

DISCUSSION AND SELF-QUIZ

1. You are the presiding president of a special court-martial in the case of Seaman Richard Roe, U.S. Navy. Roe has been charged with breaking restriction in violation of Article 134 and with unauthorized absence in violation of Article 86. Roe pleads guilty. His unauthorized absence was for a period of two days. The unauthorized absence occurred at the same time as the breaking restriction. What is the maximum confinement at hard labor that can be imposed in this case? See section A of Chapter XXV and paragraph 76a(5) of the MCM.

2. You are the trial counsel in a special court-martial in which the president is presiding. The accused is charged with two short periods of unauthorized absence. A glance at the accused's service record shows he has been awarded nonjudicial punishment on five different occasions. Is there any way you can initially bring these NJPs to the court's attention so that they will award an "appropriate" punishment? See paragraph 75d of the MCM.

3. You are a member of a special court-martial convened on board the USS *Awash* (DD–909). After hearing the evidence in mitigation and extenuation the court closes to deliberate on the sentence. The mitigation disclosed that the accused is an outstanding worker. If he is confined at hard labor he will have to be transferred to a shore brig, as the ship has no confinement facilities. The forfeiture of $60.00 per month for four months, reduction to E-1, and confinement at hard labor for four months seems to you to be an adequate punishment. However, you prefer he remain on board the ship, as he is vitally needed for his skills.

a. Could the court award four months' restriction in lieu of four months' confinement at hard labor?

b. Could the court award four months' hard labor without confinement in lieu of confinement at hard labor? See Chapter XXV of the MCM.

4. You are the trial counsel in a special court-martial case. The accused pleads guilty and the pre-sentencing procedure begins. In the accused's service record is a record of previous conviction of a non-BCD special court. It has been reviewed by the convening authority but not the supervisory authority. Can you enter the conviction into evidence as to the sentence to be awarded for this present offense? See paragraph 75b(2) of the MCM.

5. You are a Marine company commander. Your company is presently located in CONUS. Private Jones desires to talk to you about military justice. Jones has been told by his civilian friends that "it is well-known that a serviceman seldom can obtain a free lawyer to defend him." Is this true?

6. You are a member of a special court-martial. The charge is larceny. After hearing all the evidence and arguments in the case, the members of the court believe beyond a reasonable doubt that the accused is only guilty of wrongful appropriation, a lesser included offense of larceny. Draft the court's findings in this case. See paragraph 1304 of this chapter.

CHAPTER XIV

Administrative
Fact-Finding Bodies

An administrative fact-finding body (commonly called a JAG Manu.
Investigation) may be any one of a number of administrative entities en
ployed to collect and record information respecting some subject. Th
primary purpose of all administrative fact-finding bodies is to provic
convening and reviewing authorities adequate information upon whic
to base decisions in the matters involved. These bodies are not judicia
Their reports are purely advisory and their opinions, when expresse
do not constitute final determinations or legal judgments. Their recon
mendations, when made, are not binding upon convening or reviewin
authorities. The basic directive which discusses administrative fact-findin
bodies is the JAG Manual. It is applicable to both the Navy and Marir
Corps.

The primary function of all administrative fact-finding bodies is t
search out, develop, assemble, analyze, and record all available inform.
tion relative to the matter under investigation. The collateral functio
of a court of inquiry, and (when so directed by the convening authorit)
a formal investigation, is to afford a hearing to any person whose condu
or performance of duty is subject to inquiry or who has a direct intere
in the subject of the inquiry.

1401   Necessity of Administrative Fact-Finding Bodies

The collection and preservation of important information by fac
finding bodies convened under JAG Manual regulations are vitally nece
sary and useful in many respects. For example:

1. *Efficient Command or Administration.* Fact-finding reports ma
provide convening and reviewing authorities with information essenti.

to the efficient operation and readiness of the fleet or improve some facet of administration within the Department of the Navy. For example, they may become the bases for:

a. Reevaluation of operational practices or standards;

b. Redesign and improvement of material or equipment;

c. Modification or adoption of instructions, regulations, and procedures;

d. Timely and accurate reply to inquiries concerning incidents of legitimate public interest, with accompanying improved public relations.

2. *Proper Disposition of Claims for or Against the Government.*

3. *Personnel Determinations.* Fact-finding reports may provide information which is usable in connection with various personnel actions arising out of the conduct or performance of individuals, such as misconduct and line of duty determinations, commendatory actions, disciplinary actions, and other administrative actions.

1402 Types of Administrative Fact-Finding Bodies

There are three types of administrative fact-finding bodies: courts of inquiry, formal investigations, and informal investigations.

An administrative fact-finding body may be composed of one or several members. By statute (Article 135 of the Code) a court of inquiry must consist of three or more commissioned officers and a counsel to the court. Investigating bodies comprised of more than one member are sometimes referred to as "boards of investigation." From the standpoint of procedural requirements, administrative fact-finding bodies may be either formal or informal.

A formal fact-finding body is one which utilizes a formal hearing procedure, ordinarily takes all testimony under oath and maintains a verbatim record of all evidence, and may be authorized to designate parties. An informal fact-finding body normally employs the preliminary inquiry method of gathering evidence, using telephone inquiries, correspondence, and informal interviews to assemble the required information conveniently and expeditiously.

An informal fact-finding body may not be authorized to designate parties. A court of inquiry must necessarily be a formal fact-finding body. Article 135 of the Code gives it the power to designate parties and requires a record of the proceedings. Courts of inquiry ordinarily take all testimony under oath. On the other hand, a formal investigation might proceed informally to the extent that the appointing order may specify that a verbatim record is not required and either no party is in fact designated or no party insists upon adherence to court-type procedure.

1403 Selection of Type of Fact-Finding Body

The type of fact-finding body to be ordered should be determined in large measure by the powers which the fact-finding body will require, the paramount purposes of the inquiry, the relative seriousness of the subject of the inquiry, the probable complexity of the factual issues involved, and other such factors. Much must be left to the judgment and sound discretion of officers in command. In general, however, the following guidelines should be considered in the selection of the type of fact-finding body to be employed.

Where it appears that the incident under investigation involves substantial loss of life or where significant international or legal consequences may be involved, either a court of inquiry or a formal board of investigation should be employed. A court of inquiry should be utilized whenever it may be necessary to compel by subpoena the appearance and examination of persons outside the armed forces. Other serious incident requiring investigation, such as grounding of a ship, collision, flooding and other major afloat casualties, particularly if significant loss of life resulted, should ordinarily be investigated by a formal board or formal single officer investigation, but in such cases the requirement of a verbatim record need not invariably be imposed. In other less serious cases an informal investigation will ordinarily be adequate. Doubt as to the type of fact-finding body which should be ordered may be referred to superior in command for advice.

1404 Parties

A "party" is an individual who has properly been designated as such in connection with a court of inquiry or formal fact-finding body. *No person may be designated a party before an informal fact-finding body.*

Generally, there are two occasions when a person is designated a party before a fact-finding body:

1. *When the person's conduct or performance of duty is "subject to inquiry".* This would occur when the person is involved in the incident under investigation in such a way that disciplinary action may follow, that his rights or privileges may be adversely affected, or that his personal reputation or professional standing may be jeopardized.

2. *When the person has a "direct interest" in the subject of inquiry.* This occurs (1) when the findings, opinions or recommendations of the fact-finding body may, in view of his relation to the incident or circumstances under investigation, reflect questionable or unsatisfactory conduct or performance of duty, or (2) when the findings, opinions, or recommendations may relate to a matter over which the person has a duty or right to exercise official control. Section 0302 of the JAG Manual discusses when parties are designated and who may designate them.

A person designated as a party has the following rights:

1. To be given due notice of such designation;
2. To be present during the proceedings;
3. To be represented by counsel;
4. To examine and to object to the introduction of physical and documentary evidence and statements or testimony of witnesses;
5. To cross-examine witnesses other than his own who have offered testimony;
6. To introduce evidence;
7. To testify as a witness;
8. To refuse to incriminate himself; and if accused or suspected of an offense, to be informed of the nature of the accusation and advised that he does not have to make any statement regarding the offense of which he is accused or suspected and that any statement made by him may be used as evidence against him in a trial by court-martial;
9. To make a voluntary statement, oral or written, to be included in the record;
10. To make an argument at the conclusion of presentation of the evidence.

In courts of inquiry, a party has two additional rights:

11. To challenge members of the court of inquiry for cause stated to the court;
12. If charged with an offense, to be a witness at his own request and not to be called as a witness in the absence of his own request.

The party is entitled to be represented during the proceedings by civilian counsel provided by himself at no cost to the government or by military counsel of his own selection if reasonably available, or by military counsel appointed for him by appropriate military authority. Upon request for appointed military counsel, counsel qualified under Article 27(b) of the Code should be appointed, if practicable, and *must* be appointed if the court or investigation is to be used as a pretrial investigation for a general court-martial required by Article 32 of the Code. There are no special legal qualifications required of civilian counsel provided by the party himself or of military counsel selected by him.

It is the duty of counsel for the court of inquiry or board to call witnesses and conduct the direct examination of all witnesses except those requested or called by a party. He also administers oaths or affirmations to all members and witnesses and supervises the recording of the proceedings and preparation of the record. His primary responsibility is to explore all sources of information in order to bring out all the facts in an impartial manner without regard to the favorable or unfavorable effect on persons concerned.

There are differences of opinion among service lawyers as to the effect of a failure to accord an individual the rights of a party to a formal investigative proceeding. Such failure will at best entail delay in completing such action as imposition of nonjudicial punishment, incorporating the record of investigation by reference into a personnel record, or making a final determination that an injury was due to the misconduct of the injured person or was not incurred in the line of duty. Such failure may preclude use of the investigation as a pretrial investigation in accordance with Article 32 of the Code.

Rights which a party can choose to exercise or not to exercise are conclusively waived by the party's failure to exercise them.

1405   Courts of Inquiry

The most formal and "highest" of the JAG Manual fact-finding bodies is the court of inquiry. The principal distinguishing features of a court of inquiry are:

1. It consists of at least three commissioned officers as members and a commissioned officer as counsel for the court;

2. It is convened by a written appointing order;

3. Whether or not directed in the appointing order, it *must* take all testimony under oath and record all proceedings verbatim;

4. Persons subject to the Code whose conduct is subject to inquiry must be designated parties;

5. Persons subject to the Code or employed by the Department of Defense who have a direct interest in the subject of inquiry must be designated parties upon a request therefor to the court;

6. It possesses the power to subpoena civilian witnesses; and witnesses failing to appear or to testify or to produce evidence are subject to prosecution in a federal district court.

Any person authorized to convene a general court-martial or any other person designated by the Secretary of the Navy for that purpose, may convene a court of inquiry (Article 135 of the Code).

As all testimony is taken under oath and recorded verbatim, a court of inquiry is similar in its proceedings to a general court-martial. Although the court is not strictly bound by the rules of evidence, the rights of all witnesses and parties shall be carefully safeguarded. Should a member object to the senior member's ruling on any matter, a vote will be taken. In the event of a tie vote, the decision of the senior member shall rule.

When all the evidence and testimony have been duly considered, and all statements and arguments submitted, the court will close and make its determinations according to instructions in the appointing order. It will first consider the findings of fact and then, if requested by the appointing order, will render opinions based on these facts. If requested, it will make such recommendations as are specifically directed and any others that, in its opinion, are appropriate and advisable in view of the nature of the facts found and the opinions expressed. The opinion of the majority of the court will determine the above. If a member does not agree, he may append a minority report and therein state explicitly those parts wherein he disagrees and the reasons therefor.

1406 Formal Investigations

The principal distinguishing features of a formal investigation are:

1. It consists of one or more commissioned officers as member or members;

2. It is convened by a written appointing order;

3. The appointing order may direct that the body take all testimony under oath and record all proceedings verbatim;

4. It normally utilizes a formal hearing procedure;

5. Persons whose conduct is subject to inquiry or who have a direct interest in the subject of inquiry may *not* be designated parties unless such designation is expressly authorized in the appointing order;

6. It does *not* have the power to subpoena civilian witnesses.

Generally, any "officer-in-command" authorized to convene any type of court-martial or to administer nonjudicial punishment may order a formal board of investigation. This includes an "officer-in-charge." Additionally, the appointing order of a fact-finding body other than a court of inquiry may be issued or subscribed by an officer who holds a delegation of authority for such purpose from the convening authority.

As a general rule, the principles and rules of procedure of a court of inquiry are to be applied to a formal fact-finding body. Chapter V of the JAG Manual sets out appropriate modifications to these principles and rules of procedure applicable especially to formal fact-finding bodies. There is no right of challenge, as there is to a member of a court of inquiry, but an investigating officer who does not feel that he can act impartially should make this fact known and request that another serve in his stead.

It is not mandatory that a counsel be appointed for a board; if one is not, then the junior member shall so act. It is highly desirable, if matters under consideration involve a high degree of technical knowledge, that the counsel or assistant counsel possess knowledge in this area.

A formal one-man investigation consists of one commissioned officer and may be convened by any officer in command. By its nature, it is rather uncommon in the naval service today. The rules and principles governing the operation of a formal board are also applicable to the formal one-man investigation.

1407   Informal Investigations

The principal distinguishing features of an informal investigation are

1. It may consist of one or more officers, senior enlisted persons, o civilian employees of the Department of the Navy as member or members
2. It may be convened orally or in writing (see Appendix 21);
3. It is ordinarily not directed to take testimony under oath or t record testimony verbatim;
4. It utilizes informal procedures in collecting evidence;
5. It may not designate any persons or parties to the investigation
6. It does not possess the power to subpoena civilian witnesses.

Informal investigations may be convened by any officer in comman authorized to convene a formal investigation. As a rule of thumb, if com missioned officers are not appointed to conduct the investigation, it wil always be informal. Ordinarily, counsel is not appointed for an informa fact-finding body. The appointing order should in every case direct th fact-finding body to report findings of fact despite the circumstance tha this duty is present in every appointment. It should, when desired, ex pressly direct that opinions, or opinions and recommendations, be sub mitted. The appointing order may also direct that some or all of th testimony be taken under oath and/or be recorded verbatim, but in tha event, to avoid confusion, the convening authority should indicate tha he is appointing an informal fact-finding body.

As an informal fact-finding body does not perform the collateral func tion of affording a hearing for a party (as there are *no* parties), it is fre to determine and utilize the most effective methods of seeking out, un covering, collecting, analyzing, and recording all information which is or may be, relevant to a determination of all the facts and circumstance of the subject under inquiry.

For example, two or more officers may assign witnesses and evidentiar facets of the inquiry for an individual member to develop, holding n collective meeting until an initial review is made of all the informatior collected. An informal investigation may collect information either for mally or by informal personal interview, correspondence, telephone in quiry, or other means. In short, an informal fact-finding body ma employ any method which it finds most efficient and effective in per forming its investigative function. Facts and circumstances of an inciden or matter under investigation are most often proved or disproved by (1 real evidence, (2) documentary evidence, and (3) witnesses.

1. *Real Evidence.*   Whenever the condition, location, or other char acteristic of an item of real evidence is of value in proving the existenc or nonexistence of a fact, an item or a photograph, a description or othe suitable reproduction thereof should be included in the report of investi gation. Statements of witnesses identifying the item and certifying to th

accuracy of the reproduction should be included. If the physical layout of a room, etc., is relevant, the investigation should consider the desirability of including in the report plans or charts of the space. Area photos, if interrelated areas are relevant, may be of value.

The investigator should not overlook *his own value as a witness*. If a member observes items and gains impressions not adequately portrayed by a photograph, chart, map or other representation, he should record his impressions respecting the items and include such statement as an enclosure to the report.

2. *Documentary Evidence.* Documentary evidence is that taken from records, documents, letters, etc. This type of evidence should be attached to the record (either the original or a copy thereof).

3. *Witnesses.* Ordinarily, statements of witnesses will be obtained during an informal interview in which a witness relates his knowledge and it is then reduced to writing and signed. If this method is utilized, the investigator or board should assist the witness in preparing his written statement to avoid excessive inclusion of irrelevant material or the omission of important facts and circumstances. However, any suggestion of coaching or indicating the existence or nonexistence of facts to the witness must be scrupulously avoided.

Ordinarily, the single investigator or board should collect all relevant information from all available sources other than persons suspected of an offense for which prosecution is contemplated. After the collection of all available evidence, if the scope of the inquiry dictates that an interview with a person or persons so suspected should be conducted, such persons should be accorded the rights prescribed in paragraph 307 of *Military Law.* If the only issue is the line of duty/misconduct status of an injured serviceman, such a person need only be advised of the nature of the inquiry; the possible effect of an adverse line of duty/misconduct determination; and the opportunity to seek advice from someone not connected with the government side of the investigation.

An informal fact-finding body is not bound by the formal rules of evidence applicable before courts-martial, and may collect, consider, and include in the record any matter of reasonable believability or authenticity, where necessary. A statement of a witness is not required to be in writing. If it is not in writing and signed, it should be certified to be the true substance or verbatim transcript of an oral statement made by a witness.

1408 Investigative Report

In all cases, an investigative report in letter form shall be submitted. It shall consist of a preliminary statement, findings of fact, enclosures, and when directed by the convening authority, opinions and recommendations.

1. *Preliminary Statement.* The purpose of the preliminary statement is to inform the convening and reviewing authorities that the requirements as to procurement of all reasonable available evidence and directives of the convening authorities have been met. After setting forth the nature of the investigation, it will set forth in detail the difficulties encountered in the investigation, if any; any limited participation in the investigation by a member; and any other information necessary for a complete understanding of the case.

2. *Findings of Fact.* The findings of fact represent the evaluation of the evidence and information received and collected. The findings must be as specific as possible as to times, places, persons, and events. Each fact may be made a separate finding, or facts may be grouped into a narrative.

3. *Opinions.* Opinions are the logical inferences or conclusions which flow from the facts. The investigation will express its opinions when directed to do so by the convening authority. For guidance as to the opinions normally required in specific situations, see Chapters VIII and IX of the JAG Manual.

4. *Recommendations.* Recommendations will be made only when the convening authority has so directed in his appointing order. If required, such recommendations as are specifically directed and those which appropriately flow from the findings of fact and expressed opinions shall be made. If trial by court-martial is recommended, a charge sheet, signed and sworn to by a member joining in the recommendation, shall be prepared and submitted as an enclosure to the investigative report. See paragraphs f and g of section 0608 of the JAG Manual as to the enclosures, signing, and authentication for the investigative report. The JAG Manual contains a sample informal investigative report. (See Appendix 22.)

1409 Summary

Fact-finding bodies perform an essential function within the military. The proper investigation of incidents that occur in the service is essential to the efficient operation of the fleet. Investigative bodies facilitate the disposition of claims for or against the government and provide information for line of duty and misconduct determinations.

The JAG Manual discusses three basic fact-finding bodies: courts of inquiry, formal investigations, and informal investigations.

The court of inquiry is the most formal of the three. The informal investigation is the type most often conducted in the military. Its method of collecting information upon which to base its facts may be very informal.

DISCUSSION AND SELF-QUIZ

1. You are the legal officer on board your ship, which is steaming independently in a remote area. Your ship is involved in a collision with a foreign freighter. As a result, ten men on board your ship are killed. Your commanding officer wants to know if an informal board of investigation will suffice. What is your advice? (See paragraph 1403 of this publication.)

2. What are the two situations when a person is designated a "party" before a fact-finding body? (See paragraph 1404 of this publication.)

3. You have been appointed to conduct an informal investigation. One of the "key" witnesses to the incident has been transferred 3,000 miles to another duty station. How can you complete your investigation? (See paragraph 1407 of this publication.)

CHAPTER XV

Line of Duty and Misconduct Determinations

The line of duty and misconduct investigation is familiar to every Navy and Marine Corps officer, as it is the most common JAG Manual investigation held in the military. An unfavorable line of duty and misconduct determination may result in the necessity for the injured serviceman to make up the time lost because of hospitalization. He may also lose retirement or separation pay or disability compensation.

Assume that Private Jones, USMC, shot himself in the foot with a semi-automatic rifle while attempting to adjust the malfunctioning of its ejection mechanism. He had been target practicing when a round of ammunition jammed in the weapon. With the gun aimed at his foot, he cleared the jammed round from the weapon by pulling back on the bolt and releasing it. This had the additional effect of placing a new round in the chamber. As soon as the new round entered, the gun discharged. The bullet penetrated his foot. He sustained permanent injuries. A line of duty/misconduct investigation would be required in this case.

However, the JAG Manual has been revised in recent years so that there are *many* cases in which a complete line of duty and misconduct investigation is *not* required. When first assigned such an investigation, the officer should study the rules and regulations very carefully to determine if such an investigation really is required.

If it is not, the commanding officer or his legal representative should be so informed. If the commanding officer concurs with the investigating officer's analysis of the JAG Manual requirements, he may decide not to investigate the case as such investigations are very time-consuming. He may desire that the investigator conduct a preliminary inquiry (see Chapter III) if there is a question of disciplinary action yet to be resolved.

However, in this case it would be best to conduct a preliminary inquiry rather than the informal investigation. The reason for this is that non-judicial punishment cannot be awarded on the basis of an investigation at which the accused was not accorded the rights of a party. Informal investigations cannot designate parties.

Therefore, it is important to determine just *when* a complete line of duty and misconduct investigation is required and when more expeditious methods will achieve the same result.

Prior to resolving the issue of whether a report is required, it is vital that misconduct and line of duty be discussed.

1501 Misconduct/Line of Duty

1. *Misconduct.* "Misconduct" is present, within the meaning of the JAG Manual, when it is established by clear and convincing evidence that the injury or disease was either intentionally incurred or was the proximate result of such gross negligence as to demonstrate a reckless disregard of the consequences.

To determine if the intentional, grossly negligent or willful conduct was so closely connected with the injury or disease so that the one resulted in the other, the test of "proximate cause" is used.

When the conduct either sets in motion or directly results in the force causing the injury or disease and when this force is the reasonably foreseeable result of such wrongful conduct, it is said to be the proximate result of the injury or disease.

For example, the general rule is that injury or death incurred as the proximate result of voluntary participation in a fight, in which the person is at least equally at fault with his adversary in starting or continuing the fight, is the result of misconduct.

The reason for this is that fighting normally involves a danger of injury so great and so apparent that participation therein shows a reckless disregard for personal safety. It is reasonably foreseeable that a person could be injured by another when he voluntarily participates in a fight.

However, the test of proximate cause must be met. Reread the Private Jones case in the introductory paragraph relating to the rifle incident. It has been held that firearms are inherently dangerous and their use demands the highest degree of care. Under the circumstances, the injured man's act of aiming the rifle at his foot, knowing it was loaded and was not functioning properly, showed such lack of caution and circumspection, that it amounted to gross negligence. His injuries were considered to have been incurred as the result of his misconduct and not in line of duty.

Assume in the rifle case that while Jones was involved in attempting to adjust the malfunctioning of the ejection mechanism, he was, through no fault of his own, shot by another rifle. In this event, his lack of caution would not be the "proximate cause" of the injury. In such a case, his injuries might be held to have been incurred in the line of duty and not due to his own misconduct as long as there is no negligence on his part, such as placing himself or remaining in the line of fire of the other rifle.

It is presumed that a person's injury did not occur as a result of his own misconduct unless there is clear and convincing evidence to show that the person's misconduct was the proximate cause of the injury.

2. *Line of Duty.* The determination of whether or not the injury or disease occurred in the line of duty must also be made. In the absence of clear and convincing evidence to the contrary, it is presumed that an injury or disease was incurred in line of duty. Any injury or disease is considered to have been incurred in line of duty unless it is found to have been incurred under any one of the following conditions:

a. As a result of the person's own misconduct;

b. While avoiding duty by deserting the service;

c. While the person was absent without leave, which absence materially interfered with the performance of his military duties;

d. While confined under a court-martial sentence which involved an unremitted dishonorable discharge;

e. While confined under sentence of a civil court following a conviction of a felony as defined by the laws of the jurisdiction where convicted.

An opinion relating to misconduct must in every case precede the line of duty determination. This is because any determination that the injury or disease resulted from the person's own misconduct must further result in a determination that it was incurred *not* in the line of duty. The opposite is not true and it may be determined that an injury or disease was not the result of misconduct but was *not* incurred in the line of duty. The classic example is an injury incurred during a prolonged period of unauthorized absence, but through no fault on the part of the one injured.

Whether absence without leave materially interferes with the performance of required military duties necessarily depends upon the facts of each situation, to which must be applied a standard of reality and common sense.

However, absence in excess of 24 hours generally constitutes a material interference unless there is evidence to establish the contrary. Similarly, an absence of shorter duration will not be considered to be a material interference unless there is clear and convincing evidence to establish the contrary. The commanding officer, division officer, or other responsible official should sign a statement as to whether or not an absence without leave constituted a material interference with the performance of required military duties.

This statement shall be included in the investigative report. The question of whether an unauthorized absence interferes with the performance of military duties is material only as regards eligibility for Veterans Administration benefits. For example, Section 1207 of Title 10, U.S. Code, a statutory provision administered by the naval service, bars disability retirement or disability severance benefits to a member of the armed forces for any disability incurred during a period of unauthorized absence, regardless of duration or noninterference with performance of duty.

In summary any one of the following determinations can be made:

   a. In line of duty, not due to own misconduct;
   b. Not in line of duty, not due to own misconduct;
   c. Not in line of duty, due to own misconduct.

1502   The 24-Hour Rule

Once the terms "line of duty" and "misconduct" have been defined, it is possible to determine what type of report or investigation, if any, is required. This can be done by relating the facts of any particular case to the provisions in the JAG Manual.

Line of duty/misconduct findings only need to be made in each case in which a member of the naval service incurs an injury which results in his physical inability to perform his regularly established duty or work for a period exceeding 24 hours. This 24-hour period is measured from 2400 on the day of the injury. A service member cannot perform his regularly established duties if he is reassigned to duties of a less demanding nature as a result of the injury (OPNAVINST 5100.11).

Periods of hospitalization for evaluation or observation are excluded in computing this time period. The only exception to this general rule would be when the injury incurred is likely to result in permanent disability. In that event, findings as to line of duty/misconduct would be required.

For example, assume that a serviceman sustains minor nonpermanent injuries when he mishandles a firearm. Generally, this would require an investigative report. However, if he is only required to stay in the hospital for an hour so that his toe can be bandaged, of if the hospital keeps him for a period of hospitalization for observation or evaluation, *no findings are required*.

1503   Investigation Requirement

The mere fact that line of duty/misconduct findings are required does *not* mean that an investigation of the scope of those discussed in

Chapter XIV of *Military Law* is necessary in every case. On the contrary, an unofficial inquiry is generally all that is conducted in most accident or death cases. The reason is that an investigation is generally only *required* when:

1. An injury or death occurs under circumstances which suggest that a finding of misconduct or of not in line of duty might result; or

2. A *death* occurs under peculiar or doubtful circumstances or as the result of an apparent suicide; or

3. Medical care is furnished by the government for an injury to a member of the naval service in which a third party might be subject to a claim by the government for hospitalization costs. (As an example, assume that a member of the naval service is injured and hospitalized for two months as the result of a car accident in which a civilian is negligent. An investigation would be required to furnish the government facts upon which it may assert a claim against the civilian and/or his insurance company); or

4. A member of the Navy or Marine Corps Reserve is injured or killed en route to or from a period of active duty, training duty, or an inactive duty training (drill) period.

Of course, in *any* case the convening authority or higher authority may require an investigation. Generally, if the only issue is the injury or death of a single service member and the case does not require a higher investigation for any other reason, an informal investigation will suffice. See paragraph 1407, *Military Law*.

1504 Responsibilities When Investigation Is Not Required

If findings are required, and an investigation is *not* necessary, one of a number of simpler methods may be used to report line of duty/misconduct findings. Prior to utilization of these methods, the commanding officer and the medical officer (or representative of an afloat medical department) must agree that the circumstances of the incident do not suggest that a finding of misconduct or not in line of duty might result if an investigation were held.

These simpler methods are discussed in detail in the JAG Manual, in OPNAV Instructions 5100.11 and 5100.9 and in Marine Corps Order 5101.8.

1505 Diseases

Findings as to whether a particular disease was or was not contracted in the line of duty and as the result of a member's own misconduct *must* be made when:

1. The disease results in the member's inability to perform duties for a period of 24 hours (this does not include hospitalization for evaluation or observation); and

2. If the disease is attributable to vicious habits, intemperance, or other factors suggesting misconduct or under circumstances suggesting not in line of duty.

Otherwise, investigation is not required as adequate information regarding such disease normally is available in the individual's health and service records and in medical reports. If there is permanent disability and a claim for disability benefits, the determination for eligibility would be based upon the findings in physical disability retirement or separation proceedings which are governed by the Disability Separation Manual (NAVEXOS P1990).

1506 Convening Authority's Action

In each case in which an injury or disease is investigated by informal investigation the convening authority can either:

1. Return the action for further investigation;
2. If he is of the opinion that the injury or disease was incurred in the line of duty and not as the result of misconduct or that evidence is not available to rebut this presumption, he should forward the case, expressing such a finding in his endorsement;
3. If he has substantial doubt that the injury or disease was incurred in line of duty or believes it was caused by misconduct, he must grant the individual a hearing which will provide the individual certain fundamental rights. He shall consider the result of this hearing in making his decision. The hearing will consist of the following:

a. The service member must be advised that his disease or injuries are believed to have been incurred as the result of his misconduct and not in the line of duty; and

b. Where the service member might be charged with a violation of the Code, he must be advised of his Article 31 and *Miranda-Tempia* rights (see paragraph 307, *Military Law*); and

c. The service member will be given the opportunity to inspect the investigative report and enclosures; and

d. The service member must be given the opportunity to present any matters in refutation, explanation, or rebuttal respecting the disease or injury. A reasonable time will be given the member to prepare for such a presentation.

1507 Summary

Misconduct is present when an injury or disease was either intentionally incurred or was the proximate result of such gross negligence as to demonstrate a reckless disregard of the consequences.

If an injury is incurred as the result of misconduct, it is *never* in the line of duty. A determination as to line of duty is generally required if a service member injures himself while absent without leave. If the absence materially interferes with the performance of his military duties, it is not considered to have been incurred in the line of duty.

There are many instances when findings as to line of duty/misconduct are not required. *No* findings are required if the injury does not result in a person's physical inability to perform duty for a period exceeding 24 hours, unless the injury is likely to be permanent. A careful analysis of the JAG Manual may eliminate many man-hours spent investigating incidents for which a fact-finding body may not be required.

DISCUSSION AND SELF-QUIZ

1. You are conducting a line of duty and misconduct investigation into the permanent injuries sustained by Seamen Brown and Smith, both members of your command. Your investigation discloses that Brown and Smith were sitting in a bar when some local men entered. Brown began arguing with one of the men over a girl friend. A fist fight soon developed between the two.

    a. One of the local men's friends struck Smith who was in no way involved in the fight. Smith was then attacked with a broken bottle, and in his own defense, struck his assailant. However, the bottle severely lacerated his arm. Smith's arm required five days' hospital treatment.

    b. Brown, in the meantime, had wearied of the fight and retreated outside. There, after several minutes of searching for him, his assailant found him and stabbed him in the back. Brown had offered no resistance and was trying to avoid a fight at the time the knifing occurred. Brown sustained permanent back injuries as the result of the knife wound.

Were Seaman Brown's injuries and Seaman Smith's injuries due to their own misconduct and not in the line of duty?

2. Private John Doe, U.S. Marine Corps, fell asleep while driving his new car, drove off the road and collided with a telephone pole. Doe stated that he had gone without sleep for 15 hours, but that he had rested for a few hours prior to the time he started driving. Doe stated that he did not realize that he was tired when he fell asleep.

    a. Is there any checklist in the JAG Manual that would apply to this type of incident?

    b. From the facts disclosed, do you believe his injuries were due to his own misconduct and consequently were not incurred in the line of duty?

3. Seaman Peter Roe, U.S. Navy, a member of your command, was informed that the ship was to depart for operational exercises at 0700 on 10 March 19___. On the evening of 9 March 19___, he consumed three quarts of beer and a half bottle of whiskey. Witnesses, who saw him that evening, state that at 2045 he was staggering, his speech was slurry, and, in their opinion, Roe was "drunk." As

Roe left the bar at 2100, he collapsed on the sidewalk, seriously injuring his head. The evidence indicates the alcohol caused him to collapse. You have been appointed investigating officer. Were Roe's injuries sustained in the line of duty and not due to his own misconduct?

4. Petty Officer Third Class Brown, in a liberty status, is returning to his home after work. His vehicle is struck from the side by a vehicle that ignored a red light. Brown has been hospitalized for several months in the local Navy hospital. It is obvious to you that Brown's injuries were sustained in the line of duty and not due to his own misconduct. Is a fact-finding investigation required under these circumstances?

Appendices

SAMPLE LOCALLY PREPARED REPORT FORM

USS NEVERSAIL (DD234)
Fleet Post Office
New York, New York

REPORT OF OFFENSE

INSTRUCTIONS FOR USE: Fill in as many blanks as possible with the known
information and deliver to the Discipline Office.

THE FOLLOWING NAMED MAN IS HEREBY PLACED ON REPORT:

_____

name   rate   division

DESCRIPTION OF OFFENSE:

Date: Place

CIRCUMSTANCES:

WITNESSES: (Give name, rate, division)

Date: SIGNED _____

name   rate   division

REPORT AND DISPOSITION OF OFFENSE(S)
NAVPERS 2696 (Rev. 8-63)

To: Commanding Officer, __USS SLUG (DL-901)_____   Date of Report: __31 August 19___

1. I hereby report the following named man for the offense(s) noted:

NAME OF ACCUSED	SERIAL NO.	RATE/GRADE	BR. & CLASS	DIV/DEPT
ROE, Richard M.	B01 00 00	SA	USN	2nd Div.

PLACE OF OFFENSE(S)	DATE OF OFFENSE(S)
1. USS SLUG (DL-901)	1. 30 AUG 19_
2. HI-HO Bar & Grill, Newport, R.I.	2. 31 AUG 19_

DETAILS OF OFFENSE(S) *(Refer by article of UCMJ, if known. If unauthorized absence, give following info: time and date of commencement, whether over leave or liberty, time and date of apprehension or surrender and arrival on board, loss of ID card and/or liberty card, etc.):*

1. Viol. Art. 86, UCMJ -UA from 0730, 30 AUG 19_, until apprehended by the
    Shore Patrol at 2100, 31 AUG 19_
2. Viol. Art. 92, UCMJ - (1) Failure to have liberty card in his possession
    while off-station on 31 AUG 19_ (2) Being in an establishment that is
    off-limits to servicemen, to wit: HI-HO Bar & Grill in Newport on
    31 AUG 19_.

NAME OF WITNESS	RATE/GRADE	DIV/DEPT	NAME OF WITNESS	RATE/GRADE	DIV/DEPT
Just U. WRITE	BMC	SPHQ			
James J. JONES	BM2	SPHQ			
Matt C. DILLON	Detective, Newport Police Department				

BMC, USN, Shore Patrol
(Rate/Grade/Title of person submitting report)

/s/ Just U. Write
JUST U. WRITE
(Signature of person submitting report)

I have been informed of the nature of the accusation(s) against me. I understand I do not have to answer any questions or make any statement regarding the offense(s) of which I am accused or suspected. However, I understand any statement made or questions answered by me may be used as evidence against me in event of trial by court-martial (Article 31, UCMJ).

Witness: /s/ Jack N. Box
JACK N. BOX, LCDR, USN
(Signature)

Acknowledged: /s/ Richard M. Roe
RICHARD M. ROE
(Signature of Accused)

PRE-MAST RESTRAINT	☐ CONFINED FOR SAFEKEEPING	☒ RESTRICTED: You are restricted to the limits of _USS SLUG (DL-901)_
	☐ NO RESTRICTIONS	_____in lieu of arrest by order of the CO. Until your status as a restricted man is terminated by the CO, you may not leave the restricted limits except with the express permission of the CO or XO. You have been informed of the times and places which you are required to muster.

/s/ Jack N. Box
JACK N. BOX, LCDR, USN, Discipline Off.
(Signature and title of person imposing restraint)

/s/ Richard M. Roe
RICHARD M. ROE
(Signature of Accused)

INFORMATION CONCERNING ACCUSED

CURRENT ENL. DATE	EXPIRATION CURRENT ENL. DATE	TOTAL ACTIVE NAVAL SERVICE	TOTAL SERVICE ON BOARD	EDUCATION	GCT	AGE
1 JUN 19_	3 MAY 19_	27 mos.	13 mos.	9th grade	39	21

MARITAL STATUS	NO. DEPENDENTS	CONTRIBUTION TO FAMILY OR QTRS ALLOWANCE (Amount required by law)	PAY PER MONTH (Including sea or foreign duty pay, if any)
Single	None	None	$187.10

RECORD OF PREVIOUS OFFENSE(S) *(Date, type, action taken, etc. Nonjudicial punishment incidents are to be included.)*

SCM - 1 JUN 19_ Viol. Art. 86, UCMJ (Failed to go to appointed place
          of duty). Sentenced to reduction from SN to SA and to
          forfeit $35.00 per month for one month.

CO NJP - 5 AUG 19_
          Viol. Art. 134, UCMJ (Appearing in unclean uniform).
          Awarded: 2 weeks restriction.

Substantially reproduced from Naval Justice School materials.

PRELIMINARY INQUIRY REPORT

From: Commanding Officer

To: __LT Josh E. WATCH, USN__   Date: __1 SEP 19___

1. Transmitted herewith for preliminary inquiry and report by you, including, if appropriate in the interest of justice and discipline, the preferring of such charges as appear to you to be sustained by expected evidence.

REMARKS OF DIVISION OFFICER *(Performance of duty, etc.)*

ROE has been in the 2nd Division only one month. While under close supervision, he is a good worker.

NAME OF WITNESS	RATE/GRADE	DIV/DEPT	NAME OF WITNESS	RATE/GRADE	DIV/DEPT
Just U. WRITE	BMC	SPHQ	Gaylord P. SWANBY	BM2	2nd DIV
James J. JONES	BM2	SPHQ			

RECOMMENDATION AS TO DISPOSITION:

[X] REFER TO COURT MARTIAL FOR TRIAL OF ATTACHED CHARGES
(Complete Charge Sheet (DD Form 458) through Page 2)

[ ] DISPOSE OF CASE AT MAST   [ ] NO PUNITIVE ACTION NECESSARY OR DESIRABLE   [ ] OTHER

COMMENT *(Include data regarding availability of witnesses, summary of expected evidence, conflicts in evidence, if expected. Attach statements of witnesses, documentary evidence such as service record entries in UA cases, items of real evidence, etc.)*

Summary of Evidence: Statements of WRITE and JONES (enclosures (1) and (2)) stated they apprehended ROE in the HI-HO Bar & Grill, an out-of-bounds establishment in Newport. Statement of SWANBY (enclosure (3)) supports the fact that ROE was absent from quarters for muster at 0730, 30 Aug 19_. ROE's service record contains entries to establish the commencement and termination of the absence. It is recommended that ROE be tried by summary court-martial on the charges set forth in enclosure (4).

                                        /s/ Josh E. Watch
                                        LT JOSH E. WATCH

                                        (Signature of Investigation Officer)

ACTION OF EXECUTIVE OFFICER

[ ] DISMISSED   [X] REFERRED TO CAPTAIN'S MAST

SIGNATURE OF EXECUTIVE OFFICER /s/ John L. Sullivan
JOHN L. SULLIVAN, CDR, USN

RIGHT TO DEMAND TRIAL BY COURT-MARTIAL
(Not applicable to persons attached to or embarked in a vessel)

I understand that nonjudicial punishment may not be imposed on me if, before the imposition of such punishment, I demand in lieu thereof trial by court-martial. I therefore (do) (do not) demand trial by court-martial.

WITNESS _____   SIGNATURE OF ACCUSED _____

ACTION OF COMMANDING OFFICER

[ ] DISMISSED	[ ] CONF. ON _____ 1, 2, OR 3 DAYS
[ ] DISMISSED WITH WARNING (Not considered NJP)	[ ] CORRECTIONAL CUSTODY FOR _____ DAYS
[ ] ADMONITION: ORAL/IN WRITING	[X] REDUCTION TO NEXT INFERIOR PAY GRADE
[ ] REPRIMAND: ORAL/IN WRITING	[ ] REDUCTION TO PAY GRADE OF _____
[X] REST. TO USS SLUG FOR 45 DAYS	[X] EXTRA DUTIES FOR 45 DAYS
[ ] REST. TO _____ FOR _____ DAYS WITH SUSP. FROM DUTY	[ ] PUNISHMENT SUSPENDED FOR _____
[X] FORFEITURE: TO FORFEIT $ 42.00 PAY PER MO. FOR 2 MO(S)	[ ] RECOMMENDED FOR TRIAL BY GCM
[ ] DETENTION: TO HAVE $ _____ PAY PER MO. FOR (1, 2, 3) MO(S) DETAINED FOR _____ MO(S)	[ ] AWARDED SPCM [ ] AWARDED SCM

DATE OF MAST:	DATE ACCUSED INFORMED OF ABOVE ACTION:	SIGNATURE OF COMMANDING OFFICER
3 SEP 19_	3 SEP 19_	/s/ John A. Law
JOHN A. LAW, CAPT, USN

FINAL ADMINISTRATIVE ACTION

WHERE NJP INVOLVED, APPEAL RIGHTS EXPLAINED AND UNDERSTOOD:	APPEAL SUBMITTED BY ACCUSED DATED: 3 SEP 19_	FINAL RESULT OF APPEAL:
[X] YES [ ] NO /s/ RMR *(Initials)*	FORWARDED FOR DECISION ON 4 SEP 19_	Punishment as awarded by CO approved

APPROPRIATE ENTRIES MADE IN SERVICE RECORD AND PAY ACCOUNT ADJUSTED WHERE REQUIRED	/s/ PN PN *(Initials)*	FILED IN UNIT PUNISHMENT BOOK:	/s/ PN PN *(Initials)*
DATE: 3 SEP 19_		10 SEP 19_ DATE:	

NAVPERS 2696 (Rev. 8-63)

SUSPECT'S RIGHTS ACKNOWLEDGEMENT/STATEMENT

FULL NAME (ACCUSED/SUSPECT)	FILE/SERVICE NO.	RATE/RANK	SERVICE (BRANCH)
ACTIVITY/UNIT	SOCIAL SECURITY NUMBER		DATE OF BIRTH
NAME (INTERVIEWER)	FILE/SERVICE NO.	RATE/RANK	SERVICE (BRANCH)
ORGANIZATION		BILLET	
LOCATION OF INTERVIEW		TIME	DATE

RIGHTS

I CERTIFY AND ACKNOWLEDGE BY MY SIGNATURE AND INITIALS SET FORTH BELOW THAT, BEFORE THE INTERVIEWER REQUESTED A STATEMENT FROM ME, HE WARNED ME THAT:

    (1)   I AM SUSPECTED OF HAVING COMMITTED THE FOLLOWING OFFENSE(S): _____

_____

_____ ☐

    (2)   I HAVE THE RIGHT TO REMAIN SILENT; ------------------------------------- ☐

    (3)   ANY STATEMENT I DO MAKE MAY BE USED AS EVIDENCE AGAINST ME IN TRIAL BY COURT-MARTIAL; --- ☐

    (4)   I HAVE THE RIGHT TO CONSULT WITH A LAWYER PRIOR TO ANY QUESTIONING.   THIS LAWYER MAY BE A CIVILIAN LAWYER RETAINED BY ME AT MY OWN EXPENSE; OR, IF I WISH, NAVY OR MARINE CORPS AUTHORITY WILL APPOINT A MILITARY LAWYER TO ACT AS MY COUNSEL WITHOUT COST TO ME; --- ☐

    (5)   I HAVE THE RIGHT TO HAVE SUCH RETAINED CIVILIAN LAWYER OR APPOINTED MILITARY LAWYER PRESENT DURING THIS INTERVIEW. ------------------------------------- ☐

WAIVER OF RIGHTS

I FURTHER CERTIFY AND ACKNOWLEDGE THAT I HAVE READ THE ABOVE STATEMENT OF MY RIGHTS AND FULLY UNDERSTAND THEM, --- ☐
AND THAT,

    (1)   I EXPRESSLY DESIRE TO MAKE A STATEMENT; ------------------------ ☐ 1

    (2)   I EXPRESSLY DO NOT DESIRE TO CONSULT WITH EITHER A CIVILIAN LAWYER RETAINED BY ME OR A MILITARY LAWYER APPOINTED AS MY COUNSEL WITHOUT COST TO ME PRIOR TO ANY QUESTIONING;-- ☐ 2

    (3)   I EXPRESSLY DO NOT DESIRE TO HAVE SUCH A LAWYER PRESENT WITH ME DURING THIS INTERVIEW;-- ☐ 3

    (4)   THIS ACKNOWLEDGEMENT AND WAIVER OF RIGHTS IS MADE FREELY AND VOLUNTARILY BY ME, AND WITHOUT ANY PROMISES OR THREATS HAVING BEEN MADE TO ME OR PRESSURE OR COERCION OF ANY KIND HAVING BEEN USED AGAINST ME. ------------------------------------- ☐ 4

SIGNATURE (ACCUSED/SUSPECT)	TIME	DATE
SIGNATURE (INTERVIEWER)	TIME	DATE
SIGNATURE (WITNESS)	TIME	DATE

THE STATEMENT WHICH APPEARS ON THIS PAGE (AND THE FOLLOWING _____ PAGE(S), ALL OF WHICH ARE SIGNED BY ME), IS MADE FREELY AND VOLUNTARILY BY ME, AND WITHOUT ANY PROMISES OR THREATS HAVING BEEN MADE TO ME OR PRESSURE OR COERCION OF ANY KIND HAVING BEEN USED AGAINST ME.

                                     SIGNATURE (ACCUSED/SUSPECT)

_____

_____

_____

Reproduced from JAG Manual.

RECORD OF AUTHORIZATION FOR SEARCH

1. At _____ on _____ I was
              Time   Date

approached by _____
                          Name

in his capacity as _____ who advised
                       Duty [1]

me that he suspected _____ of
                        Name

_____ and requested permission to
         Offense

search his _____
                  Object or Place [2]

for _____

_____
                 Items [3]

2. The reasons stated to me for suspecting the above named person were: [4]

RECORD OF AUTHORIZATION FOR SEARCH (continued)

3. After carefully weighing the foregoing information, I was of the belief

that the crime of _____ [had been]

[was being] [was about to be] committed, that _____

was the likely perpetrator thereof, that a search of the object or area stated

above would probably produce the items stated and that such items were [the

fruits of crime] [the instrumentalities of a crime] [contraband] [evidence].

4. I have therefore authorized _____

_____ to search the place named for the

property specified, and if the property be found there to seize it.

_____   _____   _____
      Grade   Signature   Title

_____
    Date and time

INSTRUCTIONS

1. Although the person bringing the information to the attention of the
Commanding Officer will normally be one in the execution of investigative
or police duties, such need not be the case. The information may come from
one as a private individual.

2. The area or place to be searched must be specific, such as wall locker,
wall locker and locker box, residence or automobile.

3. A search may be authorized only for the seizure of certain classes of
items: (1) Fruits of a crime (the results of a crime such as stolen objects);
(2) Instrumentalities of a crime (example: search of an automobile for a
crowbar used to force entrance into a building which was burglarized);
(3) Contraband (items, the mere possession of which is against the law--
marijuana, etc.); (4) Evidence of crime (example: bloodstained clothing
of an assault suspect).

RECORD OF AUTHORIZATION FOR SEARCH (continued)

4. Before authorizing a search probable cause must exist. This means reliable information that would lead a reasonably prudent and cautious man to a natural belief that:

    a. An offense probably is about to be, is being or has been committed; and

    b. Specific fruits or instrumentalities of the crime, contraband or evidence exist; and

    c. Such fruits, instrumentalities, contraband or evidence are probably in a certain place.

In arriving at the above determination it is generally permissible to rely on hearsay information, particularly if it is reasonably corroborated or has been verified in some substantial part by other facts or circumstances. However, unreliable hearsay cannot alone constitute probable cause, such as where the hearsay is several times removed from its source or the information is received from an anonymous telephone call. Hearsay information from an <u>informant</u> may be considered if the information is reasonably corroborated or has been verified in some substantial part by other facts, circumstances or events. The mere opinion of another that probable cause exists is not sufficient; however, along with the pertinent facts, it may be considered in reaching the conclusion as to whether or not probable cause exists.

If the information available does not satisfy the foregoing, additional investigation to produce the necessary information may be ordered.

CONSENT TO SEARCH

I, _____ , have been

advised that inquiry is being made in connection with _____

_____.

I have been advised of my right to not consent to a search of [my person]

[the premises mentioned below].

I hereby authorize _____

_____ [and] _____ ,

who [has] [have been] identified to me as _____

_____ Position(s) _____

to conduct a complete search of my [person] [residence] [automobile] [wall

locker] [   ] [   ] located at _____

_____.

I authorize the above listed personnel to take from the area searched any

letters, papers, materials, or other property which they may desire.

This search may be conducted on _____.
                                                                    Date

    This written permission is being given by me to the above named

personnel voluntarily and without threats or promises of any kind.

                                         _____
                                                            Signature

WITNESSES

_____

_____

CHARGE SHEET

PLACE	DATE
USS GLORY (DD-902), NAVAL STATION, NORFOLK, VIRGINIA	13 June 19--

ACCUSED (Last name, First name, Middle initial) (List aliases when material)	SERVICE NUMBER	GRADE OR RANK SA
DOE, John J.	B00 00 00	AND PAY GRADE E-2

ORGANIZATION AND ARMED FORCE (If the accused is not a member of any armed force, state other appropriate description showing that he is subject to military law)	DATE OF BIRTH	PAY PER MONTH	
	30 AUGUST 1944	BASIC	$179.10
U.S. NAVY	CONTRIBUTION TO FAMILY OR QUARTERS ALLOWANCE (MCM, 126h (2))	SEA OR FOREIGN DUTY $	8.00
USS GLORY (DD-902) NAVAL STATION	$40.00		
NORFOLK, VIRGINIA		TOTAL	$187.10

RECORD OF SERVICE

INITIAL DATE OF CURRENT SERVICE	TERM OF CURRENT SERVICE
20 DECEMBER 19--	TWO YEARS FROM 20 DECEMBER 19--

PRIOR SERVICE: __04__ __01__ __15__ (As to each prior period of service, give inclusive dates of service and Armed Force, if available.)
          YEARS MONTHS DAYS

5 NOVEMBER 1962 - 19 DECEMBER 1966 - U. S. ARMY

DATA AS TO WITNESSES
(Summary Court Officer will line out and insert names as applicable (MCM, 79g) and initial changes)

		WITNESSES FOR	
NAME OF WITNESS	ADDRESS	PROSECUTION	ACCUSED
NONE			

DOCUMENTS AND OBJECTS

LIST AND DESCRIBE (If not attached to charges, note where it may be found)

Service Record
Service pages 13(7) through 13(11)

The above documents are retained at the Legal Office, USS GLORY (DD-902)

DATA AS TO RESTRAINT

NATURE OF ANY RESTRAINT OF ACCUSED	DATE	LOCATION
Restriction in Lieu of Arrest	5/1/- -5/19/-	USS GLORY (DD-902)
Confinement for Safekeeping	6/11/-	NAVAL STATION, NORFOLK, VIRGINIA

DD FORM 458
1 JUL 62   REPLACES EDITION OF 1 NOV 1957, EXISTING SUPPLIES WILL BE ISSUED AND USED UNTIL 1 JULY 1963 UNLESS SOONER EXHAUSTED

Charge   I   : Violation of the Uniform Code of Military Justice, Article 86

Specification 1: In that Seaman Apprentice John J. Doe, U.S. Navy, USS GLORY,
did, on or about 4 April 19__, without authority, absent himself from his
unit, to wit: the USS GLORY, located at the Naval Station, Norfolk,
Virginia, and did remain so absent until on or about 30 April 19__.

Specification 2: In that Seaman Apprentice John J. Doe, U.S. Navy,
USS GLORY, did, on or about 19 May 19__, without authority, absent
himself from his unit, to wit: the USS GLORY, located at the Naval
Station, Norfolk, Virginia, and did remain so absent until on or about
5 June 19__.

Charge II: Violation of the Uniform Code of Military Justice, Article 134

Specification: In that Seaman Apprentice John J. Doe, U.S. Navy, USS GLORY,
having been duly restricted to the limits of said ship, did, on board
the USS GLORY, at the Naval Station, Norfolk, Virginia, at or about 2152
on 19 May 19__, break said restriction.

If this space is insufficient for all charges and specifications, they will be set forth numerically, front to back, on separate sheets attached to
this page.

NAME, GRADE, AND ORGANIZATION OF ACCUSER	SIGNATURE
ENS J.L. SMITH, U.S. NAVY	/s/ J.L.SMITH

AFFIDAVIT

Before me, the undersigned, authorized by lay to administer oaths in cases of this character, personally appeared the above-named accuser this ___13___ day of _____JUNE_____, 19 _- , and signed the foregoing charges and specifications under oath that he is a person subject to the Uniform Code of Military Justice, and that he either has personal knowledge of or has investigated the matters set forth therein, and that the same are true in fact, to the best of his knowledge and belief.

LT, U.S. NAVY	/s/ S.R. BELL
GRADE AND ORGANIZATION OF OFFICER	SIGNATURE

SUMMARY COURT-MARTIAL	S.R. BELL
OFFICIAL CHARACTER, AS ADJUTANT, SUMMARY COURT, ETC. (MCM, 29*g*, and Article 30*a* and 136)	TYPED NAME

Officer administering oath must be a commissioned officer.

13 JUNE 19-
DATE

I have this date informed the accused of the charges against him *(MCM, 32f(1))*.

ENS R. U. RIGHT, U.S. NAVY	/s/ R. U. RIGHT
NAME, GRADE, AND ORGANIZATION OF IMMEDIATE COMMANDER	SIGNATURE

USS GLORY (DD-902), NAVAL STATION, NORFOLK, VIRGINA	14 JUNE 19-
DESIGNATION OF COMMAND OF OFFICER EXERCISING SUMMARY COURT-MARTIAL JURISDICTION	PLACE DATE

The sworn charges above were received at ___1500___ hours, this date *(MCM, 33b)*.

XXXXXXXXXX

COMMANDER J.G. JOHNSON, USN COMMANDING OFFICER	/s/ J. G. JOHNSON
NAME, GRADE, AND OFFICIAL CAPACITY OF OFFICER SIGNING	SIGNATURE

¹ST INDORSEMENT

USS GLORY (DD-902), NAVAL STATION, NORFOLK, VIRGINIA	14 JUNE 19-
DESIGNATION OF COMMAND OF CONVENING AUTHORITY	PLACE DATE

Referred for trial to the ___SPECIAL___ court-martial appointed by ___COMMANDING OFFICER___

USS GLORY (DD-902), CONVENING ORDER CODE LE/5812/2

DATED _____, ___10 JUNE___ 19_- , subject to the following instructions:²

NONE

XXXX   XXX
XXXXXXXXXXXXXXX

COMMANDER J. G. JOHNSON, USN COMMANDING OFFICER	/s/ J. G. JOHNSON
NAME, GRADE, AND OFFICIAL CAPACITY OF OFFICER SIGNING	SIGNATURE

I have served a copy hereof on each of the above-named accused, this ___18___ day of ___June___, 19 _- .

S. D. WRIGHT, LT, USN, USS GLORY (DD-902)	/s/ S. D. WRIGHT
NAME, GRADE, AND ORGANIZATION OF TRIAL COUNSEL	SIGNATURE

¹/ When an appropriate commander signs personally, inapplicable words are stricken out. ²/ Relative to proper instructions which may be included in the indorsement of reference for trial, see MCM, 33j(1). If none, so state.

CHARGE SHEET

PLACE Place where charge sheet made out showing geographical location	**DATE** Date charge sheet is prepared

ACCUSED (*Last name, First name, Middle initial*) (*List aliases when material*)	SERVICE NUMBER	GRADE OR RANK Used by AND PAY GRADE court to determine forfeiture or reduction
Self explanatory	Self explanatory	

ORGANIZATION AND ARMED FORCE (*If the accused is not a member of any armed force, state other appropriate description showing that he is subject to military law*)	DATE OF BIRTH Considered by the court in determ. sentence		PAY PER MONTH
Shows unit or organization and Armed Force. Normally accused can be tried only by same Armed Force.	CONTRIBUTION TO FAMILY OR QUARTERS ALLOWANCE (*MCM, 126h (2)*) Minimum amount listed that accused is required by law to contribute to "Q" allotment	BASIC	$ Self-explanatory
		SEA OR FOREIGN DUTY	$
		TOTAL	$

RECORD OF SERVICE

INITIAL DATE OF CURRENT SERVICE Shows how long accused has served in the enlistment **TERM OF CURRENT SERVICE** (may mean a previous conviction not admissible) and how long accused has left on present enlistment.

PRIOR SERVICE: ___total___ ____ (*As to each prior period of service, give inclusive dates of service and Armed Force, if available.*)
YEARS MONTHS DAYS

Informs court of military experience of accused - lets the court determine whether he should have used better judgment. Also, may amount to mitigation by showing if the accused apparently intends to make the service his career.

DATA AS TO WITNESSES
(*Summary Court Officer will line out and insert names as applicable (MCM, 79g) and initial changes*)

NAME OF WITNESS	ADDRESS	WITNESSES FOR	
		PROSECUTION	ACCUSED
	Accused is entitled to know the witnesses against him. If they are listed here, he cannot assert at the trial that he wasn't informed.		
Name and grade. If a civilian, add "civilian" after name. Show Armed Force of military witness	Military address; if civilian witness, show civilian address.		"X" in appropriate column.

DOCUMENTS AND OBJECTS

LIST AND DESCRIBE (*If not attached to charges, note where it may be found*)

Accused has a right to see the objects and documents accompanying the charges. List such things here as: Statements of witnesses, Service Record entries, real evidence, etc. Also show where documents or objects are located if not attached to the charge sheet.

DATA AS TO RESTRAINT

NATURE OF ANY RESTRAINT OF ACCUSED	DATE	LOCATION
Indicate here all forms of pre-trial restraint, such as "confinement," "arrest," or "restriction in lieu of arrest." Show date of each form and places or limits of these restraints. May be used by the court in determining a sentence. Show total length of restraint.		

DD FORM **458** 1 JUL 62   REPLACES EDITION OF 1 NOV 1957, EXISTING SUPPLIES WILL BE ISSUED AND USED UNTIL 1 JULY 1963 UNLESS SOONER EXHAUSTED

Reproduced from U.S. Naval Justice School Hand Book.

Charge *   : Violation of the Uniform Code of Military Justice, Article

Specification **

Enumerate the Charges and Specifications of the offenses setting forth
the Article of the UCMJ violated and then list all the specifications
under the Charge. Note the footnote at the bottom of the page.

* Denote the Charge number in Roman numerals. If only a single
Charge, then no number is assigned.

** Denote the Specifications in Arabic numerals. If only a single
Specification under the Charge, then no number is assigned.

If this space is insufficient for all charges and specifications, they will be set forth numerically, front to back, on separate sheets attached to
this page.

NAME, GRADE, AND ORGANIZATION OF ACCUSER   SIGNATURE

May be the victim of the offense, preliminary inquiry officer or other person subject to the UCMJ who either has knowledge of or has investigated the offense(s).

AFFIDAVIT

Before me, the undersigned, authorized by law to administer oaths in cases of this character, personally appeared the above-named accuser this_____ day of____(month)____, 19___, and signed the foregoing charges and specifications under oath that he is a person subject to the Uniform Code of Military Justice, and that he either has personal knowledge of or has investigated the matters set forth therein, and that the same are true in fact, to the best of his knowledge and belief.

This shows that the accuser was sworn. Signature of the officer attests that the oath was given to the accuser. Only certain officers can administer oaths.

GRADE AND ORGANIZATION OF OFFICER   SIGNATURE

This space shows authority of the officer swearing the accuser.

OFFICIAL CHARACTER, AS ADJUTANT, SUMMARY COURT, ETC.   TYPED NAME
(MCM, 29a, and Article 30a and 136)

Officer administering oath must be a commissioned officer.

Accused is entitled to know of the charges as soon as practicable after they are sworn to. Enables him to obtain counsel quickly and prepare————————
his case.   DATE
I have this date informed the accused of the charges against him (MCM, 32f(1)).

                                        Signature attests that accused was
                                                    informed.
NAME, GRADE, AND ORGANIZATION OF IMMEDIATE COMMANDER   SIGNATURE

Self explanatory. Must be filled in.
DESIGNATION OF COMMAND OF OFFICER EXERCISING   PLACE   DATE
SUMMARY COURT-MARTIAL JURISDICTION

The sworn charges above were received at_____hours, this date (MCM, 33b).

                            FOR THE¹ _____
The execution of this stops the running of the Statute of Limitations. In the Navy, normally signed by the CO and the words "FOR THE" are struck out. Fill in all the spaces.
NAME, GRADE, AND OFFICIAL CAPACITY OF OFFICER SIGNING   SIGNATURE

1ST INDORSEMENT

This refers the charges to a specific court for trial.   Date must be same or subse-
                                                         quent to oath and convening
DESIGNATION OF COMMAND OF CONVENING AUTHORITY   PLACE   order.   DATE
                        type   identify the convening order as
           Referred for trial to the of court   court-martial appointed by to serial number, date, etc.

_____,_____19___, subject to the following instructions²
Trial in joinder or in common; capital case to be treated as non-capital; to be tried with other charges; etc. If no instructions insert "None".

Normally in Navy the CO signs ✗✗✗ _____ ✗✗ _____
the referral and the words struck   ✗✗✗✗✗✗✗✗✗✗✗✗✗✗✗✗
out as shown. See footnote 1/ at
bottom of page.

NAME, GRADE, AND OFFICIAL CAPACITY OF OFFICER SIGNING   SIGNATURE

I have served a copy hereof on each of the above-named accused, this _____ day of _____,
19___.   Accused, in time of peace, cannot be taken past arraignment within
          (5 days-GCM)(3 days-SpCM) after service if he objects thereto. No
          requirement this be completed in the case of SCM.
NAME, GRADE, AND ORGANIZATION OF TRIAL COUNSEL   SIGNATURE

¹ When an appropriate commander signs personally, inapplicable words are stricken out. ² Relative to proper instructions which may be included in the indorsement of reference for trial, see MCM, 33j(1). If none, so state.

Fill in blank numbers of pertinent charges and specifications or "all specifications and charges," as may be appropriate for use unless departmental regulations prevent such election (MCM, 32j(2)).

☐ THE ACCUSED HAS BEEN PERMITTED AND HAS ELECTED TO REFUSE PUNISHMENT UNDER ARTICLE 15 AS TO
Not applicable if attached to or embarked in a vessel. If ashore, fill in as appropriate.

☐ THE ACCUSED HAS NOT BEEN OFFERED PUNISHMENT UNDER ARTICLE 15 AS TO

NAME, GRADE, AND ORGANIZATION OF OFFICER EXERCISING ARTICLE 15 JURISDICTION	SIGNATURE

RECORD OF TRIAL BY SUMMARY COURT-MARTIAL	CASE NUMBER
TO BE FILLED IN BY SUMMARY COURT AS APPLICABLE	*(Inserted by convening authority)*

1. WAS THE ACCUSED ADVISED IN ACCORDANCE WITH PARAGRAPH 79d, MCM, 1951? ☐ YES Do not overlook this space

2. THE ACCUSED, HAVING REFUSED TO CONSENT IN WRITING TO TRIAL BY SUMMARY COURT-MARTIAL, THE CHARGES ARE HEREWITH RETURNED TO THE CONVENING AUTHORITY.
Fill in if applicable.

NAME, GRADE, AND ORGANIZATION OF SUMMARY COURT OFFICER	SIGNATURE

TO BE FILLED IN BY THE ACCUSED

Fill in one as appropriate.

I ☐ CONSENT ☐ OBJECT TO TRIAL BY SUMMARY COURT-MARTIAL   SIGNATURE OF ACCUSED

SPECIFICATIONS AND CHARGES	PLEAS	FINDINGS	SENTENCE OR REMARKS
SAMPLES:			SCM enters the sentence which he adjudges in the case:
Sp. 1: Ch. I	G	G	
Sp. 2: Ch. I	G	G	To be confined at hard labor
Ch. I	G	G	for one month and to forfeit
Sp. Ch. II	NG	NG	$50.00 per month for one
Ch. II	NG	NG	month.
NOTE: Prior convictions must be admissible under the rules therefor.			

NUMBER OF PREVIOUS CONVICTIONS CONSIDERED (MCM, 75b(2)) Enter number considered.

PLACE AND DATE OF TRIAL Name of command, its location & date of trial
U. S. Naval Justice School   29 March 19   DATE SENTENCE ADJUDGED

NAME, GRADE, ORGANIZATION, AND ARMED FORCE OF SUMMARY COURT OFFICER (MCM, 4g)   SIGNATURE
LT L. G. WILBER, U.S. NAVY
U. S. Naval Justice School, U. S. Naval Base, Newport, Rhode Island
Enter after signature, "Only officer present with command", if such is the case.

TO BE FILLED IN BY CONVENING AUTHORITY (MCM, 89, and app. 14g.)

ORGANIZATION	PLACE	DATE
U. S. Naval Justice School	U.S. Naval Base, Newport, R.I.	30 March 19___

ACTION OF CONVENING AUTHORITY

Here the convening authority indicates his action on the case, using the appropriate form from Appendix 14a, MCM,.   Example: (Approval of findings and part of the sentence. Only so much of the sentence as provides for confinement at hard labor for twenty (20) days and forfeiture of $10.00 per month for a period of two (2) months is approved and ordered executed. The U. S. Naval Base Brig, Newport, R. I. is designated as the place of confinement.

NAME, GRADE, AND ORGANIZATION OF CONVENING AUTHORITY	SIGNATURE
I. M. LAW, CAPTAIN, U.S. NAVY, U. S. NAVAL JUSTICE SCHOOL	

ENTERED ON APPROPRIATE PERSONNEL RECORDS IN CASE OF CONVICTION. (MCM, 91g)

NAME, GRADE, AND DESIGNATION OF OFFICER RESPONSIBLE FOR ACCUSED'S RECORDS	SIGNATURE
LT E. J. JOHNSON, U. S. Navy Personnel Officer	

NOTE: Summary of evidence, if required by the convening or higher authority, will be attached on separate pages.

* U.S. GOVERNMENT PRINTING OFFICE : 1962 O—659706

ADMINISTRATIVE REMARKS	*See Art. B-2305, BuPers Manual*

SHIP OR STATION

USS AWASH (DD-902)

2 JAN __: On unauthorized absence from 0800, 1 January 19__.
Intentions unknown.

/s/J.O. JONES
J.O. JONES, ENS, USNR, Personnel
Officer, By direction of the
Commanding Officer

- -

6 JAN __: Surrendered on board USS AWASH (DD-902) at 0730 this date.
Unauthorized absentee since 0800, 1 January 19__, a period
of about five (5) days.

/s/J.O. JONES
J.O. JONES, ENS, USNR, Personnel
Officer, By direction of the
Commanding Officer

- -

8 JAN __: COMMANDING OFFICER'S NON-JUDICIAL PUNISHMENT

DATE OF OFFENSE: 1 January 19__

NATURE OF OFFENSE: Viol. Art. 86, UCMJ:
                                         Unauthorized absence
                                         from the USS AWASH
                                         (DD-902) from at or
                                         about 0800, 1 January
                                         19__ to at or about
                                         0730, 6 January 19__,
                                         a period of about 5
                                         days.

DATE OF CAPTAIN'S MAST: 8 January 19__

NON-JUDICIAL PUNISHMENT AWARDED: Two weeks restriction
                                         to the limits of the
                                         ship without suspension
                                         from duty.

/s/ D.C. SMITH
D.C. SMITH, ENS, USN, Legal
Officer, By direction of
the Commanding Officer

NAME *(Last, First, Middle)*	SERVICE NO.	BRANCH AND CLASS
DOE, John Mark	B29 00 26	USN

ADMINISTRATIVE REMARKS—NAVPERS 601-13 (Rev. 12-61)   GPO 926-588   13

Substantially reproduced from U.S. Naval Justice School Hand Book.

PUNISHMENTS AUTHORIZED BY ARTICLE 15, UCMJ,
AS AMENDED BY PL 87-648 AND AS LIMITED BY
CHAPTER 26, MCM, AND CHAPTER I, JAG MANUAL

OFFICERS (*1)

	CO, Flag or General Officer in Command	CO, LCDR or MAJ and above	CO, LT and below
ADMONITION or REPRIMAND	YES	YES	YES
RESTRICTION	60 days	30 days	15 days
ARREST IN QUARTERS	30 days	NO	NO
FORFEITURE OF PAY	½ of 2 mos. pay	NO	NO
DETENTION OF PAY	½ of 3 mos. pay	NO	NO

ENLISTED (*1)

	CO, LCDR or MAJ and above	CO, LT and below and OINCs
ADMONITION or REPRIMAND	YES	YES
RESTRICTION	60 days	14 days
EXTRA DUTIES	45 days	14 days
CORRECTIONAL CUSTODY	30 days (only E-3 and below)	7 days (only E-3 and below)
CONFINEMENT ON B & W or DIMINISHED RATIONS	3 days (only shipboard personnel E-3 and below)	3 days (only shipboard personnel E-3 and below)
REDUCTION IN GRADE (2*)	One grade	One grade
FORFEITURE of PAY (*3)	½ 2 mos. pay	7 days pay
DETENTION of PAY (*4)	½ 3 mos. pay	14 days pay

(*1) Censure plus one or more of the listed punishments may be imposed, subject to the rules of apportionment.

(*2) CPO (E-7) in the Navy and SSGT (E-6) in the Marine Corps may not be reduced in grade by their CO.

(*3) Involves base pay plus sea or foreign duty pay.

(*4) Detention may not be imposed for a period longer than one(1) year or expiration of enlistment whichever is shorter. Involves base pay plus sea or foreign duty pay.

NOTE: For both Forfeiture and Detention of pay, if the offender is an E-4 with less than 4 years service or non-rated and has dependents the compulsory contribution from his pay must be subtracted before determining net pay subject to forfeiture or detention.

LIMITS OF PUNISHMENTS UNDER ARTICLE 15, UCMJ
(NON-JUDICIAL PUNISHMENT)
(SEE NOTES 1 & 2)

Imposed By	Imposed on	Confinement on B & W or Dim Rats (4)(12)	Correctional Custody (3)(4)	Arrest in Quarters (3)(4)	Forfeiture (5)(6)	Reduction (7)	Extra Duties (3)(4)	Restriction to Limits (3)	Detention of Pay (5)(8)	Admonition (9)	Reprimand (9)
General Ofcrs in Command	Ofcrs	No	No	30 days	½ one mo. for 2 mos.	No	No	60 days	½ one mo for 3 mos	Yes	Yes
	E-4 to E-9	No	No	No	½ one mo. for 2 mos.	1 Grade	45 days (10)	60 days (10)	½ one mo for 3 mos	Yes	Yes
	E-1 to E-3	3 days	30 days (10)	No	½ one mos. for 2 mos.	1 Grade	45 days (10)	60 days (10)	½ one mo for 3 mos	Yes	Yes
0-4 to 0-6	Ofcrs	No	No	No	No	No	No	30 days	No	Yes	Yes
	E-4 to E-9	No	No	No	½ one mo. for 2 mos.	1 Grade	45 days (10)	60 days (10)	½ one mo for 3 mos	Yes	Yes
	E-1 to E-3	3 days	30 days (10)	No	½ one mo. for 2 mos.	1 Grade	45 days (10)	60 days (10)	½ one mo for 3 mos	Yes	Yes
0-3 below and OinC's (13)	Ofcrs	No	No	No	No	No	No	15 days	No	Yes	Yes
	E-4 to E-9	No	No	No	7 days	1 Grade	14 days (11)	,14 days (11)	14 days	Yes	Yes
	E-1 to E-3	3 days	7 days (11)	No	7 days	1 Grade	14 days (11)	14 days (11)	14 days	Yes	Yes

(1) NJP may not be imposed if, before imposition of punishment, trial by court-martial is demanded by any member not attached to or embarked in a vessel.
(2) Officer who imposes punishment, or his successor in command, CO of unit to which accused is transferred, or his successor in command, and officer receiving appeal, may, at any time -
    1. Suspend probationally for up to 6 months from date of suspension or until expiration of enlistment, whichever is earlier -
       a. Any part or amount of unexecuted punishment
       b. A reduction in grade or a forfeiture, whether or not executed, except if executed the suspension must be made within 4 months of imposition
    2. Remit or mitigate any part or amount of the unexecuted punishment
    3. Set aside in whole or in part the punishment, whether executed or unexecuted, and restore all rights privileges, and property affected
    4. Mitigate reduction in grade to forfeiture or detention of pay
    5. Mitigate (provided the mitigated punishment shall not be for a greater period than the punishment mitigated) -
       a. Arrest in quarters to restriction
       b. Confinement on bread and water or diminished rations to correctional custody
       c. Correctional custody or confinement on bread and water or diminished rations to extra duties or restriction, or both
       d. Extra duties to restriction
(3) No two or more these punishments may be combined to run consecutively in the maximum amount imposable for each; must be apportioned.
(4) Any, except bread and water, may be combined to run concurrently for the maximum of the most severe
(5) Should be imposed in round dollars. May be combined by apportionment: 1½ days of detention equals 1 day forfeiture.
(6) Forfeiture, and detention of pay may not be combined unless apportioned.
(7) If grade from which reduced is within promotion authority of CO or any subordinate.
(8) Detention of pay shall be for a stated period of not more than one year, but not beyond expiration of enlistment.
(9) May be imposed in addition to or in lieu of all other punishments.   Ref: (a) P.L. 87-648, 10 U.S.C. Sec. 815
(10) 1½ days of extra duties equals 1 day of custody or 2 of restriction.   (Art 15, UCMJ)
(11) 1 day of custody equals 2 of extra duties or 2 of restriction.   (b) Executive Order 11081 (MCM,
(12) Only if embarked on or attached to a vessel.   1951, Chap 26)
(13) OinC's have NJP authority over enlisted personnel only.   (c) Sec 0101, JAG Manual

Reproduced from U.S. Naval Justice School Hand Book.

TABLE II

For combining Correctional Custody with either Extra Duties or Restriction to Limits to be served consecutively.

CC	+	R	or	ED
1	+	58	or	43
2	+	56	or	42
3	+	54	or	40
4	+	52	or	39
5	+	50	or	37
6	+	48	or	36
7	+	46	or	34
8	+	44	or	33
9	+	42	or	31
10	+	40	or	30
11	+	38	or	28
12	+	36	or	27
13	+	34	or	25
14	+	32	or	24
15	+	30	or	22
16	+	28	or	21
17	+	26	or	19
18	+	24	or	18
19	+	22	or	16
20	+	20	or	15
21	+	18	or	13
22	+	16	or	12
23	+	14	or	10
24	+	12	or	9
25	+	10	or	7
26	+	8	or	6
27	+	6	or	4
28	+	4	or	3
29	+	2	or	1

(Note #1)

CC –   Number of days of Correctional Custody.

R –   Number of days of Restriction to Limits.

ED –   Number of days of Extra Duty.

Note 1:   Restriction and extra duties may be combined to run concurrently with correctional custody to the maximum for correctional custody.

Note 2:   Extra Duties and Restriction to Limits may be combined to be served concurrently to the maximum of Extra Duties.

TABLE III

For combining Extra Duties and Restriction to Limits to be served consecutively.

ED	+	R
1	+	58
2	+	57
3	+	56
4	+	54
5	+	53
6	+	52
7	+	50
8	+	49
9	+	48
10	+	46
11	+	45
12	+	44
13	+	42
14	+	41
15	+	40
16	+	38
17	+	37
18	+	36
19	+	34
20	+	33
21	+	32
22	+	30
23	+	29
24	+	28
25	+	26
26	+	25
27	+	24
28	+	22
29	+	21
30	+	20
31	+	18
32	+	17
33	+	16
34	+	14
35	+	13
36	+	12
37	+	10
38	+	9
39	+	8
40	+	6
41	+	5
42	+	4
43	+	2
44	+	1

(Note #2)

TABLE IV

For combining Forfeiture of Pay and Detention of Pay.

FF	+	DP
1	+	43
2	+	42
3	+	40
4	+	39
5	+	37
6	+	36
7	+	34
8	+	33
9	+	31
10	+	30
11	+	28
12	+	27
13	+	25
14	+	24
15	+	22
16	+	21
17	+	19
18	+	18
19	+	16
20	+	15
21	+	13
22	+	12
23	+	10
24	+	9
25	+	7
26	+	6
27	+	4
28	+	3
29	+	1

(Notes #3 & 4)

FF –   Number of days of Forfeiture of Pay.

DP –   Number of days of Detention of Pay.

TABLE V

For combining Detention of Pay and Forfeiture of Pay.

DP	+	FF
1	+	29
2	+	28
3	+	28
4	+	27
5	+	26
6	+	26
7	+	25
8	+	24
9	+	24
10	+	23
11	+	22
12	+	22
13	+	21
14	+	20
15	+	20
16	+	19
17	+	18
18	+	18
19	+	17
20	+	16
21	+	16
22	+	15
23	+	14
24	+	14
25	+	13
26	+	12
27	+	12
28	+	11
29	+	10
30	+	10
31	+	9
32	+	8
33	+	8
34	+	7
35	+	6
36	+	6
37	+	5
38	+	4
39	+	4
40	+	3
41	+	2
42	+	2
43	+	1

(Notes #3 & 4)

Note 3:   Forfeiture of Pay and Detention of Pay must be expressed in dollars not in days.

Note 4:   In no case shall Forfeiture or Detention of Pay or a combination thereof be imposed in excess of 15 days in any single month.

Reproduced from U.S. Naval Justice School Hand Book.

TABLE I

For combining Correctional Custody, Extra Duties <u>and</u> Restriction to Limits to be served consecutively.

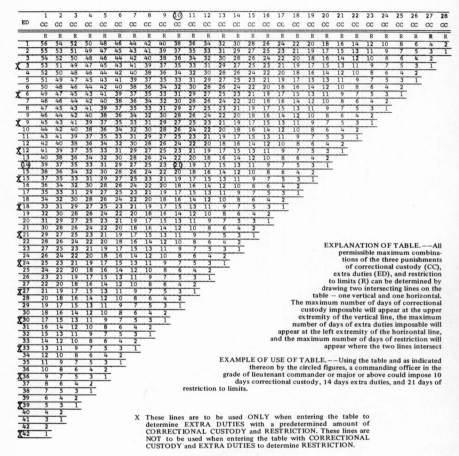

ED	1 CC	2 CC	3 CC	4 CC	5 CC	6 CC	7 CC	8 CC	9 CC	(10) CC	11 CC	12 CC	13 CC	14 CC	15 CC	16 CC	17 CC	18 CC	19 CC	20 CC	21 CC	22 CC	23 CC	24 CC	25 CC	26 CC	27 CC	28 CC
	R	R	R	R	R	R	R	R	R	R	R	R	R	R	R	R	R	R	R	R	R	R	R	R	R	R	R	R
1	56	54	52	50	48	46	44	42	40	38	36	34	32	30	28	26	24	22	20	18	16	14	12	10	8	6	4	2
2	55	53	51	49	47	45	43	41	39	37	35	33	31	29	27	25	23	21	19	17	15	13	11	9	7	5	3	1
3	54	52	50	48	46	44	42	40	38	36	34	32	30	28	26	24	22	20	18	16	14	12	10	8	6	4	2	
X 3	53	51	49	47	45	43	41	39	37	35	33	31	29	27	25	23	21	19	17	15	13	11	9	7	5	3	1	
4	52	50	48	46	44	42	40	38	36	34	32	30	28	26	24	22	20	18	16	14	12	10	8	6	4	2		
5	51	49	47	45	43	41	39	37	35	33	31	29	27	25	23	21	19	17	15	13	11	9	7	5	3	1		
6	50	48	46	44	42	40	38	36	34	32	30	28	26	24	22	20	18	16	14	12	10	8	6	4	2			
X 6	49	47	45	43	41	39	37	35	33	31	29	27	25	23	21	19	17	15	13	11	9	7	5	3	1			
7	48	46	44	42	40	38	36	34	32	30	28	26	24	22	20	18	16	14	12	10	8	6	4	2				
8	47	45	43	41	39	37	35	33	31	29	27	25	23	21	19	17	15	13	11	9	7	5	3	1				
9	46	44	42	40	38	36	34	32	30	28	26	24	22	20	18	16	14	12	10	8	6	4	2					
X 9	45	43	41	39	37	35	33	31	29	27	25	23	21	19	17	15	13	11	9	7	5	3	1					
10	44	42	40	38	36	34	32	30	28	26	24	22	20	18	16	14	12	10	8	6	4	2						
11	43	41	39	37	35	33	31	29	27	25	23	21	19	17	15	13	11	9	7	5	3	1						
12	42	40	38	36	34	32	30	28	26	24	22	20	18	16	14	12	10	8	6	4	2							
X 12	41	39	37	35	33	31	29	27	25	23	21	19	17	15	13	11	9	7	5	3	1							
13	40	38	36	34	32	30	28	26	24	22	20	18	16	14	12	10	8	6	4	2								
(14)	39	37	35	33	31	29	27	25	23	(21)	19	17	15	13	11	9	7	5	3	1								
15	38	36	34	32	30	28	26	24	22	20	18	16	14	12	10	8	6	4	2									
X 15	37	35	33	31	29	27	25	23	21	19	17	15	13	11	9	7	5	3	1									
16	36	34	32	30	28	26	24	22	20	18	16	14	12	10	8	6	4	2										
17	35	33	31	29	27	25	23	21	19	17	15	13	11	9	7	5	3	1										
18	34	32	30	28	26	24	22	20	18	16	14	12	10	8	6	4	2											
X 18	33	31	29	27	25	23	21	19	17	15	13	11	9	7	5	3	1											
19	32	30	28	26	24	22	20	18	16	14	12	10	8	6	4	2												
20	31	29	27	25	23	21	19	17	15	13	11	9	7	5	3	1												
21	30	28	26	24	22	20	18	16	14	12	10	8	6	4	2													
X 21	29	27	25	23	21	19	17	15	13	11	9	7	5	3	1													
22	28	26	24	22	20	18	16	14	12	10	8	6	4	2														
23	27	25	23	21	19	17	15	13	11	9	7	5	3	1														
24	26	24	22	20	18	16	14	12	10	8	6	4	2															
X 24	25	23	21	19	17	15	13	11	9	7	5	3	1															
25	24	22	20	18	16	14	12	10	8	6	4	2																
26	23	21	19	17	15	13	11	9	7	5	3	1																
27	22	20	18	16	14	12	10	8	6	4	2																	
X 27	21	19	17	15	13	11	9	7	5	3	1																	
28	20	18	16	14	12	10	8	6	4	2																		
29	19	17	15	13	11	9	7	5	3	1																		
30	18	16	14	12	10	8	6	4	2																			
X 30	17	15	13	11	9	7	5	3	1																			
31	16	14	12	10	8	6	4	2																				
32	15	13	11	9	7	5	3	1																				
33	14	12	10	8	6	4	2																					
X 33	13	11	9	7	5	3	1																					
34	12	10	8	6	4	2																						
35	11	9	7	5	3	1																						
36	10	8	6	4	2																							
X 36	9	7	5	3	1																							
37	8	6	4	2																								
38	7	5	3	1																								
39	6	4	2																									
X 39	5	3	1																									
40	4	2																										
41	3	1																										
42	2																											
X 42	1																											

EXPLANATION OF TABLE.—All permissible maximum combinations of the three punishments of correctional custody (CC), extra duties (ED), and restriction to limits (R) can be determined by drawing two intersecting lines on the table — one vertical and one horizontal. The maximum number of days of correctional custody imposable will appear at the upper extremity of the vertical line, the maximum number of days of extra duties imposable will appear at the left extremity of the horizontal line, and the maximum number of days of restriction will appear where the two lines intersect

EXAMPLE OF USE OF TABLE.—Using the table and as indicated thereon by the circled figures, a commanding officer in the grade of lieutenant commander or major or above could impose 10 days correctional custody, 14 days extra duties, and 21 days of restriction to limits.

X These lines are to be used ONLY when entering the table to determine EXTRA DUTIES with a predetermined amount of CORRECTIONAL CUSTODY and RESTRICTION. These lines are NOT to be used when entering the table with CORRECTIONAL CUSTODY and EXTRA DUTIES to determine RESTRICTION.

Form approved by Comptroller General, U.S.
July 18, 1951

EXEMPT REPORT   **COURT MEMORANDUM**

See ART. B-2305, BuPers Manual

DATE OF MAST	TYPE OF COURT	DATE OF TRIAL
7 April 19__	CO's NJP	

SYNOPSIS OF OFFENSE(S) DATE(S)

Viol UCMJ, Art. 86-UA from 0745, 6 March 19__ until 0902, 18 March 19__,
a period of about 12 days.

SENTENCE AS APPROVED BY CONVENING AUTHORITY (INCL. ANY TERMS OF THE C.A.'S ACTION CONCERNING EXECUTION OR SUSPENSION)

Punishment awarded: To be reduced to BM3, to forfeit $20.00 per month
for two months and to detain $20.00 per month
for three months

	MONTHLY AMOUNT	NUMBER OF MONTHS	TOTAL AMOUNT	EFFECTIVE DATE
FORFEITURE OF PAY	$20.00	Two	$40.00	7 April 19__
DETENTION OF PAY	$20.00	Three	$60.00	7 April 19__
REDUCTION IN RATE	FROM BM2	TO BM3		

DATE AND OTHER IDENTIFICATION OF CONVENING AUTHORITY'S ACTION. C. M. O. No., ETC.
N.A.

☒ MEMORANDUM ENTRY OR MARKS AND DIARY ENTRIES MADE

SIGNATURE	GRADE AND TITLE	SHIP OR STATION
D.C. SMITH	ENS, USN, Legal Off., By dir of CO	USS AWASH (DD-902)

SUPPLEMENTARY COURT MEMORANDUM

(A) FINDING AND SENTENCE APPROVED WITHOUT CHANGE BY SUPERVISORY AUTHORITY ON_____

(B) RESUME OF ACTION BY REVIEWING AUTHORITY OR UNDER ARTICLES 72, 74, OR 15 (D) OR (E), UCMJ. (ALSO ANY APPEAL OR ANY REQUEST FOR IMMEDIATE DISCHARGE)

IDENTIFY SUPPLEMENTARY COURT MARTIAL ORDER, JAG LETTER OR OTHER DOCUMENT RESULTING IN CHANGE OR MODIFICATION OF FINDING OR SENTENCE, INCLUDING DATE:

☐ SUPPLEMENTARY MARKS AND DIARY ENTRIES MADE

SIGNATURE	GRADE AND TITLE	SHIP OR STATION

NAME (*Last*)	(*First*)	(*Middle*)	SERVICE NUMBER	RATE	BRANCH AND CLASS
BROWN	JOHN	EDWARD	123 45 67	BM3	USN

COURT MEMORANDUM NAVPERS 601-6/NAVCOMPT 516 (Rev. 4-64)

PART 1—RETAIN IN SERVICE RECORD

6 ☐1

Substantially reproduced from U.S. Naval Justice School Hand Book.

```
                    U.S.S. AWASH (DD-902)
                    c/o Fleet Post Office
                 New York, New York 59000




                              5817
                              Ser: 1746
                              23 February 19__

From:  Commanding Officer, U.S.S. AWASH (DD-902)
To:    Lieutenant John B. Smith, U.S. Navy, U.S.S. AWASH (DD-902)

Subj:  Convening Summary Court-martial

1.  Effective this date, Lieutenant John B. Smith, U.S. Navy,
is detailed a Summary Court-martial.


                         (signature)
                         THOMAS M. JOHNSON
                         Commander, U.S. Navy
                         Commanding Officer
                         U.S.S. AWASH (DD-902)
```

TRIAL GUIDE FOR A SUMMARY COURT-MARTIAL

PART I - Preliminary procedures

SCM: **THE COURT WILL COME TO ORDER.** *Call to order*

SCM: ( ) (If a reporter is used): _____ has been appointed reporter for this court and will now be (sworn) (affirmed). *Swearing reporter*

SCM: Do you (swear) (affirm) that you will faithfully perform the duties of reporter to this court (so help you God)?

REP: I do.

SCM: ( ) (If accused is represented by counsel): Do you, _____, (swear) (affirm) that you will faithfully perform the duties of defense counsel in this case (so help you God)? *Swearing counsel*

DC: I do.

SCM: The accused, _____, is present, and the court is now convened. *Court convened*

SCM: I am (LCDR) _____. I have been appointed a Summary Court-Martial by Commanding Officer, _____, letter serial _____ dated _____, signed by _____, the convening authority. Certain charges against you have been properly referred to me for *Identity of Summary Court-Martial*

This material is based upon the Summary Courts-martial Guide NAVPERS 10091, 1967.

Referral of charges for trial. Court in session

trial by Summary Court-Martial. The court is now in session for the trial of your case. The charges are signed by ————, a person subject to the Uniform Code of Military Justice, as accuser, and are properly sworn to before an officer of the armed forces authorized to administer oaths. The charges allege, in general the offense(s) of ————

I now hand you your copy of the charges.

Cautioning the accused

I am now going to advise you of the rights you have at this trial. Until I have completed my explanation, I do not want you to say anything except to answer specific questions that I will ask you. Do you understand?

ACC: (Yes, sir) (————).

Duties as SCM

SCM: As a Summary Court-Martial, it is my duty to produce and examine all the evidence concerning any offense charged to which you plead not guilty, and this includes evidence both for and against you. It is also my duty to consider any evidence you may wish to present in mitigation and extenuation, that is, any evidence which might lessen the severity of the sentence if you are found guilty. I must evaluate and weigh the evidence impartially, determine your guilt or innocence of any offense to which the evidence received in court in your presence during this trial, and, if you are found guilty, adjudge an appropriate sentence. As to any offense to which you plead not guilty, you will be presumed to be innocent until your guilt is established by legal and competent evidence beyond a reasonable doubt.

The following witnesses will probably appear and testify against you:
(Lieutenant ———————————) (Chief Petty Officer ———————)
———————) (Yeoman First Class ———————
and (Mr. ———————).

Witnesses for the Government

After these witnesses have testified in response to my questions, you will have the right to cross-examine them, that is, you (or your counsel) may ask them any questions which relate to this case or, if you prefer, I will do this for you.

Right to cross-examine

You also have the right to call witnesses and to produce other evidence in your behalf. I will arrange for the attendance of any witnesses needed by you or the production of any evidence relating to your case or help you in any other way possible. [I notice that (Lieutenant ———————) (Yeoman First Class ———————) are listed as ———————) and (Mr. ——————— witnesses for you on the charge sheet and I have arranged to have them present to testify at the trial, if you so desire.]

Witnesses for the defense

As the accused in this case, you also have these rights:

First, you may be sworn and testify as a witness concerning the offense (s) charged against you. If you do that, whatever you say will be considered and weighed as evidence by me just as is the testimony of other witnesses.

Right to testify concerning the offense or offenses

Right to testify concerning less than all offenses

Right to remain silent

Matters in mitigation and extenuation

Note: The following should be used if there is only one specification:

( ) If you testify you can be questioned by me about the whole subject of the offense and about your worthiness of belief.

Note: The following should be used if there is more than one specification:

( ) If your testimony should concern less than all of the offenses charged against you, that is, you do not testify about some of the offenses charged, then you may be questioned by me about the whole subject of those offenses concerning which you do testify and concerning your worthiness of belief, but I will not question you about any offense concerning which you do not testify.

Second, you may remain silent, that is, say nothing at all. You have a right to do this, and if you do so, it will not count against you in any way and I will not consider it as an admission that you are guilty. If you remain silent, I am not permitted to question you about the offense(s).

Third, if you are found guilty, you will have the right to testify under oath concerning matters in extenuation or mitigation, or you may remain silent, in which case I will not draw any inferences from your silence. In addition, you may, if you wish, make an unsworn statement in extenuation or mitigation. The statement may be oral or in writing, or both. If you testify under oath, I may question you concerning your testimony and your worthiness of belief. If you make an unsworn statement, I am not permitted to question you upon it but I may receive evidence to contradict anything contained in the statement

Maximum punishment

If I find you guilty of (the offense) (any of the offenses) charged, the maximum sentence which I am authorized to impose is:

( )   (If the accused is above the fourth pay grade)
    (1) Reduction to the next inferior pay grade; and
    (2) Forfeiture of two-thirds pay per month for one month; and
    (3) Restriction to specified limits for two months; and
    (4) Admonition or reprimand

-or-

( )   (If the accused is in the fourth pay grade or lower)
    (1) Reduction to the lowest pay grade; and
    (2) Forfeiture of two-thirds pay per month for one month; and
    (3) Confinement at hard labor for one month; and
    (4) Admonition or reprimand

Right to refuse
Summary Court-Marial

You have the right to object to trial by Summary Court-Martial. If you object to trial by Summary Court-Martial, I will have you note your objection at the appropriate place on the charge sheet and I will return the file to the convening authority. In this event, appropriate authority may decide to refer your case to a special or general court-martial for trial. If you have any questions concerning the matter of objecting to trial, I will be glad to answer them. If you desire some time to consider whether to object to trial by Summary Court-Martial I will postpone the case for a period long enough for you to decide. Do you want some additional time to make up your mind? (No, sir) (   ).

Reading the charges to the accused

Note: If the accused desires additional time to consider whether he will object to trial by summary court-martial, recess or adjourn the proceedings for a reasonable period, advising the accused how long the period will be. If the accused objects to trial by summary court-martial, have the accused mark the appropriate box and sign his name on page 4 of each copy of the charge sheet and return the file to the convening authority after placing your signature in the appropriate space provided. If the accused consents to trial by summary court-martial, have him reflect that fact by marking the appropriate space on page 4 of each copy of the charge sheet and signing his name.

Note: When the trial is to proceed as a result of the accused's consent to trial by summary court-martial proceed as indicated below:

SCM: The charge(s) and specification(s) against you which have been referred to me for trial are as follows:

Charge (I): Violation of the Uniform Code of Military Justice, Article _____.

    Specification (1): In that _____

    Specification (2): In that _____

((Charge (II) (Additional charge): Violation of the Uniform Code of Military Justice, Article _____.

Motions to dismiss and to grant other relief

Explanation of pleas of guilty and not guilty

(Specification 1: In that _____).

_____)).

SCM: Do you understand the charge(s) and specification(s)?

ACC: (Yes, sir) (   ).

> *Note: Make certain that the accused understands the charges and specifications. It may be necessary to explain each specification in as simple language as possible, breaking it down into its essential components, or elements, and to ask the accused if he understands the explanation. Any additional explanation needed by the accused should be given.*

SCM: Before I ask you whether you are going to plead guilty or not guilty to the charge(s) and specification(s), I must advise you that any motion to dismiss (the) (any of the) charge(s) and specification(s) or to grant other relief should be made at this time.

> *Note: At this point the accused should be advised concerning any motions which examination of the file indicates he may desire to make (MCM, Ch XII). When the accused has no motions to make or if all motions have been disposed of and termination of the trial has not resulted, proceed with the trial as indicated below:*

SCM: Before you enter your pleas to the charge(s) and specification(s), I will explain your rights concerning the pleas you may make. First, you may plead not guilty to the charge(s) and specification(s) or to any of them. You have a moral and legal right to plead not guilty even though you may believe that you are guilty. A plea of not guilty merely means that you are requiring that your guilt be proved beyond a reasonable

Lesser included offenses

doubt in this trial before you may be found guilty. If you plead not guilty to (the charge and specification) (one or more of the charges and specifications), I will proceed to hear and consider the evidence as to (the charge and specification) (each charge and specification as to which you plead not guilty). Second, you may plead guilty to the charge(s) and specification(s) (or to any of them). If you plead guilty to a charge and specification, you thereby admit every essential fact, or element, of the offense stated in that specification. I am authorized to find you guilty of any charge and specification to which you plead guilty because of your plea alone without calling any witnesses or considering any evidence. However, you will still have the opportunity to have witnesses testify and introduce other evidence in mitigation or extenuation, for the purpose of lessening the severity of the sentence. Any plea of guilty you desire to make must be entirely voluntary and should be made only because you are convinced that you really are guilty and not for any other reason whatsoever.

> *Note: Explanation of plea of Guilty to Lesser Included Offense. If a less serious offense is included in an offense charged (some examples are contained in App. 12, MCM, Table of Commonly Included Offenses), advise the accused substantially as follows:*

SCM: ( )   Third, you may plead guilty to a lesser included offense, that is, to an offense included in (an) (the) offense charged which is less serious than the offense charged. Included in the offense alleged (in specification____ of charge ___) is the lesser offense of _____ . If you plead guilty to a lesser included offense, you thereby admit every essential fact, or element, of that included offense. With respect to any lesser included offense to which you plead guilty, I may find you guilty of that offense without any proof. However, I will call witnesses and will produce any other evidence available for the purpose of

Explanation of maximum sentence

determining whether you are guilty of the greater, rather than the lesser, offense.

SCM: If you plead guilty to (the) (any) offense, I may sentence you to the maximum sentence which I have advised you that I am authorized to impose. The maximum punishment which may be awarded is _____. The maximum authorized punishment may be adjudged upon conviction of the offense. I will not accept any plea of guilty unless you understand its meaning and effect.

If you desire some time to consider what your pleas will be, I will postpone the proceedings for a period long enough for you to decide. Do you understand the various pleas and the rights you have in connection with them?

ACC: (Yes, sir) (_____).

SMC: Do you want some additional time to make up you mind?

ACC: (No, sir) (_____).

> *Note: Do not proceed further until convinced that the accused understands his rights as to the pleas he may enter. If the accused desires some time to decide how he wants to plead, recess or adjourn the proceedings for a reasonable period, advising the accused how long the period will be. When the period has elapsed, call the accused before the court, advise him that the court is again in session, and ask him how he pleads.*

SCM: How do you plead?

Pleas

ACC: I plead (guilty) (not guilty) (to all charges and specifications) (to specification — of charge —) (—).

Note: If the accused pleads guilty to one or more offenses advise and question him as follows:

SCM: You have pleaded guilty to ——— . The essential facts, or elements, of (the) (each) offense to which you have pleaded guilty are:

Pleas of guilty to one or more offenses

ACC: As I said before, when you plead guilty to any offense you thereby admit every essential fact, or element, of that offense, and I may find you guilty of that offense without any proof and sentence you to the maximum punishment that I am authorized to impose. Do you understand this explanation of the meaning and effect of your pleas of guilty?

ACC: (Yes, sir.) (————).

> *Note: In order to clearly establish each element of the offense in question, the summary court-officer should question the accused specifically regarding each element. In order to avoid the receipt in evidence of extraneous comment outside the scope of the offense charged, pointed questions which bear directly on the elements should be employed. The following examples are provided:*

SCM: Did you at ———— absent yourself from your ————?

ACC: Yes (no) sir.

SCM: Was this absence without proper authority from anyone competent to give you leave?

ACC: Yes (no) sir.

SCM: What was the length of your absence?

ACC: ————————————————

SCM: ————————————————

ACC:

> *Note: If the accused's answers do not establish the existence of each element of each offense to which he has pleaded guilty, his plea to the offense in question must not be accepted.*

SCM: You should never enter a plea of guilty to any offense of which you are not, in fact guilty. A plea of guilty is the strongest form of proof known to the law. If you plead guilty this court could, on the plea of guilty alone, without receiving any evidence, find you guilty, and impose sentence. This court will not accept a plea of guilty unless you understand its meaning and effect. You have a perfect legal right to plead not guilty even though you believe you are guilty, and so leave the prosecution with the burden of proving your guilt beyond a reasonable doubt. A plea of guilty will not be accepted unless you realize that by such a plea you admit every element of the offense(s) to which you plead guilty and unless you are pleading guilty because you really are guilty. Do you understand the effect of your pleas of guilty?

ACC: Yes, sir.

SCM: Are you pleading guilty because you are in fact guilty?

ACC: Yes, sir.

SCM: _____ Do you realize that by pleading guilty you are waiving your constitutional right against self-incrimination?

ACC: Yes (no) sir.

SCM: Do you realize that your plea of guilty waives your right to a trial of the facts by a court-martial?

ACC: Yes (no) sir.

SCM: Do you realize that your plea of guilty waives your constitutional right to confront the witnesses against you?

ACC: Yes (no) sir.

SCM: And you nevertheless desire to persist in your pleas of guilty?

ACC: Yes (no) sir.

Note: If the answer to any of these four questions is no, the summary court-martial officer must ensure that the accused understands the rights he waives by his guilty plea before accepting his plea.

SCM: _____ , I (do not) find that you are knowingly, intelligently and consciously waiving your right against self-incrimination, your right of trial of the facts by this court, and your right to be confronted by the witnesses against you by your plea(s) of guilty.

SCM: Your plea(s) of guilty will (will not) be accepted.

Any plea of not guilty

Pleas of guilty to all charges and specifications

Note: If the accused does not appear to understand the meaning and effect of a plea of guilty made by him or if he desires to change that plea to one of not guilty, enter a plea of not guilty to the affected offense and proceed accordingly. Also, if the accused refuses or fails to plead guilty or not guilty to an offense charged, enter a plea of not guilty to that offense for him. All pleas should be noted at this time in the space provided on page 4 of the charge sheet.

Note: If the accused has entered a plea of not guilty to any offense charged, advise the accused as follows:

SCM: [The names of _____ , _____ , and _____ are listed on the charge sheet as being witnesses for you (and they have been notified to appear to testify for you).] If you know of any (other) witnesses you desire to have called to testify in your defense, give me their names and organizations or addresses and I will try to arrange to have them called as witnesses. What do you desire?

ACC: (_____).

Note: If the accused has entered a plea of guilty to all charges and specifications and you have accepted these pleas, you may proceed at once to announce your findings of guilty of these charges and specifications. In announcing the findings, request the accused to stand before you and announce the findings substantially as follows:

Procedure regardless of pleas

Explanation of mitigation and extenuation

SCM: I find you of (the charge and specification) (all charges and specifications): Guilty.

> Note: *The findings of guilty should immediately be noted in the space provided for findings on page 4 of the charge sheet. Next advise the accused as follows:*

SCM: (I do not intend to call any witnesses.) (I am going to call (some of) the witnesses to testify in order to obtain a better knowledge of what occurred to help me in determining the sentence.) However, you may desire to call witnesses or to introduce other matter in extenuation or mitigation, that is, for the purpose of lessening the severity of the sentence. [The names of _____, and _____ are listed on the charge sheet as being witnesses for you (and they have been notified to appear to testify for you).]

> Note: *Regardless of how the accused has pleaded, proceed as follows:*

SCM: I will now advise you particularly as to the meaning of extenuation and mitigation. You may introduce matter tending to show that you have a good character generally or tending to establish your good character, reputation, or record for efficiency, fidelity, temperance, courage, or any other traits that go to make up a good enlisted person. (You may also introduce evidence of the character of any of your former discharges from the military service.)

This is called matter in mitigation. Matter in extenuation of an offense serves to explain the circumstances surrounding the commission of the offense, including the reasons that caused you to act as you did but not amounting to a defense. Matter in mitigation or extenuation of an offense may be introduced through the testimony of witnesses, official records, or letters, affidavits, or any other written documents. If you introduce matter in mitigation or extenuation of an offense, I will have the right to call witnesses to testify, or to receive and consider other evidence, for the purpose of contradicting the matter you have introduced.

Do you want me to call witnesses for the purpose of testifying in mitigation or extenuation on your behalf (in the event you are found guilty of (the) (an) offense)? If so, furnish me with a list of their names and organizations or addresses. If you want me to get some military records that you would otherwise be unable to obtain, provide me with a list of these documents also. If you desire to introduce letters, affidavits, or other documents in mitigation or extenuation and these documents are not now in your possession, please advise me so that I can determine the time for further proceedings in this trial.

What do you desire?

ACC: (_____).

Note: If the accused desires to have witnesses called or to have certain documents or records obtained, arrange, if possible, to have the witnesses present and the documents or records produced at the time and place set for the appropriate session of the trial. However, if the accused indicates a desire to obtain letters, affidavits, or other documents not now in his possession, he may require a reasonable time to do so. In this event or in the event you are unable to arrange for the attendance of certain witnesses or the production of certain documents it will be necessary to adjourn for an appropriate period of time. In such event, inform the accused when and where you intend to resume the proceedings and arrange for his attendance. Also, notify the witnesses of the date and place you have set for the further proceedings and arrange for their attendance.

Note: If the accused has been found guilty of all charges and specifications on pleas of guilty and it appears that no evidence regarding the sentence is to be produced other than that already possessed, the court may proceed in accordance with PART III. In other situations, proceed with PART II or PART III, as appropriate, at the time set for further proceedings.

PART II - Procedure for Not Guilty Plea

PROSECUTION CASE IN CHIEF

SCM: The prosecution will begin.

> *Note: SCM should consult Chapter XXVII, MCM, and other applicable legal references for any rules of evidence which may affect the trial.*

Testimonial Evidence: *Testimonial evidence*

SCM: The prosecution calls as a witness _____.

SCM: (to the witness) Raise your right hand. Do you (swear) (affirm) that the evidence you shall give in the case now in hearing shall be the truth, the whole truth and nothing but the truth (so help you God)?

WIT: I do.

SCM: ( ) | State your full name, grade, organization and armed force.
                                            -or-
        ( ) | State your full name, occupation and address.

WIT: _____.

SCM: Do you know the accused?

WIT: I do (not).

> *Note: If affirmative, SCM continues:*

SCM: ( ) Point to him if you see him and state his name.

WIT: He is ——————— (pointing to accused).

> *Note: SCM proceeds with his direct examination of the witness. SCM then allows the accused (or his counsel) to cross-examine the witness. Be certain that the accused is afforded the opportunity to cross-examine witnesses against him, and if redirect examination is used for the prosecution, the accused must be permitted recross-examination. Upon conclusion of all testimony by the witness, he should be advised as follows:*

Warning witnesses

SCM: You are instructed not to discuss your testimony in this case with anyone except (the counsel or) the accused. You will not allow any witness in this case to talk to you about the testimony he has given or which he intends to give. If anyone, other than (the counsel or) the accused, attempts to talk to you about your testimony in this case, you should make the circumstances known to me. You are excused.

Documentary Evidence:

Documentary evidence

SCM: I intend to admit into evidence this document as prosecution exhibit (1). I will now show this document to you (and your counsel) to allow you an opportunity to object to the admission of this exhibit.

ACC: (No) Objection.

Caution: SCM must be very careful to use only documentary evidence which is relevant, material and competent.

Note: After all prosecution witnesses have testified and all prosecution evidence is in, SCM should announce that the prosecution rests its case. If the prosecution has not produced evidence bearing on all elements of the offense(s) the court may grant a defense motion for a finding of not guilty (see Chapter XII, MCM).

Other Evidence as Required:

( )

Evidence for the defense

Testimonial rights of accused

DEFENSE CASE IN CHIEF

SCM: The defense may present evidence.

Note: SCM will administer the oath to witnesses. The accused or his counsel may ask questions in direct examination, or the SCM may question the witnesses on behalf of the accused. After direct examination, the SCM may cross-examine. Redirect and recross-examination are permitted. Witnesses should be warned at the conclusion of their testimony.

SCM: (to accused) You have the following legal rights as the accused in this case:

You may be sworn and take the stand as a witness only at your own request. If you do, whatever you say will be considered and weighed as evidence by the court just as is the testimony of other witnesses and you can be cross-examined on your testimony by the court. (If your testimony should concern only one of several offenses charged and you do not testify concerning the others, then you may be cross-examined only about those offenses concerning which you do testify and your worthiness of belief, but you will not be cross-examined about any offenses concerning which you do not testify.)

You may remain silent, that is, say nothing at all. If you do so, the fact of your silence will not count against you in any way with this court. Your silence in open court is not an admission that you are guilty and I cannot infer your guilt from it.

ACC: I desire to (remain silent) (testify as a witness) (―――――――).

Note: After all defense witnesses have testified and all defense exhibits are admitted, and the defense has rested, the SCM may offer prosecution evidence in rebuttal and then offer the accused the opportunity to present defense evidence in rebuttal.

Caution: The SCM will not make argument. However, accused should be offered an opportunity to present argument.

Determination of findings

SCM: The court will be closed.

Note: The SCM will close the court to arrive at his findings. The SCM may not convict the accused of any offense, unless he believes that the guilt of the accused has been established by legal and competent evidence beyond a reasonable doubt.

FINDINGS

Call to order

SCM: The court will come to order.

Announcement of findings

SCM: Examples:

(name of accused), I find you:

( )   Of all charges and specifications (Guilty) (Not Guilty).

—or—

( )   Of specification 1 of the charge, guilty; of specification 2 of the charge, not guilty; and of the charge guilty.

—or—

( )   Of the specification of the charge, guilty except the words "_____", substituting therefor the words "_____"; of the excepted words, not guilty, of the substituted words, guilty, and of the charge, guilty.

> *Note:* *There must be a finding as to each specification under each charge and also as to the charge itself. The examples above are not exhaustive. The SCM must be sure that the findings are recorded correctly in abbreviated form in the record of trial on page 4 of the charge sheet. (See paragraph 1304, Military Law.)*

> *Caution:* *Do not explain the reasons for the findings to the accused or allow argument about them.*

> *Note:* *If the accused has been found not guilty of all charges and specifications, the court should adjourn. If any findings of guilty have been made, proceed in accordance with PART III.*

PART III- Procedure Pertaining to the Sentence

PRESENTENCING PROCEDURE

SCM: The following personal data is found on page 1 of the charge sheet:

Reading personal data

Name: _____

Service number: _____

Grade: _____

Branch of service: _____

Date of birth: _____

Organization: _____

Contribution to family or quarters allowance: _____

Pay per month: _____

Initial date of current service: _____

Term of current service: _____

Prior service: _____

Restraint: _____

Are these data correct?

ACC: (Yes, sir) (———).

> *Note: If the accused states that any of the personal data is incorrect, the SCM should seek an official determination of the challenged data and correct that which is demonstrated erroneous.*

*Previous
convictions*

*Right of accused to
present evidence,
testify, remain
silent, and make*

SCM: ( ) I have evidence of no previous convictions.

-or-

( ) I intend to introduce evidence of ____ previous conviction(s) by court-martial of (an) offense(s) committed within six years preceding the commission of any offense(s) of which the accused has been convicted at this trial.

> *Note: If the previous conviction relates to an offense committed more than 6 years prior to the date of the earliest current offense it may not be used.*

> *Caution: To be admissible as a previous conviction there must also be the final approval of the conviction.*

SCM: Do you have any objection to this evidence of previous conviction(s) by court-martial?

ACC: (No, sir) (————).

> *Caution: Evidence of the imposition of nonjudicial punishment under the provisions of Article 15 UCMJ may not be considered as matter unfavorable to the accused in determining the sentence.*

SCM: It is your right at this time to submit for the court's consideration any matters in mitigation or extenuation of the offense(s) of which you stand convicted. You may call witnesses and submit any letters, affidavits, documents and any other matters which you so desire. Earlier in this trial, I advised you concerning your right to testify under oath in

unsworn statement in mitigation and extenuation

your own behalf as to matters in mitigation or extenuation, to remain silent, and to make an unsworn statement about these matters. I will repeat this advice if you want me to. Do you want me to repeat this advice?

ACC: (No, sir) (Yes, sir).

Note: If the accused answers in the affirmative, repeat the advice set forth in PART 1 concerning his right to testify as to matters in mitigation or extenuation, to remain silent, and to make an unsworn statement about these matters. If the accused indicates that he does not desire this advice repeated or when the accused indicates that he understands his rights after it has been repeated, ask him what evidence in extenuation and mitigation he desires to present.

If the accused elects to testify under oath, administer the oath to him or remind him that he is still under oath, as appropriate. The court may cross-examine the accused on his sworn testimony. If the accused elects to make an unsworn statement, permit him to do so. Also receive any unsworn written statement that the accused may present.

Testimony or unsworn statement of accused

If the court desires witnesses in rebuttal of matters presented in mitigation or extenuation, they may be called. If witnesses in rebuttal are called, they should be sworn and examined in the same manner as any other Government witness and the accused should be extended the right to cross-examine or to request the court to cross-examine them along lines indicated by him.

Witnesses in rebuttal

ACC: I desire to _____ .

Inconsistent pleas

> *Caution: If the accused now presents matter inconsistent with pleas of guilty, the SCM must explain to the accused that his statement is inconsistent and ask the accused whether he persists in his pleas of guilty. If the accused does not withdraw the inconsistent matter, or it appears that the pleas of guilty were made improvidently, the SCM must withdraw the pleas of guilty, enter pleas of not guilty, and proceed in accordance with PART II.*

SCM: Does the accused have anything further to offer?

ACC: (No, sir) (———————).

SCM: The court will be closed.

Sentencing

Closing the court

> *Note: The SCM may use the "Table of Equivalent Punishments" found in the Manual for Court-Martial. Use of this table, however, may not result in a sentence which exceeds the maximum jurisdictional limits of the SCM nor the limitation on the use of a particular type of punishment.*

SCM: The court will come to order.

Call to order

SCM: (name of accused), it is my duty as Summary Court-Martial to inform you that the court sentences you:

Examples:

( )   To be confined at hard labor for (one month) (—— days).

( )   To be restricted to the limits of ——————————— for ————— month(s)(days).

( )   To perform hard labor without confinement for ————— days.

( )   To forfeit $ ————— pay per month for (————— month(s)) (————— days).

( )   To have $ ————— pay per month for (————— month(s)) (————— days) detained.

( )   To be reduced to pay grade E- ————— .

( )   To be reprimanded.

( )   To be admonished.

( )   To no punishment.

Note: Appropriate combinations may be adjudged.

Note: If the sentence includes confinement the accused must be advised of the substance of paragraph 88f of the MCM as follows:

SCM: You are advised that you may request in writing that the convening authority defer your sentence. The deferment is terminated and the sentence to confinement begins to run or resumes running when the sentence is approved and ordered executed.

SCM: The court is adjourned.

Note: If SCM believes further mitigation warranted he may make a recommendation for clemency to the convening authority in specific terms and should give reasons. However, the SCM should never award an excessive sentence, which he believes is inappropriate, in reliance upon the mitigating action of higher reviewing authorities.

Caution: The SCM should not attempt to explain reasons for the sentence awarded. The accused may be informed of the process of review, that is, the case must be first reviewed by the convening authority who must take action on the record of trial. Thereafter, the record of trial must be forwarded to the supervisory authority in accordance with Article 65(c), UCMJ.

Form—approved by Comptroller General, U. S.
July 18, 1951

COURT MEMORANDUM

EXEMPT REPORT

See ART. B.2305, BuPers Manual

DATE OF MAST'	TYPE OF COURT	DATE OF TRIAL
31 Dec 1965	SUMMARY COURT-MARTIAL	5 Jan 1966

SYNOPSIS OF OFFENSE(S) DATE(S)

Viol UCMJ Art 86 - UA from 0730, 10 Dec 1965 to 1700, 15 Dec 1965

SENTENCE AS APPROVED BY CONVENING AUTHORITY

Confinement at hard labor for 30 days and forfeiture of $65.00 per month for 1 month. Sentence is ordered executed. The sentence was adjudged on 5 January 1966.

	MONTHLY AMOUNT	NUMBER OF MONTHS	TOTAL AMOUNT	EFFECTIVE DATE
FORFEITURE OF PAY	$65.00	ONE (1)	$65.00	6 Jan 1966
DETENTION OF PAY				
REDUCTION IN RATE	FROM	TO		

DATE AND OTHER IDENTIFICATION OF CONVENING AUTHORITY'S ACTION. C. M. O. NO. ETC.
The CA approved SCM No. 3-66 on 6 Jan 1966. Record of Trial forwarded to COMCRUDESLANT on 7 Jan 1966.

☒ MEMORANDUM ENTRY OR MARKS AND DIARY ENTRIES MADE

SIGNATURE	GRADE AND TITLE LT, USNR	SHIP OR STATION
R A Franklin lei	Legal Officer, by dir of C.O.	USS DINWIDDLE (DDE 111)

SUPPLEMENTARY COURT MEMORANDUM   20 January 1966

(A) FINDING AND SENTENCE APPROVED WITHOUT CHANGE BY SUPERVISORY AUTHORITY ON (COMCRUDESLANT ltr ser: 21)

(B) RESUME OF ACTION ~~APPROVING FINDINGS OF SENTENCE~~ BY REVIEWING AUTHORITY OR UNDER ARTICLES 72, 74, OR 15(D)
OR (E). UCMJ

EXAMPLE OF STRAIGHT APPROVAL
OF COURT-MARTIAL THROUGH SA

IDENTIFY SUPPLEMENTARY COURT MARTIAL ORDER, JAG LETTER OR OTHER DOCUMENT RESULTING
IN CHANGE OR MODIFICATION OF FINDING OR SENTENCE, INCLUDING DATE:

☐ SUPPLEMENTARY MARKS AND DIARY ENTRIES MADE

SIGNATURE	GRADE AND TITLE LT, USNR	SHIP OR STATION
R A Franklin lei	Legal Officer, by dir of C.O.	USS DINWIDDLE (DDE 111)

NAME (Last)	(First)	(Middle)	SERVICE NUMBER	RATE	BRANCH AND CLASS
DANIELS,	Robert	Gene	411 00 01	FN	USN

COURT MEMORANDUM   NAVPERS 601-6/NAVCOMPT 516 (Rev. 2-63)
PART 1—RETAIN IN SERVICE RECORD

6 ☐1

Reproduced from U.S. Naval Justice School Hand Book.

Sample Special Court-martial Convening Order

U.S.S. AWASH (DD-902)
c/o Fleet Post Office
New York, New York 59000

5817
Ser: 2000
25 February 19__

From: Commanding Officer, U.S.S. AWASH (DD-902)
To: Lieutenant Commander John P. Anderson, U.S. Navy
      U.S.S. AWASH (DD-902)

Subj: Convening Special Court-martial

1. A special court-martial is hereby ordered to convene on board the U.S.S. AWASH (DD-902) at 0900 hours on 1 March 19__, or as soon thereafter as practicable, for the trial of such persons as may properly be brought before it. The court will be constituted as follows:

MILITARY JUDGE

Lieutenant Commander John S. Brown
JAGC, U.S. Navy

Certified in accordance with Article 26(b) and previously sworn in accordance with Article 42(a)

MEMBERS

Lieutenant Commander John P. Anderson, U.S. Navy,
Lieutenant Edward M. Sherbank, U.S. Navy,
Lieutenant (junior grade) Calvin N. Murray, U.S. Naval Reserve
Ensign Samuel F. Prescott, SC, U.S. Naval Reserve

COUNSEL

Lieutenant Larry O. Smith, U.S. Navy

TRIAL COUNSEL, certified in accordance with Article 27(b)

Ensign Roger L. Crump, U.S. Naval Reserve

ASSISTANT TRIAL COUNSEL not a lawyer in the sense of Article 27

Lieutenant J.F. Shogun, JAGC, U.S. Navy

DEFENSE COUNSEL certified in accordance with Article 27(b)

Ensign Phillip M. Dawes, U.S. Naval Reserve

ASSISTANT DEFENSE COUNSEL, not a lawyer in the sense of Article 27

(signature)
THOMAS M. JOHNSON
Commander, U.S. Navy
Commanding Officer
U.S.S. AWASH (DD-902)

```
                    U.S.S. AWASH (DD-902)
                    c/o Fleet Post Office
                  New York, New York 59000



                              5817
                              Ser: 2001
                              15 April ___

From:   Commanding Officer, U.S.S. AWASH (DD-902)
To:     Lieutenant Commander John P. Anderson, U.S. Navy, U.S.S.
        AWASH (DD-902)

Subj:   Modification to Convening Order of Special Court-martial

1.. Lieutenant (junior grade) Philip V. Wagner, U.S. Navy is
detailed as a member of the special court-martial convened
by my order serial 2000 of 25 February 19__..


                    (signature)
                    THOMAS M. JOHNSON
                    Commander, U.S. Navy
                    Commanding Officer
                    USS.AWASH (DD-902)
```

CHECKLIST FOR TRIAL COUNSEL

| Accused (Last name—First name—Middle initial) | (Rate) | (Armed Force) | (Organization) |

INSTRUCTIONS

To indicate completion of the items listed, place a check mark to the right of the checklist item; if an item is inapplicable, place a diagonal mark there. Correspondence and reports to the convening authority should be through the Judge Advocate or Legal Officer.

References are to this handbook, Articles of the Uniform Code of Military Justice, paragraphs and appendices of the Manual for Courts-Martial, United States, 1969 (Revised edition), and the JAG Manual.

SECTION A—DUTIES PRIOR TO TRIAL

1. Check the charge sheet and all allied papers in order to assure that the file is complete. _____

2. Ascertain from the indorsement on the charge sheet and the order convening the court whether the charges have been properly referred to the court for trial. _____

3. Examine the charges and allied papers to determine whether any member of the prosecution is disqualified because of prior participation in the same case (MCM 6, 44*b*). If so, the matter must be reported immediately to the convening authority prior to any action being taken. _____

4. *a.* Make certain that the data on the charge sheet are free from errors of substance or form (MCM 44*f*(1)). _____

   b. Compare the name and description of the accused in each specification with the corresponding data on page one of the charge sheet. _____

   c. Compare the charges and specifications in the charge sheet with the pertinent forms set forth in appendix 6*c* of the MCM to determine if they are in proper form, and allege offenses. _____

This material is based upon *Military Justice Handbook: The Trial Counsel and Defense Counsel* (DA Pam 27–10).

5. *a.* Report substantial discrepancies in the convening orders to the convening authority. _____

b. Examine the orders convening all courts to which the case has been referred, the charge sheet, and the accompanying papers to determine whether the military judge and counsel have the necessary legal qualifications and whether any facts appear which would disqualify the military judge or any of the counsel from acting in the case (MCM 4e, 6). _____

c. If, with respect to the qualifications of the military judge or counsel, the court is not legally constituted, notify the convening authority. _____

6. *a.* Serve or cause to be served a copy of the charge sheet and all allied papers on the accused in the presence of his defense counsel if possible. _____

b. Complete and sign the certificate of service (bottom of page 3 of charge sheet (DD Form 458)). _____

7. *a.* Examine the record of previous convictions for completeness, admissibility, and freedom from errors of form or substance. If any previous convictions would not be admissible in the case, obtain a new record of convictions showing only those which are admissible (MCM 44f(1), 75b(2). _____

b. If the court-martial is constituted with a military judge assure that any personnel records of the accused, including those that reflect his past conduct and performance, and records of nonjudicial punishment, are available for use. Appendix 8 of *Military Law* contains a sample service entry. The record of nonjudicial punishment must relate to offenses committed prior to trial, during the current enlistment of the accused, and within two years of the commission of the present offense. (Section 0117, JAG Manual). _____

8. *a.* If the defense counsel was not present when the charges were served notify him that charges have been served. _____

b. Deliver copies of the papers that accompanied the charge sheet to the defense counsel (MCM 44h, 115c). _____

c. Determine from the defense counsel whether the data shown on the first page of the charge sheet are correct. _____

d. Inform defense counsel of any papers accompanying the charges that were withheld from him by order of the convening authority. _____

9. *a.* If the accused is an enlisted person, ascertain from defense counsel whether he desires enlisted members on the court. If so, obtain a request signed by the accused therefor and advise the convening authority. _____

b. If the accused requests enlisted members, make certain that none of the enlisted persons who will sit as members of the court are members of the same unit as the accused or are junior in grade to the accused; insure that one-third of the total court membership will be enlisted persons (Article 25(c); MCM 4). _____

c. If a military judge has been detailed to the court-martial which will try the accused, determine if the accused has submitted a written request for trial by the military judge alone. (Article 16; MCM 4*a*). _____

d. Determine from appointed defense counsel whether the accused desires to be represented by individual counsel, civilian or military. If the court can adjudge a BCD, determine if the detailed defense counsel is a certified military lawyer. If a non-BCD case, determine if the accused desires a certified military lawyer. If the accused requests such counsel, he must be furnished it unless physical conditions or military exigencies prevent it. If such conditions exist, the trial counsel must obtain a written statement from the convening authority explaining why such counsel could not be obtained (MCM, 6*c*; *Military Law*, Chapter VIII). _____

10. Ask defense counsel how accused intends to plead. If the accused offers to plead guilty under a pretrial agreement, his signed offer in writing should be brought to the attention of the convening authority. (See Chapter I, JAG Manual.) _____

11. Ascertain from the defense counsel what witnesses he will need and the earliest date he will be ready for trial. Any requested delay by the defense counsel should be placed in writing. This is to preserve the record in the event the speedy trial issue should arise. _____

12. Arrange for any necessary depositions in coordination with the defense counsel. Consider appropriate stipulations of fact or of testimony with the defense counsel. (MCM 117).   _____

13. Study the elements of proof and the law relating to each offense charged (MCM, Chapter XXVIII).   _____

14. Interview prosecution witnesses and take notes.   _____

15. Interview defense witnesses other than the accused and take notes.   _____

16. Arrange with appropriate division officers to have all material witnesses available for trial; take action to insure that such witnesses will not be transferred or allowed leave so as to make them unavailable.   _____

17. Examine any documentary evidence pertaining to the case for accuracy, completeness, admissibility, and form (MCM 143-146)._____

18. Arrange to have any real evidence, such as knives, guns, money, clothing, etc., available for the trial; be prepared to establish relevance, if necessary.   _____

19. If, during the preparation of the case, new information is discovered that affects the feasibility of proceeding with the trial, advise the convening authority (MCM 44f(5)).   _____

20. If a question arises as to the sanity of the accused, refer the matter to the convening authority (MCM 121).   _____

21. *a.* Prepare proof analysis sheet.   _____

   b. Plan the order in which the evidence will be placed before the court at the trial.   _____

22. Obtain and study legal authorities concerning any possible questions of law likely to arise at the trial, particularly in connection with the instructions or special findings. A non-lawyer should seek the advice of a JAG lawyer if he has any difficulty in this area.   _____

23. Note any lesser offenses included in each specification and carefully analyze the expected evidence to determine which lesser offenses might be in issue (MCM 158).   _____

24. Prepare proposed instructions or special findings. (MCM 73*d*). _____

25. Prepare an outline of any opening statement and final argument to be made at the trial.   _____

26. Examine the order convening the court, the charge sheet, and the accompanying papers for possible grounds for challenge (MCM 62*f*).   _____

27. Consider whether the defense may make any motions or objections and, if so, make the necessary preparation to respond to them (MCM, Chapter XII).   _____

28. Have necessary photographs, maps, charts, *etc.*, prepared.   _____

29. Obtain official copies of price lists, regulations, orders, *etc.*, of which the court will be requested to take judicial notice (MCM 147*a*).   _____

30. Determine the strong points in the probable defense case and prepare to counteract them if possible.   _____

31. Outline the expected testimony of each prosecution witness and the expected cross-examination of each defense witness.   _____

32. Prepare an outline for the cross-examination of the accused in the event he elects to take the stand to testify.   _____

33. Prepare trial notes.   _____

34. If possible, stipulate with the defense counsel and the accused concerning unimportant or uncontested matters.   _____

35. *a.* If a military judge is detailed, determine the desirability of an Article 39(a) session, if applicable, and the issues to be presented to the session.   _____

b. Contact military judge to arrange time and date of the session and the uniform to be worn at the Article 39(a) session.   _____

c. Give appropriate notice of the Article 39(a) session to defense counsel.   _____

d. Arrange for the presence of witnesses and a reporter at the Article 39(a) session.   _____

36. *a.* Arrange for a military judge, if applicable. _____

b. If a court reporter is to be used, ascertain the dates that he will be available. _____

c. Ascertain from the president of the court the uniform to be worn (MCM 40*b*(1) (a)). _____

d. Confer with the military judge and/or president of the court regarding the date and time of trial (MCM 39*b*(3), 40*b*(2)). _____

37. Notify all persons concerned of the meeting of the court and the uniform to be worn, *i.e.,* members of the court, military judge, counsel, reporter and interpreter. _____

38. Arrange for the presence of civilian witnesses; if necessary, subpoena civilian witnesses for the prosecution and the defense (MCM 115*a*). Arrange with their commands for the presence of military witnesses (MCM 115*b*). _____

39. Arrange with the accused's command for the presence of the accused at the trial (MCM 60). _____

40. Inspect the courtroom and see that proper furniture is provided and is properly arranged (MCM, Appendix 8*b*). _____

41. Secure necessary stationery items; submit proposed findings and sentence worksheets, *etc.*, to the military judge for use by members of the court-martial and furnish copies to the defense counsel. _____

42. Have typewritten copies of the charges and specifications prepared by the reporter for the military judge, if applicable, each member of the court, the accused and reporter. _____

43. Go to the courtroom early and check all arrangements. _____

SECTION B—DUTIES DURING TRIAL

44. At all times during the trial, utilize trial notes and the procedural guide for trials before special courts-martial.

45. Check with the reporter concerning the time of each assembly or opening, and recess, adjournment, or closing.   _____

46. Account for the "parties to the trial" when the court opens after closing, adjourning, or recessing.   _____

SECTION C–DUTIES AFTER TRIAL

47. Arrange for proper disposition of accused, to include an armed guard if necessary (MCM 21*d*).   _____

48. Notify, in writing, the accused's commanding officer, the commanding officer of the brig in which the accused is confined, and the convening authority of the outcome of the trial (MCM 44*e*).   _____

49. Complete witness vouchers and assist witnesses in securing payment as prescribed by departmental regulations.   _____

50. If original documents are to be returned, see that certified true copies or other authorized reproductions of such documents are prepared for substitution in the record of trial (MCM, Appendix 8*b*).   _____

51. Prepare proper descriptions or photographs of items of real evidence for inclusion in the record (MCM 138*c*).   _____

52. Determine the number of copies of the record of trial to be prepared (MCM 49*b*(2)).   _____

53. Turn over to the reporter or clerical assistant exhibits and allied papers to be attached to the record of trial.   _____

54. Supervise the preparation of the record of trial (Article 38(a); MCM 82*a*).   _____

55. *a.* Check the record of trial as it is being transcribed, and, when the record has been completed, carefully review it and see that all papers are arranged and bound in the manner prescribed by secretarial regulations (MCM, Appendix 9*e*, 10*c*).   _____

   b. Note, correct, and initial errors in the record of trial.   _____

c. Submit the record of trial to the defense counsel for his examination and signature prior to authentication.   _____

d. Special Court-Martial.   _____

(1) With a military judge submit the record of trial to the military judge for authentication (MCM 83*a*).   _____

(2) Without a military judge - submit the record of trial to the president of the court for authentication (MCM 83*a*).   _____

e. If a civilian reporter was employed, check the reporter's voucher and sign it, if it is correct.   _____

f. Supply each accused with a copy of the record of trial from which any classified material has been deleted; obtain a receipt for each copy so provided and attach it to the record of trial (MCM 82*g*(1)).   _____

g. Complete the Court-Martial Data Sheet (DD Form 494).   _____

h. If appropriate, include in the record a signed letter containing reasons why declassification of classified matter in the allied papers was not accomplished prior to the dispatch of the record.   _____

i. Include immediately following the chronology sheet in all records of trial by special courts-martial in which a bad conduct discharge has been adjudged, a statement of the accused through defense counsel that he does or does not desire appellate defense counsel or, in lieu thereof, a certificate of the defense counsel that he advised the accused of his appellate rights (Articles 38(a), 66 and 70).   _____

j. Forward the record of trial to the convening authority.   _____

56. Retain all reporter's notes and other records from which the record of trial was prepared, until appellate review is completed.   _____

CHECKLIST FOR DEFENSE COUNSEL

ACCUSED (Last name - First   (Rate)   (Armed Force)   (Organization)
name—Middle initial)

INSTRUCTIONS

To indicate completion of the items listed, place a checkmark in the box to the right of the checklist; if an item is inapplicable, place a diagonal mark in the box.

References are to this handbook, Articles of the Uniform Code of Military Justice, paragraphs and appendices of the Manual for Courts-Martial, United States, 1969 (Revised edition), and the JAG Manual.

SECTION A—DUTIES PRIOR TO TRIAL

1. Check the charges and allied papers received from the trial counsel to assure that they are complete. ⎯⎯⎯⎯⎯

2. Ascertain from the first indorsement on the charge sheet and the orders convening the court whether the charges have been properly furnished to you as defense counsel. ⎯⎯⎯⎯⎯

3. Examine the charges and allied papers to determine whether any member of the defense has acted as accuser, investigating officer, military judge, court member, or for the prosecution in the same case. ⎯⎯⎯⎯⎯

4. If, because of prior participation, a member of the defense can serve only if the accused expressly requests him to do so, advise the accused of his rights in this respect and, if he wants the member to act in the case, have him sign a statement to that effect; otherwise, notify the convening authority (MCM 6*a*). ⎯⎯⎯⎯⎯

5. Interview the accused and advise him that you have been detailed as defense counsel, of your general duties, and of the confidential relationship which exists between the defense counsel and the accused. ⎯⎯⎯⎯⎯

6. *a.* Determine whether the accused desires individual counsel— civilian or military. ⎯⎯⎯⎯⎯

This material is based upon *Military Justice Handbook: The Trial Counsel and Defense Counsel* (DA Pam 27–10).

b. Advise the accused that civilian counsel cannot be provided at Government expense (MCM 48*a*). If he desires civilian counsel, assist him in making the necessary arrangements.   _____

c. If the accused desires individual military counsel, submit an immediate written request therefor (MCM 46*d*).   _____

d. If you are not a certified military lawyer, advise the accused that he has the right to be represented by a certified military lawyer. If the accused desires such counsel, advise the convening authority.   _____

7. Explain to the accused he should not discuss the case with anyone without your approval.   _____

8. Check the accuracy of the data on page one of the charge sheet concerning the accused's restraint, record of service, and personal data.   _____

9. Advise the accused of his rights, as follows:

a. Right to have enlisted personnel on the court- (if accused is an enlisted person) (Article 25(c); MCM 48*f*).   _____

b. Right to challenges for cause and one peremptory challenge._____

c. Right to assert any defense or objection (MCM, Chapters XII, XXIX).   _____

d. Right to plead not guilty (MCM 70*a*).   _____

e. Meaning and effect of a guilty plea and, if appropriate, a pretrial agreement (including the maximum punishment) (MCM 70*b*).   _____

f. Right, before findings, to testify as a witness or to remain silent (MCM 53*h*, 148*e*, Appendix 8*b*).   _____

g. Right, to introduce evidence in extenuation and mitigation and to testify, make an unsworn statement personally and/or through counsel, or remain silent (MCM 75*c*).   _____

h. Right to be tried by the military judge alone if one has been detailed (MCM 4*a*).   _____

i. Right to request convening authority to defer any confinement adjudged (MCM 88*f*). Prepare undated request if agreeable with accused.   _____

10. Unless the accused has requested individual counsel or a certified military lawyer and has indicated that he does not desire the services of detailed counsel, detailed counsel will begin the preparation of the case for trial (MCM 46*d*).   _____

11. Analyze the charges, specifications, and pretrial investigation report.   _____

12. Study the discussion contained in Chapter XXVIII of the MCM to determine the essential elements of each offense charged._____

13. Impress the accused with the necessity for a full disclosure of all the facts and circumstances surrounding the offense charged. _____

14. In the event co-accused are to be defended, advise them of any conflicting interests in the conduct of their defense which would warrant a request for other counsel (MCM 48*c*).   _____

15. Obtain from the accused the names and addresses of witnesses who may have helpful information concerning the case or his character. Contact each of these witnesses personally or write to them and obtain their version of the events that occurred or information pertaining to the accused's reputation.   _____

16. Learn from the accused the location of any documentary or real evidence applicable to the case, such as check stubs, canceled checks, letters, *etc.*, and have such evidence available for use at the trial.   _____

17. If the accused has made a confession or admission concerning any of the offenses charged, determine the circumstances surrounding such confession or admission (MCM 140*a*).   _____

18. *a.* Interview in detail witnesses for the defense.   _____

   b. Interview in detail witnesses for the prosecution.   _____

   c. Determine which prosecution witnesses probably should be, or should not be, cross-examined.   _____

d. If it appears that the prosecution has not divulged all facts or witnesses known to him, make a motion for appropriate relief for such information to the convening authority or at an Article 39(a) session to the military judge. _____

19. *a.* Determine whether accused desires to plead guilty, not guilty, or guilty of a lesser included offense (MCM 70*a*). _____

b. If the accused desires to enter into a pretrial agreement, reduce the offer to writing, witness, with another person, the accused sign it, and bring the matter to the attention of the convening authority through the trial counsel. Section 0114, JAG Manual. _____

20. Determine if the accused wishes to be tried by the military judge, if detailed, alone. _____

21. If the accused is an enlisted person, and he desires to have enlisted personnel on the court, prepare the necessary request for his signature and submit it to the convening authority through the trial counsel (MCM 48*f*). _____

22. *a.* Determine whether the military judge or any member of the court may be subject to challenge for cause. Prepare necessary voir dire examination (MCM 62*f*). See paragraph 1004 of *Military Law.* _____

b. Determine whether it will be advantageous for the accused to exercise his right to one peremptory challenge against any member of the court. _____

c. Discuss the membership of the court with the accused and determine his wishes with respect to challenges. _____

23. Determine whether there is any doubt as to accused's sanity at the time of the alleged offenses, or his mental capacity now to stand trial, and advise trial counsel accordingly (MCM, Chapter XXIV). _____

24. Prepare trial notes and take other appropriate action to prepare the case for trial. _____

25. *a.* Outline the essential elements of each offense charged. _____

b. Study and make appropriate notes concerning the rules of evidence applicable in the case (MCM, Chapter XXVII). _____

c. Determine whether each specification properly states an offense under the Code (MCM, Appendix 6). _____

d. (1) Review and outline the expected prosecution evidence. _____

(2) Note weaknesses in the prosecution's evidence. _____

(3) Determine whether such expected evidence is sufficient to establish all elements of each offense charged beyond a reasonable doubt. _____

(4) If the expected evidence does not appear to substantiate the offenses charged, determine whether the evidence substantiates any lesser included offense. _____

e. Ascertain and carefully outline any defenses available to the accused. Advise the trial counsel of any anticipated delays. _____

f. Advise the trial counsel of the names and addresses of witnesses which the defense desires to have present at the trial. _____

g. (1) Plan the order in which evidence will be introduced. _____

(2) Outline the testimony of each defense witness. _____

(3) Outline cross-examination of each prosecution witness. _____

h. Arrange with the trial counsel for the taking of necessary depositions. _____

i. Depending on the desire of the accused, stipulate with the trial counsel concerning unimportant or uncontested matters. _____

j. If appropriate, prepare a tentative outline of the opening statement. _____

k. If any motions are to be made, prepare the motions in detail and outline supporting legal authorities and supporting evidence (MCM, Chapter XII). _____

l. Have necessary photographs, maps, charts, *etc.*, prepared. _____

m. Obtain official copies of price lists, regulations, orders, *etc.*, of which the court will be requested to take judicial notice (MCM 147*a*). _____

n. Prepare a tentative final argument. _____

o. (1) Prepare a detailed summary of accused's civilian and military background. _____

(2) Outline available evidence in extenuation and mitigation to be presented in the event findings of guilty are announced. _____

p. Check for accuracy and admissibility any evidence of previous convictions (MCM 75*b*). _____

q. Note the lesser offenses included in each specification and analyze the expected evidence to determine which lesser offenses might be in issue. _____

r. Determine requested instructions or special findings as appropriate and furnish same to the military judge (or president of the special court-martial without a military judge) with copies to trial counsel. _____

s. Instruct accused as to his appearance and the manner in which he should conduct himself during the trial and make certain that he has a neat and appropriate uniform complete with all authorized ribbons, decorations, *etc.* _____

t. Obtain and prepare an outline of such legal authorities as may be necessary to support defense contentions. _____

26. *a.* Determine what matters, if any, to present at an Article 39(a) session: _____

(1) Motions for appropriate relief (MCM 69*a*). _____

(2) Motions in bar of trial (MCM 68*a*). _____

(3) Objections to admissibility of government evidence (confessions, fruits of illegal search, *etc.*). _____

(4) Challenges for cause (MCM 62*f*). _____

(5) Present request for trial by military judge without court members (MCM 4*a*).   _____

(6) Other matters.   _____

b. Inform trial counsel of defense request for an Article 39(a) session and matters to be presented, if applicable.   _____

c. Insure trial notes include all matters to be taken up at the Article 39(a) session and are so designated.   _____

SECTION B—DUTIES DURING TRIAL

27. The defense counsel will at all times during the trial utilize his trial notes and follow the approved procedure for trials before special courts-martial set forth in the appropriate naval trial guide. See Chapters XII and XIII, *Military Law*.   _____

SECTION C—DUTIES AFTER TRIAL

28. If the accused is found guilty and is sentenced, consider preparing and presenting to the court a clemency petition (MCM 48*k*(1)).   _____

29. If confinement at hard labor has been adjudged, determine whether to submit a request for its deferment to the convening authority (MCM 48*k*(4)).   _____

30. Examine the record of trial to see if it correctly reflects all of the proceedings before the court.   _____

31. As appropriate, advise the accused of his appellate rights and submit to the trial counsel a signed statement of the accused that he does or does not desire appellate defense counsel (MCM 48*k*(3)).   _____

32. If appropriate, prepare and submit an appellate brief (MCM 48*k*(2)).   _____

33. Examine post trial review and rebut it appropriately.   _____

34. Examine action of convening authority.   _____

INFORMAL ONE OFFICER INVESTIGATION APPOINTING ORDER

(File information)

_____ Feb 19_____

From: Commanding Officer, Headquarters Battalion, Marine Corps Base, Camp Pendleton, California

To: Captain X _____ Y. Z _____ , 000000/0185, USMC

Subj: Investigation to inquire into the circumstances connected with _____ which occurred at _____ on _____ February 19

Ref: (a) JAG Manual

1. You are appointed to conduct an informal investigation, in accordance with chapter VI of reference (a), as soon hereafter as practicable, for the purpose of inquiring into all the circumstances connected with _____ which occurred at _____ on _____ February 19___ .

2. You will conduct a thorough investigation into all the circumstances connected with _____ and report your findings of fact, opinions and recommendations as to the cause of_____ , the resulting damage, the injuries to members of the naval service and their line of duty and misconduct status, the circumstances attending the death of members of the naval service, and responsibility for _____ , including any recommended administrative or disciplinary action.

3. By copy of this appointing order, Commanding Officer, Headquarters Company is directed to furnish the necessary reporters and clerical assistance for recording and transcribing the testimony of witnesses and assisting you in preparing the report of the results of your investigation.

/s/ R _____ C. K _____

R _____ C. K _____
Lieutenant Colonel, U.S. Marine Corps

Copy to:
[CG, MCB, CamPen, Calif]
[CO, HQCo, HQBn, MCB, CamPen, Calif] (Signed copy)

Reproduced from JAG Manual.

INFORMAL INVESTIGATIVE REPORT *

From: Captain X _____ Y. Z _____ , 000000/0185, USMC

To: Commanding Officer, Headquarters Battalion, Marine Corps Base, Camp Pendleton, California

Subj: (Same as subject of appointing order)

Encl: (1) Appointing order and modifications thereto (if any were issued)
    (2) [Summary of (or verbatim) sworn (or unsworn) testimony of _____
       _____ , (a witness)]
    (3) [Summary of (or verbatim) sworn (or unsworn) testimony of _____
       _____ , (a witness)]
    (4) Statement of _____ , signed by witness.
    (5) Description of _____ (knife found at scene of the accident)
    (6) Photograph of _____ depicting _____ .

Note: The testimony of each witness should be a separate enclosure to the investigative report. Enclosures containing testimony or statements of witnesses should precede enclosures in the form of other documents, descriptions of real evidence, photographs, et cetera. See 0608f.

Preliminary Statement

1. Paragraph 1 of the investigative report shall contain information in the form of a "preliminary statement". Its length may make it necessary to continue on into one or more additional paragraphs, depending upon the circumstances. See 0608b. The purpose of the preliminary statement is to inform the convening and reviewing authorities that the requirements as to procurement of evidence and any directives of the convening authority have been met. Where applicable, the investigating officer will set forth the name and organization of the Judge Advocate consulted. After setting forth the nature of the investigation, he will set forth the difficulties encountered in the investigation, if any; limited participation in the investigation by a member; or any other information necessary for a complete understanding of the case. A report of the investigating officer's itinerary is not necessary.

Findings of Fact

1. _____
2. _____
3. _____

*(Unless otherwise indicated, all references are to the JAG Manual.)
Reproduced from JAG Manual.

Note: See 0608c. The findings of fact constitute the investigating officer's description of the details of the events as derived from his evaluation of the evidence. The findings must be as specific as possible as to times, places, persons, and events. Each fact may be made a separate finding, or facts may be grouped into a narrative. It is for the investigating officer to determine the most effective presentation for a particular case. Each fact set forth must be supported by either the testimony of a witness, statement of the investigating officer, or documentary or real evidence appended to the investigative report as an enclosure thereto.

Opinions

1. _____
2. _____
3. _____

Note: See 0608d. An opinion is a logical inference or a conclusion drawn from the prior factual description of the events. For guidance as to the opinions normally required in specific situations, see chapters VIII and IX. Each opinion set forth must be supported by the findings of fact. Determination of line of duty and misconduct is properly stated as an opinion.

Recommendations

1. _____
2. _____
3. _____

Note: See 0608e. If the investigating officer recommends trial by court-martial, a charge sheet, signed and sworn to by the investigating officer, shall be prepared and submitted to the convening authority with the investigative report. See MCM 1969, par. 29. If a punitive letter of reprimand or admonition or a nonpunitive letter is recommended, a draft of the recommended letter will be prepared and forwarded with the investigative report.

(Signature of investigating officer)

Answers

to Discussion

and Self-Quizzes

Chapter I

1. YES. Jones cannot be tried again, even though the new evidence would now enable the trial counsel to prove his guilt. Article 44(a) of the Code states that "no person may, without his consent, be tried a second time for the same offense." The government had its day in court and is not entitled to another under these circumstances. A more thorough investigation perhaps would have developed this evidence.

2. YES. Article 32 of the Code states that "no charge or specification may be referred to a general court-martial for trial until a thorough and impartial investigation of all the matters set forth therein has been made." This pretrial investigation is not the type of investigation the preliminary inquiry officer conducts (see Chapter III), and it is considerably more formal. It is not the equivalent of a grand jury either, as it consists of only *one* commissioned officer. However, its purposes, which are three-fold, are essentially the same. These are:

    a. To inquire into the truth of the matters set forth in the charges and specifications;

    b. To make sure the charges and specifications are in proper form;

    c. To secure information upon which to recommend proper disposition of the case to the convening authority.

3. YES. Article 57(d) provides for the military equivalent of "bail." An accused who has been found guilty by a court-martial and awarded confinement may have the confinement deferred until such time as the sentence is ordered executed (ordered into effect). There is no posting of "bond" (i.e., money or other valuables to ensure the return of the alleged offender) in military law. This deferment is optional with the convening authority and may be withdrawn at any time.

Chapter II

1. Confinement or arrest would not be required. This is a minor offense and the first one for the accused. As he surrendered himself, it is unlikely that he will commit the same offense again in the immediate future. However, if his continued presence is desired pending investigation or if you believe he will be tempted to absent himself again, it would be appropriate to put him in restriction in lieu of arrest.

2. a. No. He is not resisting apprehension. Paragraph 174a of the MCM states that mere "words of remonstrance, argument or abuse" do not constitute the offense of resisting apprehension.
    b. Yes. In this case there has been a *submission to apprehension* and control has been exercised by *official acts or orders*.

3. Simply speaking, *apprehension* is the taking of a person into custody and is the equivalent of a civilian police officer arresting you for speeding. *Arrest* under military law is a form of pretrial restraint that may be utilized following an apprehension. It is a moral restraint directing a person to remain within certain specified limits.

4. No. The restriction was not lawfully imposed. The U.S. Court of Military Appeals, in discussing paragraph 20b of the MCM, (the old and new MCM wording is exactly the same in this regard) stated that "we find no provision of the Code or the Manual which could be construed as authorizing the imposition of restriction for the *only* purpose contended here." The accused "was not then under charges, under investigation, under suspicion, nor a material witness. . . . There was an intent here to deter the accused from possibly committing further offenses, but this accused was not 'already under charges.' In short, there was no authorized ground therefor and the 'restriction' was not lawfully imposed."

5. Yes. Although the issue has not been finally decided, it is apparent that the Court of Military Appeals considers "restriction" is encompassed within the mandate of Article 10. The revisers of the MCM recognized this trend also when they described restriction, arrest, and confinement as "restraints" creating a speedy trial issue once they have been imposed.

Chapter III

1. a. Yes. The statement made by Brown is admissible in evidence against him, and the seizure is lawful. It was a spontaneous response to a proper question asked by a person subject to the Code. It was the OOD's responsibility to check into the routine matter as to why the lights were not out in the compart-

ment. Nor was the accused's response relative to the question asked. In *United States* v. *Ballard,* 17 USCMA 96, 37 CMR 360 (1967), the Court of Military Appeals stated, in a similar case, that where the question asked was not designed or geared to elicit a statement of incrimination, the response was "the ban of a guilty conscience." The seizure of the billfold would be the product of a lawful search as it was the product of a search incident to a lawful apprehension.

b. YES. Doe should have been warned of his rights under Article 31(b). When you ask a question regarding an offense of a person suspected of such an offense, the suspect's reply is a statement, whether it consists of an oral declaration or a physical act. In either case, the reply is an affirmative, conscious act on the part of the individual affected by the demand and therefore within the purview of Article 31.

In this case, it is evident that the OOD suspected the accused of using another's I.D. card to obtain liquor, as he knew he had previously done so. He should have given the accused the Article 31(b) warning.

In *United States* v. *Nowling,* 9 USCMA 100, 25 CMR 362 (1958), an air policeman suspected the accused of having committed a pass offense. When the air policeman asked to see the accused's pass, the accused produced the pass of another. The court held that the accused's conduct in producing a pass upon request was the equivalent of a statement and was consequently inadmissible in the absence of a 31(b) warning.

2. YES. The Court of Military Appeals in the *Volante* case held that evidence unlawfully seized by an individual in a purely private capacity, and not acting as a disciplinary or law enforcement agent, can be admitted into evidence against an accused. Here, the sergeant acted in a private capacity and was motivated by personal monetary interests, and not for any government interest or the desire to enforce military law. It is noted that the sergeant was not in a law enforcement capacity when he made the search.

3. It would *not* be proper to conduct a command search of an enlisted man's quarters on the beach as the quarters are not located on a military installation nor are the quarters in "occupied territory or a foreign country." It would, of course, be permissible to order a search of the locker as it is property "used, occupied by, or in the possession of, a person subject to military law" and is situated in a military "vessel." Paragraph 310, *Military Law.*

In order to search the accused's home on the beach, the local police authorities should be notified. They may obtain a search warrant. It is evident in this case that there is probable cause for the search.

4. No. The Court of Military Appeals stated the search was the product of an irrational suspicion. The mere fact that a larceny had taken place in the accused's last unit did not, in itself, provide probable cause that the accused committed the offense or had possession of the stolen goods. The court amplified further by stating that as "no action as to the missing articles having been taken for five months, it is highly doubtful whether the accused was even considered as prime suspect."

5. Yes. The court held that the "search and seizure" was lawful. The court indicated that the provisions designed to regulate the search for, and seizure of, the subjects of crime have no application to the routine military inspection that is wholly unconnected with military law enforcement. Further, it stated: "Therefore, when a purely routine military inspection conducted without any reference to recently stolen property results in the disclosure of a recently reported stolen item lying in open view, no legal bar arises to the admission in evidence of such an item."

Chapter IV

1. No. In *United States* v. *Myhre,* 9 USCMA 32, 25 CMR 294 (1958), the Court of Military Appeals did not agree with the defense counsel and upheld the conviction of the accused for unauthorized absence. It stated as follows: "Reliance upon the noncriminal nature of a juvenile proceeding is misplaced in this case. We are dealing not with the nature of the New York proceedings against the accused but with the character of his absence. As the Manual points out, an accused who 'through his own fault' is absent from his place of duty is absent without leave. Physical inability to return from leave to the place of prescribed duty is a defense to a charge of unauthorized absence. . . . However, the inability must not be occasioned by the accused's own willful act. Here, before expiration of his leave, the accused voluntarily engaged in a prohibited act which resulted in his apprehension and detention by civilian authorities. It, therefore, was his own willful and deliberate conduct which led to the events which resulted in overstaying his leave. In other words, the accused's inability to return to his place of duty was the result of his own willful misconduct. Consequently, he is responsible for the period of time that he remained away from his station without authority."

2. Charge: Violation of the Uniform Code of Military Justice, Article 86

> Specification: In that Seaman Apprentice John M. Doakes, U.S. Naval Reserve, USS *Ball,* on active duty, did on or about 4 September 19___, without authority, absent himself from his unit, to wit: the USS *Ball,* located at Newport, Rhode Island, and did remain so absent until on or about 15 September 19___.

The fact that a naval reservist is on active duty must be alleged in order to show jurisdiction. It is not necessary to allege the exact time in this case, as "on or about" a certain day is sufficient to enable the accused to understand what he is charged with. See paragraph 409 of this publication.

3. a. Seaman Stack violated Article 86(1) of the Code (absence from his appointed place of duty) rather than 92(2) of the Code.

It is true that the first element of 86(1) is an "order," in that "a certain authority appointed a certain time and place of duty for the accused." The reason why this "violation of an order" is charged under Article 86 can be found in paragraph 165 of the MCM wherein it states that Article 86 covers *"every case not elsewhere provided for in which any member of the armed forces is through his own fault not at the place where he is required to be at a prescribed time."* (Emphasis supplied.) Therefore, as the essential part of the offense is an unauthorized absence it should be charged under Article 86.

b. No.   Stack does not have a valid defense as it was foreseeable that his friend, who had been drinking, could oversleep.

c. CHARGE: Violation of the Uniform Code of Military Justice, Article 86

> SPECIFICATION: In that Seaman Joseph B. Stack, U.S. Navy, USS *Pan*, did on board said ship, at or about 0745 on 10 April 19___, without authority, fail to go at the time prescribed to his appointed place of duty, to wit: the quarterdeck watch at the forward gangway.

4. YES.   In *United States* v. *Anderson*, 17 USCMA 588, 38 CMR 386 (1968), the Court of Military Appeals determined that in November of 1964 the United States was at war in Vietnam. It sustained the conviction of the accused for unauthorized absence.

The Court based its decision on the Gulf of Tonkin resolution passed by the U.S. Congress on 10 August 1964. "The resolution is clearly more than a reminder of the existence of obligations under treaties relating to Southeast Asia. It describes the attack on United States Naval Forces in Tonkin Gulf as a violation of international law, and it specifically commits the United States 'to take all necessary steps,' including the use of armed force, to repel aggression and to assure peace in Southeast Asia. It contemplates use of the armed forces for an uncertain period of time. Thus, it directs that its provisions remain in force until either the President declares that 'the peace and security of the area' are assured, or Congress terminates them earlier by 'concurrent resolution.' The language of the resolution clearly indicates that Congress also recognized and declared, as a legislative decision, that the Gulf of Tonkin attack precipitated a state of armed conflict between the United States and North Vietnam."

5. a. It is obvious that Seaman Jones has violated Article 86, unauthorized absence. He has also violated Article 87. If the facts as recited can be proven, the accused may be charged with missing movement through design.

The proof required to convict of this offense is:

(1) That the accused was required in the course of duty to move with a ship, aircraft or unit;

(2) That the accused knew or had reasonable cause to know of the prospective movement of the ship, aircraft or unit;

(3) That, at the time and place alleged, the accused missed the movement of the ship, aircraft or unit; and

(4) That the accused missed the movement through design, as alleged.

In this case, if the facts are in dispute, there could be two lesser included offenses—unauthorized absence or missing movement through neglect.

b. Seaman Roe has violated Article 86, unauthorized absence. He also has violated Article 87, missing movement through neglect. Paragraph 166 of the MCM discusses this offense as follows. The "omission by a person to take such measures as are appropriate under the circumstances to assure that he will be present with his ship, aircraft or unit at the time of a scheduled movement, or his doing of some act without giving attention to its probable consequences in connection with the prospective movement, such as a departure from the vicinity of the prospective movement to such a distance as would make it likely that he could not return in time for the movement."

In this case, it is apparent that Seaman Roe did not exercise due diligence to assure that he would be present with his ship when it left Norfolk.

c. Neither Jones nor Roe would have "missed movement" although they would be guilty of unauthorized absence. Paragraph 166 of the MCM, in discussing the word "movement" states it does not include "minor changes in location of ships, aircraft, or units, as when a ship is shifted from one berth to another in the same shipyard or harbor. . . ."

The BUPERS Manual requires page 13 entries be made following any unauthorized absence. It further states that in "addition, the entry 'Missed sailing of this vessel from (place of sailing) on (date) en route to (destination)' shall be made in the absentee's service record. Where appropriate, the entry shall include details showing that the absentee had knowledge of the time scheduled for the movement and of either the destination or of the fact that the movement was substantial as distinguished from a mere shifting of berths in the same harbor or other minor movement."

Chapter V

1. The case would have been reversed and sent back for a retrial or it would have been dismissed. *United States* v. *O'Hara* stated that instructions "provide the court-martial with the legal framework within which it determines the accused's guilt or innocence." Paragraph 73a of the MCM requires the presiding officer to give instructions on each affirmative defense reasonably in issue. An affirmative defense is one wherein the accused admits he committed the act but denies he is guilty. In this case, the accused claimed he was not guilty because he lacked "criminal intent." His defense was a good one; however, the court apparently did not believe his story. This case also brings out the point that an act may originally be committed with no criminal intent but later the accused may develop such an intent to accompany the act—and hence be guilty of larceny or wrongful appropriation.

2. No. Jones should be charged with wrongful appropriation and not larceny. Paragraph 200a(6) of the MCM states as follows:

An intention to pay for the property stolen or otherwise to replace it with an equivalent is not a defense, even though such an intention existed at the time of the theft, and, once a larceny is committed, a return of the property or payment for it is no defense. If, however, the accused takes money or a negotiable instrument having no special value above its face value, with the intent to return an equivalent amount of money, the offense of larceny is not committed although wrongful appropriation . . . may be.

In essence what this says is that if Jones had taken Roe's watch and intended to give him its value in money or another item, this would still constitute larceny. But since he took money for money, this would only be a wrongful appropriation, as he was really intending to return the same item—money.

The reader should distinguish this case and the "friendly borrowing case" in the reading assignment. In the friendly borrowing case, the accused, if believed, would have no criminal intent. Paragraph 504, *Military Law.*

3. a. Jones may be charged with disobeying a petty officer in violation of Article 91 of the Code. Paragraph 170c of the MCM states that an order from a petty officer in the execution of his office may be inferred to be a lawful order.

The proof required to convict an accused of this offense is as follows: (a) that the accused enlisted person or warrant officer received a certain lawful order from a certain warrant officer, noncommissioned officer, or petty officer, as alleged; (b) that at the time the warrant officer, noncommissioned officer, or petty officer was the superior of the accused; (c) that the accused at the time knew that the warrant officer, noncommissioned officer, or petty officer, was his superior; and (d) that the accused willfully disobeyed the order.

b. Jones should be charged with a violation of Article 92(3) of the Code (dereliction in the performance of duties). Paragraph 171c of the MCM states that a person "is derelict in the performance of his duties when he willfully or negligently fails to perform them, or when he performs them in a culpably inefficient manner."

The proof required to convict an accused of this offense is as follows: (a) that the accused had certain prescribed duties; and (b) that he was derelict in the performance of those duties.

c. Jones has violated Article 92(2) of the Code, by violating his ship's instructions. Ship's instructions, generally signed by the commanding officer, are his order.

The proof required to convict an accused of this offense is as follows: (a) that a certain lawful order was issued by a member of the armed forces; (b) that the accused had knowledge of the order; (c) that it was the duty of the accused to obey the order; and (d) that the accused failed to obey the order.

d. Jones has violated Article 92(1) of the Code even though he was without knowledge of the provision of Navy Regulations regarding liquor on board a ship. Paragraph 171 of the MCM states that Article 92(1) "contains no requirement that any kind of knowledge be either alleged or proved in a prosecution thereunder for violating or failing to obey a general order or regulation."

The proof required to convict an accused of this offense is as follows: (a) that there was a certain general order or regulation; (b) that the accused had a duty to obey it; and (c) that the accused violated or failed to obey the order or regulation.

e. Jones has violated Article 90(2) of the Code. The order was directed to him personally. Paragraph 169b of the MCM states the following: "As long as it is understandable, the form of an order is immaterial, as is the method by which it is transmitted to the accused, but the communication must amount to an order, and the accused must know that it is from his superior commissioned officer, that is, a commissioned officer who is authorized to give the order whether he is superior in rank to the accused or not."

Smith was, in the example, merely the mode of communication used by Lieutenant Zeal to give Jones his personal order.

The proof required to convict an accused of this offense is as follows: (a) that the accused received a certain lawful command from a commissioned officer, as alleged; (b) that this officer was the superior officer of the accused; (c) that the accused willfully disobeyed the command; and (d) that the accused at the time knew the officer was his superior commissioned officer.

f. Jones has violated Article 89 of the Code in that he was disrespectful towards a superior commissioned officer.

Paragraph 168 of the MCM states that it "is not essential that the disrespectful behavior be in the presence of the superior, but in general it is considered objectionable to hold one accountable under this article for what was said or done by him in a purely private conversation. . . . Disrespect by words may be conveyed by opprobrious epithets or other contemptuous or denunciatory language. Disrespect by acts may be exhibited in a variety of modes—as neglecting the customary salute, by a marked disdain, indifference, insolence, impertinence, undue familiarity, or other rudeness in the presence of the superior officer."

See paragraph 168 for a discussion of the proof required to convict an accused of such an offense.

g. Jones has *not* violated Article 91(3) of the Code, which states that any enlisted member who "treats with contempt or is disrespectful in language or deportment toward a warrant officer, noncommissioned officer, or petty officer while that officer is in the execution of his office" violates this provision.

Paragraph 170d of the MCM states that the word "toward" read in connection with the phrase "while that officer is in the execution of his office" limits the application of this part of the article to behavior and language within the sight or hearing of the warrant officer, noncommissioned officer, or petty officer concerned.

h. Seaman Recruit Jones has violated Article 134 of the Code—the General Article. This article applies to "all disorders and neglects to the prejudice of good order and discipline in the armed forces, all conduct of a nature to bring discredit upon the armed forces, and crimes and offenses not capital. . . ."

Appendix 6c of the MCM contains the forms of specifications for these two offenses.

i. No. Jones is wrong. Failure to obey the orders of one not a superior is chargeable under Article 92(2) of the Code. Paragraph 171b of the MCM states that examples "of orders which a person might have a duty to obey, even though issued by one not a superior, are lawful orders of a sentinel or of members of the armed forces police" (or shore patrol).

Chapter VI

1. No. Section 0101c of the JAG Manual states that "commanding officers and officers in charge are authorized and expected to use nonpunitive measures, including administrative withholding of privileges *not extending to deprivation of normal liberty,* in furthering the efficiency of their commands." Of course, a man who has been assigned a task which he has failed to complete may be required to complete it during liberty hours. Also, a person who requires "extra instructions" can be given that instruction after working hours. (See paragraph 601, *Military Law.*)

2. Your commanding officer should be advised of the following: he cannot reduce more than one pay grade at Mast (0101b(7), JAG Manual); he must apportion the extra duties and restriction (paragraph 131d, MCM) or make it run concurrently; he can only forfeit not more than one-half of one month's pay although he may do it for two months; and that the admonishment is a permissible additional punishment.

Therefore, he should be informed that he can: reduce Doe to pay grade E–3; give Doe consecutively 25 days' extra duties and 26 days' restriction or concurrently 45 days' extra duties and 45 days' restriction; forfeit one-half pay per month for two months (at his reduced pay grade rate) and admonish him.

3. Section 0101e(2) of the JAG Manual has your solution. The prior punishment of restriction still has 20 days to run and *must* be completed before the correctional custody even begins to run. However, the correctional custody would not have to run until the ship reached port in ten more days for the JAG Manual provides that the commanding officer may, "when the exigencies of the service require, defer execution of correctional custody and confinement on bread and water for a reasonable period of time, not to exceed 15 days, after imposition." Seaman Apprentice Smith could therefore serve a full 30 days correctional custody when the ship returns to Norfolk, Virginia.

4. The JAG Manual provides that, as a policy matter, the commanding officer of the ship should impose nonjudicial punishment on members of a unit attached to his ship "for duty therein." The commanding officer and the squadron commanding officer would have concurrent jurisdiction. Section 0101b(3) of the JAG Manual states that this policy is not applicable where an organized unit is embarked for transportation only. See paragraph 1401, Navy Regulations.

Chapter VII

1. Although the answer is not clear, it is the author's opinion that these two punishments must be apportioned, as they are both in the nature of deprivation of liberty. Paragraph 16b, MCM, requires apportionment of restriction and confinement as they are both forms of "deprivation of liberty." Paragraph 127c

(2), MCM, reiterates this statement, but also contains another interesting statement as follows:

> . . . if the authorized punishment for an offense is confinement at hard labor for one month and forfeiture of two-thirds of one month's pay the court may, for example, by substitution adjudge hard labor without confinement for 15 days (1½ for 1), restriction to limits for 40 days (2 for 1), and forfeiture of two-thirds pay for one month.

However, this sentence did not relate specifically to summary courts and may not be applicable. The author bases his conclusion on a comparison between extra duties awarded by nonjudicial punishment and hard labor without confinement awarded by a court. Both are defined almost precisely the same in the MCM and the JAG Manual and they are, in effect, the same punishment. However, the commanding officer at Mast *must* apportion extra duties and restriction as they are "in the nature of deprivation of liberty." Paragraph 131*d*, MCM.

2. Although there are other factors that should be considered in determining whether an accused should be punished at nonjudicial punishment or referred to a summary court-martial, the commanding officer should be informed that a summary court-martial may reduce an enlisted man from E–4 to E–1 whereas at nonjudicial punishment, the accused can be reduced only one pay grade. See Chapter I of the JAG Manual.

3. Admittedly, the determination must be subjective to a certain extent. It is unquestionable that a summary court-martial is the more serious of the two. It constitutes a previous conviction which may warrant the imposition of a bad conduct discharge. See Section B of paragraph 127*c*, MCM. It is also a more formal proceeding and is one of the three types of courts-martial.

However, the MCM itself distinguishes between the two. Paragraph 129*b* of the MCM states that punishments "under Article 15 are primarily *corrective* in nature," whereas paragraph 79 of the MCM states that summary courts are applicable to offenses that are "*relatively* minor." A logical interpretation would be that nonjudicial punishment should be awarded as a means of educating military personnel as to their responsibilities in our military society. However, an offense which reflects a continued behavior or disciplinary problem and requires punishment beyond mere correction would generally warrant referral to a summary court.

4. You must find the accused not guilty of the absence which occurred during the period he was detained and subsequently acquitted by civilian authorities. If you believe him guilty (beyond a reasonable doubt) of the second offense, you may find him guilty of that offense. (See Chapter IV of this book.)

5. The summary court-martial, in this case, may award one of each:

a. Reduction one pay grade;

b. Confinement at hard labor for one month (or hard labor without confinement for 45 days, or restriction for 60 days, or an apportionment of confinement, hard labor without confinement and restriction);

c. Admonition or reprimand;

d. Forfeiture of two-thirds of one month's pay (or a fine or detention of two-thirds of one month's pay).

Of course, the nature and amount of punishment to be awarded in each case depends upon the individual and unique facts present in any particular court-martial. That is why there are those cases in which no punishment may be an appropriate sentence.

Chapter VIII

1. No. Article 27(c)(3) states that:

> . . . if the trial counsel is a judge advocate, or a law specialist or a member of the bar of a federal court or the highest court of a state, the defense counsel detailed by the convening authority must be one of the foregoing.

Paragraph 6c adds that if the trial counsel is qualified to act as counsel before a general court-martial, the defense counsel must be so qualified. Therefore, while there is a disparity in the qualifications of counsel in this case, there is no violation of the specific provisions of the Code or MCM.

In *United States* v. *Bartholomew,* 1 USCMA 341, 3 CMR 41 (1952), there was such a disparity. In discussing a similar provision in the Articles of War (the predecessor to the 1951 Code), the Court of Military Appeals found a violation of the spirit and not the letter of the law and looked deeper to see how well the counsel performed. The defense counsel was "highly effective" and, therefore, the court found that while there might have been error, there was no prejudicial error in this particular case and under these facts.

However, under the 1968 changes to the Code which went into effect in August of 1969, such detailing would result in the accused requesting that a certified military lawyer defend him, as he must be informed of this right to a qualified defense counsel both before and during the trial.

2. The commanding officer, even though he can excuse personnel from serving in one or more cases without relieving them, cannot, *once a court is assembled,* excuse a member except for physical disability or for good cause. Only critical situations, such as emergency leave or military exigencies, justify the removal of a member once the court has been assembled. The member may, of course, be challenged off the court peremptorily. On its face, it would not appear that supervising the on-loading of foodstuffs is the type of "critical situation" warranting the excusal of Ensign Jones by the convening authority. If the court had not assembled, he could have been excused orally and no "good cause" would have been required.

3. Roe should be returned to the Long Beach police for civilian trial, as the military has no jurisdiction to try him. Although Article 5 of the Code presently

states that the Code "applies in all places," the U.S. Supreme Court ruled in *O'Callahan* v. *Parker* that military law does *not* apply in a case such as Roe's.

4. a. The maximum punishment that may be adjudged includes:
1. A bad conduct discharge;
2. Confinement at hard labor for six months;
3. Forfeiture of two-thirds pay per month for six months;
4. Reduction to E–1.
Section B of paragraph 127*c* of the MCM states:

. . . if an accused is found guilty of two or more offenses for none of which dishonorable or bad-conduct discharge is authorized, the fact that the authorized confinement without substitution for these offenses is six months or more will, in addition, authorize bad conduct discharge. . . .

It states further:

. . . if an enlisted member of other than the lowest enlisted grade is convicted by a court-martial, the court may, in its discretion, adjudge reduction to any inferior grade in addition to the punishments otherwise authorized.

b. Yes. Paragraph 804 states that a bad conduct discharge may not be adjudged by a special court-martial unless a military judge is detailed to the court except when physical conditions or military exigencies prevent such detailing.
c. Yes. A certified military lawyer must be detailed to represent the accused in a case where a bad conduct discharge may be adjudged.

5. a. In *United States* v. *Beeker,* 18 USCMA 563, 40 CMR 275 (1969), the Court of Military Appeals determined the following:
1. No. The military authorities have no jurisdiction to try the accused for the importation of the marijuana and its concealment. These offenses are triable by the federal courts. (Under military law they are triable under Article 134 of the Code.) The court stated further that there were no circumstances surrounding the commission of the offenses to relate them specially to the military.
2. Yes. The military authorities have jurisdiction to try a serviceman for the possession of marijuana and narcotics either on or off the base as such possession has a special military significance warranting military jurisdiction.
3. and 4. Yes. The military authorities have jurisdiction to try the accused for the wrongful use of the marijuana as "use of marijuana and narcotics by military persons on or off a military base has special military significance." In *United States* v. *Williams,* 8 USCMA 325, 24 CMR 135 (1967), the court had previously noted that the use of these substances had "disastrous effects . . . on the health, morale, and fitness for duty of persons in the armed forces."
b. No. There is no military jurisdiction in this case. In *United States* v.

Riehle, 18 USCMA 603, 40 CMR 315 (1969), the Court of Military Appeals stated that it "is apparent that the offense of larceny was committed against the civilian community and, as a consequence, the matter was triable in the courts of the State of California. . . . The only possible 'service connection,' as reflected by the convening authority's summary, that might be found is the subsequent action of the accused in bringing the stolen property on base. While it might be contended that his action compromised 'the security of a military post' . . . we do not believe that in this case it is sufficient to clothe the court-martial with jurisdiction to try the accused for the offense of larceny."

c. YES. The military authorities have jurisdiction. In *United States* v. *Paxiao,* 18 USCMA 608, 40 CMR 320 (1969), the Court of Military Appeals stated that while "it is apparent that the crime was committed against a civilian and that civilian property was involved, the offense occurred on the Presidio of San Francisco, a military reservation. Under these circumstances, we are constrained to hold that since the crime directly affected 'the security of a military post' " (*O'Callahan* v. *Parker,* 395 US 274) "there is a sufficient basis to sustain military jurisdiction."

d. The military authorities have jurisdiction over the two bad checks cashed in the exchange but not over the bad check cashed at the local civilian grocery store. The Court of Military Appeals in *United States* v. *Williams,* 18 USCMA 605, 40 CMR 317 (1969) stated that as the offense involving the two bad checks took place on base and were cashed by a "governmental agency," these offenses were service connected. However, the grocery check was cashed in the civilian community, a civilian was victimized, and the offense was triable in the courts of North Carolina. The court stated that "under the rationale of *O'Callahan* v. *Parker* the offense was not service connected."

e. No. The Court of Military Appeals in *United States* v. *Castro,* 18 USCMA 598, 40 CMR 310 (1969) stated that while it was true that accused's possession of the weapon only became known after he entered the military hospital, his presence was not voluntary. The court stated that "we have no doubt that the need to maintain 'the security of a military post' . . . gives to the Congress of the United States the right to proscribe the charged misconduct when it occurs within the confines of a military establishment. Under the circumstances of this case, however, we do not believe that the offense is properly chargeable under the Uniform Code. Since it is an offense cognizable in the courts of the State of Washington, it should be tried there."

Chapter IX

1. YES. The Court of Military Appeals in *United States* v. *Brooks,* 12 USCMA 423, 31 CMR 9 (1961), stated as follows in reversing the case: "It has long been settled that an accused's pre-trial reliance upon his rights under" Article 31 of the Code "when interrogated concerning an offense of which he is suspected, may not be paraded before a court-martial in order that his guilt may be inferred from his refusal to comment on the charges against him."

2. No. The Court of Military Appeals stated in *United States* v. *McCants*, 10 USCMA 346, 27 CMR 420 (1959), that "we, of course, look with disfavor on the procedure employed by trial counsel in the instant case. While no fixed rule can be employed to fit all cases, unless it is absolutely necessary to a proper disclosure of the truth, no certified counsel should pit his credibility against that of other witnesses." The court did not reverse the case because it concluded that as the defense did not object and the trial counsel's testimony was in addition to similar testimony presented, the accused was not unduly prejudiced.

3. Article 35 of the Code states as follows: "In time of peace no person may, against his objection, be brought to trial or be required to participate by himself or counsel in a session called by the military judge . . . (article 39(a)), in a general court-martial case, within a period of five days after the service of charges upon him, or in a special court-martial within a period of three days after the service of the charges upon him." A failure to perform this function would give the defense grounds for a postponement (continuance) of the trial.

4. A pretrial agreement is a contractual type of agreement between the accused, his counsel, and the convening authority. Generally, the accused agrees to plead guilty if the convening authority agrees to approve only certain types or amounts of punishment. For example, Seaman Jones is charged with missing movement through neglect in violation of Article 87 of the Code. His case is forwarded to a special court-martial, which can award him a bad conduct discharge, six months' confinement at hard labor, the forfeiture of two-thirds pay per month for six months and reduction to pay grade E-1. The accused agrees to plead guilty to this charge if the convening authority will agree, upon reviewing the case, that he will not approve a BCD. The case goes to trial and Jones receives the maximum. The remainder of the sentence may be approved by the convening authority, but the BCD may not. The request must originate with the defense. The members of the court *cannot* be informed as to the existence of such an arrangement.

Paragraph 904 of this book and Chapter I of the JAG Manual contain further information on pretrial agreements. Such agreements are advantageous to the accused and the government. They guarantee the accused only so much punishment if he pleads guilty and it saves the government the time and expense of proving his guilt. *However, as a member, do not assume that because an accused pleads guilty there is a pretrial agreement.* There is no pretrial agreement in the great majority of cases.

5. Paragraph 17 of the "Duties Prior To Trial" section states that if "the accused has made a confession or admission concerning any of the offenses charged, determine the circumstances surrounding such confession or admission." It then refers to paragraph 140 of the MCM which states that "it is a general rule that a confession or admission of the accused cannot be considered as evidence against him on the question of guilt or innocence unless independent evidence, either direct or circumstantial, has been introduced which corroborates the essential facts admitted sufficiently to justify an inference of their truth."

Chapter X

1. Yes. The MCM is explicit in this area and specifically states that "a person who by his certificate has attested or otherwise authenticated an official record introduced in evidence by the prosecution, or who has authenticated any writing so introduced, is a witness for the prosecution, *even if he does not testify as a witness.*" (Emphasis supplied.) Consequently, you would be ineligible to sit any longer and the challenge must be sustained. *United States* v. *Mansell,* 8 USCMA 153, 23 CMR 377 (1957) is the case from which this question was taken.

2. Yes. Paragraph 53*d* of the MCM states as follows: "No member of a general or special court-martial shall have access to or use in any open or closed session the Manual for Courts-Martial, reports of decided cases, or any other reference material, except that the president of a special court-martial without a military judge may use these publications or materials in open session."

3. No. It is extremely unfair to the accused. If you don't believe the accused has been proven guilty, vote to acquit. If you believe, to a moral certainty, that he is guilty, vote to convict. Article 37 of the Code states that "no person subject to this chapter may attempt to coerce or, by any unauthorized means, influence the action of a court-martial or any other military tribunal *or any member thereof,* in reaching the findings or sentence in any case. . . ."

4. If the defense submits a recommendation for clemency, you may sign it if you feel so inclined.

Paragraph 77*a* of the MCM states that "mitigating circumstances which could not be taken into consideration in determining the sentence may be the basis of a recommendation for clemency by the military judge who adjudged the sentence or by individual members of the court. The recommendation should represent the free and voluntary expression of the individuals who join therein. It should be specific as to the amount and character of the clemency recommended and as to the reasons for the recommendation."

It is attached to the record and is considered by reviewing authorities when they review the sentence awarded by the court.

Chapter XI

1. The president's ruling was correct. The unauthorized absence offense may be utilized to prove the offense charged. It is relevant, as proof of the unauthorized absence goes directly to prove one of the elements of the offense: that "at the time and place alleged, the accused missed the movement of the ship." (Paragraph 1105, *Military Law.*)

Assume that the argument had been made that the unauthorized absence constitutes evidence of other offenses and that, therefore, it is inadmissible on that ground. There is no question that such evidence is admissible as it "has substantial value as tending to prove something other than" the criminal disposition of the accused (in this case, an essential element). Paragraph 138*g*, MCM.

2. The president's ruling was correct. It is not essential that the trial counsel show that the documents are true. In this chapter and in paragraph 144*b* of the MCM, it states that an official record is not "subject to objection on the ground that it is secondary evidence." The court members can decide whether they believe the entry, just as they determine which witnesses to believe. (Paragraph 1106, *Military Law*.)

3. The president's ruling was incorrect. The defense counsel should have been permitted to present evidence as to what the accused was doing on 1 January 19___ if it would be relevant. As stated in paragraph 1105 of this chapter, "evidence is relevant when the fact which it tends to prove is part of any issue in the case." Another of the elements of missing movement through design is that "the accused missed the movement through design."

4. The president's ruling was correct. The evidence was properly admitted. Missing movement through design is a specific intent crime similar to larceny in this regard. Paragraph 505 of this publication, in discussing defenses to larceny and wrongful appropriation, states as follows:

> *Voluntary Intoxication:* This is a defense if the court believes that the accused lacked the mental capacity to entertain the required specific intent.

5. The president's ruling was incorrect. As discussed in paragraph 1104, real evidence "is any physical object, such as a stolen watch, jewelry, or a weapon used in an assault." It is not necessary to authenticate by *chain of custody* so long as a piece of real evidence can be identified. Here, the witness sufficiently identified the billfold. It is relevant evidence as it tends to prove that the accused did not *intend* to miss the movement of the ship.

Chapter XII

1. You can recommend that the convening authority return the record to the court for reconsideration of the ruling. The convening authority will hear both the defense and prosecution's viewpoint on this issue. If he agrees with the prosecution, he can return it to the court for reconsideration. Paragraph 67*f* of the MCM states that "to the extent that the matter in disagreement relates solely to a question of law, as, for example, whether the charges allege an offense

cognizable by a court-martial," the presiding officer "will accede to the view of the convening authority."

2. As the result of *United States* v. *Chancelor* and similar cases, paragraph 70*b* of the MCM was revised to state that, among other matters, the accused must be informed of the "elements of the offense to which the plea of guilty relates." (Paragraph 1215, *Military Law.*)

3. a. No. Only a military judge may hear a case without members and determine an appropriate sentence. (Paragraph 1204, *Military Law.*)

b. No. Only a military judge may hold an Article 39(a) session. (Paragraph 1203, *Military Law.*)

c. No. Court members need only be given the oath once under the convening order that detailed them. (Paragraph 1209, *Military Law.*) Of course, this oath would be given the first time the court meets under a new convening order.

d. No. The president of a special court-martial without a military judge cannot rule alone upon challenges for cause. All members, except the challenged member, who will be excused, must vote. (Paragraph 1210, *Military Law.*) In a court with a military judge, the judge determines all challenges.

e. No. If a president is presiding, he conducts this hearing in the presence of the other members. If a military judge is detailed, he would hold the hearing out of the presence of the members. (Paragraph 1215, *Military Law.*)

f. Yes. Regardless of whether the president or the military judge is presiding, the president is *always* a member.

g. No. A military judge detailed to a court with members present to hear a case is not a member. The determination of guilt or innocence and the appropriate sentence to be awarded are matters that the members decide in closed session.

Chapter XIII

1. The Table of Maximum Punishments provides for one month's confinement at hard labor for breaking restriction and one month's confinement at hard labor for unauthorized absence for not more than three days. However, paragraph 76*a*(5) of the MCM states that the "general rule is that offenses are not separate unless each requires proof of an element not required to prove the other." Therefore, the maximum confinement at hard labor that could be awarded is one month because "absence without leave does not require proof of any element" not also required to prove the breaking of restriction.

2. No. Unless the defense makes a statement such as "this man has never been in trouble before," which would justify your placing these nonjudicial punishments into evidence as rebuttal, you cannot do so. Paragraph 75*d* only

permits the court members to be informed of such matters if a military judge is presiding.

3. a. No. Paragraph 126*g* of the MCM states that restriction "will not be adjudged in excess of two months. . . ."

b. No. Paragraph 126*k* states that "hard labor without confinement will not be adjudged in excess of three months."

4. No. Paragraph 75*b*(2) of the MCM states that "no proceeding in which an accused has been found guilty by a court-martial upon any charge or specification shall, as to that charge or specification, be admissible as a previous conviction until the finding of guilty has become final after review of the case has been fully completed."

5. No. The rights of a serviceman to obtain a military lawyer to defend him free of charge are broader than civilians would generally have in a state court. The civilian is seldom offered a free attorney if he appears before a justice of the peace or other lower state court. Yet, an accused can refuse nonjudicial punishment unless he is attached to or embarked on a ship. His case could next be forwarded to a summary court, where he could refuse that court-martial. If forwarded to a non-BCD special court, he must be afforded a military lawyer unless physical conditions or military exigencies preclude his obtaining one. Therefore, although he may be subjected to harsher punishments if convicted, a military man does have the right to a military lawyer in all but the most unusual cases.

6. The findings could be announced as follows:

Of the specification of the Charge: Guilty except the word "steal," substituting therefor the words "wrongfully appropriate"; of the excepted word, not guilty, of the substituted words, guilty.
Of the Charge: Guilty.

Chapter XIV

1. An informal board of investigation would probably be inappropriate in this case. As a practical matter, the decision as to the type of investigation to be held in this event will probably be made by the next senior officer in either the ship's administrative or operational chain of command. In this case, there was a substantial loss of life and there may be significant international or legal consequences involved—therefore either a court of inquiry or a formal board of investigation would be appointed. See section 0205, JAG Manual.

2. Paragraph 1404 of this publication states:

Generally, there are two occasions when a person is designated a party before a fact-finding body:

1. *When the person's conduct or performance of duty is "subject to inquiry."* This would occur when the person is involved in the incident under investigation in such a way that disciplinary action may follow, that his rights or privileges may be adversely affected, or that his personal reputation or professional standing may be jeopardized.

2. *When the person has a "direct interest" in the subject of inquiry.* This occurs (1) when the findings, opinions, or recommendations of the fact-finding body may, in view of his relation to the incident or circumstances under investigation, reflect questionable or unsatisfactory conduct or performance of duty, or (2) when the findings, opinions, or recommendations may relate to a matter over which the person has a duty or right to exercise official control. Paragraph 0302 of the JAG Manual discusses when parties are designated and who may designate them.

3. Section 0605 of the JAG Manual states that an informal investigating officer may obtain "relevant information from the witnesses by informal personal interview, correspondence, telephone inquiry, or other means. . . ." Section 0606e of the JAG Manual requires such statements to be certified to be either an accurate summary or the verbatim transcript of oral statements made by them.

Chapter XV

1. a. No. Smith's injuries were sustained in the line of duty and were not due to his own misconduct. Although the general rule is that voluntary participation in a fight is the result of misconduct, injury incurred by a serviceman acting in self-defense is not the result of his misconduct.

b. No. Brown's injuries were sustained in the line of duty and were not due to his own misconduct. This case exemplifies two more exceptions to the general rule. Injuries incurred by a person after he has completely abandoned a fight are not the result of his own misconduct. Brown, when he abandoned the fight, terminated his own misconduct.

However, even if Brown had continued the fist fight, this would not be the result of his own misconduct. This is because in a fist fight a person could reasonably expect to be injured by a fist or by falling, but could not reasonably expect to be stabbed.

2. a. YES. Section 0903 of the JAG Manual lists facts which are important and should be covered in every investigation of a vehicle accident.

b. No. The injuries were not due to his own misconduct and were incurred in the line of duty. The act of falling asleep, in itself, does not constitute gross negligence. To constitute gross negligence, there must have been such prior warning of the likelihood of sleep that continuing to drive would constitute a reckless disregard of the consequences. There must be an appreciation of the danger of falling asleep, or circumstances which would cause a reasonable, prudent person to appreciate it in order to constitute misconduct.

3. No. Roe's injuries were due to his own misconduct and were not incurred in the line of duty. Section 0809 of the JAG Manual states that an injury incurred as the proximate result of prior and specific voluntary intoxication is incurred as the result of misconduct. In order for intoxication alone to be the basis for a determination of misconduct respecting a related injury, there must be a clear showing that the person's physical or mental faculties were impaired due to intoxication at the time of the injury, the extent of the impairment, and that the impairment was a proximate cause of the injury. The intoxication (impairment) may be due to alcohol, drug or comparable origin.

4. Yes. Section 2404 of the JAG Manual requires an investigation whenever "medical care is furnished by the Department of the Navy, either in kind without reimbursement or by reimbursing another department, agency, private facility, or individual, under circumstances which may give rise to a claim against a third person, an investigation shall be conducted in the manner and form prescribed in Chapter XX" of the JAG Manual. Therefore, even though Brown was not at fault, the government may have a claim against the third party who injured him in order to reimburse them for their medical expenses. Consequently, an investigation is required.

Glossary

This glossary is designed to facilitate the reading of this book by defining those words and abbreviations that are used frequently in military law.

A

Accused—one who is charged with an offense under the Code.

Accuser—any person who signs and swears to charges, any person who directs that charges nominally be signed and sworn to by another, and any other person who has an interest other than an official interest in the prosecution of an accused.

Acquitted—the legal and formal certification of the innocence of a person who has been charged with a crime; a finding of not guilty or its equivalent.

Active Duty—the status of being in the active federal service of any of the armed forces under a competent appointment or enlistment or pursuant to a competent muster, order, call, or induction.

Additional Charges—new and separate charges preferred against the same accused while prior charges are still pending.

Admission—a self-incriminatory statement falling short of an acknowledgment of guilt. See *Confession*.

Affidavit—a statement or declaration reduced to writing and confirmed by the party making it by an oath taken before a person who has authority to administer the oath.

Aggravation—any circumstances attending the commission of an offense which increase the enormity or seriousness of the crime.

Alibi—a defense that the accused could not have committed the offense alleged because he was somewhere else when the crime was committed.

Allegation—the assertion, declaration, or statement of a party of what he expects to prove.

Allege—to state in a specification; in military law, an assertion which its maker proposes to support with evidence.

Appeal—a complaint to a superior court of an injustice done or error committed by an inferior court, whose judgment or decision the court above is called upon to correct or reverse.

Appellant—the party who appeals the decision of one court to another court. For example, the party who appeals from a decision of a Court of Military Review to the U.S. Court of Military Appeals would be the appellant.

Appellate Review—review of the records of cases tried by courts-martial. Reviewing authorities include the convening authority, the supervisory authority, the Courts of Military Review, and the U.S. Court of Military Appeals. The level to which a case proceeds for review is prescribed by the Code and the MCM.

Appellee—the party against whom an appeal is taken; in other words, the party who has an interest adverse to setting aside or reversing the judgment.

Apprehension—the taking of a person into custody. This is generally accomplished by informing the person that he is being taken into custody or being apprehended. The suspect or accused must understand that the person apprehending him intends to detain him.

Area Coordinator—the Naval District Commandant in a naval district or the appropriate fleet commander-in-chief for overseas (non-naval district) activities. For mobile units, the area coordinator is the one most accessible to the mobile unit at the time of forwarding of a record of trial or an appeal from nonjudicial punishment.

Arraignment—this brief court-martial procedure consists of: (1) the distribution of copies of the charges and specifications to the members; (2) the reading of the charges and specifications or their waiver; (3) the statement by the trial counsel of the name of the accuser and the convening authority and the fact that the charges have been properly sworn to before an officer authorized to administer oaths; (4) the stating of the day the charges were served on the accused; and (5) the asking of the accused how he pleads.

Arrest—a moral and legal pretrial restraint of a person. It is a greater restraint of freedom of movement than restriction in lieu of arrest. A person in arrest cannot be required to perform his full military duties. Arrest may be imposed on either officers or enlisted men. See *Arrest in Quarters*.

Arrest in Quarters—a punishment that may be awarded as nonjudicial punishment by a general or flag officer in command or by an officer exercising general court-martial jurisdiction. Only an officer or warrant officer can be awarded this punishment. A person in arrest in quarters cannot be required to perform his full military duties. See *Arrest*.

Article 39(a) Session—a session that is presided over by the military judge outside the presence of the members. It may be held before, during, or after the formal assembly of the court. The arraignment, defenses and objections, interlocutory matters, admittance of evidence, requests for trial by enlisted members or a military judge alone—all are matters which may be considered by a military judge in an Article 39(a) session.

Assembled—a court is assembled when, after the members have gathered in the courtroom, the presiding officer announces it is assembled. This announcement is made following the preliminary organization of the court. If the military judge presides, he may accomplish much of the preliminary organization of the court in an Article 39(a) session.

Attempt—an act or acts done with a specific intent to commit an offense under the Code amounting to more than mere preparation, and tending but failing to effect the commission of such offense.

Attesting Certificate—a method of authenticating documentary evidence. The certificate, signed by the custodian of the record or his deputy or assistant, states that the attested writing is an original or a copy and that the signer of the attesting certificate is acting in an official capacity as the person having custody of the record or as his deputy or assistant.

B

Bad Conduct Discharge—one of two types of punitive discharges that a court-martial may award an enlisted man. It is designed as a punishment for bad conduct. An accused who has been convicted repeatedly of minor offenses and whose punitive separation from the service appears to be necessary may be awarded a bad conduct discharge (BCD).

BCD Special Court-Martial—a special court-martial in which a bad conduct discharge is a possible punishment for the offenses charged. A bad conduct discharge may not be awarded unless (1) a military judge is detailed to the court (except if physical conditions or military exigencies preclude such detailing), (2) a certified military lawyer is detailed to represent the accused, and (3) a complete and verbatim record of the proceedings is made.

Beyond a Reasonable Doubt—the degree of persuasion based upon proof such as to exclude not every hypothesis or possibility of innocence, but any fair and rational hypothesis except that of guilt; not an absolute or mathematical certainty but a moral certainty.

Boards of Review—now called *Courts of Military Review*.

C

Capital Offense—an offense for which the maximum punishment includes the death penalty.

Captain's Mast—See *Nonjudicial Punishment*.

Case in Chief—See *Prosecution Case in Chief* and *Defense Case in Chief*.

Certified Military Lawyer—a "certified military lawyer" as used in this text, is a person qualified to be detailed as counsel to a general court-martial. Article 27(b) of the Code states that he: "(1) must be a judge advocate of the Army, Navy, Air Force or Marine Corps or a law specialist of the Coast Guard, who is a graduate of an accredited law school or is a member of the bar of a Federal Court or of the highest court of a state; or must be a member of the bar of a Federal Court or of the highest court of a State; and (2) must be certified as competent to perform such duties by the Judge Advocate General of the armed force of which he is a member." (It is possible that a civilian lawyer could be qualified in accordance with this definition. However, in order to reflect what will invariably be the common practice in the naval service, the words "certified military lawyer" or "JAG lawyer" will be utilized throughout the text.)

Challenge—a formal objection to a member of a court continuing as such in a court-martial case. It may be either (1) a challenge for cause—an objection based on a fact or circumstance which has the effect of disqualifying the person challenged from further participation in the proceedings, (2) peremptory challenge—an objection permitted without grounds or basis. A military judge can only be challenged for cause. See *Voir Dire.*

Challenge for Cause—See *Challenge.*

Charge—a formal statement of the article of the Code which the accused is alleged to have violated. The word "charges" is often used to identify both the charges and the specifications.

Charge and Specification—a description in writing of the offense which the accused is alleged to have committed; each specification, together with the charge under which it is placed, constitutes a separate accusation that the accused committed a certain crime.

Charge Sheet—a four-page document (DD Form 458) which basically contains the following: (1) information concerning the accused and witnesses; (2) the charges and specifications; (3) the preferring of charges and their referral to either a summary, special, or general court-martial for trial; and (4) a record of trial by summary court-martial. See Appendices 6 and 7 of *Military Law.*

Circumstantial Evidence—the evidence which tends directly to prove or disprove not a fact in issue, but a fact or circumstance from which, either alone or in connection with other facts, a court may, according to the common experience of mankind, reasonably infer the existence or nonexistence of another fact which is in issue.

Clemency—forbearance, leniency, or mercy exercised by a convening or other reviewing authority concerning a court-martial sentence. See paragraph 1308, *Military Law.*

Closed Sessions (or Closed Court)—those periods during a court-martial in which the members (or the military judge, if trial is before a military judge alone) are deliberating alone. No one else may be present when a court-martial is in closed session. In a court-martial in which the accused pleads not guilty but is found guilty there would be at least two closed sessions: the deliberations on the findings and the deliberations on the sentence.

Code—The Uniform Code of Military Justice (UCMJ). The Code is an enactment of the U.S. Congress relating to military justice. It is applicable to all three services.

Command Judge Advocate—See *Legal Officer.*

Confession—an acknowledgement of guilt of an offense. See *Admission.*

Confinement—the physical restraint of a person.

Convening Authority—the officer having authority to convene a court-martial and who convened the court-martial in question.

Convening Order—the document by which a court-martial is created. It specifies the type of court and lists the time and place of the meeting; the names of the members, trial and defense counsel; the name of the military judge, if detailed to the court; and when appropriate, the authority by which the court is created. See Appendices 14 and 17 of *Military Law*.

Counsel—a person who represents one of the sides in our adversary system of courts-martial.

Court-Martial—a military tribunal composed of one or more eligible members of the armed forces (the number depending on the court selected) or of a military judge alone. Its purpose is to decide whether a person subject to military law has violated the Code, and if it finds him guilty, to adjudge an appropriate punishment, if any, for the offense.

Court-Martial Reports (CMR)—the reference book that publishes all of the opinions of the U.S. Court of Military Appeals and selected cases decided by the Courts of Military Review.

Court of Military Appeals—See *U.S. Court of Military Appeals*.

Courts of Military Review—military appeals courts composed of not less than three officers or civilians. Each must be a member of the bar of a federal court or of the highest court of a state of the United States. See Article 66 of the Code. These courts are one step below the U.S. Court of Military Appeals.

Credibility—a witness's worthiness of belief. It may be determined from the acuteness of his powers of observation, memory, general manner, appearance, biases, prejudices, friendships, and his character as to truth and veracity. Paragraph 153, MCM.

Cross-Examination—the examination of an opposing party's witness. In general, cross-examination is limited to the issues which the witness has testified to on cross-examination and the question of his credibility.

Custody—the restraint of free movement imposed by lawful apprehension. It may be corporeal and forcible or, once there has been a submission to apprehension or a forcible taking into custody, may consist of control exercised in the presence of the prisoner by official acts or orders.

Customary Law—such usage as by common practice and long established practice becomes law. *Black's Law Dictionary*, Fourth Edition, describes custom as a "usage or practice of the people, which by common adoption and acquiescence, and by long and unvarying habit, has become compulsory, and has acquired the force of a law with respect to the place or subject matter to which it relates."

D

Defense Case in Chief—the initial presentation of defense evidence.

Defense Case in Rebuttal—evidence presented by the defense rebutting any matters raised during the *Prosecution Case in Rebuttal*.

Defense Counsel—he defends the accused.

Delict—a wrong or injury; an offense; a violation of public or private duty.

Deposition—the testimony of a witness taken out of court, reduced to writing, under oath or affirmation, before a person empowered to administer oaths, in answer to interrogatories (questions) and cross-interrogatories submitted by the party desiring the deposition and the opposite party or based on oral examination by counsel for the accused and the prosecution. The accused and counsel must be present if they desire. Depositions are seldom utilized in courts-martial today.

Dereliction in the Performance of Duties—willfully or negligently failing to perform assigned duties or performing them in a culpably inefficient manner.

Direct Evidence—evidence which tends directly to prove or disprove a fact in issue.

Dishonorable Discharge—the most severe punitive discharge that a court-martial can award an enlisted man or a noncommissioned warrant officer; reserved for those who should be separated under conditions of dishonor, after having been convicted of offenses usually recognized by the civil law as felonies, or of offenses of a military nature requiring severe punishment. Only a general court-martial can award a dishonorable discharge.

Dismissal—a general court-martial punishment consisting of separation from the service with dishonor. Only officers, commissioned warrant officers, cadets, and midshipmen may receive a dismissal. It is considered the equivalent of a dishonorable discharge. Paragraph 126d, MCM, and *United States* v. *Ellman,* 9 USCMA 549, 26 CMR 329 (1958).

Documentary Evidence—anything in writing which is offered as evidence, such as a page from the accused's service record, a letter, or a forged check.

Double Jeopardy—See *Former Jeopardy.*

Drunkenness—(1) drunkenness as an offense under the Code, is intoxication which is sufficient sensibly to impair the rational and full exercise of the mental and physical faculties.

It may be caused by liquor or drugs. (2) drunkenness as a defense claiming the lack of intent or knowledge is intoxication which amounts to loss of reason preventing the accused from knowing the nature of his act or the nature and probable consequences thereof.

E

Elements—the essential facts or ingredients of an offense which must be proved at a trial; the acts or omissions which form the basis of any particular offense; the essential components of an offense.

Execution of His Office—engaged in any act or service required or authorized to be done by statute, regulation, the order of a superior, or a military custom.

Extenuation—matter in extenuation of an offense serves to explain the circumstances surrounding the commission of an offense. This may include the reasons that motivated the accused to commit the crime. Matter in extenuation is presented in an effort to lessen the punishment that may be awarded at nonjudicial punishment or by a court-martial. It is generally presented after the accused has been found guilty. See *Mitigation.*

Evidence—the system of rules and standards by which the admission of proof at a court-martial is regulated. Court members cannot utilize inadmissible evidence in arriving at their conclusions.

F

Fact—See *Question of Fact.*

Felony—any offense of a *civil* nature punishable under the Code by death or by confinement exceeding one year is a felony. For example, unauthorized absence, a strictly military offense, is not a felony.

Findings—the resolution of the issue of guilt or innocence of an accused. The findings as to the charges may be guilty; not guilty; or not guilty, but guilty of a violation of a different article. As to the specifications, the findings may be guilty; not guilty; or guilty with exceptions and/or substitutions.

Fine—a type of punishment making the accused liable to the United States for a specified amount of money.

Forfeiture of Pay—a type of punishment depriving the accused of all or part of his pay.

Former Jeopardy—the rule of law that no person shall be tried for the same offense by the same sovereign a second time without his consent.

Former Punishment—the rule of military law that nonjudicial punishment for a minor offense may be interposed as a bar to trial by court-martial for the same offense.

G

GCM—See *General Court-Martial.*

General Court-Martial—the highest trial court within the military judicial system. It is the most serious of the three types of courts-martial.

General Intent Offense—this type of offense constitutes a violation of the Code even though there is no specific intent to actually commit the offense.

Grand Jury—in civilian law this is a group of persons (12 to 23 in number) designated to examine into accusations against an accused charged with a serious crime to determine if there is sufficient reason to bring the accused to trial. The military counterpart of the grand jury is the *Pretrial Investigation.*

Gross Negligence—a gross lack of care; a reckless disregard of the consequences.

H

Habeas Corpus—an order from a civil court which requires the custodian of a prisoner to appear before a court to show cause why the prisoner is confined or detained.

Hearsay Evidence—a statement made out of a courtroom which is offered in evidence to prove the *truth* of the matters stated therein.

I

Individual Defense Counsel—a civilian lawyer or military officer (certified military lawyer or nonlawyer) requested by the accused to act as his defense counsel for a court-martial. The accused would be required to compensate any civilian counsel retained by him. Military counsel requested by the accused will defend him, free of charge, if reasonably available.

Infra—"*U.S.* v. *O'Hara,* infra" means that the case cite (i.e., 14 USCMA 167, 33 CMR 379 (1963)) may be found *later* (below or beneath the present mention of the case).

Initiation of Charges—this is the initial report to the proper military authorities of the known, suspected, or probable commission of an offense by a person subject to the Code. Any person may initiate such a complaint. It may be oral or in writing. The initiation of charges should be contrasted with the *Preferring of Charges.*

Instructions—the law that applies to a particular court-martial case. If an accused pleads "not guilty," the members must apply the law as furnished them by the instructions of the presiding officer in their resolution of the factual issue of the guilt or innocence of the accused. If an accused is convicted, further instructions by the presiding officer will furnish the guidelines to be utilized by the court members in their determination of an appropriate sentence.

Interlocutory—a question is interlocutory unless it would terminate a court-martial case by determining guilt or innocence. Such matters as the admissibility of evidence, propriety of arguments of counsel, etc., are interlocutory questions.

J

JAG Lawyer—a member of the Judge Advocate General's Corps. See *Certified Military Lawyer.*

JAG Manual—the Manual of the Judge Advocate General of the Navy. This directive of the Secretary of the Navy contains minor variations in the manner of administering military justice which are peculiar to the Navy and Marine Corps. It is also the primary source of authority relating to administrative fact-finding bodies and claims regulations. Promotions, physical disabilities, and customs regulations are also contained in the JAG Manual.

Judicial Notice—the formal recognition by a court-martial of the existence of certain kinds of facts without the formal presentation of evidence.

Jurisdiction—the power of a court-martial to try and determine a case. In order for a court-martial to have jurisdiction in any particular case, it must meet the following requirements: (1) the court must be convened by an official empowered to convene it; (2) the court must be properly constituted as to the number of members; (3) the members of the court must be legally competent to sit on the court; (4) the court must have the power to try the accused; (5) the court-martial must have the power to try the offense charged.

L

Larceny—the wrongful taking, obtaining, or withholding, by any means, from the possession of the owner or of any other person, any money, personal property, or article of value of any kind, with intent *permanently* to deprive or defraud another person of the use and benefit of property or to appropriate it to his own use or the use of any person other than the owner.

Law—See *Question of Law.*

Law Officer—the functions of the law officer are now performed by the military judge (Military Justice Act of 1968). See *Military Judge.*

Leading Question—a question which either suggests the answer it is desired the witness shall make or which, embodying a material fact, is susceptible of being answered by a simple yes or no.

Legal Officer—the officer primarily responsible for the technical aspects and efficiency of the administration of military justice within a command. He serves as the principal adviser and special assistant to the commanding officer in matters relating to military law and other legal matters. If the legal officer is a member of the JAG Corps, he would be called the *Command Judge Advocate*.

Lesser Included Offense—an offense necessarily included, either expressly or by fair implication, in the offense charged; an offense containing some but not all of the elements of the offense charged, so that if one or more of the elements of the offense charged is not proved, the evidence may still support a finding of guilty of the lesser included offense.

M

MCM—the Manual for Courts-Martial, United States, 1969 (Revised). An executive order issued by the President of the United States that implements the Code (the Uniform Code of Military Justice). See paragraph 107, *Military Law*.

Member—a person subject to the Code who is detailed to a court-martial. to determine whether an accused has been proven guilty and to determine an appropriate sentence if the accused is found guilty. The member most senior in rank present for the hearing of the case is the president.

Mental Capacity—the ability of the accused at the time of trial to understand the nature of the proceedings against him and intelligently conduct or cooperate in his defense.

Mental Responsibility—the condition of the accused at the time of the commission of an offense. He is considered to be mentally responsible if he was so far free from mental defects, disease or derangement as to be able concerning the particular act charged both to distinguish right from wrong and to adhere to the right.

Military Judge—a commissioned officer of the armed forces on active duty. He is a member of the bar of a federal court or of the highest court of a state. He must be certified as qualified for duty as a military judge by the Judge Advocate General of the Navy. Military judges of general courts-martial must also be members of an independent judiciary (the U.S. Navy—Marine Corps Judiciary Activity). A military judge is detailed to every general court-martial. In a BCD special court-martial a military judge must be detailed unless physical conditions or military exigencies preclude such detailing. The military judge rules finally on all questions of law and on most interlocutory questions.

Mitigate—action that may be taken by a reviewing authority that reduces or lessens the quality or quantity of the punishment awarded at Captain's Mast or Office Hours or as the result of a courts-martial.

Mitigation—anything presented to a court-martial or at nonjudicial punishment which has for its purpose the lessening of the punishment to be assigned or the furnishing of grounds for a recommendation for clemency. It is generally presented after the accused has been found guilty. See *Extenuation*.

Moral Turpitude Offense—this is an offense for which a dishonorable discharge or confinement for more than one year is authorized; or an offense considered a felony under federal law or by the state in whose jurisdiction the offense occurred; or an offense involving fraud, deceit, larceny, wrongful appropriation, or the making of a false statement. See paragraph 153b(2)(b), MCM.

Motion—a request to the court, by either counsel, for particular relief. See *Motion to Dismiss, Motion to Grant Appropriate Relief,* and *Motion for a Finding of Not Guilty.*

Motion for a Finding of Not Guilty—a request to a court to return a finding of not guilty as to one or more of the offenses charged on the basis that the evidence is insufficient to sustain a conviction of that offense. "If there is any evidence which together with all inferences which can properly be drawn therefrom and all applicable presumptions, could reasonably tend to establish every essential element of an offense charged or included in any specification to which the motion is directed, the motion will not be granted." Paragraph 71, MCM.

Motion to Dismiss—a motion raising any defense or objection in bar of trial.

Motion to Grant Appropriate Relief—a motion to cure a defect of form or substance which impedes the accused in properly preparing for trial or conducting his defense.

N

Naval Law—military law that is peculiarly related to the naval service. Naval law, as a separate body of law, has been largely superceded by the Code and the MCM. Today, the JAG Manual is the principal directive which contains minor variations in the manner of administering justice peculiar to the Navy and Marine Corps.

Naval Service—the Navy and Marine Corps.

NAVPERS 2696 (Report and Disposition of Offenses)—the primary document utilized by the preliminary inquiry officer investigating alleged offenses against the Code. It is a Navy form. It is not presently used in the Marine Corps. See Appendix 2 of *Military Law.*

Navy Regulations—See *United States Navy Regulations.*

NJP—See *Nonjudicial Punishment.*

Nonjudicial Punishment—a procedure whereby a person subject to the Code may receive an official punishment if found guilty of a minor offense. It is not a court-martial. In the Navy it is called "Captain's Mast"; in the Marine Corps, "Office Hours."

Nonpunitive Measures—the corrective measures taken by a command such as administrative admonitions, reprimands, exhortations, extra-military instruction, criticisms, etc. They may be oral or in writing. They are *not* official punishments.

O

Offense—a violation of the Code (Uniform Code of Military Justice).

Office Hours—See *Nonjudicial Punishment.*

Open Sessions—those periods during a court-martial in which the members, accused, defense counsel, trial counsel, reporter, and, if detailed, the military judge, are present in the courtroom. Generally, the public is permitted to attend open sessions of a court-martial. But, see paragraph 53e, MCM.

Opinion Evidence—evidence of what a witness thinks, believes, or infers in regard to facts in dispute, as distinguished from his personal knowledge of the facts themselves.

Oral Evidence—the sworn testimony of a witness.

P

Peremptory Challenge—See *Challenge.*

Plea—the accused's response (generally made through his counsel) to each charge and each specification.

Preferring of Charges—this is accomplished by filling out a charge sheet (DD Form 458) and includes signing and swearing to the charges and specifications shown by an investigation to warrant such action. See Appendices 6 and 7 of *Military Law.* Only a person subject to the Code can prefer charges. See *Initiation of Charges.*

Preliminary Inquiry—the initial investigation of a reported or suspected violation of the Code. The preliminary inquiry should be distinguished from the pretrial investigation conducted under Article 32 of the Code. See *Pretrial Investigation.*

Preliminary Inquiry Officer—the individual, generally an officer, who conducts the preliminary inquiry.

President of a Court-Martial—the detailed senior member in ra⸴k present at a trial, whether or ⹁ot he is the senior member detailed by the convening order, is president of the court for the trial of that case.

Presiding Officer—in a special court-martial without a military judge, the president is the "presiding officer." If a military judge is detailed to a special court-martial, he is the "presiding officer." In a general court-martial, a military judge is always detailed.

Pretrial Investigation—an investigation to determine if a case should be recommended for forwarding to a general court-martial. The purpose of the investigation is "to inquire into the truth of the matters set forth in the charges, the form of the charges, and to secure information upon which to determine what disposition should be made of the case." Paragraph 34, MCM. The pretrial investigation conducted under Article 32 is much more formal than the preliminary inquiry of the preliminary inquiry officer. For example, Article 32(b) states as follows: "The accused shall be advised of the charges against him and of his right to be represented at that investigation by counsel. . . . at that investigation full opportunity shall be given to the accused to cross-examine witnesses against him if they are available and to present anything he may desire in his own behalf, either in defense or mitigation, and the investigating officer shall examine available witnesses requested by the accused. If the charges are forwarded after the investigation, they shall be accompanied by a statement of the substance of the testimony taken on both sides and a copy thereof shall be given to the accused." Appendix 7 of the MCM is an example of the Investigating Officer's Report.

Prosecution—See *Trial Counsel.*

Prosecution Case in Chief—the initial presentation of the trial counsel's case.

Prosecution Case in Rebuttal—evidence presented by the prosecution rebutting any matters raised during the Defense Case in Chief.

Punitive Articles—Articles 77 through 134 of the Code. They are discussed in Chapter XXVIII of the MCM.

Q

Question of Fact—raises an issue concerning what occurred.

Question of Law—raises an issue as to what the law is.

R

Real Evidence—any physical object, such as a stolen watch, jewelry, or a weapon.

Report and Disposition of Offenses—See NAVPERS 2696.

Report Chit—an informal expression used to describe the document used to initiate charges against an accused. See paragraph 301, and Appendices 1 and 2 of *Military Law*.

Restriction—a form of deprivation of liberty that involves moral and legal rather than physical restraint. It may be imposed either at commanding officer's nonjudicial punishment or by a summary, special, or general court-martial. It is a lesser restraint than *Arrest in Quarters* as it generally involves broader geographical limits and permits the restricted person to perform his full military duties. See *Restriction in Lieu of Arrest*.

Restriction in Lieu of Arrest—this is a form of moral and legal pretrial restraint on the liberty of an individual imposed by an order directing him to remain within certain specified limits. It is a lesser restraint than arrest as it generally involves broader geographical limits (such as a base or ship) and permits the restricted person to perform his full military duties. It is not imposed as a punishment, but is imposed either because the accused's presence during an investigation of his conduct may be necessary or to prevent further exposure to the temptation of misconduct similar to that for which he is already under charges. See *Restriction*.

S

SCM—See *Summary Court-Martial*.

Search—a quest for incriminating matter.

Seizure—to take possession of forcibly, to grasp, to snatch or to take into possession. *Black's Law Dictionary*, Fourth Edition.

Shakedown—a general exploratory inspection within a command of all or a portion thereof.

SPCM—See *Special Court-Martial*.

Special Court-Martial—the intermediate of the three types of courts-martial. This court can award up to and including six months' confinement at hard labor. It may only award a bad conduct discharge under certain circumstances. The procedure in a special court-martial when a military judge is sitting is almost identical to the procedure in a general court-martial.

Specification—a formal statement of specific acts and circumstances relied upon as constituting the offense charged; the specific facts that constitute a violation of the Code.

Specific Intent Offense—this type of offense only is a violation of the Code if the accused intended to commit the crime charged. This intent may be proven by either direct or circumstantial evidence but it must be proven, in addition to the other elements, if the accused is to be convicted of a specific intent offense.

Staff Judge Advocate—generally, a certified military lawyer attached to the staff of a convening or supervisory authority who exercises general court-martial jurisdiction.

Statute of Limitations—the rule of law which establishes the time within which an accused must be charged with an offense to be tried successfully.

Supervisory Authority—an officer exercising general court-martial jurisdiction who reviews summary or special courts-martial after the convening authority has acted.

Supra—"*U.S.* v. *O'Hara, supra*" means that the case cite (i.e., 14 USCMA 167, 33 CMR 379 (1963)) may be found in an earlier part of the case.

Stipulation—an agreement between the trial and defense counsel with the express consent of the accused as to the existence or nonexistence of any fact (a stipulation of fact) or the content of the testimony that an absent witness would give if he were present in court (a stipulation of testimony).

Subpoena—a written legal order directing a material civilian witness to appear in court to give testimony. Trial counsel and summary court officers are authorized to subpoena civilian witnesses. A subpoena is not utilized for military witnesses. Military witnesses may be ordered to appear by their superiors. See paragraph 115, MCM.

Summary Court-Martial—the lowest of the three types of courts-martial. It consists of one commissioned officer who acts as judge, jury, trial and defense counsel.

T

Trial Counsel—he prosecutes the case in the name of the government.

U

UCMJ—the Uniform Code of Military Justice. See *Code*.

United States Navy Regulations (Navy Regs)—regulations issued by the Secretary of the Navy that, among other matters, prescribe the rights, duties, and responsibilities of members of the Navy and Marine Corps.

U.S. Court of Military Appeals—a U.S. military appeals court consisting of three civilian judges who are appointed by the President of the U.S.; the highest military court; considered the military equivalent of the U.S. Supreme Court.

V

Voir Dire—the questioning of members of a court-martial by either the trial or defense counsel, or both, to determine if the members hold any biases or should otherwise be precluded from sitting in the trial of a particular case. It is a natural selection process designed to obtain a panel of members free of inclination toward *either* side of the case.

W

Wrongful Appropriation—the wrongful taking, obtaining, or withholding, by any means, from the possession of the owner or of any other person, any money, personal property, or article of value of any kind, with intent *temporarily* to deprive or defraud another person of the use and benefit of property or to appropriate it to his own use or the use of any person other than the owner.

Bibliography

Chadwick, Robert J. "The Canons, the Code and Counsel: The Ethics of Advocates before Courts-Martial," *Military Law Review,* Department of the Army Pamphlet 27-100-38 (October, 1967): 1–109.

Continental Congress. *Rules for the Regulation of the Navy of the United Colonies of North America.* 28 November 1775.

Defence of Alexander Slidell Mackenzie. New York: *Tribune* Office, 1843.

Department of the Army and the Air Force. *Military Justice Handbook—The Trial Counsel and The Defense Counsel.* DA No. 27–10 and AFP 111–1–1. November, 1962.

Department of the Army. *Military Justice Evidence.* DA 27–172. June, 1962.

Department of the Army. *Military Justice—Trial Procedure.* DA 27–173. June, 1964.

Harwood, A. A. *The Law and Practice of United States Naval Courts-Martial.* New York: D. Van Nostrand, 1867.

Hayford, Harrison. *The Somers Mutiny Affair.* Englewood Cliffs, New Jersey: 1959.

JAG Journal. Vol. XXIII, No. 2. Washington, D.C. Office of the Judge Advocate General of the Navy. September-November, 1968.

JAG Law Review. Vol. X, No. 6. Washington, D.C. Office of the Judge Advocate General of the Air Force. November-December, 1968.

Langley, Harold D. *Social Reform in the United States Navy.* Urbana, Illinois: University of Illinois Press, 1967.

Military Justice Handbook: The Trial and Defense Counsel. DA Pam 27–10, 1 August 1969.

Moyer, Homer E., Jr. "The Military Justice Act of 1968, A Look At Its Content and Implementation." *JAG Journal,* August, 1969.

Secretary of the Navy (Connally). *Manual of the Judge Advocate General.* JAGINST 5800.7, 2 June 1961.

Snedeker, James. *A Brief History of Courts-Martial.* Annapolis, Maryland: United States Naval Institute, 1954.

Tedrow, R. L. *Annotated and Digested Opinions, U.S. Court of Military Appeals.* Washington, D.C.: U.S. Government Printing Office, 1966.

United States Military Academy. "Cases and Materials on Legal Methods of Proof." West Point, New York. 1967–1968. Mimeographed.

United States Naval Justice School, Newport, Rhode Island. "Evidence Study Guide," 1 March 1967.

United States Naval Justice School, Newport, Rhode Island. "Naval Justice Hand Book," 1 January 1967.

United States Naval Justice School, Newport, Rhode Island. "Procedure Study Guide," 1 March 1967.

United States Naval Justice School, Newport, Rhode Island. "Substantive Law Study Guide," 1 March 1967.

U.S. Air Force. "Summary of Changes in the *Manual for Courts-Martial, 1969.*"

U.S. Army. "Analysis of Contents, *Manual for Courts-Martial, United States, 1968.*"

U.S. Army. "Branch Officer Career (C-22), Associate Branch Officer Career and USAR Schools Material." Charlottesville, Virginia, 1969. Mimeographed.

U.S. President (Nixon). *Manual for Courts-Martial, United States, 1969* (revised edition), (distributed in August, 1969).

U.S. President (Johnson). *Manual for Courts-Martial, United States, 1969.* 1 January 1969.

U.S. President (Roosevelt). *Navy Courts and Boards, 1937.* 1 July 1937.

U.S. President (Tyler). *Regulations for the Navy and Marine Corps.* February 19, 1841.

Van de Water, Frederic F. *The Captain Called It Mutiny.* New York: Ives Washburn, Inc., 1954.

Wolfe, M. E., and Gulick, R. I. *Military Law.* Fourth printing. Annapolis, Maryland: United States Naval Institute, 1967.

Index

The page numbers in **heavier type** indicate glossary references.

Abandoned property, as defense to larceny, 77
Absence from appointed place of duty, 70, 346–347. *See also* Unauthorized absence
  distinguished from other absence offenses, 54–55
Accused, **363**
  members, fraternizing with, 167
  personal appearance and conduct, 151
  uniform and decorations required, 142
Accused, rights of. *See also* Constitutional rights of servicemen; *individual headings*
  advice as to counsel rights in court, 209–210
  appeal rights, 236–241
  automatic review of sentence and findings, 19
  challenges, advice as to, 148
  civilian lawyer, right to retain, 122, 123
  confidential relationship with defense counsel, 197
  counsel rights explained, 145–146
  Court of Military Appeals, petition to, 240
  cross-examination cannot be denied, 186
  defense counsel, example, 249, 360
  defenses, advised as to, 148
  enlisted men as members, right to, 147–148
  former punishment, 101
  guilty plea
    hearing required prior to acceptance, 215
    waives certain rights, 216
  military judge, trial by, 147
  mitigation and extenuation advice, 150–151
  at nonjudicial punishment, 88–89, 94
  not guilty pleas, 148
  pretrial agreement advice, 149
  rehearing, if prejudicial error, 237–238
  review of record, 236–241
  self-incrimination, 196–197
  sentence hearing, 19
  summary court-martial

appeal to JAG permitted, 114
  evidence rulings, 106
  listing of, 109
  mitigation and extenuation, 111
  presumed innocent, 106
  refusal always permitted, 107
  witness, rights as, 149–151
Accuser, 106, 117, **363**
  charge sheet signed under oath by, 108
  member ineligible as, 163
  as member, must be challenged, 167
  special court cannot be convened by, 117
  summary court may be convened by, 106
Acquitted, **363**
Active duty, **363**
Adams, John, 6
Additional charges, **363**
Adjournment, 212
Administrative discharges, court-martial cannot award, 233
Admissions. *See* Confessions or admissions
Admonition
  nonjudicial punishment, 90
  nonpunitive measure, 85, 89
  special and general court may award, 234
  summary court may award, 111
Affidavit, **363**
Affirmative defenses, 348
Aggravation, 230, **363**
  drafting in specification, 64–65
  summary court conviction constitutes, 105
Alibi, **363**
  as defense, 78
Allegation, **363**
Allege, **363–364**
Allotment. *See* Basic allowance for quarters
American naval law
  Adams, John, influence of, 6
  Articles for the Government of the Navy, 6–7
  Articles of Confederation, 6
  British influence, 6
  constitutional authority for, 6
  Continental Congress, 5–6
  extinguished as separate law by Code, 7–8
  first regulations, 5–6

378

Amalfi, sea law of, 4
Appeal, **364**
Appellant, **364**
Appellate review, **364**
Appellee, **364**
Apprehension, **364**
  absentee, 57
  action following, 21
  aggravating circumstance in absentee
    case, 216
  authority for, 21
  basis for, 21
  discussed, similar to civilian arrest, 20
  distinguished from arrest, 29, 344
  initiation of charges by person appre-
    hending, 30
  probable cause requirement for, 21
  procedure, 20
  resistance of, example, 28, 344
Area coordinator, **364**. *See also* Supervisory
    authority
  reviews appeals from nonjudicial punish-
    ment, 94
Argument
  as to findings, 225
  generally, 153–154
  improper
    argument does not always require cor-
      rection, 202
    examples of, 134, 136–137
  trial counsel must argue on basis of evi-
    dence, 134
Armed force and unit or organization,
    drafting in specification, 64
Arraignment, 212–213, **364**
  Article 39(a) session may conduct, 207
Arrest, 22–23, **364**
  breaking of, mentioned, 24
  distinguished from apprehension, 29, 344
  Navy Regulations as a source of law, 11
  as nonjudicial punishment, 90
  as pretrial restraint, 22–23
  release from, 23–24
  restrictions on nature of, 23
Arrest in quarters, **364**. *See* Arrest
Article 39(a) session, **364**
  discussion, 207–208
  integral part of trial, 207
  service of charges should precede, 207
  utilized to discuss findings instructions,
    224–225
Article 69 relief, 240–241
Assembled. *See* Assembly
Assembly, 163–164, **365**
  convening order amendment after, gen-
    erally, 119
  member cannot receive lectures at, 125
  member excused after, 130, 353
Attempt, 228, **365**
  example of findings of, 229
Attesting certificate, **365**
  authentication
    copy of document, 189
    original of document, 187

  discussed, 187
  example of, 189
Attorney-client communications, 197
Authentication of records of trial, 235
  general courts, 235
  special courts, 235
  summary courts, 112

Bad conduct discharge, 232–233, **365**
  acceleration clauses, effect of, 121
  combination of offenses may warrant, 121
    example of, 131, 354
  commuted to confinement or forfeiture,
    238
  conditions for special court to adjudge,
    121
  convictions (prior) may authorize, 121,
    215–216
  instruction required, 232
  discussion, 232–233
  dishonorable discharge is more serious,
    121
  offense may warrant, 121
  summary court cannot award, 111
  summary court convictions may permit,
    105
Bancroft, George, mentioned, 17
Barcelona, sea law of, 4
Basic allowance for quarters, 107–108
  court-martial consideration of, 107–108,
    233–234
  nonjudicial punishment consideration of,
    92
Basic pay, 234
BCD special court-martial, **365**. *See* Special
    court-martial
Best evidence rule, 195
  official records are exceptions to, 195
    example, 204, 358
  original, 195
Beyond a reasonable doubt, **365**
Black Book of Admiralty, 4–5
Boards of review, **365**
Bread and water
  combination with other restraints pro-
    hibited, 93
  as nonjudicial punishment, 90–91
  summary court may award, 111
Burden of proof, 168
  findings, instruction as to, 226

Capital case, **365**
  all members must concur in death sen-
    tence, 234
  all members must concur in findings, 229
  guilty plea not permitted, 215
  military judge may not try alone, 208
  special court cannot award, 119
  summary court cannot try, 107
Captain's Mast. *See* Nonjudicial punish-
    ment
Certificate of correction, 236
Certified military lawyer, **365–366**
  BCD special court requires, 120–122

civilian law comparison mentioned, 19
confessions or admissions, advice prior to,
　33–35
general court counsel is always, 206
non-BCD special court, 122–123
oath only taken when originally certified,
　210
required if trial counsel lawyer, 123
right of accused to, 249, 360
trial advice to accused concerning, 209–
　210
Chain of custody, 187
may authenticate original of document,
　187
Challenges, **366**
advice to accused concerning, 148
cause, 166–167
　discussion, 179
　mandatory that certain members be
　　challenged, 167
　may be made at any stage of trial, 211
　members determine if president pre-
　　sides, 175
　military judge determines, 176, 212
　president of court cannot determine,
　　212
　voir dire, 167
charges given to refresh memory of mem-
　bers, 211
disclosure of grounds at trial, 211
member must disclose grounds, 166
peremptory, 166
　each accused and prosecution entitled
　　to one, 211
summary court cannot be challenged,
　106–107
voting procedure, 212
Character, good, as defense, 78. *See also*
　Moral character
Charge, **366**
Charge sheet, **366.** *See also* Charges and
　specifications
closed session, may not be taken into, 169
errors
　minor, 108, 138
　substantial, 108, 138
legal officer may assist in preparation, 126
must be served prior to 39(a) session, 207
service on accused, 138
summary court record, 112
trial counsel's initial examination, 137–
　138
Charges and specifications, **366.** *See also*
　Charge sheet; Initiation of charges
Appendix 6c of MCM should be fol-
　lowed, 138
closed sessions, copies taken into, 169
constitutes violation drafter believes
　committed, 63
distribution to members during arraign-
　ment, 212
drafting, 62–65, 69–70, 346
　aggravation, 64–65

armed force and unit or organization,
　64
facts constituting offense, 64
larceny specification, 78–79
name, 63
rate or rank of accused, 63
sample absence specification, 63, 69–70,
　346
time and place of offense, 64
wrongful appropriation specification,
　78–79
each specification is separate accusation,
　65
elements discussed, 55–56
findings, 227–230
　example of, 249, 360
initial report of, 30
members receive prior to challenges, 211
poorly drawn, indefinite or redundant,
　214
preliminary inquiry officer may prefer, 41
reading during trial, 212
service of
　as constitutional right, 18
　importance, 161, 356
specification, **374**
unsworn, accused may object, 108
withdrawal of, 140–141, 212
Check, bad
intent to defraud essential, 219
jurisdiction if cashed on base, 131, 355
Chief petty officer, nonjudicial punishment
　cannot reduce, 91
Circumstantial evidence, 182, **366**
compared with direct evidence, 170
example of, 182
larceny case, 75
Civilian law. *See also* Civilian police;
　Jurisdiction
civilian lawyer, accused's right to retain,
　122, 123
compared with military law, 3, 8, 12, 18–
　20, 46–48, 85
former jeopardy inapplicable if different
　sovereign, 61
jailing may also constitute unauthorized
　absence, 59
juvenile conviction as unauthorized ab-
　sence, 69, 346
military jurisdiction limited, 118–119
Civilian police. *See also* Civilian law
authority to apprehend absentees, 57
Clemency, **366**
discussed, 235
example of, 180, 357
sentence reduced by, 238
Closed court, 212, **366**
Closed session, **366**
Closing argument, as to findings, 225
Code, **366.** *See also* Uniform Code of Mili-
　tary Justice
Coercion, defense to specific intent crime,
　77

Collateral issue, accused may limit testimony to, 197
Command influence
   coercion prohibited, 124
   criticism prohibited, 124
   discussed, 124–126
   examples of, 14–17, 128–130
   fitness reports, 125
   instruction or information courses limited, 124–125
Command judge advocate. *See* Legal officer
Commanding officer. *See also* Convening authority
   accuser if he direct charges be preferred, 41–42
   alternatives of judge and counsel requirements cannot be met, 122
   command influence, 124–125
   convening authority, 116–117
   court-martial, nonjudicial punishment hearing not required prior to, 43
   delegation of pretrial restraint authority, 22
   dismissal before nonjudicial punishment, 43
   duty to make preliminary inquiry, 32
   indorsement on charge sheet signed by, 108
   legal officer's advice, 127
   Meritorious Mast, 98
   nonjudicial punishment
      advises accused of appeal rights, 94
      authority to impose, 87
      conduct of, 88–89
      jurisdiction over units on board ship, 104, 351
      must resolve cases, 89
      NAVPERS 2696 signing, 94
      reduction of punishment after, 96–97
   order of, 84, 349
   preliminary inquiry
      alternatives, 42–43
      pre-mast study of, 42–43
   pretrial investigation, NJP hearing not required, 43
   pretrial restraint authority, 22
   Request Mast, 98
   search authorized by, 36–38, 52–53, 345
   search warrant cannot be issued by, 40
   ship's instructions as order of, 84, 349
   successor to command defined, 117
Communications, privileged. *See* Confidential communications
Competent evidence, 191–192
Concurrently, 93
Conduct bringing discredit upon armed forces. *See* General Article 134
Confessions or admissions
   admissions, 33, **363**
   comparison with civilian law, mentioned, 19
   confessions 33, **366**
   discussed, 33–35
   fruit of poison tree doctrine, 40–41

hearsay evidence rule exception, 193
independent evidence necessary, 159
physical act as constituting, 52, 345
spontaneous statement, example of, 51, 344–345
voluntariness, 33–35
   Article 31(b) requirement, 33
   coercion, influences, etc. prohibited, 34–35
   Miranda-Tempia case, 33–34, 44–51
   must be finally resolved by members, 227
   spontaneous statement is voluntary, 35
Confidential communications
   attorney-client
      accused informed of, 146
      generally, 197
   husband-wife, 197
   marital privilege, 197
   priest-penitent, 198
Confinement, 22, 233, **366**
   bread and water, 90–91
   deferment discussed, 240
   discussed, 233
   distinguished from custody, 26–28
   escape from, mentioned, 24
   limitations on nature of, 23
   as pretrial restraint, 22
   released from, 23–24
   releasing without authority prohibited, 24
   special court cannot award over six months, 119, 233
   summary court may award one month, 111
Confinement order, 22
Consecutively, 93
Constitution of the U.S., source of military law, 9
Constitutional rights of servicemen. *See also* Accused, rights of
   apply unless excluded, 10
   charges must be served before trial, 138
   civilian jury not provided, 118
   counsel for defense, 18
   counsel in special court, 120–123
   deferment, military equivalent of bail, 18, 112, 343
   discussed, 46–48
   due process mentioned as, 19
   equivalents in military law mentioned, 18
   Fifth Amendment requirement, statements, 33
   former jeopardy, 18, 101, 343
   grand jury not provided, 118
   informed of nature of offense, 18
   limited purpose testimony, 149–150
      example of, 227
   nonjudicial punishment (31(b) right), 88
   pretrial investigation, grand jury equivalent, 18, 343
   search and seizure, 35

self-incrimination, 19, 149–150, 196–197
evidence cannot be presented if right exercised, 161, 134, 355
speedy trial, 18
subpoena right, 18
witness
confrontation, 18
right to obtain, 143–144
Contempt of court, summary court, 109
Contraband, object of search and seizure, 36
Convening authority. *See also* Command influence
authority to convene courts
acting commanding officer may, 117
delegation prohibited, 117
executive officer cannot, 117
general court-martial, 116
jurisdictional aspects, 118
special courts, 116–117
summary courts, 116–117
charges and specifications, withdrawal of, 140–141, 212
clemency, 235
command influence, 116, **366**
counsel, relationship with, 124
discussion, 124–125
example of, 128–130
members, relationship with, 124–125
personal views prohibited, 125
convening order, amendment of, 119–120
court-martial orders, 241
court directed to reconsider motion to dismiss, 213
defense counsel requirements, special courts, 120–124
deferment of confinement discussed, 240
discussed, 116–132
insanity (at time of offense) ruling may not be reconsidered, 213–214
jurisdiction considerations, 117–119
legal officer
advises convening authority, 127
direct communications permitted, 126
members
detailed by, 162, 164
excusal of, 130, 142, 353
selection of, 119–120
military judge
fitness reports, 176
requirement for special courts, 120–122
motion for finding of not guilty, 213
motion to grant appropriate relief, 214
review
commutation of court sentence, 238
lesser included offense may be approved, 239
mitigation of court sentence, 238
record of trial, 236–239
summary court, 112–113
Secretary of Navy may prescribe others, 10

special court, alternatives if judge and counsel requirements cannot be met, 122
summary court, 106
responsibility cannot be delegated, 113
suspension of sentence, 238
trial counsel cannot comment on views of, 134
witnesses, action on defense request, 143–144
Convening order, **366–367**
closed session, may be taken into, 169
date of trial, 164
legal officer may prepare, 126
members
detailed by, 162
notified of detailing by, 164
reporter not named therein, 143
Convictions
authentication of, 187–189
bad conduct discharge may be authorized by, 121, 215–216
instructions required, 232
finality requirement, example, 248, 360
sentence, considered, 230
summary court considers as to sentence, 111
summary court constitutes, 105
Correction, certificate of, 236
Correctional custody, 91
apportionment if punishments of same nature, 93
deferring execution of, 104, 351
discussed, 91
extra duties may run concurrently with, 93
restriction may run concurrently with, 93
Counsel, 133, **367**. *See also* Defense counsel; Trial counsel
appearance and decorum, 153
arguments of, 153–154
conduct of, 152–153
example, 154–157
ethics of, generally, 152–153
inadequacy of, 154–160
pretrial agreements, members must not be informed of, 157
witness, should not be, 157
Courses on military law. *See* Command influence
Courts-martial, **367**. *See also* General courts-martial; Special courts-martial; Summary courts-martial
barred if punished under Article 15, 100–103
date of trial, 164
meeting at unusual hours, 141, 164
nonjudicial punishment
not required prior to forwarding to court, 43
right to refuse and demand court, 87–88
place of trial, 141–142

preliminary inquiry may be referred to, 43

preliminary inquiry officer may recommend, 41

time of trial, 141–142, 207

unusual hours, 141, 164

Court-martial orders, 241

Court-Martial Reports, 367

discussed, 11

Court of Military Appeals. *See* U.S. Court of Military Appeals

Courts of Military Review, 367

review of, 239

source of military law, 10–11

Credibility, 186, 367

Crimes and offenses not capital. *See* General Article 134

Cross-examination, 367

discussed, 186

limited to witness testimony and credibility, 186

right of accused, 186

Custody, 21, 367

discussed, 21

distinguished from confinement, 26–28

escape from, mentioned, 24

examples of escape from, 28–29, 344

lasts until proper authority notified, 27

Customary law, 367

Customary law of sea

British admirals incorporated, 5

Continental Congress relied on, 6

extinguished by statutes and regulations, 6–8

incorporated into various ancient codes, 4

DD Form 553, 57

Death case. *See* Capital case

Defense argument, findings, 225

Defense case in chief, 183, 367

Defense case in rebuttal, 183, 367

Defense counsel, 133, 367. *See also* Counsel

accused

advice as to defense counsel, 209–210

advice as to rights under Code, 147–151

advised as to biases, etc., of counsel, 145

instructed as to conduct at trial, 152

arguments of

discussion, 153–154

on findings, 225

charge sheet and accompanying papers furnished to, 139

confidential communications with accused, 197

constitutional right to, 18

criticisms and coercion of, 124

defense case in chief, 183

defense case in rebuttal, 183

defenses, accused questioned concerning, 146–147

detailing

BCD special court, 120–122

non-BCD special court, 122–123

ethics

cannot assist trial counsel, 134

defenses must be asserted unless false, 136

duty to defend regardless of opinion of guilt, 135–136

fraud or chicane prohibited, 137

guilty accused, should not withdraw, 135

nonlawyer must observe, 133

fitness reports, 125

initial interview, 145–146

initial preparation, 146–147

lack of knowledge may cause reversal, 160

lawyer

accused advised concerning, 145–146

required if BCD special court, 122

required if trial counsel lawyer, 123

legal officer may advise as to law, 126

members, fraternizing with, 167

members, ineligible as defense counsel, 163

as members, must be challenged, 167

NJP, lawyer's advice not required, 34

nonlawyer

cannot be detailed if BCD special court, 122

may be detailed to non-BCD special court, 123

opening statement, 217

personal appearance and conduct of accused advice, 151

preparation, 145–152

record of trial examination, 235

right of accused to, 249, 360

selection by accused

BCD special court, 122

non-BCD special court, 123

stipulate unimportant matters, 190

in summary court, 110

theory of defense, 151

trial notes, 151

witnesses, informing accused of, 147

Defenses. *See also* Intent; *specific offenses listed*

abandoned property, 77

accused advised as to right to assert, 148

accused questioned concerning, 146–147

affirmative, 348

alibi, 78

Article 39(a) session may hear, 207

barring trial, 60–62

character, good, 78

coercion, 77

entrapment, 77

failure to allege offense, 61

former jeopardy

defense inapplicable if different sovereign, 61

discussed, 60–61

does not apply if failure to allege offense, 61

former punishment
  discussed briefly, 61
  no defense if serious offense, 100–103
generally, 57-62
identity, mistaken, 78
immunity, grant of, 62
impossibility 58–59, 69, 346
insanity, 60
instructions as to, 80–83
instructions required for each defense in
    issue, 226
intoxication, 77
  if specific intent crime, 205, 358
jurisdiction, 62
lesson teaching, 80–83
lost property, 77–78
mislaid property, 78
mistake of fact, 77, 66–69
  in general intent offense, 59
  unauthorized absence, honest and
    reasonable, 66–69
not guilty plea as, 57–58
motion for a finding of not guilty, 214
  at nonjudicial punishment, 88
order, obedience of, 77
pardon, 62
speedy trial, lack of, 24–25, 62
statute of limitations, 61–62, 70, 347
  extension by war, 70, 347
summary court must recognize, 106
teaching a lesson, 77
Deferment of confinement
  as constitutional right, 18, 343
  court-martial cannot award, 233
  discussion, 240
  summary court, 112
Delict, **367**
Delivery of absentee. *See* Unauthorized ab-
    sence
Demonstrative evidence
  discussed briefly, 189
  inflammatory matters, 198
Deposition, **367–368**
  closed session, members cannot take into,
    169
  summary court can utilize, 109
Dereliction in the performance of duties,
    368
  elements, 349
  example of, 84, 349
Desertion
  compared with unauthorized absence,
    228
  findings of lesser included offense, ex-
    ample, 228–229
  specific intent required, 67
  statute of limitations, 70
  unauthorized absence
    assistance in proving intent to desert,
      215
    lesser included offense, 70, 170, 347
Detention of pay
  apportioned if combined with forfeiture,
    93

discussed, 92
  as nonjudicial punishment, 92
  special or general courts may award, 234
  summary court may award, 111
Digest of Opinions, 11–12
Diminished rations, as NJP, 90–91
Direct evidence, 182, **368**
  compared with circumstantial evidence,
    170
  examples of, 182
Direct examination
  discussed, 184
  examples of, 185
Discipline officer
  drafter of NAVPERS 2696, 31
  dual function as legal officer, 31
  interviews accused, 31
Dishonorable discharge, **368**
  bad conduct discharge is lesser punish-
    ment, 121
  special court cannot award, 119
  summary court cannot award, 111
Dismiss, NJP retained in Unit Punishment
    Book, 95
Dismissal, **368**
  special court cannot award, 119
  summary court cannot award, 111
Disorder and neglects to the prejudice of
    good order and discipline. *See* Gen-
    eral Article 134
Disrespect
  towards petty officer, 84, 350
  towards superior officer, 84, 350
Dissent, 28
Documentary evidence, 187, **368**
  authentication of
    copy, 189
    original, 187–188
  bringing into closed session, 169
Double jeopardy. *See* Former jeopardy
Drafting. *See* Charges and specifications
Drunk, **368**
  aboard ship, 102
  defense to specific intent offense, 77
  on duty, 102–103
  example, as defense, 205, 358
  jurisdiction over off-base incident, 131
  as Officer of the Deck, serious offense,
    100–103

Elements, 226, **368**
  dereliction in the performance of duty,
    349
  disobedience of petty officer, 349
  drafting of, in specification, 64
  general order, 349
  guilty plea, informing accused of, 215
  instructions
    lesser included offenses, 226
    tailored to offense, 226
  larceny, 73–76
  lawful order, 349
  missing movement through design, 347

reasonable doubt applies to every element, 111
trial counsel must prove, 139
unauthorized absence, 55–56
Embezzlement, 73
Enlisted men
as member of court-martial
ineligible if same unit, 163
initially eligible under certain conditions, 162
if same unit as accused, must be challenged, 167
Entrapment, as defense, 77
Error, rehearing possible when prejudicial, 237–238
Evidence 181–200, **368**. *See also individual headings*
Article 39(a) session may determine admission, 207
President of U.S. may prescribe rules of, 9
purposes of, 182–183
relevancy, 190
summary court uses same rules of, 106
Executive officer
cannot convene court-martial, 117
designates space for NJP, 86
legal officer's relationship with, 126
legal responsibilities, 126
review of preliminary inquiry, 42
Execution of his office, **368**
Expert witness, 196
opinions may be expressed by, 196
Extenuation and mitigation. *See* Mitigation and extenuation
Extra duties
apportioned if combined with same type punishment, 93
correctional custody may run concurrently with, 93
discussed, 91
restriction may run concurrently with, 93
Extra military instruction, nonpunitive measure, 86

Fact-finding bodies. *See also* Line of duty and misconduct determinations
courts of inquiry, 254–255
formal investigations, 255
informal investigations, 256–257
investigative report, 257–258
parties, 252–254
preliminary inquiry may recommend, 41
selection of, 252
substitution for NJP hearing, 89
types of, 251
Fact, question of, 174, **374**
distinguished from question of law, 175
military judge rules finally on interlocutory, 176
exception, mental responsibility, 176
presiding president's rulings subject to objection, 174–175

Failure to allege offense
discussion, 61
motion to dismiss, 213
example of, 223, 258–259
Failure to obey lawful order. *See* Order
False pretenses, 73
Federal law, as basis for military law, 8, 9
Felony, **368–369**
Findings, **369**. *See also* Guilty plea; Not guilty plea
example of, 249, 360
instructions, 82
Fine, **369**
special or general court may award, mentioned, 234
summary court may award, 111
Fitness reports
discussed, 125
military judges, 176
Flag or general officer
Court of Military Appeals reviews cases concerning, 240
general courts convened by, 116
nonjudicial punishment
authority as to amount, 92
delegation of authority, 87
officer in charge may be designated by, 87
special or summary courts convened by, 116–117
Flogging, abolition of, 6, 17
Forfeiture, **369**
apportioned if combined with detention, 93
basic allowance for quarters, 107–108
court-martial, 233
computation of, 233–234
general court amount, 233
special court amount, 119, 233–234
summary court amount, 111
as nonjudicial punishment, 92
Former jeopardy, **369**
applicable if charges dismissed, 237
constitutional right, 18
discussion, 60–61
distinguished from former punishment, 101
inapplicable if jurisdictional defect, 237
motion to dismiss, 213
Former punishment, **369**
bars court-martial if minor punishment, 100–103
distinguished from former jeopardy, 101
mentioned, 61
motion to dismiss, 213
Fruit of the poison tree doctrine, 40–41

General Article 134, mentioned, 350
General court-martial, **369**
convening authorities, 116
discussion, 206–207
as graduated response, 13
military judges are independent judiciary, 176

new trial petitions, 241
president is never presiding officer, 206
reduction permitted in every case, 234
review, mentioned, 240
service of charges prior to 39(a) session, 207
General court-martial convening authority. *See also* Supervisory authority
reviews NJP appeals, 94
General intent offenses. *See* Intent
General or flag officer. *See* Flag or general officer
Good cause, 164
Good character. *See* Moral character
Graduated response, nonpunitive measures, 85
Grand jury, defined, 18, **369**
Gross negligence, **369**
Guilty plea
accused defending self cannot plead guilty, 215
aggravating circumstances may be presented, 216, 230
discussion of, 218–222
hearing required prior to acceptance, 215–216

Habeas corpus, **369**
constitutional right mentioned, 19
Hard labor without confinement
limit as to amount court may award, 248, 360
summary court may award 45 days, 111
Hearsay evidence, 192, **369**. *See also* Evidence; Original evidence
discussed, 192–193
exceptions to, 193–195
Husband-wife communications, 197

Identification card, false, 84, 350
Identification, real evidence, 187
example, 205, 358
Identity, mistaken, as defense, 78
Immunity, grant of, 62
Individual defense counsel, **369**
advice of accused's right to, 209, 145–146
Inflammatory matters, rule prohibiting, 198
Influence, command. *See* Command influence
Infra, **369**
Initiation of charges, 30, **369–370**
requirement to, 8, 31
who may initiate, 30
Insanity
discussed, 60
time of offense
convening authority may not return to court, 213–214
military judge rules subject to objection on, 176
Inspections. *See* Search and seizure
Instructions, ship's as orders, 84, 349
Instructions to court, 224, **370**
defenses, 81–83, 348
findings, 168–172, 225–227

purpose of, 82
sentence, 231–232, 243–248
Intent
general intent offenses, 58, 76, **369**
mistake of fact, 59, 68–69
unauthorized absence, 58
proof of, exception to hearsay rule, 193–194
specific intent offenses, **374**
defenses to, 77–78
larceny and wrongful appropriation, 75, 76
missing movement through design, 205, 358
mistake of fact, 67
wrongful appropriation, 76
Interlocutory, 174–175, **370**
accused may limit testimony to, 197
Article 39(a) session may hear, 207
Intoxication. *See* Drunk
Investigating officer. *See also* Preliminary inquiry officer
as member, ineligible, 163
as member, must be challenged, 167

JAG Journal, 11
JAG lawyer, **370**. *See also* Certified military lawyer and Staff Judge Advocate
JAG Manual, **370**
Court of Military Appeals may modify, 10
source of military law, 10
JAG Manual investigation. *See* Fact-finding bodies
Joy riding, 76
Judge Advocate General
certifies cases to Court of Military Appeals, 240
legal officer may communicate directly with, 126
Judicial notice, 191, **370**
authentication of original document by, 187
discussed, 191
Judiciary Activity. *See* U.S. Navy-Marine Corps Judiciary Activity
Jurisdiction, 117–118, **370**
as to accused, 118
active duty serviceman as victim, 131
another trial if no jurisdiction, 237
bad checks, depends on place of offense, 131, 355
base, offense on, 131, 354–355
command of accused, determination of, 55–56
competency of members, 118
discussed, 62, 117–119
drunk and disorderly off base, 131
examples, 130–131, 353–355
marijuana, 131, 132, 354
minor offenses, 131
motion to dismiss, 213
nonjudicial punishment authority, 87

not guilty finding, review of, 236
number of members affects, 118
as to offense, 118–119
sentence must be within power of court, 119
summary court
enlisted persons only, 107
noncapital offenses only, 107
punishments limited, 111–112
uniform facilitates crime, 132

Larceny, **370**
distinguished from wrongful appropriation, 76
general owner, 74, 78
obtaining type (false pretenses), 73
owner, 74
drafting of, 78
possession, 74
special owner, 74, 78
steal, 226–227
taking money and intending to replace equivalent, 83–84, 348–349
taking type
elements, 73–76
generally, 73
types of, 72–73
value
discussed, 75
drafting of, 79
withholding type (embezzlement), 73
wrongful appropriation is lesser included offense, 76
example, 249, 360
wrongful requirement, 74
Law center, 122
Law officer, abolished, 8, **370**
Law, questions of, 174, **374**
Court of Military Appeals reviews, 240
distinguished from question of fact, 175
military judge rules finally on, 176
presiding president's rulings as to, 174–175
Leadership, at NJP, 86–87
Leading questions, 184, **370**
examples of, 185
Lectures on military law. *See* Command influence
Legal officer, **370–371**. *See also* Certified military lawyer; Staff judge advocate
convening authority, communications with, 126
dual function as discipline officer, 31
duties of, 126–127
executive officer, relationship with, 126
preliminary inquiry filed with, 42
review of courts
discussion, 237–239
summary courts, 112–113
staff judge advocate, communications with, 126
Lesser included offense, 228, **371**
accused may plead guilty to, 214–215
attempt as, 228–229

discussed, 228
elements instructed upon if in issue, 226
findings
examples of, 228–229
instructions as to, 225–226
example of, 70, 249, 347, 360
mentioned, 170
reviewing authority may approve only, 239
wrongful appropriation is in larceny case, 76
Lesson teaching, as defense, 77, 81
Letters, authentication of original by, 187
Liberty card, taking of, 104, 351
Limited purpose testimony
accused's rights regarding, 196–197
instruction required regarding, 227
Line of duty and misconduct determinations, 260–266. *See also* Fact-finding bodies
convening authority's action, 265
diseases, 264–265
24-hour rule, 263
investigation requirement, 263–264
line of duty discussed, 262–263
misconduct, 261; discussed, 261–262
Liquor
prohibited on ships or aircraft, 11, 84
spirit ration abolished, 7
Lost property, as defense, 77–78

Mackenzie, Alexander Slidell, 14–17
Manual for Courts-Martial, **371**
Court of Military Appeals may modify, 10
member cannot utilize, 165, 180, 357
source of military law, 9
Manual of the Judge Advocate General. *See* JAG Manual
Marijuana offenses, jurisdiction, 131–132, 354
Marine Corps
JAG Manual applicable to, 10
NJP service record entries, 95
preliminary inquiry forms, 95
reduction at nonjudicial punishment, 91
review of courts, 239
Unit Punishment Book, 95–96
Marital privilege, 197
MCM. *See Manual for Courts-Martial*
Members, 162–173, **371**
absence after assembly, 164
good cause requirement, 164
accuser ineligible, 163
Article 39(a) session, request for enlisted, 207
attendance at trial, 142
attitude during trial, 165
challenges of
accuser must be challenged, 167
grounds must be disclosed, 166
member in previous trial, 167
voting procedure when president presiding, 212

clemency
    example of, 180, 357
    recommendation for, 235
competency of, affects jurisdiction, 118
confessions or admissions, voluntariness resolved by, 227
commissioned officer as, 162
convening order notifies of detailing, 164
criticisms and coercion of, 124
defense counsel ineligible, 163
discussion of case with counsel prohibited, 152
enlisted men as
    discussion, 162–163
    percentage and unit requirement, 208
    same unit, challenge required, 167
    same unit, ineligible, 163
excusals of, 130, 142, 353
fact question, president presiding, 174–175
findings
    determination of, 168–170, 227–230
    instructions, 168–172, 225–227
    matters that cannot be considered, 169–170
    president presides during, 173, 174
    reasonable doubt standard, 169–170
    voting on, 170–172, 180, 357
    voting procedure, 171
fitness reports, 125
fraternizing with parties to trial, 167
ineligible, if previously member, 163
inquiry as to facts prior to trial, 165
investigating officer ineligible, 163
language, intemperate, 177–180
law question, president presiding, 174
lectures prohibited once assembled, 125
MCM's and reference material prohibited, 165
    presiding president may use, 166
number of, jurisdictional aspects, 118
oath
    effective for duration of convening order, 211
    example, 166
objection to president's ruling, procedure for, 175
opinions, preconceived or fixed, 164
preliminary inquiry officer ineligible, 163
president is senior member present, 162
prosecution witness ineligible as, 163
rank if officer accused, 163
rehearing of case, must not be same members, 237–238
responsibilities prior to trial, 164–165
seating of, 166, 208
sentence
    deferred confinement cannot be awarded, 233
    instructions as to, 172–173, 231–232, 243–248
    procedure for determining, 172–173

    suspended sentence cannot to awarded, 233
    votes required, 234
stipulations in closed session prohibited, 191
summary court only has one, 105
trial counsel ineligible, 163
trial counsel, previously, must be challenged, 167
trial guides, use of, 180, 357
voir dire, 167
    example of, 129
warrant officer as, 162–163
witnesses
    called by, 183
    examination by, 168, 186
    for prosecution, must be challenged, 167, 180, 357
Mental capacity, **371.** *See also* Insanity
Mental responsibility, **371.** *See also* Insanity
Meritorious Mast, 98
Military judge, **371.** *See also* Presiding officer
accused, advising of right to, 147
Article 39(a) session
    only judge may conduct, 207
    request for judge without members, 207
challenges for cause determined by, 212
charges furnished to prior to trial, 141
counsel's conduct, responsibility for, 156–157
criticisms and coercion of, 124
detailing of
    BCD special court, 120–122, 131, 354
    non-BCD special court, 122
duties of, 175–176
fitness report of, 125
general court always has judge, 206
instructions as to findings consideration, 224–225
interlocutory questions, rules finally on, 176
    exception, 176
members, fraternizing with, 167
motion for finding of not guilty, rules finally, 214
NJP may be considered as to sentence, 230
oath only taken when originally certified, 210
presides in any case to which detailed, 175
seating of, 209
summarization of evidence permitted, 227
trial without members, request for, 208
voir dire, curtailment may be prejudicial, 179
Military Justice. *See* Military law
Military law, 3. *See also* Civilian law
criticisms of, 118
federal law as basis of, 8, 9

graduated responses to offenses, 12–13
history, 3–8
  ancient history, 3–5
  early American naval law, 5–7
  English influence, 4–5
  evidence, brief history of, 181
jurisdiction of civilian courts over servicemen, 117–119
officer's responsibility regarding. *See*
  Officer
publications, 11–12
  Court-Martial Reports, locating cases
    in, 11
  JAG Journal, mentioned, 11
  *United States Court of Military Ap-
    peals,* locating cases in, 11
purpose, 3
sources, 9–11
Uniform Code of Military Justice, inception of, 7–8
Minor offenses, defined, 86
Miranda-Tempia cases, 33–34
Mislaid property, as defense, 78
Missing movement
  design, 70–71, 347
    elements, 347
    sample case, 203–205
  harbor shift not constituting, 70–71, 348
  neglect, 70–71, 348
    findings of lesser included offense, 228
  service record entries, 348
Mistake of fact
  as defense to specific intent offense, 77
  discussion, 59, 66–69
  specific intent offense only need be
    honest, 67
Mitigate, defined, **371**
Mitigating, NJP, 96–97
Mitigation and extenuation
  comparison with civilian law, mentioned,
    19
  defense counsel advice to accused as to,
    150–151
  defense counsel must present evidence as
    to, 136
  extenuation, 231, **368**
  instructions as to sentence must include,
    231–232
    discussion, 243–248
  mitigation, 231, **371**
  at NJP, 88
  summary court, 109
  witness for defense, right to obtain for,
    144
Moral character. *See also* Character
  bad, prosecution cannot initially admit,
    198–199
  good, defense may present as to findings,
    198–199
Moral turpitude offense, **371–372**
Motion. 213, **372**. *See* Motion for appropriate relief; Motion to dismiss; Motion
  for a finding of not guilty

Motion for finding of not guilty, 214, **372**
  convening authority may not return to
    court, 213
  example as to when appropriate, 159–160
  military judge rules finally on, 176
  presiding president's rulings, 174
Motion to dismiss, 213, **372**
  convening authority may direct recon-
    sideration, 213
  failure to allege offense, 61
  former jeopardy, 60–61
  former punishment, 61
  immunity, grant of, 62
  insanity, 60
  jurisdiction, lack of, 62
  pardon, 62
  speedy trial, 24–25, 62
  statute of limitations, 61–62
Motion to grant appropriate relief, 214,
  372
  convening authority cannot return to
    court, 214
Motive, as hearsay evidence rule exception,
  193–194
Multiplicious offenses
  discussed briefly, 232
  example, 248, 359
  sentence limited by, 232
Mutiny, *Somers,* 14–17

Naval Academy, formation of, 17
Naval Investigative Service (NIS)
  initiation of charges by, 30
  responsibilities and limitations, 32
Naval law, **372**. *See also* American naval
  law; Sea law
  derived from previous codes, 4
  developed from sea law, 4
  English influence, 4–5
Naval service, **372**
NAVPERS 2696, **372**
  "Action of Commanding Officer" com-
    pletion, 94
  "Action of Executive Officer" completion,
    42
  appeal, may be forwarded with, 94
  Article 31 warning block completion, 31
  "Details of Offenses" portion completion,
    31
  drafting of charges and specifications, 31
  filed in Unit Punishment Book, 95
  "Final Administrative Action" comple-
    tion, 94–95
  "Information Concerning Accused" com-
    pletion, 31
  initiating charges by, 30
  investigating officer, completeness and
    accuracy of, 33
  legal officer may prepare, 126
  preliminary inquiry results on, 41
  "Remarks of Division Officer" comple-
    tion, 33
  "Right to Demand Trial by Court-Mar-
    tial" completion, 42

Navy Regulations. *See* U.S. Navy Regulations
New trial petitions, 241
Noncommissioned officer
    disrespect, presence required, 84, 350
    extra duties should not demean, 91
    order of, 84, 349
    summary court reduction limited, 111
Nonjudicial punishment, **372**
    accused's rights, 88–89
    alternatives available, 89
    appeal rights, 94–95
    authority to impose, 87
    concurrent punishments, 93
    consecutive punishments, 93
    corrective in nature, 86
    court-martial, right to, 87–88
    court-martial sentence, may affect, 230
        example, 248, 359–360
    dismiss, 89
        Unit Punishment Book would retain, 95
    dismissed with warning, 89
        Unit Punishment Book would retain, 95
    fact-finding body may substitute for hearing, 89
    as graduated response, 12–13
    hearing not required prior to court-martial, 43
    jurisdiction, units on ship, 104, 351
    legal officer's duties, 126–127
    minor offenses only, 86, 100–103
    Miranda-Tempia advice not required, 34
    mitigating punishments, 96–97
    nonpunitive measures may suffice, 85
    persons subject to, 87
    preliminary inquiry
        as basis for, 43
        may recommend, 41
        prior to, 30–53
    pre-mast screening, 42–43
    punishments
        admonishment, 90
        arrest in quarters, 90
        bread and water, 90–91, 93
        correctional custody, 91; deferring execution of, 104, 351
        detention of pay, 92
        diminished rations, 90–91
        extra duties, 91
        forfeiture of pay, 92
        reduction in rate, 91
        reprimand, 90
        restriction, 90
        self-quiz regarding, 104, 351
    remitting punishments, 96
    service record entries of, 95
    setting aside punishments, 96
    summary court cannot consider, 111
    summary court distinguished from, 115, 352
    summary court more serious than, 86
    suspending punishments, 97

Nonpunitive measures, 85, **372**
    discussed, 85–86
    as graduated response, 12, 85
Not guilty plea
    determination of guilt or innocence, 168–170
    findings
        examples of, 228–229
        jurisdiction is only issue, 236
        two-thirds of members must concur, 229
    instructions, 225–227
    meaning of, 216–217
    summary court must enter in certain cases, 110
    voting procedure, 171

Oath
    accuser must take on charge sheet, 108
    civilian attorneys must be sworn for for each trial, 211
    court personnel, requirement for, 210–211
    members, 166
    noncertified military counsel sworn each trial, 211
    who may administer, 108
    witness, 183
        authenticates testimony of, 186–187
Offenses. *See* Prior offenses; Lesser included offense; Multiplicious offenses
Office hours. *See* Nonjudicial punishment
Officer
    if accused, junior member should not try, 163
    arrest in quarters, 90
    arrested or confined, regulations concerning, 23
    convening authority. *See* Convening authority
    drunk as OOD is serious offense, 100–103
    legal officer. *See* Legal officer
    member, initially eligible as, 162
    offenses, reporting required by, 8, 31
    order of, 84, 350
    preliminary inquiry officer. *See* Preliminary inquiry
    president of court. *See* President of court-martial
    pretrial restraint authority, 22
    rank to hold summary court, 105
    restriction and arrest, served concurrently, 93
    restriction on board ship, 90
    shore patrol or security officer, mentioned, 8
    summary court cannot try, 107
    trial or defense counsel. *See individual headings*
Officer in charge, NJP authority, 87
Officer of the deck, drunk as, 100–103
Official records. *See also* Service records

as exception to
 best evidence rule, 195
 hearsay evidence rule, 194–195
 shore patrol report inadmissible as, 194
Oléron, sea law of, 4
Opening argument, findings, 225
Opening statement, 217
Open sessions, **372**
Opinion evidence, 195, **372–373**
 authentication of original document by,
  187
 inadmissible as a general rule, 195
  exceptions, 195–196
Oral evidence, 186–187, **373**
Order
 as defense, 77
 general order, failure to obey, 84, 349
  elements, 349
 lawful order, 84, 349–350
  elements, 349
 noncommissioned officer, disobedience of,
  84, 349
  elements, 350
 officer, disobedience of, 84, 350
  elements, 350
 petty officer, disobedience of, 84, 349
  elements, 349
 shore patrol member, 84, 350
Organization, 55
Original evidence, 192–193. *See also* Evidence

Pardon
 defense, 62
 motion to dismiss, 213
Petty officer
 disrespect, presence required, 84, 350
 extra duties should not demean, 91
 order of, 84, 349
 summary court reduction limited, 111
Physical conditions or military exigencies,
  124
 certified military lawyer, non-BCD court,
  122–123
 enlisted members need not be assigned if,
  162
 military judge, BCD special court, 121
Piracy, 14–17
Pleas. *See also* Guilty plea; Not guilty plea
 accused must be advised concerning, 148–
  149
 discussed, 214–215
Police. *See* Civilian police
Preferring charges, 41, **373**
 commanding officer may become accuser
  by directing, 41
 preliminary inquiry officer's duty to, 41
Preliminary inquiry. *See also* Preliminary
  inquiry officer and Investigating
  officer
 charges and specifications, drafting of,
  62–65

commanding officer, 373
 initial study of case, 42–43
 responsibility to order, 32
comment block completion, 41
executive officer's action, 42
manner of conducting investigation, 32–
  33
Marine Corps, locally prepared forms, 95
Naval Investigative Service statements as,
  32
NAVPERS 2696, results transcribed on,
  41
pretrial investigation distinguished from,
  43
questions to resolve, 32
recommendation alternatives, 41
speedy action required, 24–25
Preliminary inquiry officer, **373**. *See also*
  Preliminary inquiry
 ineligible as member, 163
 legal officer may advise, 126
 as member, must be challenged, 167
 reinvestigate if evidence insufficient, 89
President of court-martial, 162, **373**. *See also*
  Presiding officer
 Article 39(a) session may not be conducted by, 207
 language, intemperate, 177–180
 non-presiding, duties of, 173–174
 officer may become, 8–9
 presiding
  challenges for cause, members rule on,
   175, 212
  duties of, 174–175
  instructions, method of discussion of,
   225
  motion for a finding of not guilty, subject to objection, 214
  objections to rulings, procedure for,
   175
  summary of duties during trial, 217–
   218
  voir dire curtailment may be prejudicial, 179
 specifications may not be given to prior
  to trial, 141
President of the U.S.
 prescribes the MCM, 9
 relationship with Congress, 6
Presiding officer, **373**. *See also* President of
  court-martial; Military judge
 advises accused of counsel rights, 209–210
 certificate of correction, authentication
  of, 236
 guilty plea
  hearing as to, 215–216
  waiver required, 216
 initial informal inquiry, 208
 instructions
  findings, 225–227; examples of, 168–170
  sentence, 231–232
 members questioning of witnesses, procedure for, 168

military judge is always, if detailed, 173–174, 175
record of trial authenticated by, 235
time of trial set by, 207
Presumption of innocence, 168, 225
Pretrial agreements
accused must be advised concerning, 149
discussed, three types, 149
example of, 356
members must not be informed of, 157
Pretrial investigation, **373**
as constitutional right, 18, 343
distinguished from preliminary inquiry, 43
NJP hearing not required prior to, 43
NJP may forward case to, 89
preliminary inquiry case may be forwarded to, 43
preliminary inquiry distinguished from, 43
speedy action required, 24–25
Pretrial restraint. *See also* Arrest; Commanding officer; Confinement; Restriction in lieu of arrest
authority to, 22
limitations on nature of, 23
offenses connected with, 24
probable cause requirement, 21–22
release from, 23–24
requirement for, 28, 344
unlawful detention prohibited, 24
unlawful restraint mentioned, 24
Priest-penitent communications, 198
Prior offenses
not admissible against accused, 199
exceptions, 199
offense, **372**
trial counsel cannot imply there are, 134
Privileged communications. *See* Confidential communications
Probable cause
apprehension search, 21, 39
pretrial restraint, 21–22
search and seizure, 36–37, 52–53, 345
search authorized by commanding officer, 36–38
search warrant, 40
Procedure for courts-martial
Article 98, Code, 17
failure to comply with, 17
President of U.S. may prescribe rules, 9
Proceedings in revision, 237
Prosecution case in chief, 183, **373**
Prosecution case in rebuttal, 183, **373**
Publications. *See* Military law
Punishment. *See* Sentence; Nonjudicial punishment; *specific punishments*
Punitive articles, **373**

Rate of accused. *See* Charges and specifications
Real evidence, 187, **374**. *See also* Evidence
authentication, 187
example of, 205, 358
chain of custody, 187
in closed session, 169
identification, 187
inflammatory matters, 198
Reasonable doubt, 111, 169–170
findings, instruction as to, 168, 225–226
summary court must apply, 111
Recess, 212
Records of trial
authentication of, 112
discussed, 235–236
members cannot take into closed session, 169
summary court, 12, 112
trial counsel supervises, 142–143
verbatim requirement if BCD, 121
Recross examination, 186
Redirect examination, 186
Reduction
court may always award, 112
forfeiture based on reduced rate, 233–234
nonjudicial punishment
discussion, 91
mitigation to forfeiture or detention, 94, 97
suspension explained, 97
suspension permitted even if executed, 97
permitted in every special and general court, 234
summary court, 111
example, 114–115, 352
Reference material. *See Manual for Courts-Martial*
Rehearing, 238
Relevant evidence, 190
examples of, 203, 205, 357–358
Remitting, NJP, 96
Report chit, **374**
Reporter
convening order should not refer to, 143
present in special court cases, 143
Report of offenses forms, 30
Reprimand
as nonjudicial punishment, 90
as nonpunitive measure, 85, 89
special or general court may award, mentioned, 234
summary court may award, 111
Request Mast, 98
Restraint. *See* Pretrial restraint
Restriction, **374**. *See also* Restriction in lieu of arrest
court, limits may award, 248, 360
nonjudicial punishment
apportionment, if combination of same nature punishments, 93
arrest in quarters, concurrent with restriction, 93
correctional custody, concurrent with restriction, 93
discussed, 90
extra duties, concurrent with restriction, 93

summary court may award two months, 111
unlawful, example of, 29, 344
Restriction in lieu of arrest, 23, 374. *See also* Restriction
limitations on imposition as, 23
release from, 23–24
Review of courts-martial
compared to civilian law, mention, 19
discussion, 236–241
improper argument, 202
instructions of reviewing authority, 12
summary court, 112–113
special appeal to JAG permitted, 114
Revision, proceedings in, 237
Rhodes, sea law of, 4
Rocks and shoals, mentioned, 7
Rules for the Regulation of the Navy of the United Colonies, 5–6
Rum. *See* Liquor

Sea law. *See also* Naval law
American naval law influenced by, 6
reason for original development, 3–4
Seal or inked stamp, authentication of copy by, 189
Search and seizure, 374
apprehension, search during, 39, 51–52, 344–355
area search lawful under limited circumstances, 38–39
commanding officer's search, 36–38
apartment off-base, 52, 345
delegation of authority limited, 37
locker on ship, 52, 345
method of conducting, 37–38
probable cause requirement, 36–37; example, 52–53, 345
warrant search equivalent to, 40
what may be searched, 36
consent search, 39–40
discussion, 35–41
hot pursuit search, 40
fields and woodlands search, 40
fruit of the poison tree doctrine, 40–41
inspections do not constitute, 38, 53, 346
necessity search, 39
private search, 52, 345
public policy, basis for rules, 196
shakedowns, 38–39, 374
warrant search of civilian judge, 40
what may be searched for, 35–36
Search warrant, 40
probable cause requirement, 40
Self-incrimination. *See* Confessions or admissions and Constitutional rights of servicemen
defense counsel's explanation of rights as to, 149–150
guilty plea waives, 216
public policy is basis for, 196
Sentence. *See* Nonjudicial punishment; *specific punishments*
acceleration clauses may effect, 121

aggravating circumstances
admissible if guilty plea, 230
summary court conviction constitutes, 105
ancient punishments, 5
announcement of, example, 234–235
arguments, example of improper, 136–137
commuting of, defined, 238
convictions admissible if final and within 6 years, 230
early American, 6
flogging abolished in 1850, 6, 17
guilty plea, accused must be advised as to, 215–216
instructions, discussed, 231–232, 243–248
jurisdictional aspects, 119
multiplicious offenses, 232
example, 248, 359
NJP considered if judge presides, 230
procedure for determination, 172–173, 230–231
summary court, mitigation and extenuation, 109, 111
trial counsel, improper argument regarding, 134
Sergeant (E–5), NJP cannot reduce, 91
Service-connected offenses. *See* Jurisdiction
Service record entries. *See also* Official records
authentication
copy of document, 189
custodian may, 187
original document, 187–188; example, 188
stipulation, example of, 191
good character may be shown by, 198
as hearsay evidence exception, 194–195
example of, 204, 358
judicial notice of custodian's signatures, 191
legal officer may prepare, 127
missing movement, 348
NJP punishments must be recorded in, 95
summary court entries, 113
unauthorized absence proof, 65
Setting aside NJP, 96
Shakedowns. *See* Search and seizure
Shore patrol
initiation of charges by report of, 30
order of, 84, 350
report inadmissible in evidence, 194
Somers mutiny, 14–17
Sources of military law, 9–11
Special court-martial, 374
BCD court
certified military lawyer must be initially detailed, 209
new trial petitions, 241
personnel requirements, 120–122
review of, 239–240
charges must be served 3 days before trial, 139

confinement, six months is maximum, 233
convening authorities, 116–117
as graduated response, 13
jurisdictional limits of punishment, 119, 233–234
members, three required, 163
military judges of, 176
non-BCD court
Article 69 relief available, 240–241
certified military lawyer offered accused, 122–123, 145, 209
new trial petitions, 241
review of, 239
NJP, case may be forwarded from, 89
physical conditions or military exigencies, 123–124
preliminary inquiry prior to, 30–53
reduction permitted in every case, 234
service of charges 3 days prior 39(a) session, 207
Specifications. *See* Charges and specifications
Specific intent offense. *See* Intent
Speedy trial
considerations in determining reasonableness, 24–25
constitutional right, 18
delay of trial request by defense, 142
discussion, 24–25
mentioned, 62
motion to dismiss, 213
restriction requires, 29, 344
trial counsel's preparation for defense of, 139
unreasonable delay as bar to trial, 24–25
Spencer, Phillip, 14–17
Spontaneous exclamation, 193
hearsay evidence rule, exception to, 193
Staff judge advocate, 374–375. *See also* Legal officer
convening authority, direct communication with, 126
legal officer may communicate directly with, 126
review
BCD special courts, 239
NJP appeals, 94
summary and non-BCD specials, 113, 239
State of mind or body, exception to hearsay rule, 193–194
Statute of limitations, 375
discussed, 61–62, 70, 347
motion to dismiss, 213
Stipulations, 190, 375
closed session, members cannot take into, 169
discussed, 190–191, 201–202
fact
authentication of copy of document by, 189
authentication of original of document by, 187

contradiction by trial counsel, 200–202
example, 191
testimony, 190–191
Subpoena, 375
as constitutional right of accused, 18
discussion, 143–144
summary court may use, 109
use of, 143–144
Summary court-martial, 375
accused's rights, 110
accuser may convene, 106
accuser may serve as, 106
admonition, 111
apportionment of similar type punishment, 111–112, 114, 351–352
Article 69 relief available, 240–241
authentication, 112
bad conduct discharge cannot be awarded, 111
bread and water, 111
challenges not permitted, 106–107
commanding officer may forward to, at NJP, 89
confinement, not in excess of one month, 111
contempt of court, 109
constitutes conviction, 105
convening authorities, 106, 116–117
defense counsel may be permitted, 110
defenses must be recognized, 106
deferment of confinement, 112
depositions, 109
detention of pay, 111
dishonorable discharge cannot be awarded by, 111
dismissal cannot be awarded by, 111
enlisted servicemen may be tried by, 107
evidence
rules same as other courts, 106
summarization of, 12, 112
fine, 111
forfeiture limited to two-thirds of one month, 111
as graduated response, 13
hard labor without confinement limited to 45 days, 111
initial examination of case file, 107–108
jurisdiction as to persons, 118
membership, 105
mentioned, 13
minor offenses, 106
mitigation and extenuation, 109
new trial petitions, 241
noncapital cases only, 107
nonjudicial punishment
distinguished from, 115, 352
less serious than, 86
officers cannot be tried by, 107
preliminary inquiry prior to, 30–53
pretrial conference recommended, 108–109
rank of, 105
record of, 12, 112

reduction limited in certain cases, 111
 example, 114–115, 352
refusal of, 107
reprimand, 111
responsibilities
 findings, 115, 352
 generally, 106
restriction not in excess of two months,
 111
review of, 112–114, 239
rights of accused, 109
sentence
 convictions considered, 111; example
  of, 115, 352–353
 mitigation and extenuation right, 109,
  111
 NJP cannot be considered, 111
service record entries, 113
review of staff judge advocate, 113
subpoena, 109
trial counsel not detailed, 105
witnesses, 110
Supervisory authority, **375**
 court-martial orders, 241
 review of courts, 113, 239–240
 reviews after convening authority, 239
 summary court
  review, 113
  summarization requirement, 12, 112
Supra, **375**
Surrender of absentee. See Unauthorized
 absence
Suspension
 convening authority may, 238
 court cannot award, 233
 discussion, 238
 nonjudicial punishment
  discussed, 97
  reduction may be suspended, even if
   executed, 97
  vacation of, 97

Tempia case, 33–34, 44–51
Time and place of offense, drafting in specification, 64
Time of trial, determined by presiding
 officer, 207
Trial brief
 defense counsel, 151
 trial counsel, 139–140, 144
Trial counsel, 133, **375**
 accused, duty to insure presence, 142
 administrative duties, 141–143
 arguments of, 153–154, 225
 arraignment duties, 212–213
 cannot comment on accused's failure to
  testify, 196–197
 cannot contradict stipulations of fact,
  200–202
 challenges, discloses knowledge of, 211
 charge sheet
  examination, 137–138
  service on accused, 138

charges and specifications, withdrawal of,
 140–141
convening authority's views, cannot
 comment on, 134
criticisms or coercion of, 124
delay requests by defense, 142
duties during trial
 counsel qualifications announced, 209
 personnel of court announced by, 209
elements must be proven, 139
ethics
 duty is to see justice done, 134
 examples of improper statements, 134
final review prior to trial, 144
improper argument by, 202
ineligible as member, 163
initial preparation, 139–140
legal officer
 advises as to law, 126
 assists in preparation of record of trial,
  126
member, cannot be excused from trial by,
 142
as member, must be challenged, 167
members, fraternizing with, 167
motion to dismiss, action if disagreement,
 223, 258–259
noncertified lawyer as, 130, 353
opening statement, 217
parties to trial, duty to account for, 212
plan for trial. *See* Trial brief
prosecution case in chief, 183
prosecution case in rebuttal, 183
record of trial
 preparation, 235–236
 supervision of, 142–143
special court, lawyer not required as, 123
speedy trial issue must be anticipated,
 139
summary court is, 105
time and place of trial, 141–142
trial brief, 139–140, 144
witness
 counsel should not testify as, 161, 356
 duty to insure presence of, 143
 introductory questioning of, 184

Unauthorized absence. *See also* Absence
 from appointed place of duty; Defenses
absence from particular unit required, 56
after arraignment, trial may continue,
 213
aggravating circumstances, drafting of,
 64–65
apprehension as aggravation, example,
 230
Article 86 of Code, 55
commencement of, 56
compared with desertion, 228
defenses
 impossibility, 58–59
 inapplicable if already absentee, 59–60

mistake and ignorance of fact, 59
negligence is not, 58
unforeseen incident is not always, 60
elements
  discussion, 55–56
  instruction as to, example, 226
general intent offense, 58
lesser included offense of desertion, 70, 170, 347
mind at fault
  concept, 70, 346–347
  required to constitute offense, 58
proving, mention of, 65
sample absence specification, 63, 69–70, 346
statute of limitations, 70
  extension by war, 70, 347
termination
  by apprehension, 57; aggravating circumstance, 216
  casual presence does not suffice, 57
  by delivery, 57
  by return to any service, 57
  by surrender, 57
"without authority" must be alleged, 56
Uniform
accused's, at trial, 151
proper, required at trial, 142
unclean, as an offense, 84, 350
Uniform Code of Military Justice (Code), **366**
  Court of Military Appeals may modify, 10
  inception of, 7–8
  Military Justice Act of 1968, 8
  source of military law, 9
Unit, defined briefly, 55
Unit punishment book
  Marine Corps, 95
  Navy, 95
United States Court of Military Appeals, publication, 11
U.S. Court of Military Appeals, 101, **375**
  may review questions of law, 240
  review by, 240
  source of military law, 10
U.S. Navy-Marine Corps Judiciary Activity, 176
U.S. Navy Regulations, **375**
  enforceable under Article 92, 11
  a general order, 84, 349
  source of military law, 11

Variance, examples of, 26–28, 140–141
Vietnam, status as war, 70, 347

Violations of the Code. *See specific offenses listed*
Voir dire, 167, **375**
  examples of, 129, 177–180

War, status of, 70, 347
Warrant officer, as member, 162–163
Wisby, sea law of, 4
Witness
accused as witness, counsel's advice, 149–151
accused, discussion with concerning, 147
authentication of original document by, 187
constitutional right of confrontation, 18
counsel should not testify as, 157
credibility of, 186
cross-examination, 186
direct examination, 184
  example of, 185
  leading questions prohibited, 184
guilty plea waives confrontation right, 216
introductory questions, 184
member may question, 168
member, prosecution witness, must be challenged, 167
members, fraternizing with, 167
military
  funding of travel, 143
  obtaining of, 143
oath, recitation of, 183
obtaining of, 143–144
prosecution witness ineligible as member, 163
recross examination of, 186
redirect examination of, 186
summary court, 110
  may subpoena, 109
testimony, authentication of, 186–187
trial counsel must advise defense of, 139
Words of art, instruction required as to, 226–227
Wrongful appropriation, **375**
discussed, 76
distinguished from larceny, 76
drafting value, 79
general owner, 74, 78
intent to deprive temporarily, 76
lesser included offense of larceny, 76
  example, 249, 360
owner, 74, 78
possession, 74
special owner, 74
taking money, replacing equivalent, 83–84, 348–349